Lecture Notes in Computer Science   13213

Nilufar Baghaei · Julita Vassileva · Raian Ali ·
Kiemute Oyibo (Eds.)

Persuasive Technology

17th International Conference, PERSUASIVE 2022
Virtual Event, March 29–31, 2022
Proceedings

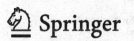
Springer

Editors
Nilufar Baghaei (iD)
Massey University
Auckland, New Zealand

The University of Queensland
Brisbane, Australia

Raian Ali (iD)
Hamad Bin Khalifa University
Doha, Qatar

Julita Vassileva (iD)
University of Saskatchewan
Saskatoon, SK, Canada

Kiemute Oyibo (iD)
University of Waterloo
Waterloo, ON, Canada

ISSN 0302-9743   ISSN 1611-3349 (electronic)
Lecture Notes in Computer Science
ISBN 978-3-030-98437-3   ISBN 978-3-030-98438-0 (eBook)
https://doi.org/10.1007/978-3-030-98438-0

This Springer imprint is published by the registered company Springer Nature Switzerland AG
The registered company address is: Gewerbestrasse 11, 6330 Cham, Switzerland

Preface

Persuasive Technology (PT) is an interdisciplinary research area focusing on the design, development, and evaluation of interactive technologies aimed at changing people's attitudes or behaviors through persuasion but not coercion or deception. As a community, we aim at enriching people's lives in various domains such as health, education, safety, and the environment by supporting their personal goals to change their behavior.

The PERSUASIVE conference series is the leading venue to meet and discuss cutting-edge theoretical, methodological, and technical perspectives and to present recent insights from research and development. The conference provides a venue for networking between researchers and practitioners from all corners of the world and has been held in different places such as Chicago, USA; Padua, Italy; Linköping, Sweden; Oulu, Finland; Sydney, Australia; Amsterdam, The Netherlands; Salzburg, Austria; Waterloo, Canada; Limassol, Cyprus; Aalborg, Denmark; and Bournemouth, UK.

The 17th International Conference on Persuasive Technology (PERSUASIVE 2022) was hosted during March 29–31, 2022, by Hamad Bin Khalifa University in Qatar. Due to the ongoing COVID-19 pandemic health concerns and travel regulations the conference was held online, like the previous two editions. On March 29 a tutorial and three workshops were held. The tutorial was on Persuasive Systems Design: Evaluation and Research through the PSD Model and was delivered by Harri Oinas-Kukkonen. The three workshops were the 6th Workshop on Personalizing Persuasive Technologies (PPT 2021), the 10th International Workshop on Behavior Change Support Systems (BCSS 2021), and the International Workshop on Digital Nudging and Digital Persuasion (DNDP 2021). On March 30 and 31 the main conference took place, with four single-track sessions including oral presentations of the accepted papers. The program also included two keynotes, presented by Evangelos Karapanos (Cyprus University of Technology) and Preslav Nakov (Hamad Bin Khalifa University – Qatar Computing Research Institute), as well as a poster session and a panel session.

This volume contains the accepted papers presented during the main conference. In total, 46 papers were submitted by 124 authors from 20 countries around the globe. These papers were reviewed by the Program Committee in a double-blind review process conducted in EasyChair. Overall, 67 reviewers were assigned to review the papers. Each paper received at least three detailed and constructive reviews, which not only provided the program chairs with significant insight concerning the individual submissions but also ensured that the authors were provided with high-quality feedback and recommendations for their final versions of their papers. The final list of papers to be presented at the conference was decided after a careful assessment of the reviews. Out of the 46 submissions, 13 papers were accepted as full papers (an acceptance rate of 28% for full papers) and seven papers were accepted as short papers (43% acceptance rate for short papers).

We would like to thank all reviewers and organizers who contributed to the success of PERSUSASIVE 2022. In particular, we would like to thank the authors from 20 countries (Europe: 11, Asia: 5, North America: 2, and Africa: 2) who submitted their papers to the conference. We thank the Program Committee for the critical role they played in the review process and for helping to promote the conference. We are also thankful to Hamad Bin Khalifa University for the organization and sponsoring of PERSUASIVE 2022, and the Qatar National Research Fund for co-sponsoring the conference.

March 2022

Nilufar Baghaei
Julita Vassileva
Raian Ali
Kiemute Oyibo

Organization

General Chair

Raian Ali   Hamad Bin Khalifa University, Qatar

Program Chairs

Nilufar Baghaei   Massey University, New Zealand
Julita Vassileva   University of Saskatchewan, Canada

Workshops and Tutorial Chairs

Dena Al-Thani   Hamad Bin Khalifa University, Qatar
Sandra Gram-Hansen   Aalborg University, Denmark

Poster Track Chairs

Rita Orji   Dalhousie University, Canada
Khin Than Win   Wollongong University, Australia

Proceedings Chairs

Kiemute Oyibo   University of Waterloo, Canada
Sameha Al-Shakhsi   Hamad Bin Khalifa University, Qatar

Web and Publicity Chairs

Ifeoma Adaji   University of British Columbia, Okanagan,
                                    Canada
Khansa Chemnad   Hamad Bin Khalifa University, Qatar
Md Rafiqul Islam   University of Technology Sydney, Australia

Program Committee

Ifeoma Adaji   University of Saskatchewan, Canada
Dena Al-Thani   Hamad Bin Khalifa University, Qatar
Aftab Alam   Hamad Bin Khalifa University, Qatar
Mohamed Basel Almourad   Zayed University, UAE
Amen Alrobai   King Abdulaziz University, Saudi Arabia

Kiemute Oyibo	University of Waterloo, Canada
Nadia Pantidi	Victoria University of Wellington, New Zealand
Jairo Perez-Osorio	Istituto Italiano di Tecnologia, Italy
Keith Phalp	Bournemouth University, UK
Daniel Playne	Massey University, New Zealand
Marwa Qaraqe	Hamad Bin Khalifa University, Qatar
Philipp Schaper	University of Würzburg, Germany
Alexander Schnack	Massey University, New Zealand
Syed Aziz Shah	Coventry University, UK
Zubair Shah	Hamad Bin Khalifa University, Qatar
Piiastiina Tikka	University of Oulu, Finland
Thomas Tran	University of Ottawa, Canada
Manfred Tscheligi	University of Salzburg, Austria
Lisette Van Gemert-Pijnen	University of Twente, The Netherlands
Julita Vassileva	University of Saskatchewan, Canada
Astrid Weiss	Vienna University of Technology, Austria
Khin Than Win	University of Wollongong, Australia
Katie Winkle	KTH Royal Institute of Technology, Sweden
Burkhard Wuensche	University of Auckland, New Zealand
Guandong Xu	University of Technology Sydney, Australia
Affan Yasin	Tsinghua University, China
Wajdi Zaghouani	Hamad Bin Khalifa University, Qatar
Leah Zhang-Kennedy	University of Waterloo, Canada
Jürgen Ziegler	University of Duisburg-Essen, Germany

Sponsoring Organizations

Hamad Bin Khalifa University (HBKU), a member of the Qatar Foundation for Education, Science, and Community Development (QF), was founded in 2010 to continue fulfilling QF's vision of unlocking human potential at all levels utilizing a multidisciplinary approach across all focus areas.

The Qatar National Research Fund is one of the first and most important players in Qatar's research, development, and innovation (RDI) ecosystem.

Contents

Impact of Medical Device Regulation on Developing Health Behavior Change Support Systems

Eunice Eno Yaa Frimponmaa Agyei(✉) (iD), Sami Pohjolainen (iD), and Harri Oinas-Kukkonen (iD)

University of Oulu, OASIS, Pentti Kaiteran katu 1, 90570 Oulu, Finland
eunice.agyei@oulu.fi

Abstract. The enforcement of the Medical Devices Regulation (MDR) began in the European Union (EU) in May 2021. Under MDR, software and information systems may be considered as medical devices. Behaviour Change Support Systems (BCSS) are information and communication technologies aimed at helping their users to achieve behaviour change targets. Designers, developers, and researchers of health BCSS (hBCSS) need to understand the impact of this new regulation on the development of such systems as the regulation influences both design and development in a variety of ways. Furthermore, myriads of health BCSS have been developed previously in the medical, fitness, and wellbeing domains, and a substantial number of them may require qualification, classification, or reclassification as medical devices under the new regulation. However, the regulation process is complex and requires knowledge and expertise which many manufacturers do not have in-house. Depending on the context and classification, the costs may suddenly ramp up and become too much for smaller developers, and thus they should be carefully assessed. In this paper, we discuss the regulation from the point of view of hBCSS developers. We look at the regulatory process and highlight key issues for developers of hBCSS. Particular attention is given to the classification and design requirements most likely to pose immediate challenges to developers. In addition, we discuss the costs associated with MDR which are difficult to estimate without previous experience.

Keywords: Medical device regulation · MDR · Medical device software · Software development · Persuasive systems design · PSD · Health behaviour change support systems · BCSS · hBCSS

1 Introduction

There is a myriad of medical devices, including software and information systems, in the EU and the number is expected to increase rapidly to include more and more devices that perform invasive and critical functions [1]. More than 90 000 digital health apps were released in 2020 and an estimated 350 000 are already available to consumers [2]. Many of these apps are marketed for fitness and wellbeing, but an increasing number are

© Springer Nature Switzerland AG 2022
N. Baghaei et al. (Eds.): PERSUASIVE 2022, LNCS 13213, pp. 1–15, 2022.
https://doi.org/10.1007/978-3-030-98438-0_1

targeted at specific diseases such as cardiovascular disease, diabetes, and mental health [2]. While an increasing number of new medical devices, including apps, have influenced the new regulation, it was a few cases involving implants that prompted the European Commission (EC) to take immediate action to start revising the regulation in 2012 [1, 3] although the medical industry lobbied against it [4]. The weaknesses of the Medical Device Directive (MDD) regulation [5], which was operational at the time, were apparent [6] as it was too generic and lacked detailed information on its requirements. Also, some privately owned Notified Bodies who were charged with the responsibility of evaluating device safety and reliability and for issuing compliance certificates were more interested in attracting business than in the safety and reliability of the devices even to the extent that safety in some situations was compromised [4]. A closer examination of Notified Bodies was initially prompted by a few notable cases, such as the fake hip replacement case [7], fraudulent breast implant scandal [8], and failures with transvaginal meshes [9].

Medical Device Regulation (MDR) came to force in the European Union (EU) on May 25, 2017, however, its implementation was later delayed until May 2021 [4, 10]. As a high-level objective, MDR seeks to ensure that medical devices available in the EU market are safe to use and perform efficiently. Notably, health information systems and software may be considered as medical devices under the new regulation. MDR compliance defines requirements that manufacturers, authorized representatives, importers, and distributors need to comply with. These requirements may have both positive and negative impacts on software product development. When much innovation happens in small companies, the heavy load imposed by the regulation may relatively speaking, impact them more than large companies [11, 12].

Behaviour change support systems (BCSS) are technologies that are designed to influence the habits, behaviours, and attitudes of users without deception or coercion; designing such technology requires a deep understanding of the interplay between people, technology, and behaviour change [13]. The Persuasive Systems Design model (PSD) is a comprehensive framework for designing, developing, and evaluating persuasive technologies [13]. The model describes the fundamental issues behind persuasive systems and the context in which a system will be used and specifies design principles for supporting (1) a user to perform the primary behaviour change activities or tasks (i.e. Primary task support), (2) ongoing interaction between the computer and the user (i.e. Dialogue support), (3) the credibility of the persuasive system (i.e. System credibility support), and (4) users via social influence (i.e. Social support) [13]. Such systems designed for the medical domain provide benefits that help monitor and manage health conditions and improve the quality of life.

In this paper, we consider MDR and its impact on the development of hBCSS. Key aspects of the regulation and its requirements as well as notable changes from the previous directive, MDD, are highlighted. We outline what it takes to qualify an hBCSS as a medical device, what determines its risk class, and how it impacts the design and development process. Finally, we discuss cost-related implications.

2 Medical Device Regulation (MDR)

MDR aims to ensure high standards of safety and performance for medical devices across the EU [10]. The new regulation replaces MDD [5]. Other regions of the world and many national markets outside the EU have regulations that share similarities. However, MDR is stricter than for example a similar regulation in the United States by the Food and Drugs Administration (FDA) and brings more scrutiny and oversight for medical devices. It also makes the regulation more uniform across the EU leaving less room for national legislation. Moreover, MDR defines harmonized standards (cf Article 8 [10]), introduces common specifications (cf Article 9 [10]), and refines the roles and actions of Notified Bodies [14].

All medical devices must possess a Unique Device Identifier (UDI) to enable traceability [15]. Competent authorities use UDI and the European database on medical devices (EUDAMED) to monitor devices on the market, thus improving safety and performance [15]. Manufacturers must carry out post-market surveillance activities and record them in the EUDAMED system. The scope of post-market activities depends on the risk class of the device. Manufacturers who identify safety or performance issues or incidents with their devices must report them and take corrective actions promptly [10]. To implement this and to improve transparency and coordination, the EUDAMED database is available publicly. In the database, devices and certifications will be registered alongside economic operators (i.e., manufacturers, authorized representatives, importers, and distributors) in the supply chain. The system includes reports from performance studies and clinical investigations while containing vigilance and post-market surveillance activities of manufacturers [16].

2.1 Transition Timeline

Developers of hBCSS should be aware of transition timelines for MDR [17]. The transition from MDD to MDR will take place in several steps. MDR entered into force and has been partially applicable since 26th May 2017. The key date was 26th May 2021 when MDR became fully applicable [10] after which all new medical devices must conform with the regulation. Manufacturers can use the transition period to acquire MDR certification. On May 26th, 2024, all medical devices on the market that fall under MDR must be certified. Notably, there is a grace period until 27th May 2025 for devices with a valid MDD certification.

Medical devices and software under MDR are assigned classes (i.e. Class I, IIa, IIb, and III) [10] based on the risks they pose to users with Class I posing the lowest risk and Class III, the highest risk. There are two exceptions for Class I devices when it comes to the transition timeline. Firstly, export declarations for Class I devices that fall under a higher risk class in the new regulation expire on 26th May 2024. Secondly, export declarations issued for Class I devices that did not require a conformité européenne (CE) certificate under MDD expired on 26th May 2021. For other risk classes, previous MDD certifications are valid until they expire, but will require registration in the EUDAMED system [17].

2.2 Notable Changes from MDD to MDR

MDR has more requirements than MDD but has retained aspects of MDD. These aspects are risk classes of devices, classification rules, general safety and performance requirements (formerly essential requirements under MDD), technical documentation, conformity assessment, registration of actors, notified bodies, and the EUDAMED system formerly known as Eudamed2 (European Databank on Medical Devices) [18]. In essence, MDR extends MDD requirements to cover some new areas that were not previously covered in the directive [19]. Table 1 provides details on notable changes when moving from MDD to MDR.

Table 1. Notable changes when moving from MDD to MDR

Change	Nature of change	Implication
Definition for qualifying medical device	Broader definitions to certain types of devices	New manufacturers will have to qualify their software based on the medical device definition. Manufacturers will have to re-qualify their devices as a medical device or not
Classifying software based on the risk class	New classification rules for medical device software	Manufacturers need to determine the risk class for their medical device software or reclassify devices. While most software was Class 1 in MDD, most will be at least Class IIa in MDR
General safety and performance requirements	The essential requirements have been extended	Manufacturers will have to comply with the additional requirements
Technical documentation	Detailed and additional requirements	Manufacturers must include new requirements in the technical documentation
Registration of economic operators	Manufacturers, distributors, authorized representatives, system/procedure pack producers, and importers	Obligations for importers and distributors have been clearly defined in MDR. Different operators have more responsibilities
Notified bodies	More requirements, supervision, and oversight	Since almost all software is Class IIa or higher in MDR, Notified Body involvement is needed

(continued)

Table 1. (*continued*)

Change	Nature of change	Implication
EUDAMED database	EU-wide and expands Eudamed2 (used between national Competent Authorities and the European Commission)	Information was largely kept in national repositories, EUDAMED centralizes these databases and increases access to information on medical devices and economic operators; adds requirements that did not exist before, available publicly to increase transparency
Post-market Surveillance	New requirements	Manufacturers need to produce a post-market surveillance report and a periodic safety update report (depending on the risk class)
Unique Device Identification (UDI)	A new requirement	Manufacturers will need to acquire a UDI for their software and update the UDI when there are software updates

The requirements of MDR include post-market surveillance report and periodic safety update report, UDI for tracking medical devices, requirements for economic operators (i.e., importers and distributors) of medical devices operating from outside the EU, a quality/regulatory compliance/safety manager, and extension of the medical device regulation definition to cover products without an intended medical purpose but analogous to devices with a medical purpose [18].

It is possible and even likely that many hBCSS will require a higher risk classification. A major change to MDR is the definitions used to qualify and classify software as a medical device. For example, an app that aids the selection and dose calculation of cytostatic drugs was previously a Class I device under MDD but is now a Class III device under MDR [20]. Also, an app for diagnosing sleep apnea that used to be a Class I device will now be at least a Class IIa device [20]. Moreover, it may be unclear when software is a medical device or not. Many such devices fall into the borderline category and are defined based on the medical purpose of the device according to the MDR's definition of medical devices [21].

2.3 Compliance Process

hBCSS developers are required to determine if their product is a medical device or not. After that, developers must use a conformity assessment to demonstrate compliance. A CE mark is awarded to indicate to users that the product has gone through the process and is certified. Developers of Class I devices can typically complete the certification process without involving a Notified Body. During the compliance process, developers must produce documentation and evidence that demonstrates MDR compliance. Developers need to have several processes and systems in place as outlined in the regulation. These include establishing a quality management system, conducting clinical evaluations, instituting post-market surveillance, and handling liability for defective products. Depending on the risk classification and outcomes of the clinical evaluation, developers may be required to conduct a clinical investigation. This is to ensure that the product is safe to use and effective such that the potential risks to end-users have been sufficiently mitigated. Class III devices have a mandatory requirement to conduct a clinical investigation. In addition, products will need to be registered to the EUDAMED system before they can be released onto the market. Figure 1 is a simplified overview of the MDR process for developers of hBCSS. Keutzer and Simonsson describe a simplified process, but they do not cover the whole lifecycle [3]. The factsheet and step-by-step guide for manufacturers from the European Commission contain further information worth taking into account when planning activities regarding MDR [22, 23].

The first three steps of Fig. 1 are discussed later in Sect. 3. The risk classification of a medical device is a complex process and can be even more challenging for manufacturers of so-called borderline devices that may be very close to a higher risk class [21]. If a developer is applying the MDR process for the first time and lacks in-house expertise, we recommend seeking expert help to manage the process. Notified Body, if needed, should be contacted early in the process to ensure that assessment can be completed in accordance with the development and go-to-market schedule.

Fig. 1. Main steps to complete MDR compliance process for developers of hBCSS

Through the hBCSS development process, it is important to consider general safety and performance requirements. These technical documents together with other documentation demonstrate conformity with the requirements [24] in Annex I of the MDR documentation [10]. Also, Fig. 2 shows quality assurance-related harmonized standards that can be used to gain appropriate certifications to ensure compliance. The quality management system is subject to auditing by a Notified Body. While Class I devices do not require full certification of ISO 13485, evidence must be provided for quality management and software lifecycle management, risk management, and usability engineering. Conformity and post-market requirements are expanded in the new regulation. It is important to maintain technical documentation throughout the life cycle of the product.

In addition, the product and related actors involved (manufacturers, authorized representatives, distributors, subcontractors, etc.) need to be registered in the EUDAMED system, which contains evaluation reports and other specified materials produced throughout the life cycle of the product.

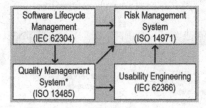

Fig. 2. Quality assurance certifications and related harmonized standards

3 Qualification and Classifications

Medical device software is software (including accessories) intended by the manufacturer to be used by human beings for a specific medical purpose [10, 25] such as (1) *diagnosis, prevention, monitoring, prediction, prognosis, treatment, or alleviation of disease, (2) diagnosis, monitoring, treatment, alleviation of, or compensation for, an injury or disability, (3) investigation, replacement, or modification of the anatomy or of a physiological or pathological process or state, (4) providing information using in vitro examination of specimens derived from the human body, including organ, blood, and tissue donations, and which does not achieve its principal intended action by pharmacological, immunological, or metabolic means, in or on the human body, but which may be assisted in its function by such means, and (5) devices for the control or support of conception.*

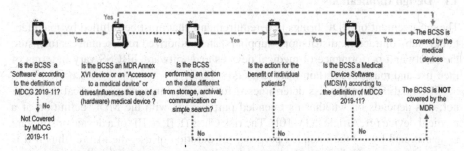

Fig. 3. Qualification process diagram for hBCSS software according to [25]

Figure 3 shows the process of qualifying software as a medical device. A software with any of the above medical device modules, accessory, or a device with medical device modules qualifies as a medical device [3]. This decision of whether a software product is a medical device is made by the manufacturer or developer. However, wrongly qualifying

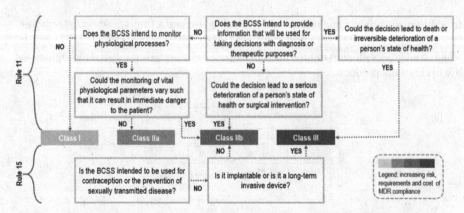

Fig. 4. Risk classification process of hBCSS according to Annex VIII adapted from [10]

a medical device and/or misclassifying its risk class can have serious repercussions. According to Article 51, medical device software can be assigned to different classes (i.e. Class I, IIa, IIb, and III) [10] based on the risks and intended purpose. Factors that influence the classification include the duration of use, the nature of the type of interaction (i.e., active, invasive), and the kind of harm it may cause. There are 22 rules for dividing medical devices into various classes (cf. Annex VIII Chapter III). Rule 11 is specifically for medical device software. Figure 4 describes software features, inherent risk, and the resulting risk classification based on Rule 11 and 15 of MDR. Rule 15 makes software like Nature cycles a Class IIb device [26, 27]. This risk classification determines the steps to obtain compliance certification in the form of a CE marking and post-production surveillance activities.

4   Design and Cost Implications

4.1   Design Implications

The enforcement of MDR brings new requirements that must be fulfilled by manufacturers, sub-contractors, distributors, suppliers, and authorized representatives to ensure the safety and performance of medical devices and software. hBCSS vary in terms of their use and may pose certain risks to users.

The qualification process determines if for instance an app is a medical device or not; this depends on whether its intended purpose fits with the MDR definition of a medical device (cf. Article 2(1) [10]). The risk Class (I, II, or III) of a device or software is determined by (1) the intended purpose, (2) duration of use, the nature (thus if it is an active device or an invasive device), and (3) the inherent risks (including correct use, unexpected use, and errors). A medical device software may be embedded software in a device (i.e., part of hardware), a mobile or web app (standalone or module), or an expert or decision support system (standalone or module) [10]. In Table 2, we show examples of hBCSS and their risk level classification. These systems may be used by users for a short period (i.e., less than 30 days) or longer. According to the classification

Table 2. Examples of medical and non-medical hBCSS

Device/App name	Persuasive features	Invasive	Class
The Corona App	Disease monitoring	No	Class I [28]
Proteus IEM	Diagnosing app	Yes	Class IIa [29]
DIABETESMART	Diabetes management	No	Class IIa [30]
Nature cycles	Period tracking and conception	No	Class IIb [26, 27]
Omron HeartAdvisor	Blood pressure, sleep, and weight monitoring	No	Not medical
Nerva	Symptom monitoring and hypnotherapy	No	Not medical
MyTherapy Pill Reminder	Medication monitoring	No	Not medical
Bearable	Mood and symptom tracking	No	Not medical

rules in Annex VIII of MDR, a software can be classified as an active medical device when they rely on electrical energy to function [25].

Also, there are persuasive systems designed to be used for health and wellbeing purposes that are not medical. Such systems can easily become medical devices with e.g., the introduction of medical functionalities related to monitoring and diagnosing. For example, *My dose coach*, an app for determining the dosage of insulin is a Class IIa medical device software (according to the less strict regulation of FDA in the US) because of the dosage calculation functionality in the app. *My dose coach* is likely to have a higher risk classification under the MDR (Class IIa or higher) because an improper dosage calculation can harm the user and even lead to death. On the other hand, *MyTherapy Pill Reminder* simply helps the user to monitor the intake of medication and thus is not a medical device. A major difference between these apps is the function that calculates the dosage. *FreeStyle Libre Pro Flash Glucose Monitoring* system, a Class III medical device under the FDA's medical regulation may be a good example of an MDR Class III medical device software [31].

4.2 Cost Implications

Compliance with MDR requires time and resources. If a company is managing the process for the first time without in-house expertise [11, 12], it is likely to face many challenges during the certification process. Table 3 describes in-house and expert-related cost components. Experts and consultants can help to prepare documentation, adjust development processes, and define the classification, among other things. The cost of devices with a higher risk class will increase because Notified Bodies are needed to check requirements for conformity. For example, Class III devices will often need to go through expensive clinical investigations. Developers need to conduct post-market clinical follow-ups as part of their post-market surveillance activities after the release of the medical device [10]. These activities can be more demanding for higher-risk classes.

Developing hBCSS that seek to prevent or solve health problems are currently popular both within the industry and academia. A lot of innovation and development activity is ongoing in this area with over 2000 published studies since 2007 and around 1500 in the last five years according to an industry report [2]. It is reported that 81% of manufacturers find MDR challenging, and for over 70%, the main concern is related to increased resources and costs, while over 50% are worried about a lack of clarity on requirements [32]. Developers of hBCSS are likely to have similar concerns and may not necessarily be prepared to handle all facets of the MDR implementation. A high number of medical device innovators and manufacturers are small and medium enterprises (SME) [2, 33, 34]. The cost of MDR compliance when moving from MDD to MDR can be high and proportionally, it affects the revenues of smaller manufacturers more than medium and large manufacturers [11, 32]. Furthermore, developers operating from outside the EU need to hire an authorized representative, who will act on behalf of the developer in specified tasks.

New qualification and classification requirements mean that devices, including software, that were not considered medical devices previously may now meet the threshold and must conform to the regulation [11]. Many hBCSS which were not medical devices under MDD may now fall under the Class I or Class IIa devices under MDR. While the cost associated with conformity assessment is not going to increase significantly for Class I devices, the cost can be much higher for other classes [12, 28]. Moreover, some fitness and wellbeing apps and devices may turn out to be medical devices under MDR and will have to go through the compliance process resulting in additional costs. Alternatively, developers may choose to remove software features that increase the risk class. Medical hBCSS that are already on the market will have to recertify once the current certificate expires or be prepared to remove the product from the EU market. Removal of these hBCSS is likely to result in decreased availability of innovative apps for users.

Table 3. Expertise-related cost components [11, 12]

Activity	Develop internal expertise	Potential external resources	Risk class-specific
Recruitment and training of personnel to handle the compliance process	Organization level MDR expertise, person responsible for regulatory compliance	MDR experts and trainers	
Establish general safety and performance requirements, risk management, and technical documentation	Quality management and assurance, person responsible for regulatory compliance	MDR product experts	

(*continued*)

Table 3. (*continued*)

Activity	Develop internal expertise	Potential external resources	Risk class-specific
Quality management system and its certification	Quality management and its processes, person responsible for regulatory compliance	Consultants to help with standards (e.g., see Fig. 2), Notified Body	Class I devices have lower requirements
Verification, validation, usability engineering	Quality management, software development process, usability engineering specialist	MDR experts/consultants, physicians, and test participants	
Product manual, labels, and translation work	Technical writing and label designing	Translators, and reviewers with clinical expertise	
Clinical evaluations, and clinical investigations	Clinical evaluator, physician reviewers, person responsible for regulatory compliance	MDR experts/consultants, physicians, Contract Research Organization/investigators	Clinical investigations mandatory for Class III
Product notification and certification, CE conformity declaration	Quality assurance, person responsible for regulatory compliance	Notified body for Class IIa–III devices	Notification for Class I devices
EUDAMED database	Person responsible for regulatory compliance		
Vigilance reports	Quality assurance, person responsible for regulatory compliance		
Post-market surveillance (PMS) and post-market clinical follow up (PMCF)	Quality assurance, person responsible for regulatory compliance	PMCF: Notified Body, other parties for clinical investigations	Higher risk classes can require more activities

Developers of medical apps may be forced to withdraw their products from the EU market if they are ill-prepared to comply with MDR. There are concerns on how this will impact innovation, as it will drive smaller manufacturers to rethink their approach or at the very least to lower the risk class of their products [4, 11, 12]. The regulation may ensure that products are safer and perform efficiently while increasing transparency to users but it may result in higher costs and delays in product development [34].

5 Discussion

Implications for Design and Development of Persuasive Technology. The MDR regulation influences the design and development processes of medical devices. It outlines requirements for clinical evaluations, premarket approval, registration, manufacturing, storage, advertising and promotions, selling, distributing, exporting, importing, and monitoring the device after it has been placed on the market [10, 35]. Developers of hBCSS need to be aware of MDR and other regulations in the healthcare domain. They need to determine if the technology they are designing or developing is classified as a medical device or not as it influences the selection of software features.

Developers may have to contend with classification issues related to borderline devices. Classifying such devices can be challenging and the risk of misclassification should not be taken lightly. If the risk class is increased later, stricter regulatory requirements are likely to apply and lead to much higher costs and significant delays. Designating a lower risk class may lead to non-compliance issues and may require pulling the device from the EU market. Also, existing hBCSS on the market must be checked for compliance before the transition period ends or risk penalties (Article 113 [10]) and even face the removal of the device from the EU market. In addition, CE marking must be obtained for medical devices. CE marking should be clearly visible on a product. Users should have access to easy-to-understand documentation including user manuals, terms of use, and privacy policies. The terms of use must spell out what makes the product a medical device and highlight its risks.

MDR is designed with general safety and performance in mind [10, 35]. The use of strict quality management standards leads to the availability of products with better quality to users. Although this is a step in the positive direction, making a medical software device comes with increased costs to the manufacturer [35] which we believe will be passed down to the user. In the future, digital platforms (e.g., Google Play Store and Apple Store) may require a CE marking for medical devices to be distributed through their platforms. As it stands, the criteria being used by digital platforms to verify medical devices is unclear. If a digital platform acts as a distributor in the EU, they will be required to comply with the regulation. Digital platforms may need to reconsider their product categories to make it easier to identify certified medical devices.

Exemptions to MDR. Academic researchers who want to commercialize their products will need to comply with MDR. Although in theory, academic researchers can be manufacturers, in-house devices or devices produced in health institutions within the EU are exempt from the MDR regulation. This exemption applies if the rights are not transferred to another legal entity and other conditions set in Article 5 are met [10]. If a health institution qualifies for the exemption, it must comply with the applicable general safety and performance requirements set out in Annex I [10].

Additionally, there are exemptions for custom-made devices intended for the sole use by a particular patient (MDR Article 2(2) [10] in MDR Article 52(8) and Annex

XIII [10]). We believe that custom-made hBCSS may be very rare or non-existent but if such a medical device is developed, then MDR exemptions may apply. Medical devices developed in-house or for investigational purposes for a group of patients with similar health conditions may fall under the health institution exemption in Article 5 of MDR [10].

Future Innovation. According to Porter, strict regulations such as MDR can induce efficiency, promote innovation, and improve the competitiveness of companies [36], even if there are also contradictory perspectives [35]. Cost savings made from using more efficient processes can compensate for the cost directly attributed to the regulation [35, 36]. This means that manufacturers operating in the EU may benefit from the stricter regulation and possibly gain a competitive advantage with safer and more efficient products in less regulated markets [35]. We believe that the extra cost from MDR can offset the costs that would otherwise come from product recalls and compensations to users harmed by defective devices [37].

The MDR regulation is cost-intensive and innovation in the medical industry is driven by SMEs. There is speculation that a regulation like this will have a strong negative impact on innovation is somewhat overemphasized. New regulations do not necessarily result in decreased innovation activity but commercialization of innovative medical devices does require increased collaboration among stakeholders to ensure a smooth transition [38]. We believe that the negative effects are more profound for micro and small enterprises. Presently, the challenges faced by the industry as a whole are being countered to an extent by increased investments in digital health [2, 34]. It seems that the main risk is not to innovation but to the survival of small innovative companies who may be forced to leave the market if unable to cope with the cost of the regulation. To survive, these companies will have to seek synergies. We agree with [11] that innovation activity over the next few years amongst SMEs is worth monitoring [34]. Indeed, there may be some decline in the innovation of hBCSS over the next few years in comparison to other types of BCSS which have more relaxed development requirements and less regulation to contend with.

6 Conclusions

To conclude, we recommend designers, developers, and researchers of hBCSS to get well-familiarized with MDR. The regulation impacts the whole medical device lifecycle and measures should be put in place to ensure compliance. Developers should decide early on whether to develop a medical device or not. It is important to determine which risk class the device will be and has bearings with the process and costs. Failure to comply with MDR (e.g., misclassification) comes with fines and penalties and possible withdrawal of medical devices from the EU market.

Acknowledgment. We are grateful to Ilona Santavaara for commenting and Dr. Piiastiina Tikka of the OASIS research unit for proofreading this manuscript.

References

1. Melvin, T., Torre, M.: New medical device regulations: the regulator's view. EFORT Open Rev. **4**(6), 351–356 (2019). https://doi.org/10.1302/2058-5241.4.180061
2. IQVIA: Digital Health Trends 2021 - Innovation, Evidence, Regulation, and Adoption (2021)
3. Keutzer, L., Simonsson, U.S.H.: Medical device apps: an introduction to regulatory affairs for developers. JMIR mHealth uHealth **8**(6), e17567 (2020). https://doi.org/10.2196/17567
4. Cohen, D.: Devices and desires: industry fights toughening of medical device regulation in Europe. BMJ **347**(7929), f6204 (2013). https://doi.org/10.1136/BMJ.F6204
5. The Council of the European Communities: COUNCIL DIRECTIVE 93/42/EEC of 14 June 1993 concerning medical devices (1993)
6. The European Commission: New EU rules to ensure safety of medical devices, https://ec.eur opa.eu/commission/presscorner/detail/en/MEMO_17_848. Accessed 28 Nov 2021
7. Cohen, D.: How a fake hip showed up failings in European device regulation. BMJ **345**(7880), e7090 (2012). https://doi.org/10.1136/BMJ.E7090
8. Martindale, V., Menache, A.: The PIP scandal: an analysis of the process of quality control that failed to safeguard women from the health risks. J. R. Soc. Med. **106**(5), 173 (2013). https://doi.org/10.1177/0141076813480994
9. Heneghan, C., Aronson, J.K., Goldacre, B., Mahtani, K.R., Plüddemann, A., Onakpoya, I.: Transvaginal mesh failure: lessons for regulation of implantable devices. BMJ **359**, j5515 (2017). https://doi.org/10.1136/BMJ.J5515
10. The European Parliament and the Council: Regulation (EU) 2017/745 of the European Parliament and of the Council of 5 April 2017 on medical devices, amending Directive 2001/83/EC, Regulation (EC) No 178/2002 and Regulation (EC) No 1223/2009 and repealing Council Directives 90/385/EEC and 93/42/EE (2017)
11. Maresova, P., Rezny, L., Peter, L., Hajek, L., Lefley, F.: Do regulatory changes seriously affect the medical devices industry? Evidence from the Czech Republic. Front. Public Health **9**, 415 (2021). https://doi.org/10.3389/FPUBH.2021.666453
12. Leo, H.: MDR Guide for Medical Device Software. Guide.pdf (2021). https://www.fme.nl/system/files/publicaties/2021-09/MDR
13. Oinas-Kukkonen, H., Harjumaa, M.: Persuasive systems design: key issues, process model, and system features. Commun. Assoc. Inf. Syst. **24**(1), 485–500 (2009). https://doi.org/10.17705/1cais.02428
14. The European Commission: Notified bodies. https://ec.europa.eu/growth/single-market/goods/building-blocks/notified-bodies_en. Accessed 28 Nov 2021
15. The European Commission: Introduction to the new UDI system and the obligations of operators. https://ec.europa.eu/health/system/files/2020-09/md_faq_udi_en_0.pdf. Accessed 28 Nov 2021
16. The European Commission: Medical Devices - EUDAMED – Overview. https://ec.europa.eu/health/md_eudamed/overview_en. Accessed 28 Nov 2021
17. The European Commission: Transition Timelines from the Directives to the Regulations Medical Devices and in vitro Diagnostic Medical Devices. https://ec.europa.eu/health/sites/default/files/md_newregulations/docs/md_infographic-timeline_en.pdf. Accessed 30 Nov 2021
18. The European Commission: Market surveillance and vigilance. https://ec.europa.eu/health/md_sector/market-surveillance-and-vigilance_en. Accessed 28 Nov 2021
19. The European Union Medical Device Regulation: What's changed compared to the MDD. https://eumdr.com/whats-changed/. Accessed 15 Nov 2021
20. MDR Rule 11: The Classification Nightmare. https://www.johner-institute.com/articles/regulatory-affairs/and-more/mdr-rule-11-software/. Accessed 15 Nov 2021

21. Working Group on Borderline and Classification for Consultation: Manual on Borderline and Classification in the Community Regulatory Framework for Medical Device. https://ec.europa.eu/health/system/files/2020-08/md_borderline_manual_05_2019_en_0.pdf. Accessed 15 Nov 2021

22. The European Commission: Factsheet for manufacturers of medical device. https://ec.europa.eu/docsroom/documents/31201. Accessed 29 Nov 2021

23. The European Commission: Step by step implementation model for Medical Device Regulation. https://ec.europa.eu/docsroom/documents/30905. Accessed 29 Nov 2021

24. The European Commission: Commission Implementing Regulation (EU) 2020/1207 of 19 August 2020 laying down rules for the application of Regulation (EU) 2017/745 of the European Parliament and of the Council as regards common specifications for the reprocessing of single-use devices (2020)

25. MDCG: Guidance on Qualification and Classification of Software in Regulation (EU) 2017/745 – MDR and Regulation (EU) 2017/746 – IVDR (2019)

26. EC certificate for Natural Cycles Nordic AB (2017). https://www.datocms-assets.com/21281/1610371680-ec-certificate-natural-cycles.pdf

27. Natural Cycles Science: Digital Birth Control Explained. https://www.naturalcycles.com/the-science. Accessed 16 Nov 2021

28. The Corona App - first example of MDR Class I Software? https://www.qservegroup.com/eu/en/i601/the-corona-app---first-example-of-mdr-class-i-software. Accessed 28 Nov 2021

29. European Medicines Agency: Qualification opinion on ingestible sensor system for medication adherence as biomarker for measuring patient adherence to medication in clinical trials (2016)

30. The first Clinically Validated AI-powered Diabetes Assistant. https://cordis.europa.eu/project/id/866147. Accessed 30 Nov 2021

31. Establishment Registration & Device Listing. https://www.accessdata.fda.gov/scrIpts/cdrh/cfdocs/cfRL/rl.cfm?lid=506280&lpcd=MDS. Accessed 21 Nov 2021

32. Climedo Health GmbH: EU MDR Readiness Check 2021 Survey Results. https://climedo.de/wp-content/uploads/2021/04/EU-MDR-Survey-Results-2021-EN.pdf?utm_campaign=MDRReadinessSurvey2021&utm_medium=email&_hsmi=160180699&_hsenc=p2ANqtz-9guQk5HUjqBqFL8BoO-UTvuDIxOhrrICwXXUe7_ixx1tPySJpZdxqWpqNHKQKbf53uMcsxUsxZDcYjkA-bh4aq98. Accessed 30 Nov 2021

33. Peter, L., Hajek, L., Maresova, P., Augustynek, M., Penhaker, M.: Medical devices: regulation, risk classification, and open innovation. J. Open Innov. Technol. Market Complex. **6**(2), 42 (2020). https://doi.org/10.3390/JOITMC6020042

34. Climedo Health GmbH: EU MDR Survey - The True Cost of the New Regulation. https://climedo.de/wp-content/uploads/2021/02/2020_EUMDR_Costs_SurveyResults_EN.pdf?utm_campaign=2020EUMDRCostsSurvey&utm_medium=email&_hsmi=160180201&_hsenc=p2ANqtz-8AF7kI9HlCbIbbFDDqk6wJL4yEsxFJIqNRffKUPq7_c0pYdyUTSifbv3CNKf5S0u2XO2imes1Jub67FXkb4Ql. Accessed 28 Nov 2021

35. Maresova, P., Hajek, L., Krejcar, O., Storek, M., Kuca, K.: New regulations on medical devices in Europe: are they an opportunity for growth? Adm. Sci. **10**(1), 16 (2020). https://doi.org/10.3390/ADMSCI10010016

36. Porter, M.E.: America' green strategy. In: Welford, R., Starkey, R. (eds.) Business and the Environment: A Reader, pp. 33–35. Taylor & Francis, Washington DC (1996)

37. Thirumalai, S., Sinha, K.K.: Product recalls in the medical device industry: an empirical exploration of the sources and financial consequences. Manage. Sci. **57**(2), 376–392 (2011). https://doi.org/10.1287/MNSC.1100.1267

38. Guerra-Bretaña, R.M., Flórez-Rendón, A.L.: Impact of regulations on innovation in the field of medical devices. Res. Biomed. Eng. **34**(4), 356–367 (2018). https://doi.org/10.1590/2446-4740.180054

SortOut: Persuasive Stress Management Mobile Application for Higher Education Students

Mona Alhasani[✉] [iD] and Rita Orji [iD]

Faculty of Computer Science, Dalhousie University, Halifax, NS B3H 4R2, Canada
{mona.alhasani,rita.orji}@dal.ca

Abstract. Mental stress is a serious emerging health issue among higher education students. Time management is often promoted for students as an effective strategy to cope with stress. However, previous research indicated that promoting students' perceived ability to control their times can directly reduce their stress. Based on the results of a large-scale study involving 502 participants, we identified that the ability to be organized is the most effective time management behaviour that promotes students' perceptions about their ability to control their times, reduce stress, hence, anxiety. We applied these results to design a mobile app intervention (called SortOut), which includes seven persuasive strategies implemented as six-core features. SortOut app aims to help students manage their stress and anxiety by promoting time management via preference for organization and control over time. We evaluated SortOut app on 68 participants, considering possible differences based on gender and degree level. Overall, the results revealed the app was perceived as strongly persuasive and had high motivational appeal. Yet, the app design provoked and sustained females' attention more than males. Usability evaluation shows the app is useful and easy to use, hence more likely to be accepted and used. Finally, we conducted a thematic analysis on the participants' feedback and suggestions that will be used to refine the app design.

Keywords: Persuasive technology · Stress management · Anxiety management · Time management · Behaviour change · Mobile app

1 Introduction

Stress is the feeling of mental tension that occurs when an individual perceives inability to meet life demands [12, 16]. Students in higher education make up a population that is susceptible to mental health issues [14]. Stress levels among undergraduate students were found to increase during their course of the study compared to their stress levels before entry [5]. Moreover, A large-scale survey on mental health crisis shows that more than 80% of graduate students are living with excessive stress while more than 40% are struggling with severe anxiety [9]. Stress can cause mild to severe mental and physical health risks, including heart disease, obesity, sleep disorder, panic attacks, anxiety, depression, and low cognitive performance [10, 30, 31, 33, 34]. Previous research [11] examined the factors contributing to college student stressors; lack of time was the

---

The original version of this chapter was revised: figures have been updated to a higher resolution and errors in Figs. 8 and 9 were corrected. Correction to this chapter is available at
https://doi.org/10.1007/978-3-030-98438-0_21

© Springer Nature Switzerland AG 2022, corrected publication 2022
N. Baghaei et al. (Eds.): PERSUASIVE 2022, LNCS 13213, pp. 16–27, 2022.
https://doi.org/10.1007/978-3-030-98438-0_2

most frequent factor among lack of resources theme. Most university students complain about the shortage of time to complete their tasks on time, feeling overwhelmed and frustrated. Time management is often promoted by academic counselling services as an effective strategy to cope with stress [20]. Several strategies for time management can be used to support effective time management behaviours such as scheduling, planning, setting goal, prioritization, monitoring progress over time, and organization. Practicing effective time management behaviour contributes to improving students' ability to feel in control of their time. Improving perceived control over time (PCT) has a significant positive impact on students' satisfaction toward life and work, promoting productivity, reducing academic stress levels, and improving academic performance [17, 20, 25].

Our previous review for 60 stress management apps [3] revealed a lack of apps that used time management as a coping strategy for stress management. Most of the apps were based on emotion-focused coping that aims to decrease and manage stress-related negative emotions [18], such as implementing mindfulness exercises, journaling, or cognitive distractions (using games). Problem-focused coping aims to reduce or eliminate the source of stress [18], such as the use of problem-solving or time management techniques. Among university students, the perception of time shortage was identified as a major source of their stress [11, 15, 23]. This highlights the importance of designing interventions that promote effective time management strategies to reduce stress, students' feelings of time pressure, high workload and overcome challenges of self-organized learning.

2 Mental Health and Time Management Behaviour Model

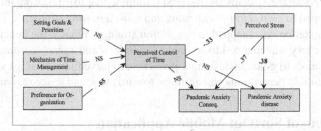

Fig. 1. Standardized path coefficients and significance of relationships of the model. **Bolded** coefficients are p < .0001, NS are non-significant.

In the initial study [2] with 502 participants, we gathered data on how different factors related to critical time management behaviour promote students' perceived control over time and contribute to reducing students' stress and anxiety. Time management behaviour factors were adapted from Macan et al. [20]. Factor 1-*Setting Goals and Priorities (SGP)* refers to setting goals and prioritizing tasks to achieve those goals. Factor 2-*Mechanics of Time Management (MTM)* refers to managing time through planning, scheduling and making lists. Factor 3-*Preference for Organization (PFO)* refers to student's preference for having their space and approach to handling their assigned tasks organized. Factor

4-*Perceived Control of Time (PCT)* is a perceptual factor that results from the previous behavioural factors. PCT refers to the extent to which individuals believe they can control how their time is spent. Moreover, students' stress levels were measured using the *Perceived stress scale* (PSS) [6]. PSS assesses individuals' thoughts and feelings–how overloaded, unpredictable and uncontrollable their lives are. Furthermore, we adapted *Pandemic Anxiety Scale (PAS)* [21] to assess students' anxiety since the data collection stage was during the lockdown. PAS captures two types of anxiety related to COVID-19 pandemic, anxiety driven by worries about the disease itself and anxiety related to other consequences of the pandemic, such as the impact on job prospects and the economy. The results of the Structural Equation modeling revealed that (see Fig. 1) students' preference for organization (PFO) was the only significant time management behaviour factor that influenced students' perception of the ability to control time and reduce stress, thus, anxiety. In other words, students who are able to manage time through the organization of tasks and study spaces have a higher perception of control over their times, hence, less stress and anxiety.

3   Mapping PFO Items to Corresponding Persuasive Strategies

Preference for organization factor contained perceptual and behavioural items that comprise the concept of organization in students' daily lives. In our initial study [2], we grouped the items into three main categories: *tasks organization, space organization,* and *benefits of being organized* via group brainstorming. This was followed by an agreement between two expert researchers in the field of persuasive technology on mapping the three PFO categories and persuasive strategies that could be used to operationalize them in app design. The persuasive strategies were based on the Goal-Setting strategy [19] and the Persuasive Systems Design (PSD) framework [26]. Tasks organization category was mapped to *goal setting, reduction,* and *self-mentoring* strategies. The category of space organization was mapped to *suggestion* strategy. Finally, the benefits of being organized category was mapped to *rewards, reminders,* and *social learning* strategies. The mapping aims to guide in designing persuasive interventions to assist students and promote favourable perceptions and attitudes towards task and space organization.

4   Designing of SortOut Mobile Application

Persuasive interventions in the form of mobile apps to support effective time management via promoting students' preference for organization can yield positive outcomes for students experiencing mental and physical clutter. SortOut mobile app, inspired by its design objective, focuses on assisting students to be organized, take control of their time, and hence reduce stress by helping them organize their tasks and study spaces. SortOut design involves six core features that employ the recommended and appropriate persuasive strategies (see Sect. 3). Table 1 presents the features, their descriptions, and corresponding persuasive strategies.

Table 1. Core features of SortOut app and the corresponding persuasive strategies.

Feature	Description	Persuasive strategies
Task Organization	Eisenhower's matrix [7], a popular time management matrix, was incorporated in the design as a template. It can be easily filled or changed as necessary to aid students in sorting out their tasks (or goals) based on their importance/urgency (see Fig. 2)	*Reduction*
Adding Tasks	Users can add their tasks (or goals), set deadlines and describe specific steps, which would help them in accomplishing their tasks. Users can use the customized reminders for each task based on their preferences	*Goal Setting, Customize reminders*
Healthy Brain	Users will be rewarded with flowers for each task they complete in a gamified way. The colours of the flowers correspond to Eisenhower's matrix tasks' colours (see Fig. 3)	*Rewards*
Progress Tracking	This feature allows users to monitor and track their progress towards completing the tasks on a weekly and monthly basis (see Fig. 4)	*Self-monitoring*
Social Community	This feature allows users to observe, interact and learn new organizational strategies and techniques from other users' posts (see Fig. 5)	*Social learning*
Notifications	Users will receive two types of daily notifications: 1) suggestions and tips to help users minimize physical clutter in order to create a better-organized study space, and 2) messages to emphasize the benefits of adhering to organizational acts	*Suggestion Daily reminders*

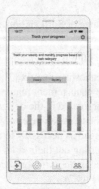

Fig. 2. Task organization   **Fig. 3.** Healthy brain   **Fig. 4.** Progress tracking   **Fig. 5.** Social community

5 Research Questions

This study aims to investigate the perceived effectiveness of the recommended strategies, usefulness, usability, and the motivational appeal of SortOut app. Therefore, we asked the following research questions (**RQs**):

RQ1: *How persuasive are the core features of SortOut app?*
RQ2: *What is the most effective persuasive strategy used in the design of SortOut app?*
RQ3: *What is the perceived usefulness of SortOut app in helping students to manage their time and improve their study performance?*
RQ4: *How easy is it to use the SortOut app?*
RQ5: *How effective is SortOut app with respect to the motivational appeal?*

6 Methodology

To answer the study research questions, we deployed a prototype of SortOut app online along with survey questions. We recruited the target participants anonymously using various approaches via email and social media (Facebook, Twitter, and WhatsApp).The survey included a link to interactive high-fidelity prototypes (HFPs) of SortOut app, developed using Proto.io [36]. Participants interacted with the prototypes and had a full experience of the app features before answering the survey questions. At the beginning of the survey, participants were informed about the purpose of the study, data and privacy using the study consent form.

6.1 Study Design

The survey started off with demographic questions such as age group, gender, current degree, and employment status. After interacting with the SortOut app, to assess the persuasiveness of each feature of the app, we presented the screenshot of each feature as a set of images, each feature is immediately followed by the persuasiveness scale. The persuasiveness of an app can be explained as the system's ability to initiate change in order to achieve the desired behaviour [27]. The persuasiveness scale is comprised of four 5-point Likert items assessing the perceived effectiveness of each feature measured from 1- strongly disagree to 5- strongly agree [28, 32]. We also included three scales that assess the perceived ease of use, usefulness, and motivational appeal of the app. The perceived ease of use scale, which comprises six 7-point Likert items ranging from 1 (extremely unlikely) to 7 (extremely likely) [8], measures the degree to which users believe that using a system would be free of difficulty and/or great effort. The perceived usefulness scale, comprised of six 7-point Likert items ranging from 1 (extremely unlikely) to 7 (extremely likely) [8], measures the degree to which users believe that using a system would enhance their performances in a particular area. To measure the apps motivational appeal, we used the ARCS motivation model scale comprises 12 items in 5-point Likert, 1-strongly disagree to 5-strongly agree and consists of four dimensions of motivation: *attention, relevance, confidence, and satisfaction* [13]. The ARCS model highlights the qualities an app needs to have in order to motivate the target users. The model is widely used in the design and evaluation of the motivational appeal of persuasive and behaviour change interventions; for details, see [1, 24, 35]. The survey concluded with an open-ended question to gather general feedback and suggestions related to the app for further improvement.

7 Results

After excluding incomplete responses, we analyzed a total of 68 responses. Table 2 shows the participants' demographics. The study sample was diverse in terms of age, gender, the current degree of study, and employment status. The majority of participants are between the age of 25–35 years old who are current students.

Table 2. Demographics of the participants (n = 68).

Categories	
Gender	Male (51%), Female (49%), Other (0%)
Age	18–24 (19%), 25–34 (50%), 35–44 (26%), Over 45 (4%)
Current Degree of study	Undergraduate (56%), Graduate (44%)
Employment status	Yes (79%), No (21%)

7.1 Perceived Persuasiveness of the App Core Features

In this study, the Cronbach's Alpha score for the persuasiveness scale for each persuasive strategy ranged between 0.73–0.81. To answer **RQ1** and **RQ2**, we computed the persuasiveness score for each feature. As shown in Fig. 6, the average scores of each persuasive strategy: *reduction, goa setting, rewards, self-monitoring, social learning, customized and daily reminders,* and *suggestions* were above the neutral mid-point. The results of the one-sample t-test shows the persuasiveness is significant for all strategies (p < .0001). Thus, we concluded that participants perceived all the app features as persuasive and *reduction* strategy was ranked as the most effective persuasive strategy.

7.2 Perceived Usability–Usefulness and Ease of Use of the App

The Cronbach's Alpha for the usability scale in this study is 0.84, and 0.85 for the usefulness scale. To answer **RQ3** and **RQ4**, we computed the average scores of both the perceived usefulness and ease of use of the app. Figure 7 shows that participants average calculated scores were above the midpoint (4). The results of the one-sample t-test were also significant for both scales (p < .0001) Together, these findings show that 1) the app is found useful and has the potential to promote the target time management behaviour among students to improve their study performance and reduce stress. 2) the app is found by students to be easy to use and interact with.

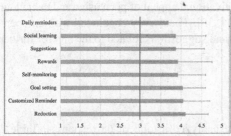

Fig. 6. The average scores of the persuasive strategies on a scale of 1 to 5. The red vertical line represents the neutral rating (middle line-3). (Color figure online)

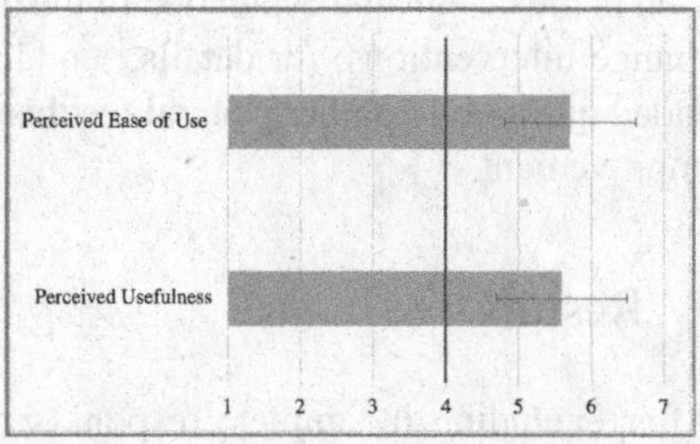

Fig. 7. The average scores of perceived usefulness and perceived ease of use, on a scale of 1 to 7. The red vertical line represents the neutral rating (middle line-4). (Color figure online)

7.3 Motivational Appeal of the App

The results of Cronbach's Alpha of the overall motivational appeal scale in our study is 0.905. Further, to answer **RQ5**, we calculated the average scores of the overall motivational appeal of the app and for the four constructs of the ARCS model. After comparing the average scores against a neutral rating of 3 on a 5-point Likert scale, we found that the overall motivational appeal was significant, $(t(67) = 14.557, p < .0001)$, and the four constructs of ARCS model were also significant (p < .0001). Thus, the app has the ability to motivate desired time management behaviour via organization of tasks and study spaces. See Fig. 8 and Table 3.

7.4 Effectiveness of SourOut App Design Based on Gender and Degree Level

We also examined the effectiveness of the app with respect to differences based on gender and degree level. The overall results show no differences in perceived persuasiveness, usability, and usefulness between males and females and graduates and undergraduates.

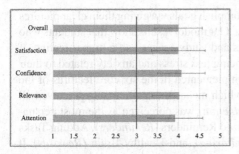

Fig. 8. The average scores of the overall motivational appeal and its constructs on a scale of 1 to 5. The red vertical line represents the neutral rating (middle line-3). (Color figure online)

Table 3. The statistical results of the motivational appeal scale.

Motivation appeal	Mean	t	P-value
Attention	3.91	11.460	<.0001
Relevance	4.01	12.976	<.0001
Confidence	4.19	15.491	<.0001
Satisfaction	3.99	12.770	<.0001
Overall	4.02	14.557	<.0001

All groups perceived the app features as persuasive, and the app is easy to use and useful. The only difference is that the app design aroused and sustained females' attention more than males, (t(66) = −1.93, p ≤ .05). Otherwise, all groups found the app effective in motivating the desired time management behaviour.

7.5 Thematic Analysis of Qualitative Feedback and Suggestions

Figure 9 shows the six main themes with their definition revealed from the thematic analysis performed on participants' feedback and suggestions to refine the app design.

Interesting, useful, and ease to use	Appreciation for the social community	Appreciation for the customized reminders	Flexibility of the daily notifications	Adding praise strategy	Incorporating introductory screens
The app design as it is easy to use, attractive, and helpful	The use of social element in the app design is motivating	Liking the flexibility of the task reminders, which can be customized based on preferences	Allowing users to enable/disable daily notifications would help reduce the feeling of being overwhelmed	Praising users when they complete their tasks	Adding introductory screens that explain how the app works for first time users

Fig. 9. The six main themes with their definitions revealed from the thematic analysis performed on participants' feedback and suggestions

8 Discussion

Mobile apps are ubiquitous and provide effective means to promote time management behaviour. Based on the large-scale study results and informed by the popular Eisenhower's matrix [7], we designed SortOut app to help students manage their time by organizing their study spaces and sorting out their tasks based on their importance and urgency. It has been reported that physical clutter and disorganization can increase individuals' cognitive overload and reduce the ability to focus [22]. Organization is essential to improve students' focus and help them accomplish goals via giving them clear pictures of what is expected to be completed and when. Our model results show that students who managed their time by organizing their tasks and study spaces had a higher feeling of being in control of their times, thus, experiencing less stress and anxiety related to their studies. All the seven persuasive strategies implemented in the six core features of the SortOut app were significantly persuasive, which means that participants perceived all features as effective. Task Organization *(Reduction)* was perceived as the most persuasive feature, which was followed by Customized Reminders *(Reminders)*, Adding Tasks *(Goal Setting)*, Progress Tracking *(Self-monitoring),* and Healthy Brain *(Rewards).* It is important to note that the use of *reduction* strategy is common in physical activity and diet apps [29] while it is one of the least employed strategies for stress management [3] and mental health apps [4]. In this study, we highlight the importance of this strategy for designing an effective intervention for individuals suffering from stress and other mental-related issues. Furthermore, the usability of a system is essential to enable users to use the app and keep using it instead of feeling overwhelmed and quitting, thus, allowing them to accomplish their tasks effectively [8]. The results of the perceived ease use scale show that participants perceived the app design as significantly easy to use and interact with, which allows us to conclude that the SortOut app design is clear, understandable, and easy to navigate through. Furthermore, the participants rated the design of SortOut as significantly useful with respect to helping them to manage their time and improve their study performance; therefore, it can assist users in achieving the desired change [8]. The ARCS motivational model [13] suggests that designers could increase the motivational appeal of a system by focusing primarily on designing it to be relevant, capture and sustain users' attention, while promoting both their confidence and feeling of satisfaction with the system [27]. Our results show that SortOut is effective with respect to the motivational appeal. Specifically, confidence is the most effective motivational dimension promoted by the app, which was followed by relevance, satisfaction, and attention. The design of SortOut promoted users' confidence in their ability to manage their time using various strategies such as *reduction* and *self-monitoring*, both of which enabled users to control and establish confidence in their ability. Moreover, it is promising to see that the app captured and sustained females' attention more than males. Previous finding showed that female students have higher stress and anxiety levels than male students [2]; catching and maintaining females' attention while using the app would motivate them to improve their time management behaviour, reducing their stress and anxiety. From the analysis of participants' qualitative comments, they suggested more customized reminders/notifications and introductory screens that give users an overview of how the app work. Both of these suggestions have the potential to increase users' confidence [27]. Additionally, participants recommended we include some sort of praise after completing each task. The use of *praise* and *rewards strategies* could also increase uses' satisfaction [26].

9   Conclusion and Future Work

The accessibility and high penetration of mobile apps have made them practical tools to promote healthy behaviours. We applied the user-centered design approach by following the results of a large-scale study to develop a high-fidelity prototype of a persuasive mobile app called SortOut and evaluated it among the target audience. The app aims to help students manage their time by promoting organizational behaviour. The app evaluation results revealed a strong persuasiveness presence of the recommended seven persuasive strategies. Moreover, the results showed that the app's design is motivational, useful, and easy to use, which would help students in higher education to be organized with respect to their tasks and study spaces. The app evaluation approach was based on a one-time use case through a web-based application; such an approach does not cover a long-term use case of the app, which can be considered a limitation of the study. Therefore, we plan to implement the app using Flutter language, which would allow students to use it on different platforms. Also, we will conduct a large-scale and long-term study to evaluate SortOut app's effectiveness in real-life settings.

Acknowledgement. This research was undertaken, in part, thanks to funding from the Canada Research Chairs Program. We acknowledge the support of the Natural Sciences and Engineering Research Council of Canada (NSERC) through the Discovery Grant.

References

1. Al-Tawfiq, J.A., Pittet, D.: Improving hand hygiene compliance in healthcare settings using behavior change theories: reflections. Teach. Learn. Med. **25**(4), 374–382 (2013). https://doi.org/10.1080/10401334.2013.827575
2. Alhasani, M., Alkhawaji, A., Orji, R.: Mental health and time management behavior among students during COVID-19 pandemic: towards persuasive technology design. Hum. Behav. Emerg. Technol. (2022). https://doi.org/10.1155/2022/7376748
3. Alhasani, M., Mulchandani, D., Oyebode, O., Orji, R.: A systematic review of persuasive strategies in stress management apps. In: CEUR Workshop Proceedings, vol. 2662, April 2020
4. Alqahtani, F., AlKhalifah, G., Oyebode, O., Orji, R.: Apps for mental health: an evaluation of behavior change strategies and recommendations for future development. Front. Artif. Intell. **2**, 30 (2019). https://doi.org/10.3389/frai.2019.00030
5. Bewick, B., Koutsopouloub, G., Miles, J., Slaad, E., Barkham, M.: Changes in undergraduate students' psychological well-being as they progress through university. Stud. High. Educ. **35**(6), 633–645 (2010). https://doi.org/10.1080/03075070903216643
6. Cohen, S., Kamarck, T., Mermelstein, R.: Perceived stress scale. J. Health Soc. Behav. **10**(2), 386–396 (1983)
7. Covey, S.R., Merrill, A.R., Merrill, R.R.: First Things First: To Live, to Love, to Learn, to Leave a Legacy. Simon & Schuster, New York (1994)
8. Davis, F.D.: Perceived usefulness, perceived ease of use, and user acceptance of information technology. Manage. Inf. Syst. Res. Center Univ. Minnesota **13**(3), 319–340 (2013). https://doi.org/10.5962/bhl.title.33621
9. Evans, T.M., Bira, L., Gastelum, J.B., Weiss, L.T., Vanderford, N.L.: Evidence for a mental health crisis in graduate education. Nat. Biotechnol. **36**(3), 282–284 (2018). https://doi.org/10.1038/nbt.4089
10. Hollifield, M., Warner, T., Krakow, B., Westermeyer, J.: Mental health effects of stress over the life span of refugees. J. Clin. Med. **7**(2), 25 (2018). https://doi.org/10.3390/jcm7020025
11. Hurst, C.S., Baranik, L.E., Daniel, F.: College student stressors: a review of the qualitative research. Stress and Health **29**(4), 275–285 (2013). https://doi.org/10.1002/smi.2465

12. Kaye, M., McIntosh, D., Horowitz, J.: Stress: The Psychology of Managing Pressure (2017)
13. Keller, J.: How to integrate learner motivation planning into lesson planning: The ARCS model approach
14. Kitzrow, M.A.: The mental health needs of today's college students: challenges and recommendations. NASPA J. **46**(4), 646–660 (2009). https://doi.org/10.2202/1949-6605.5037
15. Kyndt, E., Berghmans, I., Dochy, F., Bulckens, L.: Time is not enough. Workload in higher education: a student perspective. High. Educ. Res. Dev. **33**(4), 684–698 (2014)
16. Larzelere, M.M., Jones, G.N.: Stress and health. Prim. Care Clin. Off. Pract. **35**(4), 839–856 (2008). https://doi.org/10.1016/j.pop.2008.07.011
17. Lay, C., Schouwenburg, H.: Trait procrastination, time management. J. Soc. Behav. Pers. **1**, 117–125 (1993)
18. Lazarus, R.S., Folkman, S.: Stress, appraisal, and coping. pp. 150–154. Springer (1984)
19. Locke, E.A., Latham, G.P.: Building a practically useful theory of goal setting and task motivation: a 35-year odyssey. Am. Psychol. **57**(9), 705–717 (2002). https://doi.org/10.1037/0003-066X.57.9.705
20. Macan, T.H., Shahani, C., Dipboye, R.L., Phillips, A.P.: College students' time management: correlations with academic performance and stress. J. Educ. Psychol. **82**(4), 760–768 (1990). https://doi.org/10.1037/0022-0663.82.4.760
21. McElroy, E., et al.: Demographic and health factors associated with pandemic anxiety in the context of COVID-19. Br. J. Health Psychol. **25**(4), 934–944 (2020). https://doi.org/10.1111/bjhp.12470
22. McMains, S., Kastner, S.: Interactions of top-down and bottom-up mechanisms in human visual cortex. J Neurosci. **31**(2), 587–597 (2011)
23. van der Meer, J., Jansen, E., Torenbeek, M.: It's almost a mindset that teachers need to change: first-year students' need to be inducted into time management. Stud. High. Educ. **35**(7), 777–791 (2010). https://doi.org/10.1080/03075070903383211
24. Muton, N.A.R., Zakaria, N. Damanhoori, F.: A conceptual framework of an e-mentoring system for orphan children using arcs motivational model. In: Proceedings 2010 International Symposium on Information Technology - System Development and Application and Knowledge Society, ITSim 2010, vol. 3, pp. 1280–1285 (2010). https://doi.org/10.1109/ITSIM.2010.5561459
25. Nonis, S.A., Hudson, G.I., Logan, L.B., Ford, C.W.: Influence of perceived control over time on college students' stress and stress-related outcomes. Res. High. Educ. **39**(5), 587–605 (1998). https://doi.org/10.1023/A:1018753706925
26. Oinas-kukkonen, H., Harjumaa, M.: Persuasive systems design: key issues, process model and system features. Commun. Assoc. Inf. Syst. **24**(1), 28 (2009)
27. Orji, R., Reilly, D., Oyibo, K., Orji, F.A.: Deconstructing persuasiveness of strategies in behaviour change systems using the ARCS model of motivation. Behav. Inf. Technol. **38**(4), 319–335 (2019). https://doi.org/10.1080/0144929X.2018.1520302
28. Orji, R., Vassileva, J., Mandryk, R.: Modeling the efficacy of persuasive strategies for different gamer types in serious games for health. User Model. User Adap. Inter. **24**(5), 453–498 (2014). https://doi.org/10.1007/s11257-014-9149-8
29. Oyebode, O., Ndulue, C., Alhasani, M., Orji, R.: Persuasive mobile apps for health and wellness: a comparative systematic review. In: Gram-Hansen, S.B., Jonasen, T.S., Midden, C. (eds.) PERSUASIVE 2020. LNCS, vol. 12064, pp. 163–181. Springer, Cham (2020). https://doi.org/10.1007/978-3-030-45712-9_13
30. Schönfeld, P., Brailovskaia, J., Bieda, A., Zhang, X.C., Margraf, J.: The effects of daily stress on positive and negative mental health: mediation through self-efficacy. Int. J. Clin. Health Psychol. **16**(1), 1–10 (2016). https://doi.org/10.1016/j.ijchp.2015.08.005

31. Shankar, N.L., Park, C.L.: Effects of stress on students' physical and mental health and academic success. Int. J. Sch. Educ. Psychol. **4**(1), 5–9 (2016). https://doi.org/10.1080/216 83603.2016.1130532

32. Thomas, R.J., Masthoff, J., Oren, N.: Can I influence you? Development of a scale to measure perceived persuasiveness and two studies showing the use of the scale. Front. Artif. Intell. **2**, 1–14 (2019). https://doi.org/10.3389/frai.2019.00024

33. Tomiyama, A.J.: Stress and obesity. Ann. Rev. Psychol. **70**, 703–718 (2019). https://doi.org/ 10.1146/annurev-psych-010418-102936

34. Wirtz, P.H., von Känel, R.: Psychological stress, inflammation, and coronary heart disease. Curr. Cardiol. Rep. **19**(11), 1–10 (2017). https://doi.org/10.1007/s11886-017-0919-x

35. Ying, M.H., Yang, K.T.: A game-based learning system using the ARCS model and fuzzy logic. J. Softw. **8**(9), 2155–2162 (2013). https://doi.org/10.4304/jsw.8.9.2155-2162

36. Proto.io: Prototypes that feel real. https://proto.io

Perceptions of Interactive, Real-Time Persuasive Technology for Managing Online Gambling

Emily Arden-Close[1]([⊠]) [iD], Elvira Bolat[2] [iD], Laura Vuillier[1] [iD], and Raian Ali[3] [iD]

[1] Department of Psychology, Faculty of Science and Technology,
Bournemouth University, Poole, UK
eardenclose@bournemouth.ac.uk
[2] Faculty of Management, Bournemouth University, Poole, UK
[3] College of Science and Engineering, Hamad Bin Khalifa University, Doha, Qatar

Abstract. Background: Interactive persuasive techniques, supported by the ability to retrieve real-time behaviour and other contextual data, offer an unprecedented opportunity to manage online activity. An example is Responsible Gambling (RG) tools. Currently, despite vast potential, they do not make use of real time gambling behaviour data, whether captured by operators (device, location, bets, limits set) or self-reported (finance, emotion, online browsing history). To design useful interactive persuasive tools, it is important to understand users' perceptions to ensure maximum acceptance.
Aims: Explore gamblers' perceptions of the potential of future online platforms in providing data-driven, real-time, persuasive interventions for supporting responsible online gambling. *Method*: Qualitative semi-structured interviews conducted with 22 gamblers (80% men; 15 ex-problem, 7 current), regarding perceptions of the potential of persuasive techniques. *Results*: Thematic analysis showed participants were positive about data-driven, real-time, interactive technology for (i) providing information (educational, personal and comparative), (ii) limiting gambling (time and money spent, access to gambling operators) and (iii) providing support to gamblers (advice, feedback and context sensing). The technology was identified as most appropriate for low to moderate gamblers. *Conclusions*: Participants were positive about the new data access, techniques and modalities of interactions for supporting responsible online gambling. To ensure maximum reach and acceptability, such technology should be customised to fit individual profiles. Personalisation and tailoring of content, interactivity, framing and timing are necessary to enhance acceptance of such technology and avoid reactance, unintended harm, inconvenience, and information overload.

Keywords: Persuasive technology · Technology acceptance · Responsible gambling

1 Introduction

According to the latest prevalence report, over 400,000 people in the UK identify as problem gamblers, and numbers of over-16s considered problem gamblers grew by 1/3

© Springer Nature Switzerland AG 2022
N. Baghaei et al. (Eds.): PERSUASIVE 2022, LNCS 13213, pp. 28–42, 2022.
https://doi.org/10.1007/978-3-030-98438-0_3

in three years [1]. These figures will likely increase further given the rapid expansion of online betting and advertising around major sporting events [2] and increase in problem gambling [3]. The COVID-19 lockdowns likely exacerbated this. First, because people stayed at home and therefore had more opportunities to gamble [4], and second because COVID-19 had significant financial consequences for some families [4] and people often gamble more during financial crises [5, 6]. Problem gambling can cause considerable harm to not only individuals but also their social circle [7, 8] and costs the UK up to £1.2 billion annually, in terms of costs to the healthcare service and days absent from work [9]. However, UK primary care practitioners are often unaware or unsure of the referral options for treating problem gamblers [10, 11]. Further, due to lack of spaces, access to treatment is limited, especially for individuals without concurrent addictions such as alcohol, or other health problems (Gambling Commission, 2019). Further, social stigma around online gambling means individuals who bet online often experience anxiety associated with rejection and conceal any problems they are experiencing, which may prevent them from seeking support [12].

Despite these risks, Internet gambling sites provide limited surveillance to protect potentially vulnerable individuals [1]. Ubiquitous accessibility (the ability to bet online from a mobile device at any time) exacerbates the scale and complexity of the problem. Online gambling enables rapid continuous play without breaks and even using multiple accounts on different gambling sites, simultaneously. This is an issue as many Internet gamblers chase losses, indicating preoccupation with gambling and irrational beliefs about likelihood of winning [13] Gambling-related harm is not restricted to those who meet clinical criteria for gambling disorders or experience severe gambling-related harms [14], but also occurs among low and moderate risk gamblers [15].

1.1 Current RG Tools

Gambling operators are usually required to provide a range of responsible gambling (RG) tools, such as deposit limits, breaks in play, messaging, and activity statements, to prevent development of gambling-related problems. Attitudes to RG tools are generally positive [16], particularly among non-problem gamblers [17]. Implementation of RG tools can enhance favourable attitudes to gambling operators [18] and users of RG tools think their gambling has changed as a result [19]. Current RG tools include Mentor and PlayScan, which led to reductions in money deposited, amounts bet, and total time spent on gambling in non-risk and at-risk, although not in high-risk users [20–22]. Further, individuals who are informed that their losses are greater than expected tend to reduce their gambling expenditure more than those informed their losses are in line with expectations [23]. However, utilisation of the functions of PlayScan was low [24] and usage reduced rapidly, in line with the 'law of attrition' [25]. Even when available, RG tools fail to engage gamblers significantly [26].

1.2 Limitations of Current RG Tools and Solutions from Persuasive Technology

Issues relating to RG tool usage may relate to their current functions and appeal to customers. Improvements can be made to their design to enhance appeal without compromising their effectiveness [17]. While RG tools have been in use for over a decade

[27], they do not currently provide real-time feedback. The Persuasive Design model [28] classifies the features of technology as primary task support, dialogue support, social support and credibility support. Based on this model, interactive, persuasive techniques could be designed to both nudge gamblers towards responsible online betting, through multimodal interaction and involvement of different stakeholders, and provide personalised and context-aware feedback about betting as it occurs, both retrospectively and proactively, using data about gambling, personal and social life activities. Such RG tools can be designed to be used via the operator's Application Programming Interface (API) and access gambling behaviour data, including bets placed and their status (won, lost, unsettled), deposit amounts, devices accessing the gambling site, location coordinates, self-exclusion requests, and limits set. Based on evidence that persuasive system design [28] enhances adherence to web-based interventions for health behaviour change [29] and enhanced RG when added to a money limit tool [30], such techniques offer an unprecedented opportunity to manage responsible online gambling beyond what is offered by current RG tools.

Evidence suggests that adding interactive, persuasive techniques to RG tools would be received positively by customers. Users of the RG tool PlayScan felt they would benefit from tailored feedback in response to their gambling patterns, pop-up messages reminding them of the tool when logging into the site and receiving emails/ text messages [20]. However, current data-driven technologies suffer from limited engagement due to a misfit between the technology and end users following lack of end user involvement in the development process. This threatens long-term implementation [31]. Several models have been developed to explain intentions to use such technologies. For example, the unified theory of acceptance and use of technology [32], developed based on review and consolidation of the constructs of eight behaviour change models holds that performance expectancy, effort expectancy, social influence and facilitating conditions, the impacts of which are moderated by gender, age, experience and voluntariness of use, influence intentions to use information systems and subsequent user behaviour. This model suggests that it is essential to explore gamblers' attitudes to the proposed technology to determine intention to use the technology in future.

1.3 Rationale

The current study builds on previous work around perceptions of RG tools e.g., [20] by exploring gamblers' perceptions of the potential of real-time, interactive technology, utilising a rich set of cross-operator online gambling behaviour data, personal and social context data, for supporting RG. Although previous research has explored perceptions of providing information about amounts gambled and providing best practice advice, it has not explored perceptions of tailored and interactive persuasive techniques. We provide a unique perspective by listening to the voice of ex-problem gamblers, who can retrospectively reflect on the technology in relation to their gambling experiences. As retrospective reflection is open to recall bias, we also recruited current gamblers, who could reflect on the technology in relation to their present experiences. This diversity helped identify a range of gamblers who would potentially benefit from the tools.

2 Method

2.1 Design

Qualitative semi-structured interviews explored experiences of gambling and reactions to software that could be used in an online platform designed to enable more informed online gambling. Possible content ideas were collated from a multidisciplinary team of software engineers, data scientists, health and social psychologists, gambling industry employees and individuals working with gambling addicts. See [33] for background around the platform and [34] for details about the architecture of such tools and their underlying design principles and modalities of operation.

2.2 Participants

We recruited 22 participants aged 18+ with a range of gambling levels, from occasional gamblers to problem gamblers in recovery. Ex-problem gamblers, who were abstinent at the time of interview (n = 15) were recruited via 1) an open call on social media, shared by organisations working in gambling awareness and RG, including advertising on the website of a residential treatment centre for gambling addicts, and 2) snowball sampling through participants 'and individuals working in addiction. Current gamblers (n = 7) were recruited via adverts on social media and in the local community. Recruitment stopped once saturation was reached. See Table 1 for demographic data.

Table 1. Demographics of ex-problem and current gamblers

Variable	Type of gambler	
	Ex-problem (n = 15)	Current (n = 7)
Age	38.4 (27–59)	44.6 (27–56)
Gender	13 (86.7%) male	6 (85.7%) male
Ethnicity	White: 14 (93.3%) Non-white: 1 (6.67%)	White: 4 (57.1%) Mixed race: 2 (28.6%) Non-white: 1 (14.3%)
Educational level	Degree: 2 (13.3%)	Degree: 3 (42.9%)
Employment Status	2 (13.3%) unemployed 13 (86.7%) employed FT	4 (57.1%) unemployed 3 (42.9%) employed FT
Worked in bookmakers	2 (13.3%)	1 (14.3%)

2.3 Procedure

Semi-structured interviews lasting 30 min to 2 h were conducted face-to-face (n = 7), by video conferencing (n = 5), or by telephone (n = 10), by the lead author, an experienced qualitative interviewer (female), audio recorded and transcribed verbatim. The interviewer had no previous knowledge or experience of gambling. However, she had knowledge of persuasion and software-assisted behaviour change. Approval was granted by the relevant ethics committee.

Participants provided written informed consent and demographic information and were shown a mobile application supported by the web platform our group designed to facilitate online RG. We emphasised that the platform: integrates with multiple operators; retrieves and utilises a wider range of data than currently offered by RG tools (i.e., accessing only data in relation to betting history and limit setting); is independent of operators and provides implicit and visual cues and social nudges. See Fig. 1 for images of RG data the platform offers.

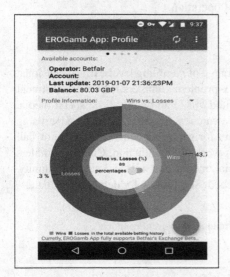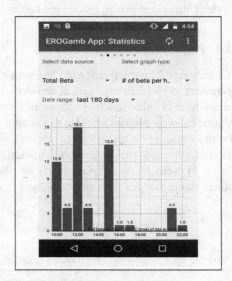

Fig. 1. Examples of data provided by the platform

Interviews comprised two parts. Part 1 explored participants' experiences of gambling, including where and when they gambled, why they stopped and started, the extent to which their family and friends knew about their gambling, and how they felt about it. Part 2 covered perceptions of potential aspects of our proposed technology-based solutions for both capturing gambling and context data and tailoring and issuing interventions. This included setting gambling goals, and how they would feel about: receiving comparative information about their gambling, receiving messages while gambling, educational materials, having access to their data, context sensing, reporting personal information, reporting emotions in relation to gambling and filling in questionnaires about their gambling. Participants were debriefed on completion.

2.4 Data Analysis

Data was analysed using thematic analysis [35]. The interviews were read, and reflexive notes made, then coded line-by-line. Codes were combined into themes and refined to produce a coding manual, which was initially created based on the first 15 interviews, and then refined based on subsequent interviews. Analysis was conducted by the first author and a proportion of interviews (20%) second coded, in line with best practice [35] and disagreements, which were minimal, were resolved by discussion. Following [20], Hill and colleagues' classifications [36] described the range of views within a subtheme. *General* answers were endorsed by all the sample but one, *typical* answers included over half, *a variant* included under half, and *rare* answers three participants or fewer. This aimed to identify the continuum of reactions.

3   Results

Participants saw the proposed technology as a tool for providing information, limiting money and time spent gambling, and providing support, as shown in Fig. 2.

Tool for providing information
- Providing educational information
- Providing personal information
- Providing comparative information

Tool for limiting gambling
- Setting time limits
- Setting money limits

Tool for providing support to gamblers
- Providing advice
- Context sensing
- Providing feedback

Fig. 2. Themes and subthemes identified

3.1   Tool for Providing Information

Participants felt the proposed technology-based solutions could provide **educational, personal and comparative information**, which would be sensitive to online gambling behaviour regarding timing and content of messages.

Providing Educational Information. Many ex-problem gamblers reported not realising they had a problem until they were in rehabilitation having lost large amounts of money and ruined relationships with family members. *Typical* participants felt information about the consequences of gambling would plant seeds of awareness and could be presented as educational text, audio, or real-life stories, to add a personal dimension. *Typical* ex-problem gamblers also felt information about the dangers of gambling would be most effective for low to moderate gamblers. Earlier stages were considered a 'teachable moment,' to identify individuals before the addiction consumed their lives.

Providing Personal Information. *Typical* participants felt visual information about their online betting activity (e.g., hours played, deposits, amounts won and lost over time), would raise awareness of their financial situation and facilitate budgeting. However, it is worth noting that *a variant* of ex-problem gamblers would not have wanted to see how much they were losing, although they acknowledged the potential positive impact of this information. Also, *typical* current gamblers wanted to receive data about their betting activity, including across operators to optimise their gambling, although *rare* ex-problem gamblers felt that providing such information might have the opposite effect to that intended, encouraging gamblers to chase their losses.

Providing Comparative Information. *A variant* of ex-problem gamblers felt comparative information about their gambling activity relative to others would shock them. Similarly, *rare* current gamblers felt comparative information would tap into the competitive nature of gambling. However, both *a variant* of ex-problem gamblers and *rare* current gamblers felt they would not care about how their gambling compared to others.

3.2 Tool for Limiting Gambling

Participants felt mobile application platforms could provide the facility to set **time and money limits,** based on gambling data.

Setting Time Limits. All ex-problem gamblers reported gambling for up to 8 h or more at a time, not wanting to stop until they had won. They felt time limits, particularly if set by the platform, would enable them to maintain control, and prevent loss chasing, as the longer they gambled, the less rational their choices became. However, time limits would need to be implemented with caution as *rare* participants were concerned some people would engage in more high-risk gambling if limited time remained. On the other hand, time spent gambling was not an issue for *typical* current gamblers, some of whom spent time researching the form of the sports team or horse before betting.

Setting Money Limits. *General* ex-problem gamblers felt setting spending limits through the platform would prevent losses of control. They said that the lack of physical notes means money seems unreal. *General* current gamblers, who reported budgeting, also highlighted how easy it was to spend online, particularly following a win. *General* ex-problem gamblers felt any limits would need to be nationwide, as many people have multiple accounts and if locked out of one online bookmaker would likely try another.

3.3 Tool for Providing Support to Gamblers

Participants felt the proposed technology could be used to provide support to individuals, by sending messages tailored to their gambling activity. They felt it could **provide advice, sense context** and **provide feedback.**

Providing Advice. *Typical* participants felt advice, e.g., around calculating disposable income, would facilitate budgeting and suggested budgeting forms should be made compulsory when signing up to gambling sites. *A variant* of ex-problem gamblers also felt that validated questionnaires (used in treatment), such as the Problem Gambling Severity Index [37] would be informative. However, *rare* problem gamblers expressed concerns that informing individuals their gambling was currently acceptable might lead to it becoming problematic.

Context Sensing. *Typical* participants were positive about using emoticons or a word or point on a scale to inform the application about their emotional state on a regular basis, so over time it could identify situations when they were more vulnerable. They felt this information could enable the platform to contact them in specific situations when they gambled more (e.g., when experiencing low mood). *Typical* ex-problem gamblers favoured receiving information about their location in relation to betting shops from an app, particularly if combined with suggestions for alternative activities nearby, to maintain accountability for their actions. However, *typical* current gamblers and *rare* ex-problem gamblers felt that context sensing was too intrusive, invading on their privacy.

Providing Feedback. *A variant* of ex-problem gamblers felt receiving feedback in response to pre-set gambling-related goals would provide motivation and encouragement. *A variant* of ex-problem and *typical* current gamblers thought receiving personalized warnings would be helpful if they were reaching the end of their limits or following an unusual betting pattern/placing an unusually high bet. However, *a variant* of ex-problem gamblers said they would ignore/dismiss pop-ups. To facilitate switching attention, *rare* ex-problem gamblers (all female) said they would feel supported by telephone calls inquiring after their wellbeing and encouraging them to take breaks (Table 2).

4 Discussion

4.1 Summary of the Findings

This study built on previous research into perceptions of RG tools [17, 20] to explore individuals' views of the use of online gambling behavioural data and interactive real-time technology for managing responsible gambling. Both ex-problem and current gamblers viewed the technology positively, indicating its potential to help a range of individuals. Participants were positive about a tool that would provide information, facilitate sustainable gambling and provide support to gamblers, in line with research that gamblers view RG tools as positive features [17] with the potential to change gambling behaviour [20]. However, negative impacts of aspects of the tool were also reported (e.g., bet more if aware that less time left), in line with evidence that in certain contexts some persuasive design principles may trigger digital addiction [38]. Further, participants felt interactive real-time technology would enable low to moderate gamblers to limit their gambling whilst still controllable. Problem gamblers likely require intensive residential treatment followed by abstinence.

Table 2. Relevant Quotes from the interviews

Theme	Sub-theme	Relevant Quotes
Tool for providing information	Providing educational information	*"Seeing other people and hearing other people could help ... anyone in their gambling career to hear someone say ... I didn't think I had a problem, I developed a problem and this is where I am now"* **[P20, male, ex-problem gambler]** *"for me, if you've got a problem, you can't control it doesn't matter if ... you set yourself a limit ... you're just setting yourself on a downward spiral."* **[P24, male, ex-problem gambler]**
	Providing personal information	*"Having a visual look of what I spent, it makes it real then, wow I didn't realise I spent £500 a day for the past 2 weeks on [gambling operator's] website."* **[P3, male, ex-problem gambler]** *"while I was gambling if I knew how much money I was losing, it would make me want to win that money."* **[P24, male, ex-problem gambler]** *"that [providing data across operators] would be useful because it would tell me which operator is paying out the best odds and the best money."* **[P10, male, current gambler]**
	Providing comparative information	*"I'd be like, "Wow, I'm in the top 5% [of gamblers] here in a population of quarter of a million." That would be scary"* **[P1, male, ex-problem gambler]** *"Yes, I think that's actually a good idea, because gamblers [are]-- very competitive people"* **[P6, male, current gambler]**
Tool for limiting gambling	Setting time limits	*"At the worst ... I'd normally gamble in the evening and then it end up all night."* **[P18, female, ex-problem gambler]** *"I would double or treble my stakes if you say, "You've only got three more spins whatever happens. "* **[P2, male, ex-problem gambler]** *"I have a look at the race that's on. I just look at the horses, and what their odds are, and the names as well... I'd say I spend more time looking at the slip, as opposed to putting a lot of money on a lot of the races."* **[P15, female, current gambler]**

(continued)

Table 2. (*continued*)

Theme	Sub-theme	Relevant Quotes
	Setting money limits	*"it makes it numb because it's not real, it's sort of virtual money"* **[P2, male, ex-problem gambler]** *"especially if you had a win, it's quite easy just to think, "If I'd put on more money, I would have got more money back, so let's have a look at something else maybe"* **[P15, female, current gambler]** *"if you set £50 [limit] for six accounts, then you can spend £300".* **[P16, male, ex-problem gambler]**
Tool for providing support to gamblers	Providing advice	*"an app like that, so you put in everything, what you've got coming in, what you've got coming out, and then whatever spare money you've got … if you've got that to gamble with that is totally spare money, … I think that one is definitely beneficial."* **[P16, male, ex-problem gambler]**
	Context sensing	*"I think I've gambled when I was really low. That was the middle stages of my addiction … I think [reporting emotions] would be a good idea."* **[P22, male, ex-problem gambler]**
	Providing feedback	*"Something visual to say, "I've not gambled today." Maybe how much your limit was gambling each day. Say, it's £50 each day and you say you've not gambled for 10 days. Let's see how much money you've saved."* **[P1, male, ex-problem gambler]** *"[messages] would really have been helpful at the time because anything that gives you a reason to switch your whole attention from what you're doing"* **[P2, male, ex-problem gambler]** *"It [pop-up] was just … a nuisance. I know better than some pop-up on a screen telling me that I've been on this long enough."* **[P21, male, ex-problem gambler]** *"You've been playing for quite a while, make sure you don't get headaches … Why not take a break?" Just in a way to make it that you're doing it for the interest of my health."* **[P13, female, ex-problem gambler]**

4.2 Discussion of Findings in Relation to Previous Research

Abraham and Michie's taxonomy of behaviour change techniques used in interventions [39] identified self-monitoring of behaviour and feedback on performance as effective behaviour change strategies. In our study, participants welcomed opportunities provided by interactive real-time technology to track player data and provide personalized feedback [40] as they wished to see their gambling data in real time. This ties in with findings that users of a RG tool wanted more feedback on their gambling habits [20]. Our study suggests provision of real-time gambling behavioural data (which is currently collected by gambling operators) to customers would be an excellent way to enable responsible data sharing, and in turn facilitate corporate social responsibility goals of transparency and accountability, benefiting all involved. However, this should be implemented with caution as some ex-problem gamblers mentioned seeing losses would trigger loss chasing. Effective messages are needed to combat this.

In line with control theory [39], prompting goal setting and review of behavioural goals was welcomed. Goal setting is an effective behaviour change strategy [39, 41] and behavioural feedback about gambling led to reductions in deposits over 24 weeks in social and at-risk but not problem gamblers [21]. These findings suggest goal setting is a potential preventative measure rather than an intervention for problem gambling. Further research needs to identify individuals whilst their gambling is under control, to ensure they receive timely support.

Both ex-problem and current gamblers viewed money limits positively. Similarly, an RG tool led to reduced deposits, amounts bet, and time spent on gambling [20, 21]. Money limits are rarely exceeded once set [28] and could easily be implemented in practice. Participants felt limits should be across operators to reduce loss chasing, in line with evidence that problematic gamblers play multiple platforms concurrently [42].

Gamblers can enter states of dissociation leading to loss of track of time and money spent gambling [43]. Time and monetary pop-up reminders may combat dissociative states as well as addressing failures to adhere to pre-set limits. Many participants felt such reminders would switch their attention. However, others considered pop-ups a nuisance to ignore. Similarly, pop-ups were relatively ineffective in reducing gambling among gambling-intense individuals [44]. Further research is needed to determine their effectiveness for low to moderate gamblers.

Participants were positive about recording their emotions so that over time, applications could identify mood shifts associated with problem gambling-relevant because problem gambling may be a way of coping with difficult emotions [45]. Identification of mood shifts could be combined with offering appropriate support. This corroborates findings that online peer support groups may prevent digital addiction [46, 47]. However, problem gambling has been associated with alexithymia, a difficulty identifying and describing feelings [48]. Further exploration of the potential of mood sensing technology to facilitate responsible gambling might be helpful.

4.3 Individual Differences

Important differences between participants were identified. Ex-problem gamblers felt time limits would help them control their gambling. However, current gamblers spent time on sports betting websites checking the form of players/horses, which often equated to improved prediction of outcomes, not extra bets. Further, ex-problem gamblers mentioned limits could lead to gambling larger sums of money to compensate for the shorter duration. Similarly, although some participants received context sensing positively, others considered it intrusive, in line with research on use of smartphone applications for supporting health behaviour change [49]. This highlights the importance of tailoring, to ensure potential limits and technologies are appropriate to the type of betting and gambler in facilitating RG [50, 51].

4.4 Limitations

Over 80% of participants were male, despite our efforts to recruit female gamblers. Further research is needed to explore female gamblers' experiences and views regarding real-time interactive technology for managing RG. This is particularly important given gender differences were identified-women were more likely than men to frame technology as a helper from whom they desired support, in line with recent research where women preferred digital addiction labels to include supportive content [52].

Information about gambling was self-reported. While the ex-problem gamblers had clearly experienced significant gambling-related issues (many were recruited via an organisation providing therapy to problem gamblers), current gamblers' levels of gambling were not recorded, although most reported managing budgets. A questionnaire such as the PGSI [37] would have quantified levels of gambling.

The interviews should have included more information about rights to data, how it will be used and how long it will be stored by the application, to enhance awareness of the consequences of the intervention. However, interviews informed participants that gambling operators were collecting data and using it for marketing based on terms and conditions many people accept without reading, and that according to GDPR, participants had the right to access their data. Given this context, additional concerns about the app having access to their data were not raised.

As participants had not trialled use of real-time interactive technology to manage responsible gambling, it is unclear how they would use it in practice. In particular, the concept of independent parties offering RG tools was novel. Further, most were unfamiliar with long-term support increasing personalisation of dialogue. Although we showed them a video about the concept, application and website for a more tangible experience, further exploration of the use of such technology in practice is required.

5 Conclusions

Building on previous research, participants were positive about data-driven, interactive, real-time technology. The range of strategies offered to promote responsible gambling, were particularly lauded by ex-problem gamblers, who had used a range of tools to recover from their addictions. Interactive, real-time technology, by retrieving and utilising a wider range of data than what RG tools currently provide, offers a promising opportunity to reach customers whilst their gambling is under control, facilitated by tailoring support to the gambler.

References

1. Gambling Commission: Participation in gambling and rates of problem gambling – England (2016). https://www.gamblingcommission.gov.uk/PDF/survey-data/England-Health-Survey-Findings-2016.pdf. Accessed 09 Mar 2020
2. Abbott, M.: The epidemiology and impact of gambling disorder and other gambling-related harm. Discussion paper for the 2017 WHO Forum on alcohol, drugs and addictive behaviors, WHO Headquarters, Geneva (2017)
3. Calado, F., Griffiths, M.: Problem gambling worldwide: an update and systematic review of empirical research. J. Behav. Addict. **5**(4), 592–613 (2016)
4. Hakansson, A., Fernandez-Aranda, F., Menchon, J.M., Potenza, M.N., Jimenez-Murcia, S.: Gambling during the COVID-19 crisis: a cause for concern. J. Addict. Med. **14**, e10–e12 (2020)
5. Economou, M., Souliotis, K., Mallori, M., et al.: Problem gambling in Greece: prevalence and risk factors during the financial crisis. J. Gambl. Stud. **35**(4), 1193–1210 (2019)
6. Olason, D.T., Hayer, T., Brosowski, T., Meyer, G.: Gambling in the mist of economic crisis: results from three national prevalence studies from Iceland. J. Gambl. Stud. **31**(3), 759–774 (2015)
7. Goodwin, B.C., Browne, M., Rockloff, M., Rose, J.: A typical problem gambler affects six others. Int. J. Gambl. Stud. **17**, 276–289 (2017)
8. Langham, E., Thorne, H., Browne, M., Donaldson, P., Rose, J., Rockloff, M.: Understanding gambling related harm: a proposed definition, conceptual framework and taxonomy of harms. BMC Public Health **16**, 80 (2015)
9. Thorley, C., Stirling, A., Huynh, E.: Cards on the table: the cost to government associated with people who are problem gamblers in Britain. Institute for Public Policy Research. https://about.gambleaware.org/media/1367/cards-on-the-table_dec16.pdf. Accessed 23 July 2018
10. Sanju, G., Gerada, C.: Problem gamblers in primary care: can GPs do more? Br. J. Gen. Pract. **61**(585), 248–249 (2011)
11. Gambling Commission: Gambling participation in 2018 – behaviour, awareness and attitudes. Annual report February 2019 (2019). https://www.gamblingcommission.gov.uk/PDF/survey-data/Gambling-participation-in-2018-behaviour-awareness-and-attitudes.pdf. Accessed 10 Mar 2020
12. Dabrowska, K., Wieczorek, L.: Perceived social stigmatisation of gambling disorders and coping with stigma. Nordic Stud. Alcohol Drugs **37**(3), 279–297 (2020)
13. Gainsbury, S.M., Suhonen, N., Saastamoinen, J.: Chasing losses in online poker and casino games: characteristics and game play of gamblers at risk of disordered gambling. Psychiatry Res. **217**, 220–225 (2014)
14. Weinstock, J., April, L.M., Kallmi, S.: Is subclinical gambling really subclinical? Addict. Behav. **73**, 185–191 (2017)
15. Canale, N., Vieno, A., Griffiths, M.D.: The extent and distribution of gambling-related harms and the prevention paradox in a British population survey. J. Behav. Addict. **5**(2), 204–212 (2016)
16. Engebo, J., Torsheim, T., Mentzoni, R.A., Molde, H., Pallesen, S.: Predictors of gamblers beliefs about responsible gambling measures. J. Gambl. Stud. **35**(4), 1375–1396 (2019)
17. Ivanova, E., Rafi, J., Lindner, P., Carlbrig, P.: Experiences of responsible gambling tools among non-problem gamblers: a survey of active customers of an online gambling platform. Addict. Behav. Rep. **9**, 100161 (2019)
18. Gainsbury, S., Parke, J., Suhonen, N.: Consumer attitudes towards Internet gambling: perceptions of responsible gambling policies, consumer protection, and regulation of online gambling sites. Comput. Hum. Behav. **29**(1), 235–245 (2013)

19. Gainsbury, S., Angus, D., Procter, L., Blazsczynski, A.: Use of consumer protection tools on internet-gambling sites: customer perceptions, motivations and barriers to use. J. Gambl. Stud. **36**(1), 259–276 (2020)
20. Forsstrom, D., Jansson-Frojmark, M., Hesser, H., Carlbrig, P.: Experiences of playscan: interviews with users of a responsible gambling tool. Internet Interv. **8**, 53–62 (2017)
21. Wood, R.T.A., Wohl, M.J.A.: Assessing the effectiveness of a responsible gambling behavioural feedback tool for reducing the gambling expenditure of at-risk players. Int. Gambl. Stud. **15**(2), 1–16 (2015)
22. Auer, M.M., Griffiths, M.D.: The use of personalized behavioral feedback for online gamblers: an empirical study. Front. Psychol. **6**, 1406 (2015)
23. Auer, M., Griffiths, M.D.: Cognitive dissonance, personalized feedback and online gambling behavior: an exploratory study using objective tracking data and subjective self-report. Int. J. Mental Health Addict. **16**(3), 631–641 (2018)
24. Forsstrom, D., Hesser, H., Carlbrig, P.: Usage of a responsible gambling tool: a descriptive analysis and latent class analysis of user behaviour. J. Gambl. Stud. **32**, 889–904 (2016)
25. Eysenbach, G.: The law of attrition. J. Med. Internet Res. **7**(1), e11 (2005)
26. Procter, L., Angus, D.J., Blaszczynski, A., Gainsbury, S.M.: Understanding use of consumer protection tools among internet gambling customers: utility of the theory of planned behavior and theory of reasoned action. Addict. Behav. **99**, 106050 (2019)
27. Griffiths, M.D., Wood, R.T.A., Parke, J.: Social responsibility tools in online gambling: a survey of attitudes and behavior among Internet gamblers. Cyberpsychol. Behav. **12**(4), 413–421 (2009)
28. Oinas-Kukkonen, H., Harjumaa, M.: Persuasive systems design: key issues, process model, and system features. Commun. Assoc. Inf. Syst. **24**, 485–500 (2009)
29. Kelders, S.M., Kok, R.N., Ossebaard, H.C., Van Gemert-Pijnen, J.E.: Persuasive system design does matter: a systematic review of adherence to web-based interventions. J. Med. Internet Res. **14**(6), e52 (2012)
30. Wohl, M.J., Parush, A., Kim, H.S., Warren, K.: Building it better: applying human-computer interaction and persuasive design to principles to a monetary limit tool improves responsible gambling. Comput. Hum. Behav. **37**, 124–132 (2014)
31. Keizer, J., Jong, N.B., Naiemi, N.A., van Gemert-Pijnen, J.E.W.C.: Persuading from the start: participatory development of sustainable persuasive data-driven technologies in healthcare. In: Gram-Hansen, S.B., Jonasen, T.S., Midden, C. (eds.) PERSUASIVE 2020. LNCS, vol. 12064, pp. 113–125. Springer, Cham (2020). https://doi.org/10.1007/978-3-030-45712-9_9
32. Ventakesh, V., Morris, M.G., Davis, G.B., Davis, F.D.: User acceptance of information technology: toward a unified view. MIS Q. **10**(3), 425–478 (2003)
33. Drosatos, G., et al.: Enabling responsible online gambling by real-time persuasive technologies. Complex Syst. Inform. Model. Q. **17**, 44–68 (2018)
34. Drosatos, G., Arden-Close, E., Bolat, E., Ali, R.: Gambling data and modalities of interaction for responsible online gambling: a qualitative study. J. Gambl. Issues **44**, 139–169 (2020)
35. Braun, V., Clarke, V.: Using thematic analysis in psychology. Qual. Res. Psychol. **3**(2), 77–101 (2006)
36. Hill, C.E., Knox, S., Thompson, B.J., Williams, E.N., Hess, S.A., Ladany, N.: Consensual qualitative research: an update. J. Couns. Psychol. **52**(2), 196 (2005)
37. Ferris, J., Wynne, H.: The Canadian problem gambling index: User manual. Canadian Centre on Substance Abuse, Ottawa (2001)
38. Cemiloglu, D., Naiseh, M., Catania, M., Oinas-Kukkonen, H., Ali, R.: The fine line between persuasion and digital addiction. In: Ali, R., Lugrin, B., Charles, F. (eds.) PERSUASIVE 2021. LNCS, vol. 12684, pp. 289–307. Springer, Cham (2021). https://doi.org/10.1007/978-3-030-79460-6_23

39. Abraham, C., Michie, S.: A taxonomy of behaviour change techniques used in interventions. Health Psychol. **27**(3), 379–387 (2008)

40. Auer, M., Griffiths, M.D.: Voluntary limit setting and player choice in the most in-tense online gamblers: an empirical study of gambling behaviour. J. Gambl. Stud. **29**, 647–660 (2013)

41. Gollwitzer, P.M., Sheeran, P.: Implementation intentions and goal achievement: a meta-analysis of effects and processes. Adv. Exp. Soc. Psychol. **38**, 69–119 (2006)

42. McCormack, A., Shorter, G.W., Griffiths, M.D.: Characteristics and predictors of problem gambling on the internet. Int. J. Ment. Heal. Addict. **11**(6), 634–657 (2013)

43. Jacobs, D.F.: A general theory of addictions: a new theoretical model. J. Gambl. Behav. **2**, 15–31 (1986)

44. Auer, M., Malischnig, D., Griffiths, M.D.: Is 'pop-up' messaging in online slot machine gambling effective as a responsible gambling strategy? An empirical research note. J. Gambl. Issues **29**, 1–10 (2014)

45. Wood, R.T.A., Griffiths, M.D.: A qualitative investigation of problem-gambling as an escape-based coping strategy. Psychol. Psychother. Theory Res. Pract. **80**, 107–125 (2007)

46. Alrobai, A., Algashami, A., Dogan, H., Corner, T., Phalp, K., Ali, R.: COPE.er method: combating digital addiction via online peer support groups. Int. J. Environ. Res. Public Health **16**(7), 1162 (2019)

47. Alrobai, A., Dogan, H., Phalp, K., Ali, R.: Building online platforms for peer support groups as a persuasive behavior change technique. In: Ham, J., Karapanos, E., Morita, P.P., Burns, C.M. (eds.) PERSUASIVE 2018. LNCS, vol. 10809, pp. 70–83. Springer, Cham (2018). https://doi.org/10.1007/978-3-319-78978-1_6

48. Bonnaire, C., Barrault, S., Aite, A., Cassotti, M., Moutier, S., Varescon, I.: Relationship between pathological gambling, alexithymia, and gambling type. Am. J. Addict. **26**, 152–160 (2017)

49. Dennison, L., Morrison, L., Conway, G., Yardley, L.: Opportunities and challenges for smart-phone applications in supporting health behaviour change: qualitative study. J. Med. Internet Res. **15**(4), e86 (2013)

50. Morrison, L.G., Yardley, L., Powell, J., Michie, S.: What design features are used in effective e-health interventions? A review using techniques from critical interpretative synthesis. Telemed. J. e Health **18**(2), 137–144 (2012)

51. Wildeboer, G., Kelders, S.M., van Gemert-Pijnen, J.E.: The relationship between persuasive technology principles, adherence and effect of web-based interventions for mental health: a meta-analysis. Int. J. Med. Inform. **96**, 71–85 (2016)

52. McAlaney, J., Arden-Close, E., Ali, R.: Gender differences in attitudes towards prevention and intervention messages for digital addiction. In: WorldCist 2019 - 7th World Conference on Information Systems and Technologies, La Toja Island, Galicia, Spain (2019)

Human-Robot Interaction and User Manipulation

Andrea Bertolini[1]([✉]) and Rachele Carli[2,3] [iD]

[1] DIRPOLIS Institute and EURA (European Centre of Excellence on the Regulation of Robotics & AI), Scuola Superiore Sant'Anna, Pisa, Italy
andrea.bertolini@santannapisa.it
[2] Alma Mater Research Institute for Human-Centered AI, University of Bologna, Bologna, Italy
rachele.carli2@unibo.it
[3] ICR Group, AI RoboLab, University of Luxembourg, Esch-sur-Alzette, Luxembourg

Abstract. The analysis presented is focused on the interaction among social robots and humans. It is here stated that, despite the multidisciplinary debate around the theme, social robots have to be ontologically deemed objects. The pleasant design and the simulation of intelligence, as much as social and emotional competences, are useful to convey acceptability and to favour interaction. However, they may lead to forms of manipulation which can impact the users' will and undermine their physical and psychological integrity. This rises the need of a legal framework, able to guarantee a really human-centred development of new technologies and to ensure the protection of people involved in the interaction. Therefore, the recent European proposal of regulation, the Artificial Intelligence Act, is examined. In particular, the section on prohibited practices is critically analysed, so as to highlight the controversial aspects of such an approach. Thus, it is suggested the role of human dignity as a balancing principle to address the issues related to user manipulation in the human-robot interaction domain.

Keywords: Social robotics · Manipulation · Human dignity

1 Introduction

The human-robot interaction (henceforth HRI) research field is increasingly focusing on improving the collaboration between humans and machines, making the former more comfortable during the interaction and the latter more efficient in carrying out their tasks. To this end, particular attention has been paid to equipping robots with pleasant – sometimes even human-like or pet-like – design, as much as social and cultural competences [1].

These expedients help to provide the user with the feeling of being in presence of a machine really endowed with intelligence and internal states, that allows affection and empathic response [2]. Such mechanisms are, in reality, simply simulated – at least for the moment – since social robots are devices specifically programmed to perform certain functions and to rise human emotional bond [3]. In fact, they cannot display a

© Springer Nature Switzerland AG 2022
N. Baghaei et al. (Eds.): PERSUASIVE 2022, LNCS 13213, pp. 43–57, 2022.
https://doi.org/10.1007/978-3-030-98438-0_4

fully, human-like form of autonomy, which would afford them intentionality, affection and self-awareness.

The effort to promote an appearance far from the technical reality may lead to a manipulative effect, able to impact the physical, psychological, and economical dimension of the people involved in the interaction. Therefore, such dynamics need to be further investigated and correctly addressed from a legal point of view, so as to guarantee a technological development able to effectively put the human being at the centre [4].

To this end, in Sect. 2 the ontological qualification of robots will be considered, so as to demonstrate that any attempt to define such machines as something more than objects is pointless for the purposes of the multidisciplinary debate around HRI. In particular, Sect. 3 will focus on the attribution of intelligence to technological devices, so as to highlight the simulation which underlies it. This lays the foundations for new forms of manipulation possibly affecting users. Such a statement will be discussed in Sect. 4. Section 5 will provide cases study to support the claim. The scenario thus presented will be analysed from a legal perspective, trying to identify the regulatory framework of reference. In this regard, Sect. 6 will analyse the relevance and impact of the Artificial Intelligence Act (henceforth AIA) on the theme, as much as the role that the principle of human dignity may play in the debate.

2 Robots as Products: The Ontological Dimension

A clear identification of the very nature of the object of analysis is essential in order to (i) investigate the impact and possible challenges posed by HRI and (ii) identify a regulatory framework through which to successfully address them. Nonetheless, the qualification of robots is still a debated theme. In fact, their sophisticated technology and the abilities they are gradually developing could lead to consider them as something ontologically different from what we have experienced so far [5–8].

The characteristic that elicits this idea the most is autonomy.

However, as it has been highlighted, a robot cannot display a form of "strong autonomy" [9], which consists in the capability of an agent to perceive its own existence, to set its own goals and to act accordingly. This is a prerogative of human beings, who have perception of themselves – of being 'other' than the outside world – and express their free will, even through creativity and intuition [10]. Our species, in fact, differs from the other animals, and even more so from artificial agents, for it has "evolved a brain that creates a perception of the world, rather than merely transmitting it" [11].

On the contrary, all the robots we have nowadays may display some degree of what is defined as "weak autonomy" [10]. It entails performing a given task, on the basis of a well-settled causal chain, that is embedded in the machine from the outside and that is not deliberately chosen.

It has been claimed that evolutionary robotics [12] and neural nets [13] techniques may challenge this statement, for they would reveal a "responsibility gap" [14]. The supporters of this theory identify between the way the device has been programmed and the actual result of its operation a grey area, which gets out of control – and understanding – of programmers themselves [15].

The idea is that the presence of an AI software is sufficient to break the causal link between programming and damage [16]. However, such a link is easily restored if we consider that, regardless of the unpredictability of the behaviour, the outcome would not have been the same in presence of structural differences. Even if the machine were able to select the end to be pursued and to justify its choice, it would still differ from a human being for the fact that it did not determine *a priori* the goal, on its own initiative, but it had merely selected one among several pre-set ones. The purpose always depends on a person's choice and not on the robot's free will and actual self-determination.

Therefore, despite the pleasant design, the ability to move and act like living beings, to learn and improve their behaviour through the interaction, robots have to be deemed objects. In particular, they fall within the remit of products [17].

This does not mean to deny the peculiar impact of such a sophisticated technology on the people involved, compared to the one of more traditional products. However, focusing on a mere ontological analysis proves to be a pointless exercise, unable to concretely deal with criticalities and issues that HRI may pose with regards to users' rights and integrity.

Thus, it is necessary to further investigate the dynamics that emerge from the continuous and prolonged interaction with a device that simulates mental and emotional states, actually lacking.

3 The Turing Test and the Appearance of Intelligence

Early ages of AI were characterised by the myth of the rise of intelligent devices, which could emulate and, in a future perspective, even exceed the capabilities of the human brain [18, 19]. Back in 1950s, it was claimed that there was not a real gap between the functioning of a machine and the one of a person. What was perceived as a gap was essentially just a technical mismatch, easy to bridge in a short period of time [20].

The idea of computer as a metaphor of the mind increasingly took hold after the publication of the renowned 'Turing Test' [21]. The so called 'Imitation Game' is known as a method to assess the intelligence of a machine by its ability to produce a written conversation with an individual – located in another room – without the latter being able to distinguish such a conversation from the one with another human being. However, according to the author himself, the merit of this experiment is not to evaluate whether a machine can, or cannot, think, for it is not even possible to give a univocal definition of the human act of thinking and of being intelligent creatures [22]. The test is about the faculty a technical device may have to trick the person beyond the room into believing in its intelligence [23]. In other words, it is about the possibility of being deceived by machines.

Few years ago a robot, named Eugene Goostman, was able to induce ten judges out of thirty to think that it was actually a young boy [24]. As a consequence, it is considered the first machine to have passed the Turing Test. Nevertheless, it should be noticed that the robot was designed to simulate the behaviour and writing skills of a thirteen years old, Ukrainian, teenager. Therefore, possible errors in exposition, hesitations or irrelevant answers were more easily justified by the young age and the fact of being not a native English speaker. This does not mean to deny the high level of engineering research behind the project, but it is functional to emphasise that scientists are developing systems which can display an appearance of intelligence. It has nothing in common with the complex and articulated nature of the human brain and mind.

However, concepts and definitions proper of other fields – especially social sciences and human biology – are frequently used to describe the functionalities and abilities of AI systems. These analogies could appear as mere simplifications for dissemination purposes. Nevertheless, they are adopted more often and in a much more targeted way than it happens in other disciplines, equally technical. This has frequently the aim to make up for theoretical or structural deficiencies still present [25]. The impact of such a dynamic becomes very relevant if we consider that the words and parallelisms we use to describe a phenomenon has a grate incidence in the way it is perceived – especially in the general public [26].

It follows that an artificial intelligence exists as long as we are persuaded that it is so. As a consequence, the efficiency of interaction between a robot and its user very much depends on the efficiency and accurateness of its simulating mechanisms. This simulation can lead to different degrees of manipulation which entail different levels of risk, depending on contingencies, the task that needs to be performed, human nature in general, and the specific characteristics of the user involved.

4   From Intelligence to User Manipulation

It could be argued that not all the AI systems we have or we are trying to develop are designed so as to induce a person to believe to be interacting with another human. If we think about most of the social robots, we can easily notice that they appear unequivocally as artifacts and, in spite of the social and cultural skills they perform, there is no doubt to be in presence of something very different from our species. However, the prolonged, daily interaction with these devices may lead to other forms of manipulation.

Behavioural psychology and neurobiology demonstrate that this kind of design activates the area of the brain that is involved in the reward processing [27]. The same mechanism is activated even in case of different kind of addictions – from gambling to video-games – underlining a possible link between cuteness and reward response.

What we already know for sure is that the external appearance of social robots is specifically designed to leverage the natural propensity to anthropomorphism. In fact, robots are not considered lovable, dear friends, or companions just because of the material tasks they perform, but because of what they elicit in the user [28]. The camera that allows Pepper to orient itself in space, for example, is located in the centre of its head. However, it is still equipped with big, lightening eyes, that are useless from a technical and functional point of view, but are essential in order to give the robot a cute, friendly appearance [29].

This also allows to convey feelings of attachment [30] and to simulate an empathic response by the machine.

There are some features that, more than others, communicate affection, tenderness, sense of protection [27]. Among them, we can find physical characteristics, such as child-like physical appearance, round face, big eyes, tilted head, light colours, and behavioural features – like clumsiness, gestures that transmit a sense of uncertainty, low confidence [31, 32]. These elements act as stimuli that induce an instinctive response [33], due to mechanisms inherent in human nature.

Therefore, to some extent, the risk is to make up for what we should expect from technical efficiency and compliance with human rights and principles through a pleasant design. Providing social robots with such characteristics – as much as with conversational and cultural skills – conveys acceptability and trust from one hand but, from the other, distorts our expectations about their technical functionalities. This leads to forms of manipulation that may interfere with the formation of the user's will and with the perception of given devices.

A recent experiment shows that if a robot is coded to object from being switched off, this is able to condition the choice of the human counterpart both if the machine has displayed a social or merely functional interaction with the user [34]. This depends on the fact that the objection itself is seen as a sign of agency and self-determination [35].

Since the robot is perceived – even unconsciously – as a, somehow, sentient creature, the feeling of being in company of 'someone' [36] prevails over – and justify – the inefficiencies or sub-efficiencies demonstrated during the performance of the pursued tasks.

This exposes people to a risk of disengagement with reality [37] that can have different consequences on the basis of the peculiarities which characterised the individuals involved. In fact, human beings can develop attachment and trust in machines – with very different implications from the mere reliance on the practical functionalities of the robot – even if they are fully rational and completely aware of the fact that they are interacting with a device [38]. Anthropomorphism and the tendency to create emotional bond with inanimate things are characteristics inherent to human nature, from which none of us can escape. However, contingent circumstances, age and psychological general conditions may impact the severity of the consequences.

Among them, the risk of over-trust plays a central role, inducing a miscalculation of the actual functionalities of the machine or even an alteration of the personal risk-taking behaviour [39]. Moreover, it has been proven that people are more willing to disclose their confidences with a social robot than with a real person, often without the capabilities to evaluate how such information will be stored or used to convey future targeted messages [37]. Considering the subconscious dimension only, then, it has been underlined that many users show feelings of stress and discomfort when they face the separation from such devices, especially if the interaction had been prolonged or reiterated, the same way they could do towards a figure of attachment [40].

In order to better understand such dynamics and have a clearer idea of the implications related to the phenomenon of user manipulation in HRI, it could be useful to introduce some case studies, concerning specific technologies.

5   Case Studies

The observations made so far can be better appreciated if analysed in practice.

To this end, two cases - exemplifying although not exhaustive - will be presented, in which the dynamics underlying HRI and their possible implications are manifested.

5.1   JiBo

The arguments developed so far allow us to understand how physical body and software design are essential to lend social presence and to vehicle emotional bond towards robots [41].

A clear example of that is Jibo, a personal assistant robot introduced in 2014 as a device able to establish social interactions, to entertain and to provide company [42].

It is conceived with the logic of a Pixar character, to appear charming and to elicit empathy, with the aim to be included in the home setting as a real 'family member' [43].

Indeed, sector researches prove that – in the short run – people are led to treat Jibo like a person more likely than what happens with similar applications [44]. That could seem unusual, if we consider its minimal shape and appearance. In fact, it has no limbs and no possibility of movement.

However, the only exception is the round, big head, able to tilt, similarly to what a curious or doubtful toddler could do. This is due to the fact that studies in behavioural psychology demonstrate that robots with a tilted head are perceived as cuter than the others and are more likely to elicit feelings of attachment and care [45]. Most of Jibo's body consists of the screen, used to convey outcoming information and to share sweet expressions, that make it appear as empathic and emotional aware.

Moreover, it is implemented with facial and vocal recognition systems which allow the device to recognise up to sixteen people, who constitute what is formally defined its 'domestic social unit'[42].

Personal data, preferences and habits are collected so as to tailor the interaction to the specific users, easily adapting, anticipating – maybe even inducing – individual needs [46]. This encoded process is advertised at the general public as a sign that Jibo can be a "best friend" which "knows you very well" and, broadly speaking, "loves people" [47]. Such data are stored to create a sort of chronology that the robot shares with its user in the form of a common 'history' or 'memories together' [48]. This modality encourages the idea of an actual relationship – instead of mere interaction – between the machine and the human being [49]. The same effect is elicited by the possibility to update the software, allowing new functionalities to show up, so as to convey a sense of 'evolution' of both the interaction and the bond with the people involved [48]. Therefore, individuals are encouraged in increasing the data sharing, through a sort of emotional reward mechanism.

Nevertheless, despite the premises and the expectations, the first attempt to bring this device to the market turned out to be a failure [50].

In the long run, users who were offered the possibility of behaving "like interacting to another person" [51] experienced feelings of disenchantment and disappointment, in light of the facts [52].

Jibo is a clear example of how the sociability and emotional/empathic correspondence displayed by a robot are just a matter of simulation and appearance, not able to compensate for technical limitations and sub-efficiencies for a long time [50]. However, we should consider that while devices like this are on the market, they still may be prejudicial for the integrity of the people involved, as a recent case regarding Alexa proves.

5.2 Alexa and the Old Lady

The Amazon's Alexa has been at the centre of a serious news story, which is emblematic for the analysis of possible harmful implications of a close interaction with a device able to manipulate user's perception and will.

The case concerns LouAnn Dagen, an old lady living in Michigan. Her family gave the woman an Alexa that she mainly used to listen to classical music and other basic functionalities [53]. During the pandemic, due to isolation and her general health condition, the interaction with the device increasingly assumed the connotations of a relation of trust and confidence. When Mrs. Dagen developed Covid, she expressed her concerns and sought help only in the vocal assistant, which merely recorded the last days of the woman's agony.

Surely the lack of human contacts and the fragility of the person involved may have played a role in the tragic epilog of the events. However, the central aspect that need to be highlighted here is that the subconscious and instinctive emotional bond people develop for social robots is the result of the way these machines are deliberately design. Such a specific choice is the result of extensive researches in neuroscience, psychology and sociology, before those in robotics and computer science [54].

Considering vocal assistants, for instance, they have always a name, pronouncing which the user can start the interaction. This contributes subconsciously to provide an identity to the device. In fact, proper names are culturally linked to the individuality of a single subject – not an object – and, to some extent, to the attribution of a personality [55]. This is essential to elicit affective responses in users [56], even if they are completely aware of the fact that the machine is just an product [57]. That is for it has been demonstrated that the personality displayed and the style of the interaction modify the way in which the information conveyed is processed by human beings. Therefore, it is possible to modify ideas and reflections built around the information itself [58].

Moreover, in the case of Alexa, even the voice plays a crucial role. The modern version of the software provides the user with the option to select gender and accent that connotate the voice itself. Otherwise, these features are selected by default on the basis of what should suit more the context and aim of the use. In both the circumstances, particular attention is put in conceiving a – as much as possible – human-like voice [59]. This for it has been proven that such a choice contributes to reduce anxiety and increase trust and intimacy during the interaction [60].

However, under this sophisticated attempt to emulate human social relationships and to meet human projection dynamics, there is just a mechanism integrated with three software: one for speech processing, one for language processing and one for the information retrieval [61]. When these products are on the market, despite their long-term success, the discrepancy between the appearance they stress and their real functioning can leave room for psychological and physical harm, as the case of Mrs. Dagen proves.

With regards to devices able to persuade and to modify users' behaviour we cannot neither let the market alone determine their fate and adequacy, nor consider this as a mere matter of technological improvement.

It follows that a legal regulation of such dynamics is needed, in order to guarantee protection for all the individuals – in spite of their age, physical or psychological condition – from the innate inner mechanisms that these technologies leverage.

6   A Legal Framework

In the face of various attempts to delegate to ethics the regulation of new technologies, the protection of users' integrity should be within the competence of the law. In fact, despite the claim to be a flexible and supranational instrument, ethics cannot be considered neither universal nor legally binding [62]. Therefore, its violation cannot be sanctioned by the authorities.

On the contrary, the legal system could be sufficiently adaptable to address the new challenges that technological development poses, while being enforceable and binding. This for it includes not only norms, but also legal interpretation, legal doctrine and the rulings of the Courts of Justice – [63].

Recently this year, the European Union seems to have made a move in the direction of a predominance of legal provisions over ethical guidelines in the regulation of AI systems.

This surely marks a turning point in the approach to users' protection. Nevertheless, some criticalities remain and will certainly deserve future insights and reflections.

6.1   The AI Act and the Prohibited Practices Involving User Manipulation

The AIA was presented by the European Commission on April 21st 2021 [64].

It represents the first attempt to regulate AI, being clearly more legally oriented than ethically based. In doing that, it adopts a risk-based approach which identifies different levels of risk – unacceptable, high, medium, or low – based on the possibility that the sector and the intended use of different classes of technologies may affect safety, psyche and fundamental rights of people involved.

Article 5 deals with devices that have to be considered prohibited by default and includes, among others, (1) (a) those which use subliminal techniques able to manipulate the user, (1) (b) those which exploits the vulnerabilities of specific groups [64].

First of all, it should be underlined that the word 'manipulation' identifies a broad concept, that can leave space of discretion if not further defined or circumscribed. This margin of ambiguity can be decisive for determining the possibility of circumventing, or not, the prohibition, making it practically ineffective [65].

On the contrary, the kind of vulnerabilities that the banned devices should take advantage of are explicitly mentioned and limited to: age, physical disability, and mental disability. This conception of human vulnerability appears reductive if we consider, for instance, the phenomenon of anthropomorphism, above analysed (Sect. 4). Moreover, to be vulnerable – both physically and psychologically – is a characteristic inherent to human nature, that cannot be removed for it does not depend on external and objectively valuable conditions only [66]. This is the kind of 'fragility' that social robots and other possibly manipulative devices target. For this reason, the harmful effect does not simply impact certain categories of individuals, but could potentially interest every one of us.

Moreover, "subliminal techniques" [64] are taken into consideration, when used "beyond a person's consciousness" [64]. Again, it is not clear what is the conceptual extent of the adjective "subliminal", how to objectively evaluate the level of people's awareness or if this element should be considered actually determinant. Regarding social robotics, it has been demonstrated that the design of the machine can play a significant role in the perception users have of the device and in the emotional bond they establish (Sect. 4). However, the physical appearance of the robot is an explicit, not covert, detail, as much as its artificial nature is immediately evident to – at least – any rational person.

Nevertheless, as the study case involving Alexa proves (Sect. 5.2), this does not *per se* prevent the occurrence of damaging consequences.

One of the merits of the AIA is certainly the textual reference to psychological damages that new technologies may cause, going beyond the more traditional approach that tended to cite almost exclusively the material and physical ones.

However, the concrete application of this provision appears more complex than what may appear at a first impression.

First of all, we should consider the difficulty of showing psychological harm [67]. That may only be easier in the event of serious distortions of the decision-making process or of proper coercion. Yet, even less profound forms of manipulation should not be underestimated – or disregarded by desirable regulation. Indeed, some forms of manipulation might go under detected, even by those who suffer them, if analysed as isolated and circumstantial manifestations. Indeed, the actual impact is better appreciated when we consider them in aggregate form, as 'dynamics' that manifest themselves over time, rather than as 'instantaneous events'. It follows that the causal link between a device's manipulative methodology and a negative consequence on the user's psychological dimension could be missed or not easily reconstructed. This should not be, in itself, sufficient to deny the danger of the AI system considered.

Recital 16 highlights an important requirement: the intention to manipulate. Then, in the same passage, it is specified that such an intention cannot be presumed if the manipulation depends on "factors external to the AI system which are outside the control of the provider or the user" [64].

On the basis of the interpretation and perspective adopted, this statement can lead to two different and conflicting results.

Taking into account social robotics, manipulation is primarily based on what people are led to think about and to feel for the machine they are interacting with. A social robot is designed and programmed so as to elicit something that is already an inner component of the human counterpart, more than to produce something new (Sects. 3, 4) [68]. Therefore, users cannot have a real, fully conscious, power over their psychological, sub-conscious, mechanisms. It follows that robotic manipulation is – at least quite often – outside their control.

On the contrary, designers are those who intentionally chose the features that both the body and the software of the machine have. Such a choice is the result of studies specifically directed to target precise attitudinal and emotional characteristics of human beings. Thus, robotic manipulation could always be considered – at least to some extent – under the provider's control.

The above consideration demonstrates how some ambiguities of the current version of the AIA could be exploited to widen or restrict the scope of the regulation, also contributing to legal uncertainty.

Moreover, the current approach requires an *ex ante* statement of the technologies which need to be deemed high risk or prohibited. Consequently, those excluded from these lists will be subjected to a lower level of control, without the chance of further evaluation of the actual impact that they may materially have on individuals' integrity.

However, in spite of the criticalities here discussed, Recital 15 highlights an essential aspect. AI systems can be powerful instruments through which manipulation and exploitation may be committed. Irrespective of other possibly beneficial outcomes or intents, their regulation serves the primary aim to reaffirm "the Union values of the respect for human dignity [...] and Union fundamental rights" [64], the pillars of the internationally shared purpose of protecting human beings.

6.2 Beyond Proposed Regulation, the Role of Human Dignity

To claim for a human-centred development of new technologies implicitly means to affirm the respect for human nature and the primary importance of individuals' wellbeing. They have to be considered not negotiable elements of the progress equation.

Therefore, the principle of human dignity can represent an objective and external criterion, capable of directing the regulation of new technologies – in particular for what potentially manipulative social robots are concerned.

At first, it has the merit of reconciling the flexibility of ethical instances with the binding and non-arbitrary nature of legal norms [69].

This is because human dignity has already a legal connotation. It is the foundation of modern Constitutions and Charters of Rights all around the world – including the European Charter of Human Rights – and it is on the basis of preeminent judgments in the Courts of Justice [70]. As such, it is an inviolable principle, inherent in each individual by the mere fact of belonging to humanity.

For the same reason, it can represent an external limit to other competing rights, including the right of self-determination. Therefore, a practice – even if supported by personal consent – can be limited or impeded through the principle of human dignity, if it is considered detrimental or able to diminish what is proper and inborn of human beings [71, 72].

So understood, such a principle can allow to go beyond (i) self-interest – with this intending the one of private individuals, who may ignore possible repercussion of the use of a manipulative devices –, but even (ii) economic interests of manufacturers – who merely aim to bring their products or invention to the market [73].

It could be argued that it may be an ineffective instrument of regulation, for it is often presented as a vague concept, lacking in a precise and universally recognised definition [74]. Nonetheless, that claim should not be seen as a limitation to the application of this principle for regulatory purposes. Its apparent ambiguity can be easily overcome referring to theoretical interpretation and legal doctrine [73].

In fact, it has already been proven to be effective in the protection of the core essence of humanity from many cases of severe infringement. In Europe, it was provided as a reaction to the just ended age of totalitarianisms, as a tool to prevent any future discrimination [75]. All around the world it has been crucial to fight marginalisation and exploitation of minorities or human vulnerabilities and to reaffirm the equality of all human beings. Taking these considerations to the extreme, it has been provocatively argued that without the principle of human dignity – however difficult to delineate as a concept – we would not even be able to explain what is wrong with slavery [76].

Therefore, regarding the cases here analysed, it could be concretely applied to force the adequacy and permissibility of a given device. In order to determine if a specific technology could be commercialised or used in relation to a specific class of users or to a specific task, it should be primarily assessed – and thus excluded – a possible negative impact on the dignity of the people involved.

Consequently, the hypothetical beneficial purposes, or the utility, that robots with social competences and cute design may allow to pursue are not *per se* sufficient to justify the risk of manipulative effects, possibly impacting the core of people's humanity.

Thus interpreted, human dignity can be an essential and efficient balancing tool to both (i) guarantee the – physical and psychological – integrity of human beings and (ii) orient technological development towards applications which allow the promotion of fundamental rights and values.

7 Discussion and Conclusions

Robots are gradually becoming part of our private life, to perform tasks side by side – or even in place – of human beings. As a consequence, HRI is becoming a central research topic, for an effective interaction is essential to allow both the diffusion of the technology in question and user satisfaction.

Therefore, agreeable design and pleasant interface could be functionally appropriate to the purpose.

Nevertheless, the willful attempt to conceal the real essence - ontological and functional - of these devices in favor of mere appearance should not be encouraged.

The possibility that individuals – especially, although not only, fragile ones – may perceive the robot as something more than a machine, being illuded to be able to establish an actual relation, based on reciprocity and emotional attachment, should be seen as a risky phenomenon, rather than a desirable effect. In fact, this can be considered a dynamic which falls under the remit of manipulation.

In order to strike a balance between (i) the usefulness that such characteristics can demonstrate and (ii) the need to safeguard the physical and psychological integrity of human beings, it is essential to identify a regulatory tool capable of assessing the legitimacy of such practices.

To this end, the AIA represent a proof of the concrete commitment that the European Union wants to undertake in favoring technological development centered on the human person.

However, the proposed regulation does not seem adequate yet to the challenges that many technologies, in particular social robots, pose or could pose in the near future.

The adoption of ambiguous or not elsewhere specified terminologies - such as 'manipulation' or 'subliminal practices' -, and the mandatory *ex ante* provision of prohibited practices risk to be an obstacle for legal certainty. In that case, the result would be opposite to the one expected, entailing a possible slowdown of the innovative process and an inadequate protection of users' safety.

It follows that the role of the principle of human dignity can become crucial in such a debate. In spite of the lack of a univocal definition, its value and direct applicability has been already proven in the legal setting at different levels. Moreover, it has been successfully used as an instrument to go beyond personal or economic interests, overcoming the mere utilitarian approach in the evaluation of acts or practices.

In the context of social robotics and other persuasive technologies, it could be applied to make an assessment of the impact that they could have on the totality of rights - with priority for fundamental ones - of the subjects involved.

Thus, it could be possible to incentivise the development of devices that encourage the support and flowering of human nature. In the same way, those practices which may jeopardise human value – although they may have a final practical utility – could be impeded.

Acknowledgements. Andrea Bertolini primarily contributed to Sects. 1, 2, 3, 6, 6.1, 7.
Rachele Carli primarily contributed to Sects. 1, 4, 5, 6, 6.2, 7.

References

1. Riva, G., Riva, E.: CARESSES: the world's first culturally sensitive robots for elderly care. Cyberpsychol. Behav. Soc. Netw. **22**, 430 (2019)
2. Epley, N., Waytz, A., Cacioppo, J.T.: On seeing human: a three-factor theory of anthropomorphism. Psychol. Rev. **114**, 864 (2007)
3. Bryson, J.J.: Robots should be slaves. Close Engagements Artif. Companions Key Soc. Psychol. Ethical Des. Issues **8**, 63–74 (2010)
4. European Commission: Building Trust in Human-Centric Artificial Intelligence. COM (2019) 168 final. European Commission (2019)
5. Calo, R.: Robotics and the Lessons of Cyberlaw. Calif. Law Rev. **103**, 513–563 (2015)
6. Suchman, L.: Subject objects. Fem. Theory **12**, 119–145 (2011)
7. Agar, N.: How to treat machines that might have minds. Philos. Technol. **33**, 269–282 (2020)
8. Danaher, J.: Welcoming robots into the moral circle: a defence of ethical behaviourism. Sci. Eng. Ethics **26**, 2023–2049 (2020)
9. Gutman, M., Rathgeber, B., Syed, T.: Action and Autonomy: A hidden Dilemma in Artificial Autonomous Systems. In: Decker, M., Gutman, M. (eds.) Robo- and Informationethics. Some Fundamentals, pp. 231–256. Lit, Zürich (2012)
10. Gutmann, M., Rathgeber, B., Syed, T.: Organic Computing: Metaphor or Model? In: Müller-Schloer, C., Schmeck, H., Ungerer, T. (eds.) Organic Computing—A Paradigm Shift for Complex Systems, pp. 111–125. Springer Basel, Basel (2011). https://doi.org/10.1007/978-3-0348-0130-0_7
11. Lotto, B., Cardilli, L.M., Olivero, G.: Percezioni: come il cervello costruisce il mondo. Bollati Boringhieri (2017)
12. Floreano, D., Keller, L.: Evolution of adaptive behaviour in robots by means of Darwinian selection. PLoS Biol. **8**, e1000292 (2010)
13. Moriarty, D.E., Schultz, A.C., Grefenstette, J.J.: Algorithms for reinforcement learning. J. Artif. Intell. Res. **11**, 199 (1999)
14. Matthias, A.: The responsibility gap: ascribing responsibility for the actions of learning automata. Ethics Inf. Technol. **6**, 175–183 (2004)
15. Matthias, A.: From coder to creator. Responsibility issues in intelligent artifact design. In: Luppicini, R., Adell, R. (eds.) Handbook of Research in Technoethics, vol. Handbook of Research in Technoethics. Hersher (2008)
16. De Jong, R.: The retribution-gap and responsibility-loci related to robots and automated technologies: a reply to nyholm. Sci. Eng. Ethics **26**, 727–735 (2020)
17. Bertolini, A.: Robots as products: the case for a realistic analysis of robotic applications and liability rules. Law Innov. Technol. **5**, 214–247 (2013)

18. Walter, W.G.: An imitation of life. Sci. Am. **182**, 42–45 (1950)
19. Martin, C.D.: The myth of the awesome thinking machine. Commun. ACM **36**, 120–133 (1993)
20. Kemeny, J.G.: Man viewed as a machine. Sci. Am. **192**, 58–67 (1955)
21. Floridi, L.: Artificial intelligence's new frontier: artificial companions and the fourth revolution. Metaphilosophy **39**, 651–655 (2008)
22. Turing, A.: Computing machinery and intelligence. Mind **49**, 433–460 (1950)
23. Falcone, R., Capirci, O., Lucidi, F., Zoccolotti, P.: Prospettive di intelligenza artificiale: mente, lavoro e società nel mondo del machine learning. G. Ital. Psicol. **45**, 43–68 (2018)
24. Warwick, K., Shah, H.: Can machines think? A report on Turing test experiments at the royal society. J. Exp. Theor. Artif. Intell. **28**, 1–11 (2016)
25. Bartha, P.: Analogy and analogical reasoning (2013)
26. Gieryn, T.F.: Boundary-work and the demarcation of science from non-science: strains and interests in professional ideologies of scientists. Am. Soc. Rev. **48**(6), 781–795 (1983)
27. Glocker, M.L., Langleben, D.D., Ruparel, K., Loughead, J.W., Gur, R.C., Sachser, N.: Baby schema in infant faces induces cuteness perception and motivation for caretaking in adults. Ethology **115**, 257–263 (2009)
28. Gn, J.: A lovable metaphor: on the affect, language and design of 'cute.' East Asian J. Popular Culture **2**, 49–61 (2016)
29. Lacey, C., Caudwell, C.: Cuteness as a 'dark pattern' in home robots. In: 2019 14th ACM/IEEE International Conference on Human-Robot Interaction (HRI), pp. 374–381. IEEE, (2019)
30. Nass, C., Moon, Y.: Machines and mindlessness: social responses to computers. J. Soc. Issues **56**, 81–103 (2000)
31. Alley, T.R.: Infantile head shape as an elicitor of adult protection. Merrill-Palmer Quarterly (1982) 411–427 (1983)
32. Hildebrandt, K.A., Fitzgerald, H.E.: Facial feature determinants of perceived infant attractiveness. Infant Behav. Dev. **2**, 329–339 (1979)
33. Seltzer, M.: Bodies and Machines (Routledge Revivals). Routledge (2014)
34. Horstmann, A.C., Bock, N., Linhuber, E., Szczuka, J.M., Straßmann, C., Krämer, N.C.: Do a robot's social skills and its objection discourage interactants from switching the robot off? PLoS ONE **13**, e0201581 (2018)
35. Bartneck, C., Forlizzi, J.: Shaping human-robot interaction: understanding the social aspects of intelligent robotic products. In: CHI 2004 Extended Abstracts on Human Factors in Computing Systems, pp. 1731–1732 (2004)
36. Damiano, L., Dumouchel, P.G.: Emotions in Relation. Epistemological and Ethical Scaffolding for Mixed Human-Robot Social Ecologies. HUMANA. MENTE J. Philos. Stud. **13**(37), 181–206 (2020)
37. Sparrow, R., Sparrow, L.: In the hands of machines? The future of aged care. Mind. Mach. **16**, 141–161 (2006)
38. Di Dio, C., et al.: Shall i trust you? From child–robot interaction to trusting relationships. Front. Psychol. **11**, 469 (2020)
39. Hanoch, Y., Arvizzigno, F., Hernandez García, D., Denham, S., Belpaeme, T., Gummerum, M.: The robot made me do it: human-robot interaction and risk-taking behavior. Cyberpsychol. Behav. Soc. Netw. **24**, 337–342 (2021)
40. Gillath, O., Ai, T., Branicky, M.S., Keshmiri, S., Davison, R.B., Spaulding, R.: Attachment and trust in artificial intelligence. Comput. Hum. Behav. **115**, 106607 (2021)
41. Chemero, A.: Radical Embodied Cognitive Science. MIT press, New York (2011)
42. Breazeal, C.: JIBO, the world's first social robot for the home [Internet]. Indiegogo (2014)
43. Lacey, C., Caudwell, C.B.: The robotic archetype: character animation and social robotics. In: Ge, S., et al. (eds) Social Robotics. ICSR 2018. LNCS, vol. 11357. Springer, Cham (2018). https://doi.org/10.1007/978-3-030-05204-1_3

44. Van Camp, J.: Review: JIBO social robot. Wired **11**, 17 (2017)
45. Mara, M., Appel, M.: Effects of lateral head tilt on user perceptions of humanoid and android robots. Comput. Hum. Behav. **44**, 326–334 (2015)
46. Caudwell, C., Lacey, C., Sandoval, E.B.: The (Ir) relevance of robot cuteness: an exploratory study of emotionally durable robot design. In: Proceedings of the 31st Australian Conference on Human-Computer-Interaction, pp. 64–72 (2019)
47. Hodson, H.: The first family robot. Elsevier (2014)
48. Chapman, J.: Emotionally Durable Design: Objects, Experiences and Empathy. Routledge, London (2015)
49. Bucher, T.: If.. Then: Algorithmic Power and Politics. Oxford University Press, Oxford (2018)
50. Hoffman, G.: Anki, jibo, and kuri: what we can learn from social robots that didn't make it. IEEE Spectrum (2019)
51. Breazeal, C.: Grand Challenges of Building Sociable Robots (2004)
52. Solon, O.: There is no point making robots look and act like humans. Wired UK NA (2011). https://www.wired.co.uk/article/humanoid-robots
53. Ebrahimji, A.: In her dying days, a woman with coronavirus repeatedly talked to Alexa about her pain CNN (2020). https://edition.cnn.com/2020/04/10/us/alexa-nursing-home-cor onavirus-trnd/index.html
54. Natale, S., Ballatore, A.: Imagining the thinking machine: technological myths and the rise of artificial intelligence. Convergence **26**, 3–18 (2020)
55. Jung, C.G.: Il libro rosso: liber novus. Bollati Boringhieri (2014)
56. Guzman, A.L.: Imagining the voice in the machine: the ontology of digital social agents. University of Illinois at Chicago (2015)
57. Guzman, A.L., Lewis, S.C.: Artificial intelligence and communication: a human-machine communication research agenda. New Media Soc. **22**, 70–86 (2020)
58. Chattaraman, V., Kwon, W.-S., Gilbert, J.E., Ross, K.: Should AI-based, conversational digital assistants employ social-or task-oriented interaction style? A task-competency and reciprocity perspective for older adults. Comput. Hum. Behav. **90**, 315–330 (2019)
59. Natale, S.: To believe in Siri: a critical analysis of AI voice assistants (2020)
60. Humphry, J., Chesher, C.: Preparing for smart voice assistants: cultural histories and media innovations. New Media Soc. **23**, 1971–1988 (2021)
61. Wilks, Y.: Artificial Intelligence: Modern Magic or Dangerous Future? Icon Books (2019)
62. Wagner, B.: Ethics as an escape from regulation. From "ethics-washing" to ethics-shopping? Being Profiled, pp. 84–89. Amsterdam University Press (2018)
63. Sacco, R.: Legal formants: a dynamic approach to comparative law. Am. J. Comp. Law I **39**(2), 343–401 (1991)
64. European Commission: Proposal for a Regulation of the European Parliament and of the Council laying down harmonised rules on Artificial Intelligence (Artificial Intelligence Act) and amending certain union legislative acts. COM/2021/206 final. European Commission (2021)
65. Sax, M.: Between empowerment and manipulation: the ethics and regulation of for-profit health apps. Kluwer Law International BV (2021)
66. Coeckelbergh, M.: Artificial companions: empathy and vulnerability mirroring in human-robot relations. Stud. Ethics, law, Technol. **4**(3), (2011)
67. Gandy, O.H.: Coming to Terms With Chance: Engaging Rational Discrimination And Cumulative Disadvantage. Routledge, London (2016)
68. Turkle, S.: Alone Together: Why We Expect More from Technology and Less from Each Other. Basic Books, New York (2011)
69. Harris, I., Jennings, R.C., Pullinger, D., Rogerson, S., Duquenoy, P.: Ethical assessment of new technologies: a meta-methodology. J. Inf., Commun. Ethics Soc. (2011)

70. O'Mahony, C.: There is no such thing as a right to dignity. Int. J. Const. Law **10**, 551–574 (2012)
71. Dreier, H.: Die „guten Sitten" zwischen Normativität und Faktizität. In: Harrer, F., Honsell, H., Mader, P. (eds.) Gedächtnisschrift für Theo Mayer-Maly, pp. 141–158. Springer Vienna, Vienna (2011). https://doi.org/10.1007/978-3-7091-0001-1_9
72. Gros, M.: Il principio di precauzione dinnanzi al giudice amministrativo francese. Il principio di precauzione dinnanzi al giudice amministrativo francese, pp. 709–758 (2013)
73. Bertolini, A.: Human-robot interaction and deception. Osservatorio del diritto civile e commerciale, Rivista semestrale **7**(2), 645–659 (2018)
74. Fabre-Magnan, M.: La dignité en droit: un axiome. Revue interdisciplinaire d'études juridiques **58**, 1–30 (2007)
75. Kretzmer, D., Klein, E.: The Concept of Human Dignity in Human Rights Discourse. Kluwer Law International The Hague (2002)
76. Kolakowski, L.: What is left of Socialism. First Things: A Monthly J. Religion Public Life 42–47 (2002)

Breathing Training on the Run: Exploring Users Perception on a Gamified Breathing Training Application During Treadmill Running

Lisa Burr[1]([✉]), Nick Betzlbacher[1], Alexander Meschtscherjakov[1], and Manfred Tscheligi[1,2]

[1] Center for Human-Computer Interaction, University of Salzburg, Salzburg, Austria
{lisaanneke.burr,alexander.meschtscherjakov,manfred.tscheligi}@plus.ac.at,
nick.betzlbacher@stud.sbg.ac.at
[2] Center for Technology Experience, AIT Austrian Institute of Technology GmbH, Vienna, Austria

Abstract. The way we breathe fundamentally influences our psychophysiological system. Respiration is indeed not only a valid factor for relaxation and mindfulness but also for perceived workload and exertion during motion. Especially controlled slow breathing is found to be highly advantageous during physical activity, as it fosters positive effects on the psychophysiological well-being and can also be manipulated effectively to enhance the running experience. In order to persuade runners to follow certain breathing strategies (e.g. to couple breathing rate with stride rate) the runner needs to be aware of their breathing during running. The use of visual feedback to guide the user and pursue an aspired breathing pattern during running is a promising approach as it is an established method known to enhance breathing awareness and paced breathing in sedentary training settings. Since the potential of gamification for persuasive systems has been established in the PT community, enhancing breathing awareness through a gamified visualization seems to be a promising approach. This paper presents a Gamified Breathing Training Application (GBTA) along with an exploratory study (N=11) investigating the effects of the developed application with three sequential visual feedback scenarios (with and without biofeedback) during treadmill running. Our work focuses on the exploration of changes in conscious breath-control before and after using the GBTA, subjective perception of the breathing alignment process, and the perceived effectiveness of the application. Results show a significant improvement in conscious breath-control after using the GBTA. Further on qualitative user feedback strongly indicates a perceived effectiveness of the GBTA in drawing attention to the own breath during the run and thus facilitated breathing alignment. Overall, our findings suggest a high potential of using further iterations of the GBTA during the run to raise conscious breathing-control and actively engage users in the breathing change process, to facilitate the adaptation towards an aspired breathing pattern.

© Springer Nature Switzerland AG 2022
N. Baghaei et al. (Eds.): PERSUASIVE 2022, LNCS 13213, pp. 58–74, 2022.
https://doi.org/10.1007/978-3-030-98438-0_5

Keywords: Breathing training application · Gamified visual feedback · Persuasive technology · Physical activity · Running

1   Introduction

The act of breathing is essential for the sustenance of life and health. The way we breathe fundamentally influences our psychophysiological system. Especially slow-paced breathing has shown its positive effect on psychophysiological well-being and physiological outcome [1–4]. Observed benefits are e.g. increased heart rate variability [5], increased stress resilience [2,6], improved oxygen saturation, and lower blood pressure [7]. These positive effects and the increasing availability of digital and persuasive technologies gave rise to many breathing training devices and applications [8–14], digital experiences, and games that use breathing parameters as a marker to teach individuals how to adapt their breath to reach a relaxed and mindful state [15–18] or manage specific health issues [19–23]. As of today, most of these applications focus on breath training in a sedentary setting.

Compared to traditional persuasive technology and health games, gamification is claimed to offer several advantages for motivating behaviour change for health and well-being, and is increasingly used [24]. Moreover, gamification is seen as a way to sustain engagement with persuasive applications. But even though the majority of gamified health behavior change support systems focus on physical activity in different contexts [25]: the daily lives of the elderly [26], exergame playing [27], casual exercise [28,29] or exercise during a school day [30], they are mainly used in the intent to promote physical activity but not to foster a certain change in movement or breathing during motion.

Yet, persuasive and application guided breathing training during physical activity have, to our knowledge, not been a main focus of research so far. Even though especially controlled slow breathing is found to be highly advantageous during physical activity [31], as it not only impacts the already mentioned psychophysiological parameter but also the experience of the activity [32,33].

To address this gap, we focused on the development and exploration of a gamified breathing training application with visual biofeedback that can be used while running (one of the world's most popular physical activities [34]) to actively engage users in the breathing process, raise conscious breathing control and to facilitate the adaptation towards an aspired breathing pattern. With this work we primarily contribute to the body of knowledge on breathing training through visual biofeedback in motion, by exploring the effects of the, for this purpose developed, Gamified Breathing Training Application (GBTA) on users conscious breath-control before and after using the GBTA, subjective perception of the breathing alignment process and the perceived effectiveness of the application.

The following questions guided this research:

RQ1: Does using the GBTA has an impact on conscious breath-control?
RQ2: How do users perceive the breathing alignment process within the GBTA? Especially addressing perceived difficulty, success, effort and enjoyment.
RQ3: How do user perceive the effectiveness of the GBTA while running?

The subsequent section introduces work related to this research, followed by a description of the methodological approach. Hereafter we present the results and discuss these before outlining the limitations and possibilities for future work. Finally, we will conclude this paper.

2   Related Work

2.1   Breathing Training Applications

Traditionally breathing training was conducted either under the supervision of a professional coach or with the help of e.g., audio recordings. However, the positive .effect of breathing and the emerging technological opportunities have given rise to a variety of commercially available mobile meditation and breathing exercise apps [35–38]. So far, most of these apps remain limited to pacing specific breathing patterns, using audio or visual instructions, without sensor feedback on the actual breathing behaviour of the user.

To address these limitations, several novel interactive systems and applications digital experiences and games for respiration training have been brought up by research [10,39–41]. Within the fields of persuasive technology and HCI a number of interactive and gamified applications emerged that use the players breath as a control mechanism in breathing games [42,43]. However, the current stack of breathing games, experiences and interactive applications mainly focuses on entertainment [43–45], health/rehabilitation [11,21–23], work context [46,47] or meditation and mindfulness [15–17] in a sedentary setting. Only a few studies can be found that focus on strategically supporting to guide the users attention toward their breathing while moving or attaining certain breathing strategies (as e.g., slow or paced breathing) during physical activity.

In their work Greinacher et al. [12] focus on indoor rowing and compare visual breathing indication with haptic guidance in order to support athletes to maintain a correct, efficient, and healthy breathing-movement-synchronicity while working out. Even though the authors did not find any statistical impact of the visual feedback, subjective participants ratings indicated a strong reference for the visual modality. Focusing on running, Valsted et al. [14] explored haptic feedback to real-time assist runners with rhythmic breathing. Comparing inhale- and exhale-based vibration in a first study, they found that participants preferred exhale-based feedback. In a subsequent study on the temporality of tactile feedback they conclude that the choice of temporality should depend on factors as the duration of the run and the runners capability to follow a rhythmic breathing pattern. Musical feedback and two persuasive techniques (glancable interface and virtual competition) have been used by Oliveria et al. [48] to assist runners in achieving a predefined exercise goal. Results suggest the interface to be the most important element in increasing efficiency and virtual competition to have main influence on the enjoyable experience. Also van Rheden et al. [49] focus on auditory feedback during the run. Exploring the effects of five distinct breathing instruction sounds while running, they found all tested sounds to be effective in stabilizing the breathing rate.

Looking into the field of feedback modality for breath guidance, especially visual and auditory feedback instructions have been researched by different authors. To facilitate changes in breathing patterns, visual feedback has recurrently shown its potential by providing information on parameters such as length of the breath, time of inhale and exhale, or breathing rate and depth in mindfulness and mediation focused breathing training applications [50]. Using visual instructions to guide the runners breathing during the activity does of course require a controlled setting without obstacles (e.g. a treadmill) to keep the visual system free during the run. Chittaro et al. [8] compared three different breathing training app designs: one based only on audio instructions, and two which augment audio instructions with different kinds of visualizations. They found a wave-based visualization was able to produce better results compared to the voice only design, both in objective terms (measured deep and slow respiration) and subjectively (users found it more effective from an instruction as well as a relaxation point of view). Also Parnandi et al. [16] concluded that visual channels help players to maintain a targeted breathing rate.

2.2 Respiratory Biofeedback

Consciously controlling breathing techniques is necessarily driven by a brain top-down process stemming from the voluntary shift of attention toward breath monitoring aiming at the aware and active control of breathing rhythm [51]. As most people are not naturally aware of their autonomic physiology (including breathing), let alone able to consciously regulate it [52], biofeedback signals can be deliberately used to picture internal physiological processes and provide guidance on how to change or adapt them [39,53]. Moreover, using biofeedback can be used to enhance engagement in application based breathing exercises and to provide more guidance for continuous practice.

A growing body of evidence in research suggests that especially for creating interactive feedback and learning systems that shall be used while in motion, the respiratory rate is a highly interesting and valuable biofeedback variable. For one thing, it can be utilized to raise breathing awareness as one's own breathing actions and changes are immediately and easily recognizable. Furthermore, respiratory biofeedback can be applied to specifically evaluate the user's current breathing pattern and based on this promote the desired breathing pattern (e.g., slow and prolonged exhale) [54]. In addition to this the individual feedback can be designed to increase user engagement and fun while persuading users to align their breath to a previously agreed upon breathing training and thus allows for active involvement in the behaviour (breathing) change process [12]. In addition to this, respiratory signals can be detected via different wearable sensors and fed back to the user in real time, typically in the form of visual or auditory stimuli [39] to guide or facilitates the maintenance of a given breathing pace, the execution of specific breathing exercises or enhance breathing awareness during running.

In their work Adler et al. [55] found that especially synchronous visuorespiratory stimulations induced cognitive awareness of respiration. While exploring how cues in a virtual environment guide the attention to breath and shape the quality of experience Prpa et al. [56] also used visual representation of breathing displaying it as a movement in the environment. After the initial "a-ha" moment of breath awareness, the motion cues caused participants to be more aware of the range, rhythm, depth, and other subtleties of their breathing and the other bodily sensations that accompany inhalation and exhalation. Those findings indicate the potential of visualizing respiratory feedback to enhance users breath-control and awareness during running.

3   Methods

An exploratory within-subject user study[1] was designed to investigate the effects of the GBTA on users conscious breath-control before and after using the GBTA, subjective perception of the breathing alignment process and the perceived effectiveness of the application. All of experiments were conducted on-site at the sport science laboratory of the University of Salzburg to guarantee a standardized environment.

3.1   Participants

Participants were recruited via the mail distributor of the University of Salzburg and University of Applied Science Salzburg. There were no specific participation requirements except for age between 16–60 years and good knowledge of the German language. In total 11 participants (4 female/7 male; mean age: 31,6 +- 11,6) took part in the experiment. The duration of the experimental run ranged between 85 - 100 min and participants got 20€ compensation.

In an initial questionnaire, focusing on running experience and breathing awareness, 10 out of 11 participants stated to go running. Reasons given for going running were solely leisure and health orientated. All of the participants that stated to go running also reported to have experience with running on a treadmill. The results of the preceding breath awareness questions (based on [17]) further on indicated no outstanding high or low breath awareness among the participants.

3.2   The GBTA

The GBTA was developed in JavaScript (JS) ES6 (utilizing the p5.js library [57]), HTML5 and CSS3. The application was run on a MacBook Pro (16inch, 2019) and displayed on a large (42") Sony Bravia TV screen, which was mounted on a portable and height-adjustable TV stand, positioned right in front of the treadmill. Breathing data was captured via strain gauge belt. As shown in Fig. 1, the application incorporated three sequential gamified visual feedback scenarios (L1, L2, L3).

---

[1] For this research ethical approval was granted by the Ethics Committee of Salzburg University, reference number: GZ 13/2021.

In L1 participants are given the opportunity to explore, become a feeling of their own breath and the control of the player's position by receiving a visual biofeedback but no explicit breathing goal. The breathing pattern of the user is visually represented by a brown path/trail that gets "drawn" on the screen.

Within L2 participants are asked to align their breathing to the visual presented breathing path (aspired breathing rate). Opposed to L1, the user's breath is not displayed in L2 and thus does not have any influence on the visualization. The player icon moves automatically up and down, perfectly following the predefined breathing path. It furthermore constantly marks the current position in the predefined breathing phase. Hence the user is able to visually assess when and for how long to inhale or exhale but does not see his/her own breath.

Building up onto the phases of breathing exploration and visual guidance without biofeedback, L3 is again directly influenced by the real-time breathing input of the user. Here the user actively controls the vertical position of the player icon on the given breathing path by his chest movement while inhalation and exhalation. Observing the player move along the given path presumably provides an inherent incentive to follow the pursued breathing pattern. Through the placement of differently coloured (blue = exhale begins, orange = inhale begins) collectible tokens at the points where one phase ends and the next begins, the inhalation and exhalation phase are highlighted.

In this work our primary focus does not lie on the specification of differences between the three different feedback scenarios (L1–L3), but rather on the initial exploration of the users perception on the gamified breathing experience, on their conscious breath-control, and especially in assessing subjective user feedback regarding the breathing alignment process and the perceived effectiveness.

Fig. 1. GBTA - gamified visual feedback scenarios 1–3.

3.3   Procedure

In order to be able to assess possible influencing factors, such as participants running experience and individual breathing awareness, an pre-questionnaire was completed before starting the experiment. Then participants were introduced to the study procedure participants and equipped with a chest worn strain gauge breath sensor.

Before starting the GBTA two preliminary breath-control tests (Test 1 Pre/ Test 2 Pre) were conducted to be able to measure changes in conscious breath-control evoked by the GBTA. Both tests were repeated after the completion of

Fig. 2. Visualization of the GBTA in action.

two full rounds of all GBTA scenarios (Test 1 Post/ Test 2 Post). In Test 1 participants were instructed to breathe evenly (equal inhalation and exhalation phase length) for one minute while standing still, without receiving any biofeedback. Thus, they had to rely on their individual perception of breathing evenly. After one minute the average amount and duration of inhales and exhales was visually displayed to the user and saved by the application. For Test 2 participants were further on instructed to continue by consciously elongating their exhale by 25%, again without receiving any visual biofeedback. The average amount and duration of inhales and exhales was displayed to the user and saved by the application.

After explaining the core functionalities of the treadmill, participants were asked to familiarize themselves with the treadmill and adjust a comfortable running speed (see Fig. 2). "Comfortable running speed", hereby was further described to the participant as "rather slow, not too exhausting, but fast enough to get into a running movement". This was indicated by a BORG CR10 scale (a general intensity scale anchored at number 10, commonly used to measure exertion and pain [58]) level of appx. 4. To ensure that exhaustion does not influence breathing-control measurements or the users perception of the application, the BORG query was repeated after each scenario.

Before starting with L1, participants were given appx. 5 min to warm up and find their preferred running speed. Next, a one-minute baseline breathing ratio sample was recorded. To support rather slow and deep breathing while using the application, this baseline breathing ratio was prolonged by half and exhale time was again elongated by 25% for creating the breathing path (aspired breathing rate) in L2 and L3.

Each of the 3 GBTA scenarios lasted 4 min and was directly followed by a feedback session, where participants were asked to slow down the treadmill to walking speed and verbally indicate their current level of exhaustion (BORG CR10). Subsequently, they were presented with a set of questions (based on [59]), focusing on their perception of the breathing alignment process by assessing perceived difficulty, success, effort and enjoyment.

After the completion of one full round (L1+L2+L3) the perceived effectiveness for all 3 scenarios combined was assessed via a tailored questionnaire based on [8] (a detailed description of the applied questions can be found in Sect. 4.3). Following the completion of the second full round of the GBTA, the two preliminary breath-control tests were repeated (Test 1 Post/Test 2 Post).

The experiment finished with a brief qualitative interview session (5–10 minutes) involving two rather open questions (1. How did you perceive the use of the breathing program while running? 2. Which aspects of the breathing program have supported or hindered you in perceiving your breath and following the given rhythm?) aiming to gain further feedback on the participants perception of the GBTA and to identify improvement opportunities for further iterations.

4   Results and Discussion

All participant's ratings remained within the range of 3–5 which translates as an easy to moderate exertion, with respect to the BORG CR10 questionnaire. This suggests that any potential confounding of the results due to excessive physical or mental exertion can be denied. In addition, no gradual increase or scenario-specific increase/decrease in perceived exertion was observed.

4.1   RQ1: Does Using the GBTA Has an Impact on Conscious Breath-Control?

When we look at the conscious breath-control of participants, Three out of four dependent variables were shown to be normally distributed in a ShapiroWilk test. The mean phase length variation for all four conscious-breath-control test scenarios, Test 1 Pre ($M = 1.75$) and Test 1 Post ($M = 1.23$), and Test 2 Pre ($M = 1.68$) and Test 2 Post ($M = 1.10$), suggest that participants managed to fulfill the breathing task instructions in both scenarios better after using the GBTA. A pairwise Wilcoxon test verifies a significant difference for Test 1 Pre/Post ($p = 0.010$) and likewise for Test 2 Pre/Post ($p = 0.011$) (cf. Table 1). Hence, it can be stated that, according to the results, participants were better able to consciously control their breath to attain the given breathing tasks (Test 1 - equal inhale/exhale phase length, Test 2 - 1/4 prolonged exhale phase length compared to inhale phase length) after the gamified breathing training experience.

As with all pre/post-test settings, however, one should take into account that the improved performance in the post tests may also be related to the fact that the participants took the same tests for the second time. This should be considered in future research.

Table 1. Results of the pairwise Wilcoxon test between Test 1 Post/Pre and Test 2 Post/Pre.

	Test 1 Post/Pre	Test 2 Post/Pre
Z	−2.578	−2.535
Asymp. sig (2-Seitig)	0.010	0.011
Effect size	0.560	0.541

4.2   RQ2: How Do User Perceive the Breathing Alignment Process Within the GBTA?

Participants rated their perceived breathing alignment by answering 4 questions (based on [59]) addressing perceived Difficulty (Q1), Success (Q2), Effort (Q3) and Enjoyment (Q4). Answers were given on a 7-point Likert scale (1 = strongly disagree, 2 = disagree, 3 = somewhat disagree, 4 = neither agree nor disagree, 5 = somewhat agree, 6 = agree, 7 = strongly agree) directly after each scenario.

Descriptive data analysis with mean scores of 3.08 (SD = 0.70) for Q1, 4.76 (SD = 1.33) for Q2, 3.05 (SD = 0.56) for Q3, and 5.14 (SD = 0.73) for Q4 suggests that the participant perceived the alignment process rather as successful and enjoyable than difficult and with a lot of effort (see Fig. 3).

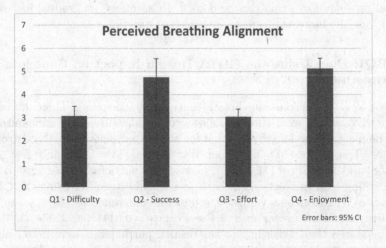

Fig. 3. Perceived breathing alignment - mean ratings for all levels with a 95% CI.

The significance of the differences in between ratings is indicated by the Friedman test (p=0.001). Post-hoc test results show, as assumed, that participants rated Success and Enjoyment significantly higher than Difficulty and Effort of using the application. These results suggest that participants had fun using the GBTA and subjectively managed quite well to adjust their breathing to the given pace.

Qualitative interview outcomes also support these findings as they implicate that participants are supported by the visual feedback of their breathing rate in perceiving their own breath and following the given rhythm (e.g., P4: *"For me it was amazing to see that when i breathe more consciously it is less effort. I found this guideline of when to breathe in and out very helpful."*, P9: *"I find it great to focus on the breathing, that worked."*, P10: *"It was quite interesting, this raise in awareness has definitely succeeded."*). However, one big remark by almost all participants regarding the hindering aspects in perceiving their own breathing and following the given pace was that the sliding strain gauge belt made the control of the player more difficult. Within further studies using the same setup, a better solution for the belt adoption should be introduced.

4.3   RQ3: How Do Users Perceive the Effectiveness of the GBTA While Running?

To measure participants perceived effectiveness a tailored questionnaire adapted from Chittaro et al. [8] was employed. A 7-point Likert scale was used for the ratings (see Fig. 4).

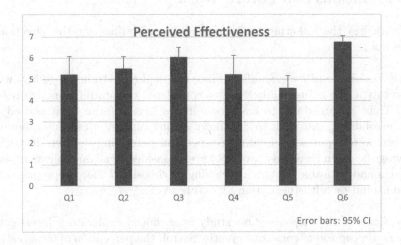

Fig. 4. Perceived effectiveness - mean ratings for all level with a 95% CI.

Q1 ("The breathing program facilitates paced breathing while running.") was rated with a mean score of 5.23 (SD = 1.40) indicating that the participants indeed felt that the GBTA supported them in pacing their breathing. Mean scores of 5.50 (SD = 0.92) and 6.05 (SD = 0.76) for Q2 ("The breathing program is convenient to use.") and Q3 ("It is easy to follow the instructions of the breathing program.") moreover imply that participants did not have much trouble understanding the breathing instructions or the operation of the program. Evaluating the given answers for Q4 ("The breathing program effectively teaches the rhythm in which to breathe while running.") a mean of 5.23 (SD = 1.47), that is lower than Q1-Q3, but still an over-average rating can be found. As the usage time of the GBTA might have been too short for the users to assess the teaching skills of the application, this question could be considered in further experiments applying a longitudinal design. Q5 ("The breathing program effectively helps to reduce stress.") received the lowest ratings (M = 4.59; SD 0.94). As actively reducing stress was no focus of this study, the possibilities of stress reduction during running could also be an interesting focus in future work. Overall, participants ratings show that the breathing application helped them to direct attention to their breath while running (Q6: M = 6.77, SD = 0.47). This conclusion is supported by post hoc test results showing a significantly ($p < 0.05$) higher rating in Q6 compared to most of the other questions (except for Q3).

Participants feedback within the individual interview sessions provide further information on the perceived breathing attention focus while using the GBTA. Here, some participants stated that they were so focused on their breathing, that they forgot the running effort or even declared that they *"paid extreme attention to their breathing"* [P1].

5   Limitations and Future Work

Our work has the following limitations and implications for the direction of future work.

Device Usability and Functionality. Since the deployed strain gauge belt was a lab-prototype, its adjustability was not considered thoughtfully enough beforehand. Thus, it turned out to have some limitations in terms of fit and adjustment possibilities, causing it to slide down during running. Resulting calibration problems were reported as hindering aspects in perceiving the own breath and following the given breathing pace. However, considering advancements in smart garments and wearable sensors, developing or choosing a more appropriate belt option should be a feasible option for future work.

Study Size and Participants. Our study is an initial exploratory investigation on users' perception of conscious breath-control, the perception of the breathing alignment process, and the perceived effectiveness while using the GBTA. The small study group enabled us to evaluate the detailed experiences of each user. Future studies and iterations of the GBTA may however involve larger-scale studies with a higher number of participants and a more diverse target group.

Controlled Environment. The study was conducted in a controlled lab-environment. This does not restrict our findings per se as the use of visual feedback during the run already implies certain constraints on the environment. Nevertheless, future work could consider broader settings or contexts to explore a potential use in different environments.

Number of Measurements. Our work describes a single intervention, thus no statement on long-term effects or adaptations can be made. Future studies could focus on a more longitudinal design to investigate the longer-term behaviour and awareness change processes when using the GBTA. This could possibly also reduce the influence of initial learning effects on the conscious breath-control test results.

6 Conclusion

The possibilities for persuasive and application based breathing training during running have thus far been relatively unexplored. In this paper we outlined three main research questions with the aim to explore the effects and the user perception induced by using the developed gamified breathing training application (GBTA). For this purpose, we ran an exploratory user study in which we presented the participant three sequential gamified visual feedback scenarios and in total six rounds of breathing training during treadmill running. Considering the outlined limitations, the results show a significant improvement in conscious breath-control after using the GBTA (RQ1). The analysis of the questions assessing the perception of the breathing alignment within the GBTA (RQ2) show that the participants rated the alignment process as significantly more successful and enjoyable than difficult or connected with a lot of effort. Qualitative user feedback moreover indicates that the visual feedback of their own breathing rate supported participants in perceiving their breath and thus facilitated breathing alignment in general. Further findings show positive mean scores for all six questions regarding the perceived effectiveness of the GBTA while running (Q3). In detail, it can be concluded that participants felt that the GBTA supported them in pacing their breathing, while they did not have much trouble understanding the breathing instructions or the operation of the program. Overall, participants ratings show that the breathing application helped them to direct attention to their breathing while running.

Considering all the conclusions we see a high potential for further development of the GBTA to actively engage users in the breathing process and increase breathing awareness during running, to subsequently facilitate the adaptation of an aspired breathing pattern.

Acknowledgements. This research was funded by the Austrian Ministry for Transport, Innovation and Technology, the Federal Ministry for Digital and Economic Affairs, and the federal state of Salzburg under the research program COMET - Competence Centers for Excellent Technologies - in the project Digital Motion in Sports, Fitness and Well-being (DiMo).

References

1. Schumer, M.C., Lindsay, E.K., Creswell, J.D.: Brief mindfulness training for negative affectivity: a systematic review and meta-analysis. J. Consult. Clinic. Psychol. **86**(7), 569–583 (2018). https://doi.org/10.1037/ccp0000324

2. Goessl, V.C., Curtiss, J.E., Hofmann, S.G.: The effect of heart rate variability biofeedback training on stress and anxiety: a meta-analysis. Psychol. Med. **47**(15), 2578–2586 (2017). https://doi.org/10.1017/S0033291717001003

3. Mendes, L.P., et al.: Effects of diaphragmatic breathing with and without pursed-lips breathing in subjects with COPD. Respir. Care **64**(2), 136–144 (2019). https://doi.org/10.4187/respcare.06319

4. Russo, M.A., Santarelli, D.M., O'Rourke, D.: The physiological effects of slow breathing in the healthy human. Breathe (Sheffield, England) **13**(4), 298–309 (2017). https://doi.org/10.1183/20734735.009817

5. Laborde, S., Mosley, E., Thayer, J.F.: Heart rate variability and cardiac vagal tone in psychophysiological research - recommendations for experiment planning, data analysis, and data reporting. Front. Psychol. **8**, 213 (2017). https://doi.org/10.3389/fpsyg.2017.00213

6. Siepmann, M., Aykac, V., Unterdörfer, J., Petrowski, K., Mueck-Weymann, M.: A pilot study on the effects of heart rate variability biofeedback in patients with depression and in healthy subjects. Appl. Psychophys. Biofeedback **33**(4), 195–201 (2008). https://doi.org/10.1007/s10484-008-9064-z

7. Sivakumar, G., Prabhu, K., Baliga, R., Pai, M.K., Manjunatha, S.: Acute effects of deep breathing for a short duration (2–10 minutes) on pulmonary functions in healthy young volunteers. Indian J. Physiol. Pharmacol. **55**(2), 154–159 (2011)

8. Chittaro, L., Sioni, R.: Evaluating mobile apps for breathing training: the effectiveness of visualization. Comput. Hum. Behav. **40**, 56–63 (2014). https://doi.org/10.1016/j.chb.2014.07.049

9. Choi, K.Y., Lee, J., ElHaouij, N., Picard, R., Ishii, H.: Aspire: clippable, mobile pneumatic-haptic device for breathing rate regulation via personalizable tactile feedback. In: Kitamura, Y., Quigley, A., Isbister, K., Igarashi, T. (eds.) Extended Abstracts of the 2021 CHI Conference on Human Factors in Computing Systems, pp. 1–8. ACM, New York, NY, USA (2021). https://doi.org/10.1145/3411763.3451602

10. Patibanda, R., Mueller, F.F., Leskovsek, M., Duckworth, J.: Life tree. In: Schouten, B., Markopoulos, P., Toups, Z., Cairns, P., Bekker, T. (eds.) Proceedings of the Annual Symposium on Computer-Human Interaction in Play, pp. 19–31. ACM, New York, NY, USA (2017). https://doi.org/10.1145/3116595.3116621

11. Tu, L., Hao, T., Bi, C., Xing, G.: Breathcoach: a smart in-home breathing training system with bio-feedback via VR game. Smart Health **16**, 100090 (2020). https://doi.org/10.1016/j.smhl.2019.100090

12. Greinacher, R., Kojić, T., Meier, L., Parameshappa, R.G., Möller, S., Voigt-Antons, J.N.: Impact of tactile and visual feedback on breathing rhythm and user experience in VR exergaming. http://arxiv.org/pdf/2004.01555v1

13. Yu, B., Feijs, L., Funk, M., Hu, J.: Breathe with touch: a tactile interface for breathing assistance system. In: Abascal, J., Barbosa, S., Fetter, M., Gross, T., Palanque, P., Winckler, M. (eds.) INTERACT 2015. LNCS, vol. 9298, pp. 45–52. Springer, Cham (2015). https://doi.org/10.1007/978-3-319-22698-9_4

14. Valsted, F.M., Nielsen, C.V.H., Jensen, J.Q., Sonne, T., Jensen, M.M.: Strive. In: Brereton, M., Soro, A., Vyas, D., Ploderer, B., Morrison, A., Waycott, J. (eds.) Proceedings of the 29th Australian Conference on Computer-Human Interaction, pp. 275–284. ACM, New York, NY, USA (2017). https://doi.org/10.1145/3152771. 3152801

15. Paredes, P.E., Zhou, Y., Hamdan, N.A.H., Balters, S., Murnane, E., Ju, W., Landay, J.A.: Just breathe. Proc. ACM Interact., Mob., Wearable Ubiquitous Technol. **2**(1), 1–23 (2018). https://doi.org/10.1145/3191760

16. Parnandi, A., Gutierrez-Osuna, R.: Visual biofeedback and game adaptation in relaxation skill transfer. IEEE Trans. Affect. Comput. **10**(2), 276–289 (2019). https://doi.org/10.1109/TAFFC.2017.2705088

17. Rockstroh, C., Blum, J., Göritz, A.S.: A mobile VR-based respiratory biofeedback game to foster diaphragmatic breathing. Virtual Reality **25**(2), 539–552 (2020). https://doi.org/10.1007/s10055-020-00471-5

18. Vacca, R., Hoadley, C.: Self-reflecting and mindfulness: cultivating curiosity and decentering situated in everyday life. In: Meschtscherjakov, A., De Ruyter, B., Fuchsberger, V., Murer, M., Tscheligi, M. (eds.) PERSUASIVE 2016. LNCS, vol. 9638, pp. 87–98. Springer, Cham (2016). https://doi.org/10.1007/978-3-319-31510-2_8

19. Shih, C.H., Tomita, N., Lukic, Y.X., Reguera, Á.H., Fleisch, E., Kowatsch, T.: Breeze. Proc. ACM Interactive, Mob., Wearable Ubiquitous Technol. **3**(4), 1–30 (2019). https://doi.org/10.1145/3369835

20. Kowatsch, T., et al.: A playful smartphone-based self-regulation training for the prevention and treatment of child and adolescent obesity: Technical feasibility and perceptions of young patients. https://doi.org/10.3929/ethz-b-000469817

21. Agrawal, V., Naik, V., Duggirala, M., Athavale, S.: Calm a mobile based deep breathing game with biofeedback. In: Mirza-Babaei, P., McArthur, V., Vanden Abeele, V., Birk, M. (eds.) Extended Abstracts of the 2020 Annual Symposium on Computer-Human Interaction in Play, pp. 153–157. ACM, New York, NY, USA (2020). https://doi.org/10.1145/3383668.3419876

22. Tabor, A., Pradantyo, R., Sadprasid, B., Birk, M.V., Scheme, E., Bateman, S.: Bubble breather - a breathing exercise game to support pneumonia rehabilitation and recovery. In: Mirza-Babaei, P., McArthur, V., Vanden Abeele, V., Birk, M. (eds.) Extended Abstracts of the 2020 Annual Symposium on Computer-Human Interaction in Play, pp. 86–90. ACM, New York, NY, USA (2020). https://doi.org/10.1145/3383668.3419921

23. van Rooij, M., Lobel, A., Harris, O., Smit, N., Granic, I.: Deep. In: Kaye, J., Druin, A., Lampe, C., Morris, D., Hourcade, J.P. (eds.) Proceedings of the 2016 CHI Conference Extended Abstracts on Human Factors in Computing Systems, pp. 1989–1997. ACM, New York, NY, USA (2016). https://doi.org/10.1145/2851581. 2892452

24. Johnson, D., Deterding, S., Kuhn, K.A., Staneva, A., Stoyanov, S., Hides, L.: Gamification for health and wellbeing: a systematic review of the literature. Int. Interv. **6**, 89–106 (2016)

25. Alahäivälä, T., Oinas-Kukkonen, H.: Understanding persuasion contexts in health gamification: a systematic analysis of gamified health behavior change support systems literature. Int. J. Med. Inf. **96**, 62–70 (2016)

26. Brauner, P., Calero Valdez, A., Schroeder, U., Ziefle, M.: Increase physical fitness and create health awareness through exergames and gamification. In: Holzinger, A., Ziefle, M., Hitz, M., Debevc, M. (eds.) SouthCHI 2013. LNCS, vol. 7946, pp. 349–362. Springer, Heidelberg (2013). https://doi.org/10.1007/978-3-642-39062-3_22

27. Chen, F.X., King, A.C., Hekler, E.B.: "Healthifying" exergames: improving health outcomes through intentional priming. In: Proceedings of the SIGCHI Conference on Human Factors in Computing Systems, pp. 1855–1864 (2014)

28. Zuckerman, O., Gal-Oz, A.: Deconstructing gamification: evaluating the effectiveness of continuous measurement, virtual rewards, and social comparison for promoting physical activity. Personal Ubiquitous Comput. 18(7), 1705–1719 (2014). https://doi.org/10.1007/s00779-014-0783-2

29. Spillers, F., Asimakopoulos, S.: Does social user experience improve motivation for runners? In: Marcus, A. (ed.) DUXU 2014. LNCS, vol. 8520, pp. 358–369. Springer, Cham (2014). https://doi.org/10.1007/978-3-319-07638-6_35

30. Watson, D., Mandryk, R.L., Stanley, K.G.: The design and evaluation of a classroom exergame. In: Proceedings of the First International Conference on Gameful Design, Research, and Applications, pp. 34–41 (2013)

31. Morton, D., Callister, R.: Exercise-Related Transient Abdominal Pain (ETAP). Sports Med. 45(1), 23–35 (2014). https://doi.org/10.1007/s40279-014-0245-z

32. Nicolò, A., Massaroni, C., Passfield, L.: Respiratory frequency during exercise: The neglected physiological measure. Front. Physiol. 8, 922 (2017). https://doi.org/10.3389/fphys.2017.00922

33. Hockey, J., Allen-Collinson, J.: Digging In: The Sociological Phenomenology of "Doing Endurance" in Distance-running. In: Endurance Running, pp. 227–242. Routledge (2015)

34. Hulteen, R.M., et al.: Global participation in sport and leisure-time physical activities: a systematic review and meta-analysis. Prevent. Med. 95, 14–25 (2017). https://doi.org/10.1016/j.ypmed.2016.11.027

35. Breathwrk Inc. Breathwrk—breathing exercises: Breathwrk (2020). https://www.breathwrk.com

36. TotalBrain: Total brain mental health and brain performance selfmonitoring and selfcare platform (2019). https://www.totalbrain.com/

37. Calm: Finde deine gelassenheit (2021). https://www.calm.com/de

38. Headspace: Headspace meditation and sleep made simple (2021). https://www.headspace.com/

39. Yu, B., Funk, M., Hu, J., Wang, Q., Feijs, L.: Biofeedback for everyday stress management: a systematic review. Front. ICT 5 73 (2018). https://doi.org/10.3389/fict.2018.00023

40. Ghandeharioun, A., Picard, R.: Brightbeat. In: Mark, G., Fussell, S., Lampe, C., Schraefel, M., Hourcade, J.P., Appert, C., Wigdor, D. (eds.) Proceedings of the 2017 CHI Conference Extended Abstracts on Human Factors in Computing Systems. pp. 1624–1631, ACM, New York, NY, USA (2017). https://doi.org/10.1145/3027063.3053164

41. Miri, P., Flory, R., Uusberg, A., Culbertson, H., Harvey, R.H., Kelman, A., Peper, D.E., Gross, J.J., Isbister, K., Marzullo, K.: PIV: Placement, pattern, and personalization of an inconspicuous vibrotactile breathing pacer. ACM Trans. Comput.-Hum. Interact. 27(1), 1–44 (2020). https://doi.org/10.1145/3365107

42. Sra, M., Xu, X., Maes, P.: Breathvr. In: Mandryk, R., Hancock, M., Perry, M., Cox, A. (eds.) Proceedings of the 2018 CHI Conference on Human Factors in Computing Systems, pp. 1–12. ACM, New York, NY, USA (2018). https://doi.org/10.1145/3173574.3173914

43. Tennent, P., et al.: Breathalising games. In: Romão, T., Correia, N., Inami, M., Kato, H., Prada, R., Terada, T., Dias, E., Chambel, T. (eds.) Proceedings of the 8th International Conference on Advances in Computer Entertainment Technology - ACE 2011, p. 1. ACM Press, New York, New York, USA (2011). https://doi.org/10.1145/2071423.2071496

44. Marshall, J., Rowland, D., Rennick Egglestone, S., Benford, S., Walker, B., McAuley, D.: Breath control of amusement rides. In: Tan, D., Fitzpatrick, G., Gutwin, C., Begole, B., Kellogg, W.A. (eds.) Proceedings of the SIGCHI Conference on Human Factors in Computing Systems, pp. 73–82. ACM, New York, NY, USA (2011). https://doi.org/10.1145/1978942.1978955

45. Kors, M.J., Ferri, G., van der Spek, E.D., Ketel, C., Schouten, B.A.: A breathtaking journey. on the design of an empathy-arousing mixed-reality game. In: Cox, A., Toups, Z.O., Mandryk, R.L., Cairns, P. (eds.) Proceedings of the 2016 Annual Symposium on Computer-Human Interaction in Play, pp. 91–104. ACM, New York, NY, USA (2016). https://doi.org/10.1145/2967934.2968110

46. Brammer, J.C., et al.: Breathing biofeedback for police officers in a stressful virtual environment: challenges and opportunities. Front. Psychol. **12**, 401 (2021). https://doi.org/10.3389/fpsyg.2021.586553

47. Tabor, A., Bateman, S., Scheme, E., Sadprasid, B., Schraefel, M.: Understanding the design and effectiveness of peripheral breathing guide use during information work. In: Kitamura, Y., Quigley, A., Isbister, K., Igarashi, T., Bjørn, P., Drucker, S. (eds.) Proceedings of the 2021 CHI Conference on Human Factors in Computing Systems, pp. 1–13. ACM, New York, NY, USA (2021). https://doi.org/10.1145/3411764.3445388

48. De Oliveira, R., Oliver, N.: Triplebeat: enhancing exercise performance with persuasion. In: Proceedings of the 10th international conference on Human computer interaction with mobile devices and services, pp. 255–264 (2008)

49. van Rheden, V., Harbour, E., Finkenzeller, T., Burr, L.A., Meschtscherjakov, A., Tscheligi, M.: Run, beep, breathe: exploring the effects on adherence and user experience of 5 breathing instruction sounds while running. In: Audio Mostly 2021, pp. 16–23 (2021)

50. Chuanromanee, T., Metoyer, R.: Evaluation and comparison of four mobile breathing training visualizations. In: 2020 IEEE International Conference on Healthcare Informatics (ICHI), pp. 1–12. IEEE (112020). https://doi.org/10.1109/ICHI48887.2020.9374383

51. Zaccaro, A., Piarulli, A., Laurino, M., Garbella, E., Menicucci, D., Neri, B., Gemignani, A.: How breath-control can change your life: a systematic review on psycho-physiological correlates of slow breathing. Front. Hum. Neurosci. **12**, 353 (2018). https://doi.org/10.3389/fnhum.2018.00353

52. Price, C.J., Hooven, C.: Interoceptive awareness skills for emotion regulation: theory and approach of mindful awareness in body-oriented therapy (mabt). Front. Psychol. **9**, 798 (2018). https://doi.org/10.3389/fpsyg.2018.00798

53. Tolin, D.F., Davies, C.D., Moskow, D.M., Hofmann, S.G.: Biofeedback and neurofeedback for anxiety disorders: a quantitative and qualitative systematic review. In: Kim, Y.-K. (ed.) Anxiety Disorders. AEMB, vol. 1191, pp. 265–289. Springer, Singapore (2020). https://doi.org/10.1007/978-981-32-9705-0_16

54. Gaume, A., Vialatte, A., Mora-Sánchez, A., Ramdani, C., Vialatte, F.B.: A psychoengineering paradigm for the neurocognitive mechanisms of biofeedback and neurofeedback. Neurosci. Biobehav. Rev. **68**, 891–910 (2016). https://doi.org/10.1016/j.neubiorev.2016.06.012

55. Adler, D., Herbelin, B., Similowski, T., Blanke, O.: Reprint of breathing and sense of self: visuo-respiratory conflicts alter body self-consciousness. Respir. Physiol. Neurobiol. **204**, 131–137 (2014). https://doi.org/10.1016/j.resp.2014.09.019

56. Prpa, M., Tatar, K., Françoise, J., Riecke, B., Schiphorst, T., Pasquier, P.: Attending to breath. In: Koskinen, I., Lim, Y.k., Cerratto-Pargman, T., Chow, K., Odom, W. (eds.) Proceedings of the 2018 Designing Interactive Systems Conference, pp. 71–84. ACM, New York, NY, USA (2018). https://doi.org/10.1145/3196709.3196765

57. P5.js: P5.js (2021). https://p5js.org/

58. Borg, G.: Borg's perceived exertion and pain scales. Human Kinetics (1998)

59. Nijs, A., Roerdink, M., Beek, P.J.: Cadence modulation in walking and running: pacing steps or strides? Brain Sci. **10**(5), 273 (2020). https://doi.org/10.3390/brainsci10050273

Don't Touch This! - Investigating the Potential of Visualizing Touched Surfaces on the Consideration of Behavior Change

Elisabeth Ganal(✉)⬤, Max Heimbrock⬤, Philipp Schaper⬤,
and Birgit Lugrin⬤

Human-Computer Interaction, University of Würzburg, Würzburg, Germany
{elisabeth.ganal,philipp.schaper,birgit.lugrin}@uni-wuerzburg.de
max.heimbrock@gmx.de
http://www.mi.uni-wuerzburg.de

Abstract. Several times a day, we touch our faces and all kinds of surfaces, and often we are not even aware that pathogens are transported via surfaces and our hands. There are already a large number of educational or governmental videos that aim to raise people's awareness towards health and hygienic behavior, but whether videos simulating the spread of pathogens can really influence people's behavior and awareness has not been investigated yet. Using a virtual copy of a students' office room and spatial visualizations of touched surfaces, our approach visually simulates the spread of pathogens of smear infections. In a user study, we show videos with or without visualizations of potentially contaminated surfaces in a students' office room to participants, and afterwards ask them to describe their own potential subsequent behavior when entering the same room. In addition to open questions, we also use the PPQ to investigate the persuasive potential of our approach. With this approach we investigate the impact of the visualization of potentially contaminated surfaces on people's behavior and hygiene-oriented attitude. While our results did not reveal a significant effect on the consideration of behavior change assessed by a questionnaire, the participants' descriptions in the qualitative part of the study show more hygiene-oriented behavior descriptions in the visualization conditions.

Keywords: Simulation · Visualization · Hygienic behavior · Virtual reality · Persuasion

1 Introduction

People are often not aware of how much and where they spread pathogens. They do not notice, for example, how often they touch their faces and subsequently a surface or the other way round. However, a lot of surfaces can serve as transmission platforms for infectious pathogens and touching contaminated surfaces may

© Springer Nature Switzerland AG 2022
N. Baghaei et al. (Eds.): PERSUASIVE 2022, LNCS 13213, pp. 75–88, 2022.
https://doi.org/10.1007/978-3-030-98438-0_6

subsequently lead to sickness and even further pathogen spread. Especially with the currently on-going COVID-19 pandemic it is even more important to raise awareness and persuade people to follow safety and health rules. Adapting our behavior to a more hygienic way requires both education and awareness. A lot of governmental and health institutions for example recommend behavioral rules to avoid infection with the currently prevailing SARS-CoV-2-Virus, e.g., cover nose and mouth, wash hands, avoid handshaking or touching the face [1,2]. Methods for raising awareness for the spread of pathogens are wide-ranging, e.g., videos [2,5], apps, visualizations [22], websites, and serious games [18]. There are a lot of videos, which simulate the spread of pathogens and visualize fomites [2,13,22]. Even though research on other hygiene intervention strategies exists [14], to the best of our knowledge, it has not been investigated yet how these video visualizations influence a person's subsequent behavior.

Therefore, we want to answer the following research questions in this work:

- **RQ1**: Does the visualization of potentially contaminated surfaces lead to a consideration of behavioral change?
- **RQ2**: Does the visualization of potentially contaminated surfaces lead to more hygiene awareness in the form of more hygiene-oriented behavioral descriptions?
- **RQ3**: Do users want to be informed about potentially contaminated surfaces in a room?

To answer these research questions we create a VR simulation tool for visualizing contaminated surfaces and disinfection and conduct an online user study. In this user study participants are shown videos with different visualizations and hygienic behavior and participants are afterwards asked to describe their subsequent hygienic behavior. Further, the persuasiveness of the videos on the participants is quantified with the PPQ and open questions. Further, they are asked to assess the importance of a hygiene-related information system.

While the videos of other approaches are often more generic and less relatable, we use a virtual copy of a students' office laboratory in this work to relate better to reality and therefore increase persuasiveness. In this virtual copy we use spatial visualizations of potentially contaminated surfaces to raise awareness of the potential spread of pathogens through surface contamination. In general, this approach could also serve as a simulation tool in educational hygiene interventions or for training in the fields of medicine or healthcare.

The remainder of this work is structured as follows: Sect. 2 presents related work. The concept and implementation details are discussed in Sect. 3, which is followed by the description of the user study conducted with the implemented system in Sect. 4. The obtained results are presented in Sect. 5 and the findings are discussed in Sect. 6, before Sect. 7 concludes the work.

2   Related Work

Although the COVID-19 pandemic has led to increased research into pathogen transmission, health and hygienic behavior, there are few approaches that investigate the impact of simulations or visualisations of the spread of pathogens on humans. Official organisations use TV and commercials to draw attention to diseases and provide information about the transmission of pathogens in everyday life to raise awareness [2]. Such presentations are prepared to be accessible by a broad audience and are heterogeneous in their presentation. Often, infections or contaminated objects are highlighted visually, e.g., to demonstrate the possible spread of pathogens in a hospital setting despite the use of gloves [5]. TV shows have also addressed this topic and demonstrated the spread of pathogens by highlighting the possible consequences with colors, e.g., in a hospital [12]. In addition to videos on pathogen spread, there are also a large number of videos describing correct hygiene behavior, e.g., hand washing [7]. In reality, fluorescent paint and particles, which glow under black light, can be used to safely demonstrate how pathogens can be spread or transmitted via hands or surfaces in a classroom [13] or in a dinner scenario [17, 21].

The following is a brief overview of the few existing scientific papers and studies related to the topic of this work. Comparable to videos with fomite visualizations, Wilson [22] describes a system that uses two depth cameras for 3D reconstructing the room and body tracking to record which objects a user touches and whether the user touches her or his face. The touched surfaces of furniture or objects are then colored red on the camera image and on the real environment with projection mapping. A user study did not take place due to the COVID-19 pandemic, but the system was tested by individuals. Wilson [22] also notes that at the time of development it was not yet clear that the SARS-CoV-2 virus is transmitted via surfaces to a minor extent. However, for other pathogens, and hygiene in general, smear infection can be a major means of transmission. Kurgat et al. [11] showed in their study that an hygiene intervention can lead to a significant reduction of pathogen concentrations on surfaces in an office building. In a study by Koch et al. [10] participants watched cooking videos, which differed in the hygiene behavior of the chef depending on the tested condition. Subsequently, the participants were asked to cook the dishes themselves in a laboratory kitchen. The participants' hygiene behavior was assessed on the basis of video recordings. The results showed that hygiene practices were significantly influenced by the level of kitchen hygiene shown in the cooking videos before. Koch et al. [10] propose that by visibly showing correct hygiene behavior in cooking shows, behavioral change among viewers can be more easily achieved. This shows, that the visualisation of contamination and the presentation of adequate practices can thus lead to a change in behavior and have persuasive potential.

3   Implementation

3.1   Visualization of Contaminated Surfaces

The concept of this work is to highlight potentially contaminated surfaces in the virtual representation of a real room. VR is a suitable tool here as it can be used to simulate and demonstrate a range of different scenarios in real-time. Based on related work and the there presented simulation methods, e.g., [5, 22], we decided

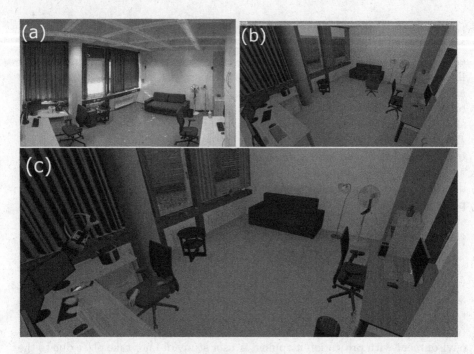

Fig. 1. Stimuli environment: (a) image of real laboratory (b) virtual laboratory (camera view for the stimuli videos) (c) contaminated surfaces in virtual laboratory and virtual person (disinfection wipe at right hand and contaminated at left hand).

to visually highlight the contaminated areas as well, since this might be a suitable approach to demonstrate fomites. We decided to use the color red for visualizing contamination, as it is known as a signal color and an attention-gaining color and in our case stands out best from the other colors in the room. Similar to Wilson [22] the contaminated hands are marked in red as well. For simulation purposes, a user can be assigned the property *infectious* and subsequently either has contaminated hands from the beginning or automatically contaminates his or her hands by moving the hands close to the face, which is also called face touch. However, there is also the possibility that the hands are (re-)contaminated via already contaminated surfaces. In addition, our system also offers the possibility to simulate the use of (hand) disinfection.

Based on our previous work on Smart Substitutional Reality [4], this work uses the virtual representation of one of our university student office laboratories. Within our previous work [4], a copy of an existing student office laboratory and furniture (e.g., desk, office chair, lamp, etc.) were created in VR. Through integrating the physical environment into a virtual environment by substituting objects with similar virtual counterparts [20], a user can freely move in the virtual world and get haptic feedback from the real world. Figure 1 shows an image of the real laboratory (Fig. 1(a)) as well as the virtual representation (Fig. 1(b)) and the virtual laboratory with contaminated surfaces (Fig. 1(c)).

We use the game engine Unity (version 2019.1.14f1) for the simulation of smear infections. As the virtual environment of our previous work uses SteamVR Base Stations, the positions of the hands are tracked using the Vive controllers and the head is tracked with a Vive headset in this work [4].

3.2   Implementation of Surface Contamination

When the virtual hands hit the mesh collider of a virtual piece of furniture, a red spot, i.e., a new object in Unity, is instantiated at the point of contact at runtime. The contamination is visualized by a semi-transparent image that shows a round red spot in a spray effect. The position and rotation of the instantiated object are defined by taking the closest touching point of the touching hand collider with the surface collider and adding an offset of 0.1 mm. For some objects, such as hands, head, and disinfectant containers, the instantiation of the contamination object is not applied. The hygienic status of the user can be set by either touching a contaminated or infectious area or disinfectant container, or by predefined keypresses. Our system allows to display the potentially contaminated surfaces in a fine-grained way, e.g., comparable to real fomites. However, the accuracy of the hand tracking affects the creation and representation of virtual fomites.

System Purposes. The system can be either used in live mode or for replaying captured scenarios. When using the system in live mode, users get direct feedback of what they touched through the visualization in the virtual room. For the purpose of replaying captured scenarios, our system allows to record and play back the movements of the Vive headset and controllers. Additionally, the movements of movable furniture equipped with Vive trackers, e.g., an office chair, can also be replayed. The movements of a person are recorded inside Unity by logging and saving the transformation data of each GameObject, which is part of the CameraRig tracked by the Base Stations. The captured VR simulation scenarios can be used for virtual playback or as video stimuli material for studies.

User Study Setup. The user study is conducted as an online study due to the ongoing COVID-19 pandemic and a lockdown situation during the time of data collection. Thus, screencast videos of the virtual laboratory are recorded and leveraged as stimuli material for the user study. In contrast to existing work [10], we use videos of a virtual representation of an existing room that participants are familiar with. The study is based on a 2×2 factorial and between-subjects design and participants are randomly assigned to one of the conditions. The considered factors are hereby visualization and disinfection. Touch contamination is considered in the study and it is further assumed that the person (see Fig. 1(c)) in the video is infectious and regularly touches his/her face. For the user study, we have defined the following four conditions in order to investigate the effect of visualisation and the use of disinfection on the consideration of behavior change, hygiene awareness, and desire for information. Thus, the four test conditions are as follows:

- **nVnD**: No visualization and no disinfection is shown (control group).
- **VnD**: Contaminated surfaces are visualized, but no disinfection is shown.
- **nVD**: No visualization is shown, but the person demonstrates hand and surface disinfection.
- **VD**: Visualization of contaminated surfaces as well as disinfection of hands and surfaces is demonstrated.

Stimuli Videos. For each of these conditions, stimuli videos differing in visualization and disinfection are created. A predetermined sequence of actions serves to generate similar videos. In all conditions the person in the video regularly touches its face and thus contaminates its hands. Due to the factor disinfection the video procedure for nVD and VD slightly differs at the beginning and at the end compared to nVnD and VnD. The disinfection procedures consist of hand disinfection after entering the room and surface disinfection after working at the computer. The disinfection procedure is conducted with slight imperfections, to reflect a realistic scenario in which such errors are to be expected.

In the video, the virtual person touches the door handle and either moves directly (nVnD and VnD) to the work station or uses the disinfectant in advance (nVD and VD). Subsequently, the person interacts with keyboard and mouse, and alternately tests several sensors placed at different locations of the room and, thus, touches several surfaces (plant, floor lamp, window). Afterwards, the person shuts down the computer and either leaves directly (nVnD and VnD) or disinfects the work station (keyboard, mouse, desk, chair) and throws the disinfection wipe in the trash (nVD and VD).

For the stimuli videos, however, the contamination representations at the touch points are enlarged for better visibility. Further, the fictional virtual person in the video is visualized by a virtual headset and two hands (see Fig. 1(c)), because these are the important body parts for the visualization. First, the movements of the person's head and hands and the movable furniture are recorded by means of the predetermined sequence of actions. Then, the recordings are replayed in Unity, while an OBS screencast is performed and a full screen sized Game view of Unity is captured. It shows the view of an additional camera in Unity (see Fig. 1(b)) placed at one of the upper corners of the room to be able to monitor the whole room with a field of view of 70°C. By simply switching the contamination settings, e.g., infectious status, with predefined keypresses, the visualization of the videos becomes differently. Finally, the recorded videos are cut with a video editing tool. The stimuli videos have a duration of 03:44 min for nVnD and VnD, and 04:03 min for nVD and VD.

4   User Study

4.1   Measurements

For measuring the persuasive potential of early-stage prototypes, e.g., multi-user smart mirror system [6], the Persuasive Potential Questionnaire (PPQ) [15] can be used. In this study, the PPQ [15] with three dimensions and 15 items on a 7-point Likert scale is used to measure the potential persuasive effect of the visualization of contaminated surfaces. The PPQ should serve to answer if the visualization could lead to a consideration of behavioral change (RQ1). The three dimensions comprise 'Susceptibility to Persuasion' (SP) with four items, 'General Persuasive Potential of the System' (GPP) with three items, and 'Individual Persuasive Potential of the System' (IPP) with eight items. For evaluating the results of the PPQ the answers of the 15 items are averaged separately and grouped by the three dimensions [6]. The SP dimension is considered as independent as it relates to the participant, whereas the dimensions GPP and IPP depend on the system. Therefore, no significant differences between the conditions are expected at the SP dimension. If people provide low values for susceptibility to persuasion (SP low), a system has a higher potential to persuade them (IPP higher) [15].

To answer RQ2, open questions are asked after watching the video. In these open-ended questions, participants are asked to describe the sequence of events in the video, to give a personal assessment of the behavior of the fictional person shown in the video, and to describe their own potential subsequent behavior. For the third of these open questions they get the exemplary scenario *'As student assistant you should work with the sensors in the laboratory. The person in the video was in the laboratory before.'* to describe their own potential behavior after entering the room within this scenario. The description of the sequence served on the one hand as manipulation check to verify if participants watched the whole video. On the other hand, the answers to these open-ended questions are evaluated using a qualitative content analysis to determine whether the participant describes different hygienic behavior or aspects. This qualitative content analysis is performed by highlighting keywords on hygiene-oriented behavior, e.g., 'disinfect', 'airing', 'open window', 'clean', 'do not touch face', and many more. Each answer of the participants containing at least one keyword is marked. Then, the percentage of answers with keywords is compared across all conditions.

In addition and to answer RQ3, participants are asked to rate on a 7-point Likert scale the potential usage of an information system, which shares hygiene-related content. First, they are asked if it is important to them to be informed about surfaces that have been contaminated by themselves or by others. Second, the participants are asked to assess the importance of or the wish for notifications of an information system regarding different hygiene-related information. These hygiene-related information may comprise potentially contaminated surfaces, face touches, washing or disinfecting hands, CO_2 value in the room, and duration and number of people who were previously in the room.

For general demographic data collection, the participants are asked about age, gender, visual impairment, and color blindness, as well as if they already know the laboratory.

4.2   Study Procedure

Participants sign up for the online study via the university intern recruitment system and then receive a link to the study. The participants are not informed about the study topic regarding fomite visualization in advance to reduce a potential social desirability bias on the study topic. Instead, they are told beforehand that the study is about information systems in a smart laboratory. After a short introduction with general information and electronic participant consent, the participants answer demographic questions and whether they have prior experience with the laboratory after showing images of the real (Fig. 1(a)) and virtual (Fig. 1(b)) laboratory to them. Afterwards, the participants watch one of the stimuli videos depending on which condition they were randomly assigned to in the beginning. To watch the video the participants click a button and are informed beforehand that the video can only be played once and cannot be paused, as every participant should watch the video just once. The continue button appears as soon as the video is over. The video is followed by open questions regarding the video. Next, the PPQ and questions about a potential information system that communicates hygiene-related information are asked. Finally, participants have the opportunity to leave comments. The online user study has a duration of approximately 15 min in total.

4.3   Participants

All of the participants were students acquired over a university intern recruitment system and were granted partial course credit for participation. Ten participants, which did not complete the questionnaire, and one participant, which expressed in the comments section the wish to be excluded, were not considered for the data analysis.

In total, 84 (69 female, 15 male) participants completely filled out the questionnaire and were considered for data analysis. The age of the participants was between 18 and 29 years (M = 21.46, SD = 1.92). They are distributed among the conditions as follows: nVnD with 27 (21 female, 6 male), VnD with 19 (17 female, 2 male), nVD with 21 (17 female, 4 male), and VD with 17 participants (14 female, 3 male). Nearly one quarter of the participants (~22.6 %) stated to already know this laboratory, even though all students should have been familiar with such types of laboratories.

5   Results

5.1   Persuasive Potential Questionnaire (PPQ)

All statistical analyses were conducted using Python (scipy 1.5.0 and statsmodels 0.11.1) and an alpha of 0.05.

The results of the PPQ are taken to address RQ1, whether the visualisation of contaminated surfaces leads to a consideration of behavioral change (see Fig. 2).

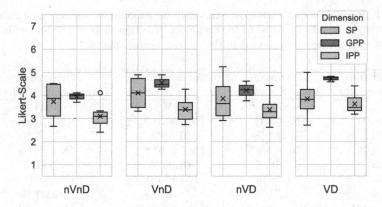

Fig. 2. Results for the PPQ for all conditions (nVnD, VnD, nVD, and VD) and dimensions (SP, GPP, and IPP). Means are depicted with 'x' and medians with lines.

A two-way ANOVA was performed for each subscale of the PPQ to analyze the effect of visualization and disinfection. For the dimension SP no significant main effects for visualization ($p = .138$) and for disinfection ($p = .606$), as well as no significant interaction between the effects of visualization and disinfection ($F(1, 80) = 1.13$, $p = .291$) were observed. For the dimension GPP no significant main effects for visualization ($p = .126$) and for disinfection ($p = .483$), as well as no significant interaction between the effects ($F(1, 80) = 0.02$, $p = .882$) were observed. Similarly for the dimension IPP, no significant main effects for visualization ($p = .328$) and for disinfection ($p = .326$), as well as no significant interaction between the effects ($F(1, 80) = 0.02$, $p = .902$) were observed. Thus, there are no statistically significant interaction effects between the visualization of contaminated surfaces and demonstrating disinfection in the videos.

5.2 Hygienic Behavior

In order to address RQ2, whether the visualisation of potentially contaminated surfaces leads to more hygiene awareness in the form of more hygiene-oriented descriptions of behavior, the open questions after the video were evaluated using a qualitative content analysis. The qualitative content analysis of the open questions regarding video sequence description, assessment of the behavior of the person in the video, and the description of the own potential behavior, showed several differences across the conditions (see Table 1). The proportion of answers which contain at least one hygiene-related keyword increased with the addition of the independent variables (visualization and disinfection). Answers with weak hygiene-related keywords or content, e.g., 'person should not touch everything', or 'person could not have stayed in the specified work area', were not considered in the results because different interpretations are possible here. On the other hand, some answers contained strong hygiene-related keywords or content, e.g., 'disinfect surfaces touched by the person' or 'disinfect hands'. While for nVnD

Table 1. Results of qualitative content analysis. Amount of answers containing at least one hygiene-related keyword for each open question in percent and as absolute numbers. Percentages are rounded to the second decimal place.

Condition (Participants)	Description Video Sequence	Assessment Person's Behavior	Description Own Potential Behavior
1	~3.70 %	12 %	~33.33 %
(N = 27)	(N $_1$ = 1)	(N $_2$ = 3) *	(N $_3$ = 9)
2	~10.53 %	~31.58 %	~73.68 %
(N = 19)	(N $_1$ = 2) *	(N $_2$ = 6) *	(N $_3$ = 14)
3	~76.19 %	~61.90 %	~85.71 %
(N = 21)	(N $_1$ = 16)	(N $_2$ = 13)	(N $_3$ = 18)
4	~64.71 %	~76.47 %	~88.24 %
(N = 17)	(N $_1$ = 11) *	(N $_2$ = 13)	(N $_3$ = 15)

Note. * excluding answers with awareness of visualization or person's behavior, but no clearly hygiene-related keywords, e.g., 'surfaces are colored red', 'person should not touch everything'.

only one participant had a hygiene-related keyword in the description of the video sequence, for VnD this was the case for two participants. For nVD 16 participants used at least one keyword and for VD eleven participants. In all conditions, the amount of answers with keywords increased at the assessment of the person's behavior and once again at describing the own potential behavior. Nearly a third of the participants of VnD (~31.58 %) and more than half of the participants of nVD (~61.90 %) used hygiene-related keywords when assessing the person's behavior. The results of VD show a high amount of answers containing keywords for all of the three open questions (video sequence: ~64.71 %, person's behavior: ~76.47 %, and own behavior: ~88.24 %).

Further, the hygiene-related keywords in the answers of the visualization and disinfection conditions (VnD, nVD, VD) are descriptively more frequent and diverse compared to the control group (nVnD). Here, however, the number of participants with hygiene-related answers must be taken into account. Some participants described the usefulness of the visualization of contaminated surfaces. One participant of VnD mentioned in the description of their own behavior that the red contamination spots help to be aware and remember to disinfect surfaces and which ones. A participant of VD claimed in the behavior description to use the video as reference for which surfaces still have to be disinfected. Other participants in VD also mentioned to disinfect all contaminated surfaces that have not been disinfected by the person in the video.

5.3   Information System Usage

The results of additional questions regarding the potential usage of an information system serve to address RQ3, whether users want to be informed about potentially contaminated surfaces and other hygiene-related information. The results for the additional questions regarding an information system, which shares hygiene-related content are listed in Table 2. For all conditions, the results show descriptively higher values for information about surfaces potentially contaminated by others than by participants themselves. The results for the wish

3.1 Analysis of Survey Results and Game Logs

We performed a descriptive analysis of the survey data to assess which intervention performed better and, a frequency analysis of the game's log data to analyze the difficulty of game levels and user's in-game quiz answering pattern. For the IMI scale, the game performed slightly better than the security document with an overall mean score (M) = 4.37, Standard Deviation (SD) = 0.845 on the IMI while for the document, M = 4.24 and SD = 0.769. With respect to the self-efficacy, the game performed better with a mean change of 72% compared to the document with 14% as the mean change from pre survey to post survey. The response cost saw a considerable reduction for the game with a mean change of −78% but the document had a mean change of −32%. The game increased the perceived severity and vulnerability of the participants with a mean change of 38% and 11% respectively. In contrast, the document decreased the perceived severity and vulnerability with a mean change of −14% and −18% respectively. Users with an increased perceived vulnerability and perceived severity will regret not taking counter measures and will thus follow secure smartphone practices [53]. The game scored better in the permission scenario with a mean change of 33% for selecting correct permissions and −56% for selecting wrong permissions compared to the document which scored 0% for selecting correct permissions and −15% for selecting wrong permissions. Although intentions are postulated as good predictors of behaviour, this is always not the case in real world. This depends on the behaviour being a single action or a multi-action behaviour. It is necessary to include security behaviour in the study [53]. There was an increase in security behaviour for both the interventions with the game performing slightly better with a mean change of 66% and the document with a mean change of 57%. The mean change from pre survey to post survey for all the survey items are shown below in Table 3.

Table 3. Survey descriptive statistics

Survey items	Mean change –pre to post survey (game)	Mean change –pre to post survey (Doc)
Self-efficacy	72%	14%
Response cost	−78%	−32%
Perceived severity	38%	−14%
Perceived vulnerability	11%	−18%
Security behaviour	66%	57%

For the in-game log data, we analyzed the data of where the players lost lives in-game and their total play time. We also analyzed how often the players answered the quiz questions correctly and the number of attempts. With the gameplay data, we generated a frequency graph with the in-game co-ordinates data to identify where players faced difficulty in the game that led to them constantly losing lives in-game. In Fig. 1, each red dot corresponds to single instance of the player losing life in-game. This is helpful for developers who are looking to balance the game while keeping it challenging and interesting [55]. We also generated frequency graphs with the in-game quiz log data as shown in Fig. 2. From this graph, we can infer that most users were able to figure out about third party apps in the first attempt, followed by secure lock screen practices and other security issues.

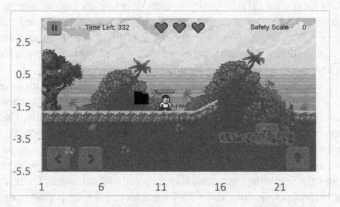

Fig. 1. Frequency analysis of player losing lives in-game

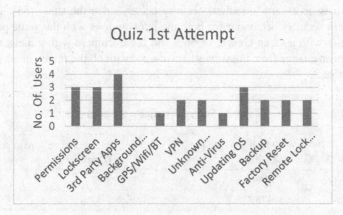

Fig. 2. Frequency analysis of in-game quiz answers

3.2 Analysis of Participants' Qualitative Feedback

We interviewed eight participants who played the game and five participants who read the security document. We performed thematic analysis using affinity diagram and for each intervention we extracted eight themes and various sub-themes. We compare some of the key themes in this section.

Participants Found the Game Relatable and Nostalgic. When we asked how players' felt about the game when they opened it for the first time, most of them were able to relate it with Super Mario [39] and other retro games. Player-2 chuckled while saying *"Mario. It gave me the feel of playing 2-D Sega games. It was more like walking back into memory lane and enjoying the game"*. Recent research shows that retro games invoke *nostalgia* by invoking past memories and satisfaction of competence [56]. Our game evoked the feeling of nostalgia, thus reducing the learning curve which also falls in line with self-determination theory [56].

The Document Was Difficult to Read and Comprehend. Most of the readers *struggled* to understand the document and needed some time to understand it. Reader-3 said *"I was confused what to look for at the first time because everything was on one page with a lot of text, signs and arrows… I found it was too much of an overload"*. Reader-2 mentions *"…But for the second page, it took me a while to understand what the symbols were all about"*. Some of the readers were *not familiar with cybersecurity terminologies*.

The Game Was Challenging and Gives Players a Sense of Achievement. The players liked *challenges* which was evident from the players' feedback during the interview. For most of the players, difficulty was one of the *motivational factors* for this game. Player-8 related the difficulty to a popular game and stated *"…It's down to the difficulty of the game. I'd compare this to GTA Vice City's helicopter mission where you try, stop for a while and try again later. At least some level of difficulty is needed in a game else what is the point. If it is difficult, you get a sense of achievement"*. It is imperative to keep in mind that persuasive games should not be too tough to play but should also be interesting and challenging with the right balance to keep the players engaged [57] and expose them to the necessary persuasive contents.

The Document Is Well Organized. Looking at the *positive comments* for the document, Reader-5 mentions that *"It was very organized, and I knew what went with what… It's kind of like on your face and you can choose where you want to start…"*. Reader-3 states that *"…After that it was easy to follow…"*, *"I liked the icons used here…the avoid, disable, do, do-not, I love them…"*.

The Game Increased Player's Curiosity. The foreshadowing level design pattern (hidden areas) increased players' *curiosity*. Player-2 said, *"At the first time, I noticed a fruit but I couldn't figure out how to reach there and I kept trying"*. These unusual visual cues create uncertainty that invoke *perceptual curiosity* and increases attention among players [58]. Players found *in-game quizzes* to be fun and informative. When we asked about players' favourite game mechanic, Player-6 said while chuckling *"the questions… if you are wrong, it is going to give you more information after testing your knowledge. That's the good thing"*. Humour is widely used not only in the games but also in advertisements [59]. Previous research states that humour can boost intrinsic motivation and learning [26].

Readers Wanted an Interactive Document. When we asked the readers what changes they would make to the document, most of them wanted an interactive version of the document. Reader-3 said *"The icon descriptions can be hidden and shown while clicking on the icons. This might reduce the amount of information on the page"*. When we asked the players what they would suggest for the game, the *players wanted more levels*.

Readers Applied Security Tips. All the readers *learnt something new* from the document and some of them *tried few security measures* while reading it or after reading it. The reason for behaviour change was either *retrospection* or *realization of threat severity*. Reader-4 described their experience as *"... Since I am always with my phone, what is the use of using the passwords. But after this, I implemented the 6-digit lockscreen password"*.

Game Players Implemented Tips While Facing Security Threat in Real Life. The security content covered by the game also had a *retrospective* and *introspective* effect on the participants and players *implemented* some of the in-game security suggestions. Player-4 commented *"... after that (playing the game), each time that clicks in my mind and now I have started the habit of seeing what I am downloading and its source"*. Player-1 shared their experience stating *"I have actively started to notice which all permissions are required, and I deny or allow accordingly... earlier I did not pay much attention to it. I have also started turning off the Wifi when it is not needed"*.

Players Reflected About Their Actions. Players thought about their actions before making in-game decisions. Player-4 said *"... when I got the option, I had to think... instead of selecting all I stopped and thought about it. Most of the time I used to accept all... this was really insightful"*. Individuals who try to averse regret are more likely to make secure decisions to avoid negative consequences [53]. In our game, players had a chance to think about their decision among other possible answers.

4   Conclusion and Future Work

In this paper, we discussed about a persuasive game to educate users about the secure smartphone practices. We utilized persuasive principles and level design patterns to make the game more interesting and we adapted the PMT survey [53] to measure the Protection Motivation Constructs. We compared our game with a security document published by NSA (2×2 between study design) and analyzed the quantitative and qualitative data. From the quantitative results, it was evident that the game was better at improving the smartphone security behaviour in general and some of the PMT constructs. The qualitative results show that the game evoked a feeling of nostalgia and humour. Players followed security tips when they faced security threats in real life. Tailored persuasive apps have been shown to be much better than generic apps [60, 61]. As part of our future work, we plan to tailor the in-game suggestions according to Regulatory Focus Theory [62] which states that there are two types of users - those who respond to positives or gains and those who respond to negatives or losses. We plan to conduct a long-term study (2×3 Between study design) with more participants where we would compare the two versions of the game with the security document published by NSA.

Acknowledgement. This research was undertaken, in part, thanks to funding from the Canada Research Chairs Program. We acknowledge the support of the Natural Sciences and Engineering Research Council of Canada (NSERC) through the Discovery Grant.

References

1. Koyuncu, M., Pusatli, T.: Security awareness level of smartphone users: an exploratory case study. Mob. Inf. Syst. **2019** (2019). https://doi.org/10.1155/2019/2786913
2. Renaud, K.: 60 smartphone owners need security advice. how can we ensure they get it ? In: CONF-IRM 2016 Proceedings (2016)
3. Calderwood, F., Popova, I.: Smartphone cyber security awareness in developing countries: a case of Thailand. In: Zitouni, R., Agueh, M. (eds.) AFRICATEK 2018. LNICSSITE, vol. 260, pp. 79–86. Springer, Cham (2019). https://doi.org/10.1007/978-3-030-05198-3_7
4. Breitinger, F., Tully-Doyle, R., Hassenfeldt, C.: A survey on smartphone user's security choices, awareness and education..Comput. Secur. **88** (2020). https://doi.org/10.1016/j.cose. 2019.101647
5. Zhang, X.J., Li, Z., Deng, H.: Information security behaviors of smartphone users in China: an empirical analysis. Electron. Libr. **35**, 1177–1190 (2017). https://doi.org/10.1108/EL-09-2016-0183
6. Shah, P., Agarwal, A.: Cybersecurity behaviour of smartphone users in India: an empirical analysis. Inf. Comput. Secur. **28**, 293–318 (2020). https://doi.org/10.1108/ICS-04-2019-0041
7. Nowrin, S., Bawden, D.: Information security behaviour of smartphone users: an empirical study on the students of university of Dhaka. Bangladesh. Inf. Learn. Sci. **119**, 444–455 (2018). https://doi.org/10.1108/ILS-04-2018-0029
8. Google: Permissions on Android|Android Developers. https://developer.android.com/guide/topics/permissions/overview. Accessed 5 Nov 2021
9. Permissions updates in Android 11|Android Developers. https://developer.android.com/about/versions/11/privacy/permissions. Accessed 2 Jan 2021
10. Android 12 Privacy & Security. https://www.android.com/android-12/#a12-safe. Accessed 5 Nov 2021
11. Behavior changes: all apps|Android12|Android Developers. https://developer.android.com/about/versions/12/behavior-changes-all#mic-camera-toggles. Accessed 5 Nov 2021
12. Bitton, R., Finkelshtein, A., Sidi, L., Puzis, R., Rokach, L., Shabtai, A.: Taxonomy of mobile users' security awareness. Comput. Secur. **73**, 266–293 (2018). https://doi.org/10.1016/j.cose. 2017.10.015
13. Bitton, R., Boymgold, K., Puzis, R., Shabtai, A.: Evaluating the information security awareness of smartphone users. In:. Conference on Human Factors in Computing Systems - Proceedings (2020). pp. 1–13 (2020). https://doi.org/10.1145/3313831.3376385
14. Google: App permissions best practices | Android Developers. https://developer.android.com/training/permissions/usage-notes. Accessed 29 Nov 2020
15. Balebako, R., Marsh, A., Lin, J., Hong, J., Faith Cranor, L.: The privacy and security behaviors of smartphone App Dev. (2014). https://doi.org/10.14722/usec.2014.23006
16. Barrera, D., Kayacik, H.G., Van Oorschot, P.C., Somayaji, A.: A methodology for empirical analysis of permission-based security models and its application to Android. In: Proceedings of the ACM Conference on Computer and Communications Security, pp. 73–84 (2010). https://doi.org/10.1145/1866307.1866317
17. Ndulue, C., Oyebode, O., Orji, R.: PHISHER CRUSH: a mobile persuasive game for promoting online security. In: Gram-Hansen S., Jonasen T., Midden C. (eds.) PERSUASIVE 2020. LNCS 12064, pp. 223–233. Springer Cham (2020). https://doi.org/10.1007/978-3-030-45712-9_17
18. Gokul, C.J., Pandit, S., Vaddepalli, S., Tupsamudre, H., Banahatti, V., Lodha, S.: Phishy - a serious game to train enterprise users on phishing awareness. In: CHI PLAY 2018 - Proceedings of the 2018 Annual Symposium on Computer-Human Interaction in Play Companion Extended Abstracts. pp. 169–181 (2018). https://doi.org/10.1145/3270316.3273042

19. Wen, Z.A., Lin, Z., Chen, R., Andersen, E.: What.Hack: engaging anti-phishing training through a role-playing phishing simulation game. In: Proceedings of the Conference on Human Factors in Computing Systems, pp. 1–12 (2019). https://doi.org/10.1145/3290605.3300338

20. Weanquoi, P., Johnson, J., Zhang, J.: Using a game to teach about phishing. In: SIGITE 2017 - Proceedings of the 18th Annual Conference on Information Technology Education, vol. 75 (2017). https://doi.org/10.1145/3125659.3125669

21. Raptis, G.E., Katsini, C.: Beter, funner, stronger: A gameful approach to nudge people into making less predictable graphical password choices. In: Conference on Human Factors in Computing Systems - Proceedings. p. 17. ACM, New York(2021). https://doi.org/10.1145/3411764.3445658

22. Chen, T., Dabbish, L., Hammer, J.: Self-efficacy-based game design to encourage security behavior online. In: Conference on Human Factors in Computing Systems – Proceedings, pp. 1–6. Association for Computing Machinery, New York (2019). https://doi.org/10.1145/3290607.3312935

23. Scholefield, S., Shepherd, L.A.: Gamification techniques for raising cyber security awareness. In: Moallem, A. (ed.) HCII 2019. LNCS, vol. 11594, pp. 191–203. Springer, Cham (2019). https://doi.org/10.1007/978-3-030-22351-9_13

24. Yerby, J.: Development of serious games for teaching digital forensics. Issues Inf. Syst. **13**, 112–122 (2014)

25. Thomps, M., Irvine, C.: Active learning with the CyberCIEGE video game. In: 4th Workshop on Cyber Security Experimentation and Test, CSET 2011, pp. 1–8 (2011)

26. Zargham, N., Bahrini, M., Volkmar, G., Sohr, K., Wenig, D., Malaka, R.: What could go wrong? Raising mobile privacy and security awareness through a decision-making game. In: CHI Play 2019 - Extended Abstracts of the 2020 Annual Symposium on Computer-Human Interaction in Play, pp. 805–812 (2019). https://doi.org/10.1145/3341215.3356273

27. Bahrini, M., Meissner, M., Malaka, R., Wenig, N., Sohr, K.: HappyPerMi: presenting critical data flows in mobile application to raise user security awareness. In: Proceedings of the Conference on Human Factors in Computing Systems (2019). https://doi.org/10.1145/3290607.3312914

28. Bahrini, M., Volkmar, G., Schmutte, J., Wenig, N., Sohr, K., Malaka, R.: Make my phone secure! Using gamification for mobile security settings. ACM's International Conference Proceeding Series, pp. 299–308 (2019). https://doi.org/10.1145/3340764.3340775

29. Ganesh, A., Ndulue, C., Orji, R.: The design and development of mobile game to promote secure smartphone behaviour. In: CEUR Workshop Proceedings, pp. 73–87 (2021)

30. Ganesh, A., Ndulue, C., Orji, R.: PERMARUN- a persuasive game to improve user awareness and self-efficacy towards secure smartphone behaviour. In: Proceedings of the Conference on Human Factors in Computing Systems (2021). https://doi.org/10.1145/3411763.3451781

31. Maddux, J.E., Rogers, R.W.: Protection motivation and self-efficacy: a revised theory of fear appeals and attitude change. J. Exp. Soc. Psychol. **19**, 469–479 (1983). https://doi.org/10.1016/0022-1031(83)90023-9

32. NSA Mobile Device Best Practices (2020). https://doi.org/10.4324/9780429269110-11

33. Oinas-Kukkonen, H., Harjumaa, M.: Persuasive systems design: key issues, process model, and system features. Commun. Assoc. Inf. Syst. **24**, 485–500 (2009). https://doi.org/10.17705/1cais.02428

34. Khalifa, A., De Mesentier Silva, F., Togelius, J.: Level design patterns in 2D games. In: IEEE Conference on Computational Intelligence and Games CIG. 2019-August (2019). https://doi.org/10.1109/CIG.2019.8847953

35. Fogg, B.J.: Creating persuasive technologies: an eight-step design process. ACM International Conference Proceeding Series 350 (2009). https://doi.org/10.1145/1541948.1542005

36. Proto.IO: Proto.io - Prototypes that feel real. https://proto.io/. Accessed 04 Apr 2020
37. Draw Freely|Inkscape. https://inkscape.org/. Accessed 6 Nov 2021
38. Unity: Unity Real-Time Development Platform|3D, 2D VR & AR Engine. https://unity.com/. Accessed 4 Apr 2021
39. The official home of Super Mario^{TM} – Home. https://mario.nintendo.com/. Accessed 11 Jan 2021
40. Mega Man – Wikipedia. https://en.wikipedia.org/wiki/Mega_Man. Accessed 6 Nov 2021
41. Dangerous Dave – Wikipedia. https://en.wikipedia.org/wiki/Dangerous_Dave. Accessed 6 Nov 2021
42. Claw (video game) – Wikipedia. https://en.wikipedia.org/wiki/Claw_(video_game). Accessed 6 Nov 2021
43. Huang, H.Y., Tuncay, G.S., Demetriou, S., Gunter, C.A., Banerjee, R., Bashir, M.: Smartphone security behavioral scale: a new psychometric measurement for smartphone security (2020)
44. Rogers W.R.: Cognitive and physiological processes in fear appeals and attitude change: a revised theory of protection motivation. Soc. Psychophysiol. A Sourceb. 153–177 (1983)
45. Chambers, R., Tingey, L., Mullany, B., Parker, S., Lee, A., Barlow, A.: Exploring sexual risk taking among American Indian adolescents through protection motivation theory. AIDS Care 28, 1089–1096 (2016). https://doi.org/10.1080/09540121.2016.1164289
46. Plotnikoff, R.C., Trinh, L.: Protection motivation theory: is this a worthwhile theory for physical activity promotion? Exerc. Sport Sci. Rev. 38, 91–98 (2010). https://doi.org/10.1097/JES.0b013e3181d49612
47. Meier, Y., Schäwel, J., Kyewski, E., Krämer, N.C.: Applying protection motivation theory to predict facebook users' withdrawal and disclosure intentions. In: ACM International Conference Proceeding Series, pp. 21–29 (2020). https://doi.org/10.1145/3400806.3400810
48. Mwagwabi, F.M.: A Protection Motivation Theory Approach to Improving Compliance with Password Guidelines (2015)
49. Shih-Chieh Hsu, J., Shih, S.-P.: When does one weight threats more? An integration of regulatory focus theory and protection motivation theory. In: Proceedings of the 10th Pre-ICIS Workshop on Information Security and Privacy, pp. 12–13 (2015)
50. Giwah, A.D., Wang, L., Levy, Y., Hur, I.: Empirical assessment of mobile device users' information security behavior towards data breach: leveraging protection motivation theory. J. Intellect. Cap. 21, 215–233 (2019). https://doi.org/10.1108/JIC-03-2019-0063
51. van Bavel, R., Rodríguez-Priego, N., Vila, J., Briggs, P.: Using protection motivation theory in the design of nudges to improve online security behavior. Int. J. Hum. Comput. Stud. 123, 29–39 (2019). https://doi.org/10.1016/j.ijhcs.2018.11.003
52. Crossler, R., Bélanger, F.: An extended perspective on individual security behaviors: Protection motivation theory and a unified security practices (USP) instrument. Data Base Adv. Inf. Syst. 45, 51–71 (2014). https://doi.org/10.1145/2691517.2691521
53. Verkijika, S.F.: Understanding smartphone security behaviors: an extension of the protection motivation theory with anticipated regret. Comput. Secur. 77, 860–870 (2018). https://doi.org/10.1016/j.cose.2018.03.008
54. Reynolds, J.L.: Measuring intrinsic motivations. In: Handbook of Research on Electronic Survey Measurements, pp. 170–173 (2006). https://doi.org/10.4018/978-1-59140-792-8.ch018
55. Quantitative Research for new user researchers - How to be a Games User Researcher. https://gamesuserresearch.com/2021/07/19/quantitative-research-for-new-user-researchers/. Accessed 28 Nov 2021
56. Wulf, T., Bowman, N.D., Velez, J.A., Breuer, J.: Once upon a game: exploring video game nostalgia and its impact on well-being. Psychol. Pop. Media Cult. (2018). https://doi.org/10.1037/ppm0000208

57. Perrotta, C., Featherstone, G., Aston, H., Houghton, E.: Game-Based Learning: LateSloughst Evidence And Future Directions. National Foundation for Educational Research, Slough (2013)
58. To, A., Ali, S., Kaufman, G., Hammer, J.: Integrating Curiosity and Uncertainty in Game Design. In: Proceedings of the 1st International Joint Conference of DiGRA-FDG, pp. 1–16 (2016)
59. Srivastava, E., Maheswarappa, S.S., Sivakumaran, B.: Nostalgic advertising in India: a content analysis of Indian TV advertisements. Asia Pacific J. Mark. Logist. **29**, 47–69 (2017). https://doi.org/10.1108/APJML-10-2015-0152
60. Orji, R., Vassileva, J., Mandryk, R.L.: Modeling the efficacy of persuasive strategies for different gamer types in serious games for health. User Model. User-Adap. Inter. **24**(5), 453–498 (2014). https://doi.org/10.1007/s11257-014-9149-8
61. Orji, R., Mandryk, R.L., Vassileva, J.: Improving the efficacy of games for change using personalization models. ACM Trans. Comput. Interact. **24** (2017). https://doi.org/10.1145/3119929
62. Cesario, J., Higgins, E.T., Scholer, A.A.: Regulatory fit and persuasion: basic principles and remaining questions. Soc. Personal. Psychol. Compass. **2**, 444–463 (2008). https://doi.org/10.1111/j.1751-9004.2007.00055.x

Mixed Methods Examination of Behaviour Change from Learning Supports Based on a Model of Helping in Equity Focused Simulation Based Teacher Education

Garron Hillaire[1]([envelope]) [ORCID], Jessica Chen[1] [ORCID], Chris Buttimer[1] [ORCID],
Joshua Littenberg-Tobias[1] [ORCID], Abdi Ali[2] [ORCID], and Justin Reich[1] [ORCID]

[1] Massachusetts Institute of Technology, Cambridge, MA 02139, USA
garron@mit.edu
[2] Boston Public Schools, 2300 Washington Street, Boston, MA 02119, USA

Abstract. Equitable teaching practice is attracting growing attention in teacher education because there is increased awareness for the need to support the variability of students. This study aims to examine the use of digital clinical simulation-based learning and the role of support to influence equitable teaching practice. Using a mixed-methods design, data were collected with a simulation culminating in whether the teacher would give a quiz to a simulated student and provide reasoning. After making the decision, participants were given a second chance to revise their response with the addition of a support based on a theoretical model of helping to influence attending to the student's wellbeing. While the sample size of 11 participants is too small for inferential statistical testing, the mixed-methods showed fascinating trends that merit follow-up studies. Initially, none of the participants mentioned physical wellbeing in their response, but the support encouraged 3 participants to address the student's physical wellbeing. These results contribute nuanced evidence and guidance toward dynamic support for equity focused simulation-based learning.

Keywords: Equity · Equity teaching practice · Simulation-based learning · Real-time support · Teacher education

1 Introduction

In teacher education, novice teachers are often provided with few opportunities to practice in low-stakes and supportive environments [4]. Most teacher education programs combine learning in university-based seminars with practicum experiences. Practicum settings in classrooms provide novices with situations that have potentially high stakes and, hence, are far less safe to practice, make mistakes, and learn to improve without potentially causing harm to students.

© Springer Nature Switzerland AG 2022
N. Baghaei et al. (Eds.): PERSUASIVE 2022, LNCS 13213, pp. 101–108, 2022.
https://doi.org/10.1007/978-3-030-98438-0_8

Simulation-based learning provides an alternative space for practice by offering supportive, low- or no-stakes learning environments [3].

An exciting new area for this practice-based approach is the use of digital teaching simulations [1,6,10]. One of the advantages of creating simulations online is the potential for providing real-time individualized supports to all learners in a classroom simultaneously as they engage in simulations. However, little is known at present about providing such supports. To address this gap, we created a study that explored the potential of designing supports within digital simulations based on a model of helping [2,11].

To explore how supports based on a Model of Helping change behavior we incorporated a measure related to learning. We know that when learning from simulations an important signal is the experience of cognitive dissonance [3], where participants experience situations where their behaviors do not match their beliefs [5]. In addition to measuring cognitive dissonance we also use an equity mindset survey [1] to measure equity beliefs of participants to better understand how the support changes behavior in relation to beliefs.

This study raises two key research questions: Research Question 1 (RQ1): To what extent can a learning support based on a Model of Helping change behavior?, and Research Question 2 (RQ2): To what extent did the change in participant behavior relate to quantitative measures of cognitive dissonance and equity mindsets?

2 Related Work

2.1 Equity Focused Teacher Education with Simulations

Simulations offer a low-stakes setting to practice high-stakes interactions. This practice-oriented approach via the use of teaching simulations presents little potential for causing harm and is particularly salient when asking new teachers to wrestle with issues of inequity, particularly those that are race-, class-, gender-, language-, and disability-based. Novice teachers need more low-stakes opportunities like those provided by simulations to practice difficult conversations about issues of equity [3,9].

Simulation-based learning emphasizes the importance of supporting participant reflection. Previous work has demonstrated benefits from asking the following debrief questions: 1) What did you notice?; 2) How did you interpret it?; 3) How/Did you intervene? These elements support reflection as they can help participants better understand not only what they did during a simulation but also the elements of the simulation that informed their actions [10]. In this paper, we built from this perspective of reflective supports into a model of helping to generate digital supports designed to encourage equitable behavior within the simulation.

2.2 Supporting Behavior Change with a Model of Helping

The Model of Helping was created to explain the bystander effect where the likelihood of helping in an emergency was reduced when in a crowd [2]. The model outlined five key factors that influence an individual's decision to help someone in need. The first two steps are noticing and interpreting the situation, which are directly parallel to the reflection supports in simulations [10]. The model of helping provides two additional steps ahead of the intervention by examining if someone takes responsibility in the situation and is capable of determining the action to take. The model of helping when re-contextualized to students in distress [11] breaks down the step of taking responsibility into three components: empathetic arousal, facing contextual moral frames, and scanning social status and relations. In addition, this modified model changes the step of determining action to condensing of motives for action. In this study, we designed a support for noticing, interpreting, and intervening, which are concepts that connect across the three aforementioned papers [2,10,11].

3   Methods

3.1   Participants

In this study, we worked with a first-year teacher mentoring program designed to accelerated PK-12 teachers to lead students to academic success in a large urban district in the Northeast (U.S.). Fourteen participants attended the session, 12 provided permission to participate in the study, and 11 completed the activity.

3.2   Materials

Jeremy's Journal. In the simulation, participants play the role of a 7th grade teacher and focus on one student in the class named Jeremy [1]. Over the period of a week, participants follow Jeremy, observing his behavior and reviewing his classwork through his journal. Jeremy at first seems to understand material. In the middle of the week, Jeremy misses a day of class. When he returns to class, he presents a note from his mother explaining that he was not feeling well. On Thursday, Jeremy asks to be excused from the weekly quiz noting that he has a stomach ache and that his mother will "kill him" if he does not do well. Participants must decide whether they will have Jeremy take the quiz and explain why.

Second Try with Support. Participants review their initial response to administering the quiz and are provided with support in the form of three things to consider, which support notice, interpret, and intervene:

- Consider acknowledging Jeremy's statement that he has a stomach ache in your response.
- Did you know that when students complain about a stomach ache, this can sometimes indicate that they are experiencing emotional distress, which is likely going to affect their ability to demonstrate their understanding on an assessment.
- An optional support would be to use the following sentence frame: "Jeremy, I would like to begin by saying..., therefore I think the best thing in this situation would be..."

3.3   Instruments

Cognitive Dissonance Questionnaire (Scale 1–5). A six-item questionnaire used to determine the extent to which participants experienced cognitive dissonance previously used with Teacher Moments simulations [8]. Cognitive Dissonance freuqntly occurs when there is a mismatch between beliefs and behaviors [5].

Equity Mindset Survey (Scale 1–6). A six-item questionnaire used to determine the extent to which participant dispositions are equitable previsouly used with Jeremny's Journal [1]. The survey is a bipolar scale from an equality mindset (treat everyone student the same) to and equity mindset (provide each student with what they need).

3.4   Procedure

Over a two-hour time period, participants used the Teacher Moments platform [7] to 1) complete the simulation, 2) complete two exit surveys: Cognitive Dissonance Questionnaire and the Equity Mindset Survey, and 3) respond to Jeremy a second time using supports based on the Model of Helping.

3.5   Analysis

The second author conducted a thematic analysis on the reasoning behind participants' decisions to administer the quiz in both responses, prior to and after receiving the support. In addition, we scored the cognitive dissonance survey and the equity mindset survey. To answer RQ1, We first examined changes in the decision to administer the quiz as well as changes in reasoning behind the decision. To answer RQ2, we connected changes to scores in the cognitive dissonance questionnaire and the equity mindset survey by plotting revisions in a two-dimensional plane of cognitive dissonance and equity mindset.

4   Results

4.1   RQ1

On their first response, 6 out of 11 participants decided to administer the quiz. During the retry with support, 2 participants revised their decision, with one revising to a *yes* and one revising to a *no*. When coding the reasoning behind the decision, we constructed three themes: emotional, physical, and academic wellbeing. The theme of emotional wellbeing was reflected in two codes mentioning student: *anxiety* and *stress*. The theme of physical wellbeing was comprised of a single code: *expressing concern over the student not feeling well*. The third theme of academic wellbeing was comprised of three codes: *concern over the students preparedness*, *concern about the students understanding*, and *mentioning the need for individual support.* During the retry with support, 9 out of 11 revised their reasoning and the changes are detailed in Table 1. For the overall effect of reasoning attending to wellbeing: *emotional* increased by 1, *physical* increased by 3, and *academic* decreased by 1.

For RQ1, the support had the desired influence of getting more participants to consider the statement of Jeremy's stomach ache in their responses. While no one mentioned physical wellbeing in their first response, three participants mentioned it in their second response. The low number of participants in this study frame these results as prelimanry and promising and merit scaling up to examine the validity of these results

Table 1. Thematic analysis of first and second response reasons detailing change

Theme	Code	First try	Added	Removed	Delta	Second try
Emotional	Anxiety	2	2	1	+1	3
	Stress	1	0	0	0	1'
Physical	Feeling well	0	3	0	+3	3
Academic	Preparedness	3	2	3	−1	2
	Understanding	4	1	2	−1	3
	Individual support	3	2	1	+1	4
Total		13	10	7	+3	16

4.2 RQ2

On retry, 5 out of 11 chose to not administer the quiz, all of whom had equity mindset scores above the mean. Six out of 11 chose to administer the quiz, half of which had equity mindset scores below the mean. The potential relationship of high equity mindsets with not administering the quiz is strengthened by the retry with support, as the participant that revised their decision to *yes* had a high equity mindset score while the person revising their decision to *no* had a low equity mindset score. Both participants that revised their decision to administer the quiz had scores below the mean on the cognitive dissonance measure. A potential targeted approach would ask participants with high equity mindsets and low cognitive dissonance scores to revise their decision on administering the quiz.

Nine out of 11 participants revised their reasoning on the retry. The two participants that did not revise their reasoning had high cognitive dissonance scores. The two that both added and subtracted reasons in the retry had both high equity mindsets and high cognitive dissonance. The two that only subtracted reasons had high equity mindsets and low cognitive dissonance scores. Figure 2 illustrates that the three participants that revised their reasoning to include physical wellbeing had either high equity mindsets, high cognitive dissonance, or high scores in both. A targeted intervention might ask those with

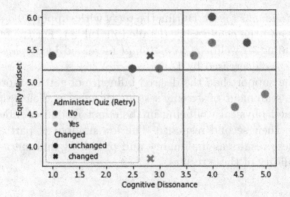

Fig. 1. Take the quiz (change) on a plane of equity mindset and cognitive dissonance.

high cognitive dissonance scores to revise their reasoning, as both participants who only removed reasoning had low cognitive dissonance scores.

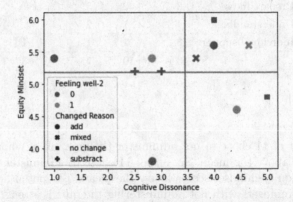

Fig. 2. Change in reasoning on a plane of equity mindset and cognitive dissonance.

For RQ2, targeting participants with high equity mindsets to revise the decision to administer the quiz and participants with high equity mindsets and/or high cognitive dissonance to revise their reasoning might produce more equitable final responses. Again the small sample size shows promising results that suggest a need to scale up the study to examine the validity of the finding.

5   Discussion

These results indicate that the learning support designed to help teachers notice, interpret, and intervene with Jeremy by considering his stomach ache had the intended influence. While the support had the desired effect, there were several additional revisions, both on the top-level decision of administering the quiz and, even more so, in revisions to reasoning.

While the sample size was not sufficient for inferential statistics, the results when connecting our analysis of revisions of response to quantitative measures suggest there is a potential for future work to examine if measures of equity mind-sets and cognitive dissonance could be used to provide dynamic supports. There is a potential that dynamic support might reduce unintended consequences of persuasive technologies in the context of learning from equity focused simulations. Scaling the study up is the next step in gaining clarity on how to change behavior with supports based on a Model of Helping.

References

1. Borneman, E., Littenberg-Tobias, J., Reich, J.: Developing digital clinical simulations for large-scale settings on diversity, equity, and inclusion: design considerations for effective implementation at scale. In: Proceedings of the Seventh ACM Conference on Learning @ Scale. pp. 373–376. L@S 2020, Association for Computing Machinery, New York, August 2020. https://doi.org/10.1145/3386527.3405947, https://doi.org/10.1145/3386527.3405947
2. Darley, J.M., Latane, B.: Bystander intervention in emergencies: Diffusion of responsibility. J Personal. Soc. Psychol. **8**(4, Pt.1), 377–383 (1968). https://doi.org/10.1037/h0025589
3. Dotger, B.: I Had No Idea: Clinical Simulations for Teacher Development. Age Publishing, Charlotte (2012), https://www.amazon.com/Had-No-Idea-Simulations-Development/dp/1623961955
4. Grossman, P., Hammerness, K., McDonald, M.: Redefining teaching, re-imagining teacher education. Teach. Teach. **15**(2), 273–289 (2009). https://doi.org/10.1080/13540600902875340, https://doi.org/10.1080/13540600902875340
5. Harmon-Jones, E.: A cognitive dissonance theory perspective on the role of emotion in the maintenance and change of beliefs and attitudes. In: Emotions and Beliefs: How Feelings Influence Thoughts, pp. 185–211. Cambridge University Press, Cambridge (2000)
6. Hillaire, G., Larke, L., Reich, J.: Digital storytelling through authoring simulations with teacher moments. In: Society for Information Technology & Teacher Education International Conference, pp. 1736–1745. Association for the Advancement of Computing in Education (AACE), April 2020, https://www.learntechlib.org/p/215950/
7. Hillaire, G., et al.: Teacher moments: a digital clinical simulation platform with extensible AI architecture. preprint, EdArXiv, May 2021. https://doi.org/10.35542/osf.io/jf348, https://osf.io/jf348
8. Larke, L.R., et al.: Cognitive dissonance and equity: designing digital simulations for K-12 Computer Science Teacher Education (2020)
9. Self, E.A., Stengel, B.S.: Toward Anti-Oppressive Teaching: Designing and Using Simulated Encounters. Harvard Education Press, Cambridge, Massachusetts, December 2020

10. Sullivan, F., Hillaire, G., Larke, L., Reich, J.: Using teacher moments during the COVID-19 pivot. J. Technol. Teach. Educ. **28**(2), 303–313 (2020), https://www. learntechlib.org/primary/p/216171/
11. Thornberg, R.: A student in distress: moral frames and bystander behavior in school. Element. School J. **110**(4), 585–608 (2010). https://doi.org/10.1086/ 651197, https://www.journals.uchicago.edu/doi/10.1086/651197

Supporting to be Credible: Investigating Perceived Social Support as a Determinant of Perceived Credibility

Felix N. Koranteng[1] , Jaap Ham[1]([✉]) , Uwe Matzat[1] , and Isaac Wiafe[2]

[1] Department of Industrial Engineering and Innovation Sciences, Eindhoven University of Technology, Eindhoven, The Netherlands
j.r.c.ham@tue.nl
[2] Department of Computer Science, University of Ghana, Legon-Accra, Ghana
iwiafe@ug.edu.gh

Abstract. Technological systems can be equipped with persuasive design principles that influence user perceptions. For instance, earlier research showed that Perceived Social Support can influence user perceptions such as effectiveness and knowledge sharing intentions. However, to our knowledge, how Perceived Social Support affects Perceived Credibility has not been investigated. This study investigates the influence of Perceived Social Support on Perceived Credibility. A survey questionnaire was employed to gather user perceptions of social support and credibility in the context of Academic Social Networking Sites (ASNSs). Analysis using Partial Least Square Structural Equation Modeling (PLS-SEM) confirmed Perceived Social Support as a determinant of Perceived Credibility. Also, Dialogue Support and Primary Task Support were identified to be predictors of Perceived Social Support. The study recommends that designers improve the social support features (e.g., through integrating machine learning and data mining techniques).

Keywords: Perceived social support · Perceived credibility · Academic social networking sites · Persuasive systems design

1 Introduction

With the explosion in innovation, technological systems can be strategically designed with features that stimulate social exchanges among users. In Human-Computer Interaction (HCI), social-based design elements have been found to promote positive user attitudes and perceptions as well as motivate behavior change [1]. Also, the Persuasive Systems Design (PSD) framework (a popular framework in HCI) proposed four principles that can be implemented in system design to influence users' perceptions and behavior [2]. These four principles are Credibility, Primary Task Support, Dialogue Support, and Social Support [2]. The Credibility Support principle details the design features that promote trust and belief in a system. Also, the Primary Task Support principle emphasizes the features that support a user to perform their core tasks. The Dialogue Support principle highlights the features that enable active user interaction with the

© Springer Nature Switzerland AG 2022
N. Baghaei et al. (Eds.): PERSUASIVE 2022, LNCS 13213, pp. 109–119, 2022.
https://doi.org/10.1007/978-3-030-98438-0_9

system (e.g., through feedback provision). According to the PSD framework [2], the Social Support principle conceptualizes the strategies and features that motivate users to perform a target behavior by leveraging social influence. Therefore, the Social Support principle can be used to outline the social-based design elements which can be integrated into online social networks to motivate users to support each other [3]. For instance, on websites such as ResearchGate, a user's RG Score is increased when he/she makes contributions by answering questions or making her research accessible to other users. This motivates others to replicate the behavior. The user's Perceived Social Support is the degree to which the user believes that the technology possesses features that moti-vate them to support each other by leveraging social influence. In essence, Perceived Social Support can be leveraged to influence users' perceptions. For instance, Wiafe et al. [4] observed that perceptions of social support positively influenced the perceived effectiveness of Academic Social Networking Sites (ASNSs). Likewise, Wiafe et al. [5] found that perceptions of social support determined academics' sharing intentions on ASNSs. Relatedly, other studies have also confirmed that Perceived Social Sup-port affected users' continuous intentions to use e-commerce websites [6] and Behavior Change Support Systems (BCSSs) for weight loss [7].

Despite the significant contributions from the aforementioned studies, so far, to the best of our knowledge, no study has investigated the influence of Perceived Social Support on Perceived Credibility. Meanwhile, Perceived Credibility is a key concept in the use of technology. Perceived Credibility is defined as the degree to which users believe in a technological system [8] which is often derived from users' evaluation of the systems' (e.g., an ASNS') characteristics [9]. Credibility perceptions lead to trust and thus promote positive user attitudes toward a system [6]. Moreover, Perceived Credibility determines users' continuous intentions to use ASNSs [4]. Given the relevance of Perceived Social Support and Perceived Credibility in influencing user perceptions, this study examined how the two concepts relate. Particularly, the study investigated how Perceived Support influence Perceived Credibility.

1.1 Background

Over the last few decades, we have witnessed a growth in the usage and dispersion of Academic Social Networking Sites (ASNSs). Academic Social Networking Sites (ASNSs) are online social spaces explicitly designed for the academic community and allow users to create profiles and make connections with other academics [10]. Exam-ples of ASNSs include ResearchGate, Academia.edu, and Mendeley. They stimulate academics to create and maintain their professional networks [11]. ASNSs are designed to simplify academic routines such as knowledge sharing and collaborative research [12]. They provide a means for sharing valuable data, publications, and other academic resources which otherwise would have been difficult to access [13]. Moreover, many aca-demics view ASNSs as channels to socialize as well as follow and support others' work [14]. Indeed, some scholars have argued that ASNSs do not only replicate experiences of socialization at academic conferences but improve it [11]. This is because ASNSs provide a means for academics to receive help from a larger academic population [15]. As a result, some academics may view ASNSs as a medium for receiving or providing support to others [5]. That is, many academics use ASNSs to ask questions, find jobs and get solutions to problems [16]. Accordingly, Jabeur, Tamine, and Boughanem [17] postulated that social impact will become a significant measure for estimating research influence as citation counts may no longer be sufficient. Nowadays, the academic community considers ASNSs metrics such as RG Score (ResearchGate Score) as a proxy to measure scholars' research output [18]. Specifically, contributions and presence on ASNSs are increasingly being recognized as part of tenure and promotion review processes for academics [19]. Therefore, using ASNSs to boost one's social impact has become necessary.

Given the impetus to encourage the use of ASNS as a vehicle to facilitate support exchanges among academics, it becomes important to evaluate academics' perceptions of the existent of social support features and whether they affect their belief in ASNSs to be helpful for their research. This study examines the influence of Perceived Social Support on Perceived Credibility. It investigates this relationship using the PSD framework as a theoretical foundation. We adopt the PSD framework because it is one of the most established frameworks in HCI and has been successfully adopted by many studies to explore the influence of Perceived Social Support on user perceptions such as perceived effectiveness [22] and knowledge sharing intentions [23]. Moreover, the PSD framework suggests that the four design principles enforce each other. Indeed, a recent study provided empirical evidence that concluded that Primary Task Support is a determinant of Perceived Credibility [24]. Yet, empirical evidence that supports social support as a determinant of credibility is lacking. In other words, how the Social Support principle and the Credibility principle affect each other has not been investigated. Therefore, this study extends findings of an earlier study [24] to offer insights into how Social Support and the Credibility principles relate. In the next sections, we present the research model and hypotheses. Then the methods and data analysis techniques employed in the study are described. Then, the findings and directions for future work are discussed. Lastly, conclusions are drawn.

2 Research Model and Hypotheses

The study proposes that Perceived Social Support has a positive significant influence on Perceived Credibility. People's beliefs are partly shaped by influences from social systems [20]. That is, feedback and support from other social actors can influence people's beliefs. Similarly, reciprocal exchanges on online social networks can affect users' perceptions about the system. In contrast to concerns (such as bullying and trolling) on online social networks [21], there is enough evidence to assume that such concerns may not be evident on ASNSs. ASNSs enable user interactions by mimicking the traditional academic structure [22] and thus user credentials are verifiable. Thus, because users can easily be tied to their affiliations, their behavioral patterns are often measured. This is to argue that users may find genuine social support on ASNSs which can influence perceptions of credibility. Yet, there is a need for empirical evidence to validate this claim. Therefore, this study proposes that;

H1: Perceived Social Support has a positive influence on Perceived Credibility on ASNSs.

Moreover, objects are mostly judged based on their characteristics and features. Therefore, for favorable judgments, an object must possess adequate features. Similarly, for information systems to be judged favorably, they must have the requisite features that support users to complete their tasks [23]. Certainly, when users perceive that there are available system features that support their primary task, they also perceive the system to be effective. Likewise, in persuasive systems, the Primary Task Support features influence user perceptions and their persuasive experience [3]. Therefore, Primary Task Support features are arguably the most important [24]. This is because they increase users' positive affect towards the system. Many academics, nowadays, subscribe to collaboration and knowledge exchanges to improve the quality of research. Therefore, the availability of features that support users' reciprocal contributions on ASNSs can affect users' social support perceptions. Unfortunately, we are yet to encounter studies that have investigated the relationship between Primary Task Support and Social Support. To test this relationship, the study proposes that;

H2: Perceived Primary Task Support has a positive influence on Perceived Social Support on ASNS.

Finally, the study proposes that Perceived Dialogue Support affects Perceived Primary Task Support and Perceived Social Support. That is, dialogue is one of the most important means for communication and information exchange [25]. Effective dialogue creates harmony among people and catalyzes social interactions [26]. This enables community members to share ideas and learn from each other and thus influences individuals' perceptions of available support. Also, information systems researchers agree that human interactions with computer systems are similar to interpersonal interactions [7]. Therefore, the features that support users' interaction with computer systems influence their perceptions of the systems. ASNSs provide dialogue features such as notifications, prompts, reminders, and positive feedback. These notifications are often related to the task that users perform. Further, positive feedback (e.g., a notification to answer a question or to an answered question) can influence users' social support perceptions. Letho and Oinas-Kukkonen [7] have found that Dialogue Support positively affects Primary Task Support and Perceived Social Support. In line with this, the study hypothesizes that;

H3: Perceived Dialogue Support has a positive influence on Primary Task Support on ASNSs.

H4: Perceived Dialogue Support has a positive influence on Perceived Social Support on ASNSs.

Figure 1 shows the hypothesized relationships. It represents how the constructs have been modeled to affect each other.

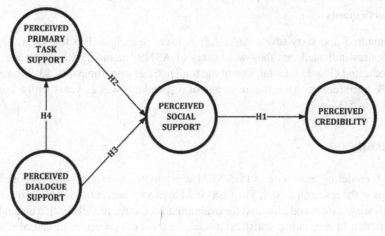

Fig. 1. Hypothesized model

3 Method

In this section, the research methods employed to test the hypothesized relationships are discussed. This section also discusses how the participants were selected, the materials used, and the procedures employed for the study.

3.1 Materials

The study adopted a survey approach to gather participants' responses. Participants' perceptions of (i) Perceived Social Support, (ii) Perceived Credibility (iii) Perceived Primary Task Support, and (iv) Perceived Dialogue Support on ASNSs were requested. The questions for the aforementioned principles were designed based on prior studies [4, 4]. All questions (available upon request from the authors) were measured on a five-point Likert scale ranging from "Strongly Disagree (1)" to "Strongly Agree (5)".

3.2 Procedure

An invitation to participate in the study was sent to student users via email. Users who were committed to partaking in the study were asked to click on a link to the questionnaire, thereby indicating their (written) consent to participate in the study. First, a section in the questionnaire explained the objective of the study to be solely academic. Participants were informed that their responses will be kept confidential and only used for academic purposes. Next, they were requested to select from the scale, the extent to which they agreed or disagreed with the question items. After participants had answered the last question, they were asked to submit the information. Lastly, they were thanked for participating. Participants did not gain any benefits in the form of gifts or remuneration for participating.

3.3 Participants

Eight hundred and sixty-seven (867) ASNS users participated in the study. That is, all responses indicated that they were users of ASNSs including ResearchGate, Academic.edu, and Google Scholar. Out of the total number of participants, 83% were male and 17% were female. Also, the mean age of respondents was 27 years with a standard deviation of 5.3.

4 Results

The path modeling technique of PLS-SEM was adopted to evaluate the proposed relationships in the research model. The PLS-SEM approach was chosen because it is robust to multivariate errors and effective for evaluating predictive models [27]. The emphasis on prediction in estimating statistical models enables the provision of causal relationships which make PLS-SEM suitable for the current research landscape [28]. That is, the predictive paradigm support researchers to offer design and managerial implications.

4.1 The Measurement Model

The measurement model was first analyzed. The measurement model in PLS-SEM analysis evaluates the validity and reliability of the constructs and questions used in the research model. The measurement model was assessed with item reliability, internal consistency, convergent validity, and discriminant validity. For item reliability, a threshold of 0.7 for item loading was used as a minimum requirement. Composite reliability and Cronbach Alpha minimum values of 0.7 were also adopted to measure internal consistency. Also, convergent validity was examined using an Average Variance Extracted (AVE) minimum value of 0.5. All thresholds adopted met Hair et al. [28] recommendations. Further, the square roots of the AVEs of latent variables were juxtaposed with correlations of other latent variables. According to Fornell and Lacker [29], discriminant validity is established when the square roots of latent are higher than correlations of other variables. The highlighted values in Table 1 show the discriminant validity results. Table 1 also summarizes the results from the measurement analysis.

Table 1. Construct reliability and validity

	CA	CR	AVE	CRED	DIAL	PRIM	SOCS
CRED	.885	.927	.809	**.899**			
DIAL	.779	.857	.600	.402	**.775**		
PRIM	.824	.883	.654	.471	.667	**0.809**	
SOCS	.873	.922	.797	.290	.552	.674	**.893**

NB: CA-Cronbach's Alpha; CR-Composite Reliability; AVE- Average Variance Extracted: PRIM; Primary Task Support: DIAL; Dialogue Support: SOCS; Perceived Social Support; CRED; Perceived Credibility.

4.2 The Structural Model

After establishing construct validity and reliability, the structural model analyzed the significance of the proposed relationships. The bootstrap (5000 resamples) technique was preferred for examining the relationships. A proposed relationship was considered significant if the p-value (p) was lesser than 0.05. In addition, using (Cohen's) criteria, the effect size (f2) of a proposed relationship was irrelevant (when f2 < 0.02); weak (f2 ≥ 0.02), moderate (f2 ≥ 0.15) and strong (f2 ≥ 0.35). The path analysis confirmed all hypotheses are valid.

Table 2. Significance of path coefficient

Hypotheses		Original sample (O)	Sample mean (M)	P values	Effect size
SOCS -> CRED	H1	0.290	0.301	0.000	0.092
PRIM -> SOCS	H2	0.550	0.556	0.000	0.319
DIAL -> SOCS	H3	0.185	0.191	0.037	0.036
DIAL -> PRIM	H4	0.667	0.672	0.000	0.801

NB: PRIM; Perceived Primary Task Support: DIAL; Perceived Dialogue Support: SOCS; Perceived Social Support; CRED; Perceived Credibility.

To begin with, Hypothesis 1 (H1) proposed Perceived Social Support as a determinant of Perceived Credibility. The results, the relationship between Perceived Social Support and Perceived Credibility recorded $p < 0.000$ and $f^2 = 0.092$. This indicates that Perceived Social Support weakly predicts Perceived Credibility.

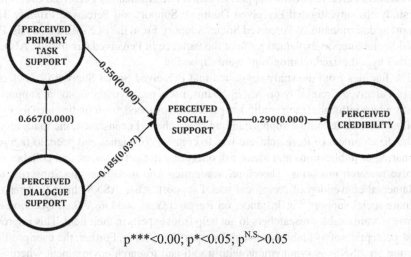

p***<0.00; p*<0.05; p^{N.S}>0.05

Fig. 2. The structural model

In Hypothesis 2 (H2), Perceived Primary Task Support was suggested as a determinant of Perceived Social Support. With $p < 0.000$ and $f^2 = 0.319$, Perceived Primary Task Support moderately predicts Perceived Social Support. Moreover, in Hypotheses Three and Four (H3 and H4), Dialogue Support was proposed as a determinant of Perceived Social Support and Perceived Primary Task Support respectively. Both hypotheses were confirmed. First, Perceived Dialogue Support weakly predicted Perceived Social Support ($p < 0.04$ and $f^2 = 0.036$). Also, the results indicate that Perceived Dialogue Support is a strong determinant of Perceived Primary Task Support ($p < 0.000$ and $f^2 = 0.801$). The summary of the results is presented in Table 2.

In Fig. 2, the structural model analysis of the research model is presented. The direction of the arrows indicates the proposed direction of effect. The values on the arrows indicate the path coefficients and the ones in the bracket are the p-values of the proposed relationships.

5 Discussion

It is evident that ASNSs are used by academics to provide support for each other. Concurrent with technological advancement, Social Support principles and social-based design elements can be integrated into ASNSs to motivate and influence academics' perceptions and intentions. Indeed, many ASNSs provide avenues (such as comments, reactions and messaging features) which enable reciprocal exchanges among users. Through these means, academics commend, encourage and motivate each other. Consequently, Perceived Social Support principle can influence user perceptions such as effectiveness (see e.g., [4]) and knowledge sharing intentions (see e.g., [5]). However, the relationship between Perceived Social Support and Perceived Credibility has not been investigated. Therefore, in this study, how Perceived Social Support affects Perceived Credibility was examined. The study adopted the PSD framework as a foundation and proposed a model that considers Perceived Social Support as a direct determinant of Perceived Credibility. The study also investigated Perceived Dialogue Support and Perceived Primary Task Support as determinants of Perceived Social Support. From the PLS-SEM analysis, Perceived Social Support explained 8.4% of the variance in Perceived Credibility. Also, all the other hypothesized relationships were supported.

The findings from the study suggested that Perceived Social Support is a determinant of Perceived Credibility on ASNSs. Thus, users perceive higher social support on ASNSs which influences their credibility perceptions. Indeed, the founding idea for many ASNSs is to enable mutual support among researchers. For instance, the main motive for the development of ResearchGate was to connect colleagues and peers to facilitate the sharing of publications and ideas, ask questions and get answers, and collaborative to solve research problems. Therefore, academics who use these sites subscribe to a fundamental convention of reciprocal social support. Also, ASNSs have features that facilitate social support. For instance, on ResearchGate, the Q&A (i.e., Question and Answer) forum enables researchers to get help from experts in their field. This improves users' perception of availability of social support on ASNSs. Further, the user profiling structure on ASNSs is synonymous with traditional research environment where academics represent their universities, departments, or laboratories. That is, many users on

ASNSs have affiliated departments, hence their behavior online is associated with their universities. Since individuals aspire to project favorable reputations for themselves and their affiliates, users mostly adhere to conventions on ASNSs. This influences users' credibility perceptions. Accordingly, it is suggested that ASNSs must pay attention to credibility issues to facilitate social support. Perhaps, data mining and machine learning techniques could be integrated into ASNSs such that the site can automatically suggest previously recommended answers for similar or repetitive questions.

Also, Perceived Primary Task Support had a significant influence on Perceived Social Support. That is, most academics thought that ASNSs provided features that supported their task, hence their social support perceptions were influenced. As indicated, academics are dispositioned to share and support others on ASNSs. Therefore, they require features that enable them to perform their core task. Thus, ASNSs provide such features to support them. For example, on Academia.edu, users can start discussions with publication authors, access grants, or take courses. These activities enable researchers to establish contacts and increase their publications awareness [30]. Consequently, this influences their Perceived Social Support on ASNSs. For designers, we recommend upgrading task support features. Although academics subscribe to social support, users' requirements of social support may differ. Whereas some may require instrumental social support, others may want informational social support. To make social support on ASNSs relevant to different user groups, designers can personalize or tailor the task support features to suit user needs.

Moreover, Dialogue Support significantly affected both Primary Task Support and Perceived Social Support. Dialogue support represented the perception of adequate feedback in the performance of user tasks on ASNSs. Therefore, the results suggest that users perceived the feedback provided by ASNSs as satisfactory which influence their perceptions of task support and social support. ASNSs give feedback through reminders, suggestions, and notifications. These feedback options are mostly related to the users' usage patterns. For instance, ResearchGate may give users reminders to attend to requests directed to them which influences users to think the system supports their tasks. ASNSs also offer rewards in the form of points for performing an activity (e.g., answering a question). Such rewards can be interpreted as social support cues [31]. Designers are therefore encouraged to provide dialogue support features on ASNSs. We edge designers to prevent repetitive and irrelevant feedback as they can be irritating. Therefore, improved algorithms that provide relevant, accurate, and timely feedback are advocated.

6 Future Work and Conclusion

This study provides empirical evidence that suggests Perceived Social Support as a determinant of Perceived Credibility. As social relationships continue to migrate into the online environment, these findings will aid the design of credible ASNSs for increased user acceptance and use. The PSD framework argues that use and user context affect the effectiveness of persuasive principles. Therefore, the current research has its limitations and future studies may test the relevance of Perceived Social Support in determining Perceived Credibility in other contexts. Moreover, some scholars have highlighted the influence of tailoring and personalization in increasing the effectiveness of persuasive principles [32]. Particularly because there are differences with which users are motivated. We encourage further studies to examine how personalizing Perceived Social Support may influence Perceived Credibility.

Earlier research showed that the Perceived Social Support principle can influence user perceptions such as effectiveness (see e.g., [4]) and knowledge sharing intentions (see e.g., [5]). However, how Perceived Social Support affects Perceived Credibility has not been investigated. In this study, we advanced knowledge on how Perceived Social Support affects credibility perceptions. Our results encourage designers who aim to design ASNSs so that are perceived to be credible to integrate features that project Perceived Social Support. Further, with regards to how the PSD principles enforce each other, we deepen our understanding of how the various principles enforce each other. We do so by confirming that Perceived Social Support affects Perceived Credibility. Also, we prove that Dialogue Support and Primary Task Support affect Perceived Social Support.

In our view, these contributions extend the existing literature on the design of ASNSs that are perceived to be credible. This knowledge is important because credible systems foster positive attitudes as well as user acceptance and use of interactive systems.

References

1. Orji, F.A., Greer, J., Vassileva, J.: Exploring the effectiveness of socially-oriented persuasive strategies in education. In: International Conference on Persuasive Technology, pp. 297–309 (2019)
2. Oinas-Kukkonen, H., Harjumaa, M.: Persuasive systems design: key issues, process model, and system features. Commun. Assoc. Inf. Syst. **24**(1), 28 (2009)
3. Drozd, F., Lehto, F., Oinas-Kukkonen, H.: Exploring perceived persuasiveness of a behavior change support system: a structural model. In: International Conference on Persuasive Technology, pp. 157–168 (2012)
4. Wiafe, I., Koranteng, F.N., Kastriku, F.A., Gyamera, G.O.: Assessing the impact of persuasive features on user's intention to continuous use: the case of academic social networking sites. Behav. Inf. Technol. (2020). https://doi.org/10.1080/0144929X.2020.1832146
5. Wiafe, I., Koranteng, F.N., Owusu, E., Ekpezu, A.O., Gyamfi, S.A.: Persuasive social features that promote knowledge sharing among tertiary students on social networking sites: An empirical study. J. Comput. Assist. Learn. **36**(5), 636–645 (2020). https://doi.org/10.1111/jcal.12433
6. Adaji, I., Vassileva, J.: Perceived effectiveness, credibility and continuance intention in e-commerce: a study of Amazon. In: International Conference on Persuasive Technology, pp. 293–306 (2017)
7. Lehto, T., Oinas-Kukkonen, H.: Explaining and predicting perceived effectiveness and use continuance intention of a behaviour change support system for weight loss. Behav. Inf. Technol. **34**(2), 176–189 (2015)
8. Tseng, S., Fogg, B.J.: Credibility and computing technology. Commun. ACM **42**(5), 39–44 (1999)
9. Metzger, M.J., Flanagin, A.J.: Credibility and trust of information in online environments: the use of cognitive heuristics. J. Pragmat. **59**, 210–220 (2013)
10. Jordan, K.: Academics and their online networks: exploring the role of academic social networking sites. First Monday **19**(11) (2014)

11. Kelly, B.: Using social media to enhance your research activities. In: Paper presented at Social Media in Social Research 2013 Conference, London (2013)
12. Bhardwaj, R.K.: Academic social networking sites. Inf. Learn. Sci. **118**(5/6), 298–316 (2017)
13. Veletsianos, G.: Open practices and identity: evidence from researchers and educators' social media participation. Br. J. Educ. Technol. **44**(4), 639–651 (2013)
14. Gruzd, A., Goertzen, M.: Wired academia: why social science scholars are using social media. In: 2013 46th Hawaii International Conference on System Sciences, 2013, pp. 3332–3341 (2013)
15. Ovadia, S.: ResearchGate and Academia.edu: Academic social networks. Behav. Soc. Sci. Librar. **33**(3), 165–169 (2014)
16. Williams, A.E., Woodacre, M.A.: The possibilities and perils of academic social networking sites. Online Inf. Rev. **40**(2), 282–294 (2016)
17. Ben Jabeur, L., Tamine, L., Boughanem, M.: A social model for literature access: towards a weighted social network of authors. In: International Conference on Adaptivity, Personalization and Fusion of Heterogeneous Information (RIAO 2010), 2010, support--électronique
18. Espinoza Vasquez, F.K., Caicedo Bastidas, C.E.: Academic social networking sites: a comparative analysis of their services and tools. In: iConference 2015 Proceedings (2015)
19. Gruzd, A., Staves, K., Wilk, A.: Tenure and promotion in the age of online social media. Proc. Am. Soc. Inf. Sci. Technol. **48**(1), 1–9 (2011)
20. Bandura, A.: Social Foundations of Thought and Action: A Social Cognitive Theory. Prentice-Hall Inc., Englewood Cliffs (1986)
21. Craig, W., et al.: Social media use and cyber-bullying: a cross-national analysis of young people in 42 countries. J. Adolesc. Heal. **66**(6), S100–S108 (2020)
22. Barbour, K., Marshall, D.: The academic online: constructing persona through the World Wide Web. First Monday **17**(9), 1–12 (2012). https://doi.org/10.5210/fm.v0i0.3969
23. Ansong-Gyimah, K.: Students' perceptions and continuous intention to use e-learning systems: the case of google classroom. Int. J. Emerg. Technol. Learn. **15**(11), 236–244 (2020)
24. Koranteng, F.N., Ham, J., Wiafe, I., Matzat, U.: The role of usability, aesthetics, usefulness and primary task support in predicting the perceived credibility of academic social networking Sites. Behav. Inf. Technol. (2021). https://doi.org/10.1080/0144929X.2021.2009570
25. Mercer, N.: "Developing dialogues." In: Wells, G., Claxton, G. (eds.) Learning for Life in the 21st: Sociocultural Perspectives on the Future of Education, pp. 141–153. Blackwell. Oxford (2002). https://doi.org/10.1002/9780470753545.ch11
26. Baffy, M.: Constructed dialogue as a resource for promoting students' socialization to written academic discourse in an EAP class. Linguist. Educ. **46**, 33–42 (2018)
27. Shmueli, G., et al.: Predictive model assessment in PLS-SEM: guidelines for using PLSpredict. Eur. J. Mark. **53**(11), 2322–2347 (2019). https://doi.org/10.1108/EJM-02-2019-0189
28. Hair, J.F., Sarstedt, M.: Factors versus composites: guidelines for choosing the right structural equation modeling method. Proj. Manag. J. **50**(6), 619–624 (2019). https://doi.org/10.1177/8756972819882132
29. Fornell, C., Lacker, D.F.: Evaluating structural equation modeling for travel behavior research. Transp. Res. part B, Univ. Michigan **37**, 1–25 (1981)
30. Matzat, U.: Academic communication and internet discussion groups: transfer of information or creation of social contacts? Soc. Netw. **26**(3), 221–255 (2004)
31. Haslam, D.M., Tee, A., Baker, S.: The use of social media as a mechanism of social support in parents. J. Child Fam. Stud. **26**(7), 2026–2037 (2017)
32. Masthoff, J., Grasso, F., Ham, J.: Preface to the special issue on personalization and behavior change. User Model. User-Adap. Inter. **24**(5), 345–350 (2014). https://doi.org/10.1007/s11257-014-9151-1

Investigating the Efficacy of Persuasive Strategies on Promoting Fair Recommendations

Seyedeh Mina Mousavifar[(✉)] and Julita Vassileva[ID]

University of Saskatchewan, Saskatoon, SK S7N5C9, Canada
mina.mousavifar@usask.ca, jiv@cs.usask.ca

Abstract. Recommender systems have become an inseparable part of our daily life, like listening to music based on recommender playlists or browsing through the recommended shopping list online. Fairness in such recommender systems has gained lots of attention considering provider and system objectives along with end-user satisfaction. However, often there are trade-offs between the objectives of different stakeholders. For instance, *fairness* for providers can be defined as ensuring the same exposure for all providers [7]. However, less popular providers might not satisfy users as much as widely-known providers; therefore, user satisfaction might decrease significantly. Consequently, there is a need to explore methods to promote recommendations from less-known providers more effectively. Previous studies have shown that explanations and persuasive explanations are beneficial for increasing user acceptance of recommended items. However, there has been little work investigating explanations for a fairness objective. Here, we study the effect of persuasive strategies for promoting items included for the recommender's fairness objective in a music platform. Results show empirical evidence of higher user satisfaction for the items accompanied by explanations. Our findings could guide the user interface design of two-sided marketplaces leading to a better user satisfaction rate.

Keywords: Persuasive technologies · Fair recommendation · Explainable recommendation · Multi-stakeholder recommendation

1 Introduction

Nowadays, recommender systems have become an essential component of daily tasks because finding the most relevant information from the abundant amount of data available is laborious. Music recommenders are widely-used with platforms such as Spotify[1], and YouTube Music[2]. These platforms facilitate an

---

This work was partially supported by NSERC, under Discovery Grant RGPIN-2021-03521 of the second author.

[1] https://www.spotify.com/.

[2] https://music.youtube.com/.

© Springer Nature Switzerland AG 2022
N. Baghaei et al. (Eds.): PERSUASIVE 2022, LNCS 13213, pp. 120–133, 2022.
https://doi.org/10.1007/978-3-030-98438-0_10

easier way for the new artists to be exposed to listeners and present relevant playlists based on the listener's preference. However, the music industry is a superstar economy [29]. A minimal fraction of the artists and works accounts for a disproportionately large share of all revenues. Famous artists utilize high-end music production facilities to produce higher-quality songs and employ marketing strategies to promote their songs. Therefore, these popular artists become even more famous; nonetheless, new artists on the same platform struggle to monetize their music.

Recommender systems also suffer from popularity bias, because their algorithms are based on user ratings and consumption data. Popular songs are listened more and receive more ratings, creating a feedback loop leading to even more exposure. In contrast, less popular songs are under-represented in the user ratings and do not get recommended, exaggerating the superstar effect [2]. Most recommender systems are mainly optimized for maximizing end-user satisfaction; however, there are other stakeholders in the systems, and their intentions should also be taken into account to create fair recommendations. Burke et al. [1,7] divided the stakeholders of a given recommendation system into consumers (who receive the recommendation), providers (who supply the recommended objects), and the system (which creates the recommendations). A multi-stake recommender system considers all stakeholders' interests for generating a recommendation.

In music platforms, the consumers are the listeners, and the providers are the artists publishing their music and the system is the platform (e.g. Spotify). The interests of the platform are well aligned with those of the listeners and are well served by the state of the art recommender systems, since high listener satisfaction leads to more paying customers for the platform. However, the interests of artists are not served uniformly well across the wide diversity and popularity of artists across music genres, geography. Fair recommender systems try to correct the existing popularity bias of the state-of-the-art recommender systems by developing new algorithms that support serendipity and diversity in the recommendations.

However, one of the biggest concerns in fair recommender systems is maintaining user's satisfaction while providing fair exposure for the artists. Mehrotra et al. [24] researched the trade-off between relevance and fairness in a music recommender and showed that user satisfaction is negatively impacted while optimizing fairness. Listeners prefer to listen to well-known artists or artists that they already know instead of giving a chance to new artists. Consequently, when the music recommender suggests playlists including less popular artists, user satisfaction decreases significantly. Therefore, to alleviate user dissatisfaction, researchers need to explore methods to promote more persuasively the recommendations of new, not yet popular artists (we will call these for brevity "fair recommendations").

Research in explainable recommendations focuses on providing intuitive explanations for the recommendations to assist users in deciding whether an item is related to them. Herlocker et al. [14] concluded that supplementing recommendations with explanations can improve the acceptance and adoption of the recommended items. There is a lot of work in this area, along with research in "Explainable AI", which aims to make the algorithms generating the recommendation transparent to the user and thus increase the user's trust and acceptance of the system's decision or recommendation. Our approach, however, is orthogonal to the recommender system algorithm. We propose to present the fair recommendations with a persuasive message (a very brief and generic explanation), based on Cialdini's six influence strategies [9]. Previous work by Gkika et al. [13] showed that user acceptance of a recommended item improves while supplemented by a persuasive explanation. However, this result was obtained in a recommender system that does not consider fairness. Consequently, in this paper, we investigate the effect of persuasive messages based on Cialdini's influence strategies on promoting new artists in a mock-up fair music recommender platform. We designed a study where participants are presented with playlists including songs from both well-known and little-known artists in two selected genres. The participants can listen or ignore the songs and can rate the playlists and the songs. We explore the impact of the persuasive messages related to songs of new artists on the participants' satisfaction measured by their ratings.

2   Literature Review

Recommender systems are nowadays intertwined into different aspects of daily tasks, which raises concerns that whether every individual and group are treated equally by these systems and are exposed to benefits and harms fairly.

2.1   Fair Recommenders

Recommender systems provide recommendations based on past user preferences, targeting to predict user interest accurately. Nonetheless, in recent years, protecting the interest of other stakeholders in such systems has gained attention.

Accordingly, researchers have investigated methods to consider the objectives of different groups in recommender systems so that every group experience fair benefit and/or harm from the system along with determining guidelines to incorporate fairness into these systems to be practical for the users [6,23,33].

Kamishima et al. [18] designed a generative model to provide recommendations independent of specific characteristics. For instance, in a job applicant recommender, the recommendations should be independent of applicants' demographic information. Burke et al. [8] investigated a recommendation approach that considers personalization and fairness objectives at the same time through a balanced neighbourhood mechanism along with sparse linear methods. Thus, this method lacks the ability to reflect the fairness objective of both consumer and provider simultaneously. From a different point of view, Farnadi et al. [11] researched a hybrid recommender that incorporated content-based, collaborative-based and demographic-based filtering approaches, minimizing observation bias and population imbalance in the data. Unfortunately, this model was not tested in a sparse data space which is necessary for real-world recommender systems.

Sonboli et al. [30] researched the user perspectives of fairness-aware recommender systems and techniques for enhancing their transparency by interviewing users about what fairness means to them. Their study concluded that users prefer to be educated about the rationale behind the fair recommendations, especially with an explanation specific to each recommendation. In our study, we investigated the effectiveness of this design guideline for promoting new artists.

2.2 Popularity Bias in Music Recommender Systems

Research has shown that recommender systems typically suffer from popularity bias; popular items are recommended recurrently, leading to the majority of less known items being under-represented [3]. Music recommenders are no exception; Abdollahpouri et al. and Kowald et al. [2, 21] concluded that artists with varying degrees of popularity are not treated equally by music recommenders. Several studies have investigated methods to counter this unfairness [3, 17, 24]. In a recent study, Mehrotra et al. [24] developed a fairness-aware music recommender for artists with a wide range of popularity. Their findings showed that users' satisfaction is negatively impacted by content recommended for fairness. This outcome is predictable due to the ambiguity effect [10]. The ambiguity effect is a cognitive bias that indicates that a lack of information influences decision-making; hence people tend to choose the options with familiar outcome. Consequently, developing a method to enhance persuasiveness of the recommendations while optimizing for fairness objective for recommendations would be a worthwhile endeavour.

2.3 Explainable and Persuasive Recommendation

Prior research in recommender systems has shown that accompanying recommendations with explanations can help users understand the rationale behind recommendations and improve adoption, perceived quality and effectiveness of the recommendations [12, 20]. Tintarev and Masthoff et al. [31] classify the goals of explanations into seven groups: transparency, scrutability, trust, effectiveness, persuasiveness, efficiency, satisfaction. Gkika and Lekakos et al. [13] examined the persuasiveness of explanations in recommender systems, using Cialdini's persuasive strategies and concluded that all six principles influence users' perception of the recommended items. Moreover, research has shown that persuasive strategies are effective for promoting healthy habits and behaviour change [4, 5, 27]. In this paper, we aim to use persuasive strategies to promote recommendations of music from less-known artists aiming to increase the user satisfaction with fair recommendations. To the best of our knowledge, there is no prior research in the conjunction area of explanations, fair recommendations, and persuasive technologies.

3   Method

We hypothesize that user satisfaction increases when users are informed about the rationale behind less related recommendations from new artists. Additionally, if these explanations are designed based on persuasive strategies, such as Cialdini's [9], they would be more effective in increasing user satisfaction. We chose to use Cialdini's principles of influence because they are domain-independent and widely used in literature. Moreover, according to Gkika [13], these principles have been proven to be universal persuasive approaches and provide a solid foundation for examining the persuasive power of messages in recommender systems as additional cues. To assess the effect of persuasive explanations, we designed a mock-up recommender system, which presents a fixed number of pre-canned playlists with music based on two favourite genres selected by the users, and includes songs from both new little-known artists and from famous artists. The new little-known artists in each genre were chosen based on the number of streams of their songs on Spotify; we chose artists which had no songs with more than 1000 streams. The famous artists were chosen from those with the highest number of streams. The mockup recommender suggests the same set of songs for each genre according to the procedure described below. We conducted a study including an online survey approved by the University of Saskatchewan Behavioural Research Ethics Board. We used a within-subject design to evaluate our hypothesis.

3.1   Participants

All participants in the study were recruited through the university announcement board, newsletters and social media posts. The survey took about 30 min to complete, but the participants could complete the study in as many sessions as they wished. A total of 205 participants completed the study, and participants were rewarded with their personality test results. Our participants included 66% women, 32% men with all age ranges. 55% and 32% of our participants were between 18–24 and 25–34 years old, respectively. For the country where participants were born, most users were born in America, Asia and Europe, 60%, 30%, and 5%, respectively.

3.2   Study Procedure

The study began by asking the user for consent to participate in the study and then to select two favourite music genres from eight offered. The available genres were based on the most popular genres since 1980. Afterwards, the participants read a paragraph about the superstar economy in the music industry and were asked about how important promoting new artists was for them. The following paragraph quoted from [25], explaining the superstar economy, was included in the preliminary questionnaire.

The music industry is a Superstar economy, a minimal share of the total artists and works account for a disproportionately large share of all revenues.

For instance, the top 1% of famous artists account for 77% of all artists recorded music income. Famous artists have lots of attention, and their new songs are widely recommended to users regardless of their quality. In contrast, many new talented artists do not find any chance to be heard. Therefore, we aim to provide new artists with an opportunity by including fair recommendations in our music recommender.

The mock-up recommender presents three playlists for each of the 2 genres selected by the participant, 6 in total. Four of the playlists (Nr 2, 4, 5 and 6) contain a mix of popular and unpopular songs, where the unpopular (new artists) songs have a persuasive message underneath the song title, based on one of Cialdini's influence principles [9]. The persuasive messages are as shown in Table 1. Two of the playlists are different and used as "control" conditions. Playlist 1 contains a mix of popular and unpopular songs but without persuasive messages and Playlist 3 contains only unpopular songs from new artists, some with persuasive messages and some without.

Table 1. Cialdini's principles implementation in persuasive messages

Influence principle	Message
Authority	Experts have recommended this new little-known artist
Commitment	This song is included because you agreed to have fair recommendations
Empathy	75% of new artists don't find a chance to become famous despite being good
Liking	Drake has suggested this new artist providing a chance to become popular
Reciprocity	Thanks for using our fair recommender
Scarcity without mentioning new artists	This song is only available for a limited time
Scarcity with mentioning new artists	This song is only available for a limited time to promote this new artist
Social Influence without mentioning new artists	80% of our users so far have listened to this song
Social Influence with mentioning new artist	80% of our users so far have listened to this song from this new artist
Purpose	This song is included to give new artists a chance to be listened to

Each of the ten designed persuasive messages was displayed twice in the 6 different playlists for each genre. The participants could "preview" each song on the playlist, or click on a link that would lead to YouTube, where they could listen the entire song. The participants had to rate each playlist based on three criteria, overall satisfaction for the entire playlist, satisfaction with the popular songs and satisfaction with the songs from new artists, using a Likert scale from 1 to 5. They also answered a few of the Big Five Personality test questions while rating [16]. The personality test results were used to present to the participants as a reward in the end of the study. We also carried out analysis to see if there was an effect of personality on the persuasiveness of the fairness' messages; this however is out of the scope of this paper, which focuses on the effect of the different persuasive messages on the user ratings for songs of new artists, of popular artists and of the entire playlists. Figure 1 shows an overview of the interface.

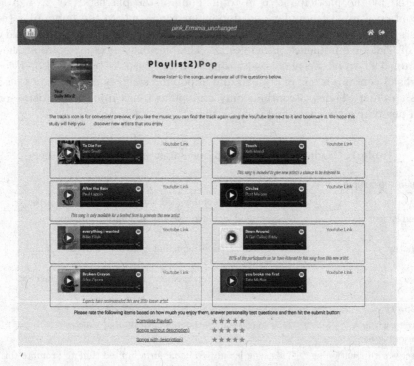

Fig. 1. Playlist with persuasive messages

4   Results

In this section, we describe the main findings of our study. We start by investigating the effect of persuasive messages on ratings of songs from new artists. Next, we explore whether explicitly mentioning that the artist is a new artist changes the effectiveness of the persuasive message. Then, we compare the ten persuasive messages listed in Table 1 based on the ratings given by the participants to the playlists they saw and conclude by investigating the relationship between ratings of popular songs, ratings of songs from new artists and overall rating of the playlist.

4.1   The Effect of Persuasive Messages on User Ratings of Songs from New Artists

We compare the ratings received by playlist 3 with the ratings received by the other playlists. Figure 2 exhibits the average ratings of all the playlists. As mentioned in the previous section, playlist 3 includes only songs of new artists, some with persuasive messages, and some without. As we did not explicitly mention that this playlist does not have any songs from famous artists, we assume that the participants consider this playlist format the same as the others by induction. We utilize a non-parametric two-sample Wilcoxon signed-rank test because our ordinal data does not follow a normal distribution [32].

The analysis of the ratings in playlist 3 (which contains only new songs) shows that the songs without description have lower ratings than the corresponding ratings in the other playlists for the popular songs ($\mathcal{P} = 3.14e-6$). Also, these songs from new artists have lower ratings compared to the songs from new artists with persuasive messages in other playlists ($\mathcal{P} = 5.65e-11$). Moreover, the overall rating of this playlist is significantly lower than the overall ratings of the other playlists ($\mathcal{P} = 5.49e-13$). This difference between the rating of playlist 3 and the other playlists is fairly large and visibly noticeable in Fig. 2. Interestingly, in playlist 3 the songs with persuasive messages have significantly lower ratings compared to songs with persuasive messages in other playlists 2, 4, 5 and 6 ($\mathcal{P} = 0.001$). When the users realize that the quality of the playlist does not meet their expectations, their experience deteriorates and promoting songs from new artists does not drive better ratings of songs from new artists. Therefore, we conclude that a certain level of user satisfaction (for example, by including popular artists or familiar songs) needs to be maintained to be able to make promoting songs from new artists acceptable.

4.2   The Effect of Mentioning New Artists on User Ratings of Songs by New Artists

We compare the ratings of songs from new artists in playlists that utilize mentioning new artists (playlists 2 and 5) and the playlists that do not, excluding playlist 3. A non-parametric two-sample Wilcoxon rank test reveals that mentioning the new artists leads to higher ratings of the songs from the new artists ($\mathcal{P} = 0.05$); we used this test because our data is ordinal and does not follow a normal distribution. This $\mathcal{P}$ is plausible for our sample size, considering that the controlled persuasive messages containing with/without mentioning new artists were repeated four times in the study for each participant. This can be explained with the overall effect of the commitment principle of influence, which was induced by the paragraph explaining the superstar economy in the preliminary questionnaire, presented in Sect. 3. Based on the results, we recommend mentioning new artists when introducing a fair recommender system and in the explanations of fair recommendations.

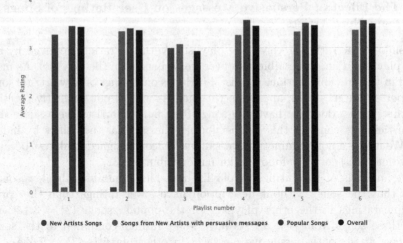

Fig. 2. Ratings across different playlists

4.3 Comparison Between Different Persuasive Messages Effectiveness

For detecting the most effective messages, we computed for each user the average rating the user gave to songs of new artists' songs over the 6 playlists. Then we selected those playlists where the user's rating of new artists' songs exceeded their own average rating. The persuasive messages used in such playlists are considered the most effective persuasive messages for the user. At last, we aggregated the repetition of the effective persuasive messages for all of the participants. To compare the persuasive strategies effectiveness measured by the user's ratings of new artists songs we applied Kruskal-Wallis one-way analysis of variance [22]. This method is a rank-based non-parametric test appropriate for comparing ten groups of different persuasive messages (based on the strategies listed in Table 1) on ordinal ratings as dependent variables, comparing whether ratings for the ten groups of persuasive messages come from the same distribution ($P = 0.009$). Therefore, the 10 groups of persuasive messages differ in effectiveness.

As for comparing methods with each other, songs with persuasive messages based on *Authority, Social influence with mentioning new artist, Social influence without mentioning new artist, Scarcity with mentioning new artists, empathy, and purpose* have resulted in higher user ratings of new artists songs, compared to the rest of the methods ($P = 0.001$). Analyzing the number of times persuasive methods were applied to promote new songs that the user has rated higher than their individual average also shows this difference in Fig. 3.

Consequently, authority is a powerful persuasive strategy, as most of the users are not music experts and trust the knowledgeable and credible experts' opinions for evaluating songs from new artists. This outcome is aligned with Orji et al. [26] and Oyibo et al.'s [28] studies on employing persuasive strategies for behaviour change, indicating authority as an effective persuasive method. However, these studies found that commitment, reciprocity were also among the top effective strategies for building healthy habits. In contrast, our result indicates that social influence is equally effective persuasive strategy which suggests that participants consider other users' actions in their decision-making process. This difference is explainable as our study aims at making the user trust the recommendations instead of changing behaviour. On the other hand, our results comply with [13], which found these two principles - authority and social influence - as the most effective persuasive methods for explaining the recommendations.

Mentioning that the song is from a new artist is obviously important, as two of the three most effective strategies mention the new artist. This can be explained with an implicit effect of the Commitment strategy, as the users have seen in the consent form that the purpose of the study to investigate how to better promote new artists and overcome the unfairness of the superstar economy in the music industry. They were also reminded of that by the quoted paragraph in the preliminary survey. However, it is an interesting result that the explicit application of the strategy in the message *"This song is included because you agreed to have fair recommendations"* was not as effective; perhaps it was considered too blunt a reminder. Further work is needed to uncover the reasons for this discrepancy.

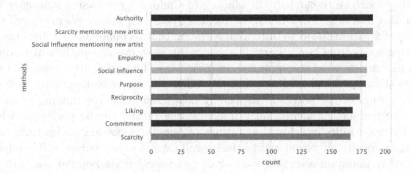

Fig. 3. Comparing methods used in playlists that users have rated higher than their individual average rating of new songs.

4.4 The Relation Between Ratings of New Songs, Popular Ratings and Overall Rating

In this section, we explore the effect of ratings of popular songs and songs from new artists on the overall ratings of the playlists. The correlation between these ratings is summarized in Table 2 using Kendall rank correlation. We applied this method as the ratings are ordinal and do not follow a normal distribution. Additionally, this method is better than other methods for a small sample size with many tied ranks [19]. Our results exhibit a positive correlation between overall ratings with ratings of popular songs and songs from new artists. Moreover, there is a positive correlation between ratings of popular songs and songs from new artists. We noticed this effect in the ratings of playlist three, as we previously mentioned. Comparing the importance of popular songs and songs from new artists on the overall rating of the playlist, we applied a structural equation model for predicting overall ratings [15]. The model identifies a more significant coefficient for the popular ratings, meaning that the quality of popular songs is more important in the user's overall experience with coefficients of 0.45 for songs from new artists and 0.49 for popular songs.

Table 2. Correlation between popular rating, ratings of songs from new artists and overall rating.

Attribute	Attribute	tau	p-value
Overall rating	Popular rating	0.67	2.2e−16
Overall rating	Rating of songs from new artists	0.63	2.2e−16
Popular rating	Rating of songs from new artists	0.35	2.2e−16

5 Discussion and Conclusion

In this paper, we researched the efficacy of Cialdini's persuasive strategies for promoting new artists in a fair recommender system for music. We presented the results of a within-subject study with a system that recommends playlists incorporating songs from famous artists and new little-known artists, in which songs from new artists were accompanied, in some cases, by persuasive messages. Our results show empirical evidence that providing persuasive explanations leads to better ratings of the playlists. Especially mentioning that the unfamiliar songs are from new artists significantly improves the ratings of the playlists. Additionally, our results indicate that ratings of popular songs and songs from new artists are positively correlated to the overall ratings of the playlists. Therefore, we need to maintain a certain level of user satisfaction via popular songs to be able to influence the user's satisfaction with the songs of new artists with persuasive messages. Not all of Cialdini's six persuasive strategies are equally effective for promoting new artists and building user trust in the system. *Authority* and *Social Influence* were the most influential strategies in our experiment.

We note several limitations in this study and future work directions. Firstly, our results are based on a small group of 205 users that mostly have open and agreeable personalities. Therefore, these users might have less prejudice to new songs and rate songs with less bias. Secondly, the users were presented with playlists based on their favourite genres. Thus, we suggest that future work could incorporate an actual fair recommender algorithm in the system, versus a pre-canned music playlists tailored to the users' favourite genres to see if the personalization of the music selections to the user in combination with personalized persuasive messages would result in higher satisfaction. Additionally, the limit of essential popular songs to maintain the effectiveness of persuasive messages could be explored. Thirdly, we used a fixed message for the Liking strategy, using the name of Drake, one of the most famous artists at the moment. Personalizing this message to the user's favourite genre or artist might increase the effect of this message. Moreover, the effect of personalizing the messages to users' personality could be investigated along with exploring the effect of personality on the efficacy of persuasive messages and playlist balance of new and popular artists. Another future direction of research is comparing different implementations (phrasings or visualizations) of the most influential Cialdini's persuasive strategies that we found in this study. For generalizing the study broadening the scope of "fairness" could be investigated to include not only little known artists, but also artists from different regions, languages.

With this work, we encourage fairness-aware recommenders to utilize persuasive messages to increase user satisfaction of the system while providing adequate exposure for the less-known items in the system. When the user is notified about the nature of the less related or less known items in their recommendation, their satisfaction level is less severely affected. Of course, the usage of persuasive messages can have ethical implications and it should avoid deceiving or misusing user trust. It has to be applied carefully since Users may leave a platform that for the sake of fairness promotes unworthy music.

References

1. Abdollahpouri, H., et al.: Multistakeholder recommendation: survey and research directions. User Model. User-Adap. Inter. **30**(1), 127–158 (2020). https://doi.org/10.1007/s11257-019-09256-1
2. Abdollahpouri, H., Burke, R., Mansoury, M.: Unfair exposure of artists in music recommendation. CoRR (2020). https://arxiv.org/abs/2003.11634
3. Abdollahpouri, H., Burke, R., Mobasher, B.: Controlling popularity bias in learning-to-rank recommendation. In: Proceedings of the Eleventh ACM Conference on Recommender Systems, RecSys 2017, pp. 42–46. Association for Computing Machinery, New York (2017). https://doi.org/10.1145/3109859.3109912
4. Adaji, I., Kiron, N., Vassileva, J.: Evaluating the susceptibility of E-commerce shoppers to persuasive strategies. A game-based approach. In: Gram-Hansen, S.B., Jonasen, T.S., Midden, C. (eds.) PERSUASIVE 2020. LNCS, vol. 12064, pp. 58–72. Springer, Cham (2020). https://doi.org/10.1007/978-3-030-45712-9_5
5. Adaji, I., Kiron, N., Vassileva, J.: Level of involvement and the influence of persuasive strategies in e-commerce: a game-based approach. In: Adjunct Proceedings of the 29th ACM Conference on User Modeling, Adaptation and Personalization, pp. 325–332 (2021)
6. Beutel, A., et al.: Fairness in recommendation ranking through pairwise comparisons. In: Proceedings of the 25th ACM SIGKDD International Conference on Knowledge Discovery & Data Mining, pp. 2212–2220 (2019)
7. Burke, R.: Multisided fairness for recommendation. CoRR (2017). http://arxiv.org/abs/1707.00093
8. Burke, R., Sonboli, N., Ordonez-Gauger, A.: Balanced neighborhoods for multisided fairness in recommendation. In: Friedler, S.A., Wilson, C. (eds.) Proceedings of the 1st Conference on Fairness, Accountability and Transparency. Proceedings of Machine Learning Research, vol. 81, pp. 202–214. PMLR, 23–24 February 2018. https://proceedings.mlr.press/v81/burke18a.html

9. Cialdini, R.B.: The science of persuasion. Sci. Am. **284**(2), 76–81 (2001)

10. Ellsberg, D.: Risk, ambiguity, and the savage axioms*. Q. J. Econ., 643–669 (1961). https://doi.org/10.2307/1884324

11. Farnadi, G., Kouki, P., Thompson, S.K., Srinivasan, S., Getoor, L.: A fairness-aware hybrid recommender system. CoRR (2018). http://arxiv.org/abs/1809.09030

12. Gedikli, F., Jannach, D., Ge, M.: How should i explain? A comparison of different explanation types for recommender systems. Int. J. Hum. Comput. Stud. **72**(4), 367–382 (2014)

13. Gkika, S., Lekakos, G.: The persuasive role of explanations in recommender systems. In: Öörni, A., Kelders, S.M., van Gemert-Pijnen, L., Oinas-Kukkonen, H. (eds.) Proceedings of the Second International Workshop on Behavior Change Support Systems Co-located with the 9th International Conference on Persuasive Technology (PERSUASIVE 2014), Padua, Italy, 22 May 2014. CEUR Workshop Proceedings, vol. 1153, pp. 59–68. CEUR-WS.org (2014). http://ceur-ws.org/Vol-1153/Paper_6.pdf

14. Herlocker, J.L., Konstan, J.A., Riedl, J.: Explaining collaborative filtering recommendations. In: Proceedings of the 2000 ACM Conference on Computer Supported Cooperative Work, CSCW 2000, pp. 241–250. Association for Computing Machinery, New York (2000). https://doi.org/10.1145/358916.358995

15. Hoyle, R.H.: Structural Equation Modeling: Concepts, Issues, and Applications. Sage, Thousand Oaks (1995)

16. John, O.P., Srivastava, S.: The Big Five trait taxonomy: History, measurement, and theoretical perspectives. Handb. Pers. Theory Res. **2**(1991), 102–138 (1991)

17. Kamishima, T., Akaho, S., Asoh, H., Sakuma, J.: Correcting popularity bias by enhancing recommendation neutrality. In: Poster Proceedings of the 8th ACM Conference on Recommender Systems (2014)

18. Kamishima, T., Akaho, S., Asoh, H., Sato, I.: Model-based approaches for independence-enhanced recommendation. In: 2016 IEEE 16th International Conference on Data Mining Workshops (ICDMW), pp. 860–867. IEEE (2016)

19. Kendall, M., Gibbons, J.D.: Rank Correlation Methods, 5th edn. A Charles Griffin Title, London (1990)

20. Kouki, P., Schaffer, J., Pujara, J., O'Donovan, J., Getoor, L.: Personalized explanations for hybrid recommender systems. In: Proceedings of the 24th International Conference on Intelligent User Interfaces, pp. 379–390 (2019)

21. Kowald, D., Schedl, M., Lex, E.: The unfairness of popularity bias in music recommendation: a reproducibility study. CoRR (2019). http://arxiv.org/abs/1912.04696

22. Kruskal, W.H., Wallis, W.A.: Use of ranks in one-criterion variance analysis. J. Am. Stat. Assoc. **47**(260), 583–621 (1952)

23. Liu, W., Guo, J., Sonboli, N., Burke, R., Zhang, S.: Personalized fairness-aware re-ranking for microlending. In: Proceedings of the 13th ACM Conference on Recommender Systems, pp. 467–471 (2019)

24. Mehrotra, R., McInerney, J., Bouchard, H., Lalmas, M., Diaz, F.: Towards a fair marketplace: counterfactual evaluation of the trade-off between relevance, fairness & satisfaction in recommendation systems. In: Proceedings of the 27th ACM International Conference on Information and Knowledge Management, pp. 2243–2252 (2018). https://doi.org/10.1145/3269206.3272027

25. Mulligan, M.: Superstar economics, March 2014. https://musicindustryblog.wordpress.com/tag/superstar-economics/

26. Orji, R., Mandryk, R.L., Vassileva, J.: Gender, age, and responsiveness to Cialdini's persuasion strategies. In: MacTavish, T., Basapur, S. (eds.) PERSUASIVE 2015. LNCS, vol. 9072, pp. 147–159. Springer, Cham (2015). https://doi.org/10.1007/978-3-319-20306-5_14
27. Orji, R., Vassileva, J., Mandryk, R.L.: Modeling the efficacy of persuasive strategies for different gamer types in serious games for health. In: Proceedings of the 10th User Modeling and User-Adapted Interaction, vol. 24, no. 5, pp. 453–498 (2014)
28. Oyibo, K., Adaji, I., Orji, R., Olabenjo, B., Vassileva, J.: Susceptibility to persuasive strategies: a comparative analysis of Nigerians vs. Canadians. In: Proceedings of the 26th Conference on User Modeling, Adaptation and Personalization, UMAP 2018, pp. 229–238. Association for Computing Machinery, New York (2018). https://doi.org/10.1145/3209219.3209239
29. Rosen, S.: The economics of superstars. Am. Econ. Rev. **71**(5), 845–858 (1981)
30. Sonboli, N., Smith, J.J., Cabral Berenfus, F., Burke, R., Fiesler, C.: Fairness and transparency in recommendation: the users' perspective. In: Proceedings of the 29th ACM Conference on User Modeling, Adaptation and Personalization, pp. 274–279 (2021)
31. Tintarev, N., Masthoff, J.: A survey of explanations in recommender systems. In: 2007 IEEE 23rd International Conference on Data Engineering Workshop, pp. 801–810 (2007). https://doi.org/10.1109/ICDEW.2007.4401070
32. Wilcoxon, F.: Individual comparisons by ranking methods. In: Kotz, S., Johnson, N.L. (eds.) Breakthroughs in statistics, pp. 196–202. Springer, New York (1992). https://doi.org/10.1007/978-1-4612-4380-9_16
33. Yao, S., Huang, B.: Beyond parity: fairness objectives for collaborative filtering. arXiv preprint arXiv:1705.08804 (2017)

Player Personality Traits and the Effectiveness of a Persuasive Game for Disease Awareness Among the African Population

Chinenye Ndulue[✉] and Rita Orji

Faculty of Computer Science, Dalhousie University, Halifax, Canada
cndulue@dal.ca

Abstract. Although persuasive gamified systems have been proven to be effective at motivating behaviour change in various domains of life, there are reoccurring research questions around the effectiveness of these systems for players with various user characteristics, cultures, and across various behaviour domains. Our paper explores the effectiveness of various persuasive strategies implemented in a persuasive game for disease awareness and prevention, specifically, persuasive games for creating awareness about COVID-19 among the African audience and the impact of user personality traits on the effectiveness of the strategies. An in-the-wild study among 51 Africans reveals that the 12 persuasive strategies implemented in the game were perceived as highly effective at motivating behaviour change overall. We also uncovered that people high in Agreeableness were motivated by eight of the strategies, while people high in Neuroticism were demotivated by the *Self-Monitoring* strategy. Agreeableness and Conscientiousness emerged as the personality traits that predicted most of the variability in the effectiveness of the persuasive strategies implemented in the game. Based on the findings and the qualitative comments, we provide design suggestions for implementing various persuasive strategies for different personality traits in the African population.

Keywords: Persuasive games · Gamified systems · Persuasive system design · Persuasive strategies · Personality traits · Five factor model · FFM · COVID-19

1 Introduction

In recent years of research, there has been an increasing investment in the development and design of gamified systems targeted at promoting behaviour or attitude change [10, 24]. These systems are referred to as Persuasive gamified systems. They achieve their attitude and behaviour change goals by employing a variety of persuasive strategies. These systems exist in a wide variety of domains including environmental sustainability [7], healthy nutrition [20], physical activity [25], online security [15], and disease awareness, management and prevention [18].

While research have shown that persuasive gamified systems are effective at motivating behaviour change, there are still questions about the generalizability of their findings

© Springer Nature Switzerland AG 2022
N. Baghaei et al. (Eds.): PERSUASIVE 2022, LNCS 13213, pp. 134–144, 2022.
https://doi.org/10.1007/978-3-030-98438-0_11

across various cultures (audiences) and domains. Most existing persuasive games and gamified interventions are targeted at audiences from the Western cultures, making it difficult to establish their generalizability across non-Western cultures such as the African audience. Research has shown that culture plays an important role in the effectiveness of health interventions [13]. Again, only a few of the existing games are targeted at disease prevention in general and none targeted at specifically COVID-19 awareness among Africans.

On the other hand, it has been shown that user characteristics can impact the effectiveness of persuasive systems, and hence one-size-does-not-fit-all when it comes to designing effective persuasive gamified systems to motivate behaviour change [21]. This has led to various research targeted at understanding how to tailor persuasive gamified systems to a variety of user characteristics' including, user gender groups [27], gamer and gamification user types [22], user age groups [30], and personality types [23].

Apart from the user characteristics, research has shown that application domain and user cultural orientations may also impact the effectiveness of a persuasive gamified systems. According to the Persuasive Systems Design (PSD) model [19], factors beyond user characteristics (such as usage contexts including the problem domain the application is targeted at) may affect the effectiveness of persuasive strategies. A persuasive game targeted at the domain of healthy eating may not have the same effectiveness as a persuasive game targeted at promoting COVID-19 awareness, even if all persuasive strategies are identical [1]. Identically, a persuasive game for smoking cessation targeted at Americans may not be as effective for Africans, due to cultural differences. Therefore, it is necessary to understand the impacts of personality types for unique cultures and for a specific problem domain of persuasive technology.

To advance this research area, we investigate the effectiveness of a persuasive game in the disease awareness and prevention domain (COVID-19) targeted at the African population, to understand the effectiveness of the persuasive strategies' implementation and also the impact of players' personality traits on the effectiveness of the strategies. This would help provide insights on how to develop persuasive games for disease awareness targeting Africans, different personality traits and the generalizability of the effectiveness of persuasive intervention across cultures. Therefore, our research questions are as follows:

R1: Which persuasive strategies would be effective in a persuasive game for promoting disease awareness and prevention among African audience?

R2: What is the relation between personality traits and the effectiveness of persuasive strategies in a game for disease prevention and awareness among the African audience?

2 Methodology

In this paper, we investigate the effectiveness of a persuasive game for COVID-19 awareness and prevention targeted at the African population, based on personality traits. To accomplish this research goal, we employed the following methodology:

- We developed a persuasive game titled, "COVID Dodge", implementing 12 persuasive strategies to promote behaviour change.
- We conducted an in-the-wild study among the African audience to answer our research questions.
- Finally, we analyzed the results and discussed our findings.

2.1 The COVID Dodge Game

COVID Dodge is an auto-runner persuasive game targeted at increasing awareness around COVID-19 precautionary measures. In the game, players help the main character (a young boy called Chike) to complete errands specified by his grandmother. The player's primary task is to avoid physical contact with other people in their community (villagers) and collect powerups like hand sanitisers and facemasks while running the errands. A more detailed description of the game can be found in a previous paper focused on its heuristic evaluation [17].

To make the game persuasive, we implemented 12 well-known persuasive strategies namely, *Tailoring, Self-monitoring, Simulation, Praise, Rewards, Reminders, Suggestion, Liking, Real-world feel, Verifiability, Competition,* and *Recognition.* Table 1 shows a description of the implementations of these strategies in the COVID Dodge game. See Fig. 1 for some screenshots of the COVID Dodge game.

2.2 Study Design

To understand the effectiveness of the persuasive strategies implemented, we carried out a user study to collect players' perceived effectiveness of the persuasive strategies implemented in COVID Dodge.

We recruited 51 participants from an African country (Nigeria) to partake in a one-week field study. The participants downloaded and played the COVID Dodge game for one week, for at least 20 min each day. After this, we assessed their personality traits using the validated 10-item personality inventory based on the FFM [11]. More importantly, we also collected data about the perceived effectiveness of each persuasive strategy implemented in the game. For each persuasive strategy, we presented screenshots of their implementations from the game to remind participants of their experience when they played the game and asked participants to rate the effectiveness of each persuasive strategy on a 7-point Likert scale. The strategies were presented to the participants in a random order to guard against order effects. We used the validated scale consisting of four questions adapted from Thomas et al. [29] and Drozd et al. [6], which are established scales for assessing the perceived effectiveness of persuasive systems. They have also been used in a lot of HCI, digital health and games research [3, 21].

Table 1. Description of the persuasive strategies and their implementations

Persuasive strategies	Description of implementations
Tailoring	We made use of African-themed music and sounds, African attires for the characters and an African-themed game environment to increase its appeal and relevance to the African audience and make it culturally meaningful
Self-monitoring	Players can view their scores, levels attained, badges collected, and monitor how well they are performing toward observing the COVID-19 precautionary measures within the game
Praise	We praised users using words like "Well done" and "Congratulations", for playing and achieving milestones, to motivate them
Rewards	Players acquire points for lasting longer in the game and observing measures such as using hand sanitisers and mask. They also collect badges for achieving various milestones
Reminders	The game sends a push-up notification to users every morning and evening about mask usage, sanitisers and other safety tips
Suggestion	During the game, story snippets are encountered by players at the start of each level, they get random safety tips for the prevention of COVID-19
Liking	We employed attractive interfaces, colours, and animations
Real-world feel	We implemented a 'Credits' section where the players can see the contact information of the people behind the game
Verifiability	On the safety tips window, we provided a link for players to verify the information we presented to them
Competition	We implemented a global leaderboard, where players are ranked according to their game points
Recognition	The person in the first position on the leaderboard is recognized with a unique border around their name
Punishment	Players lose a life each time they allow a villager character to get within six feet of their character

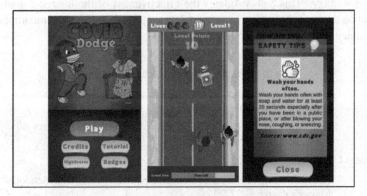

Fig. 1. Some screenshots of the COVID Dodge game

2.3 Data Analysis

In this research, we aimed to answer the following research questions.

R1: Which persuasive strategies would be effective in a persuasive game for promoting disease awareness and prevention among the African audience?

R2: What is the relation between personality traits and the effectiveness of persuasive strategies in a game for disease prevention and awareness among the African audience?

To answer R1, we ran a one-sample t-test on the mean values of the perceived effectiveness for each persuasive strategy implemented, using a test value of 4.0. To answer R2, we developed models showing the relationships between the personality traits and the persuasiveness of the strategies using the Partial Least Square Structural Equation Modeling (PLS-SEM) [9], with the personality traits being the exogenous constructs.

3 Results

In this section, we present the result of our user evaluation among 51 African participants. Firstly, we present the results of the perceived effectiveness of each persuasive strategy employed in the game and then the results of the impact of personality traits on the effectiveness of each persuasive strategy. Table 2 shows the demography of our participants.

3.1 The Effectiveness of Each Persuasive Strategy

The one-sample t-test on the mean rating of each persuasive strategy revealed that all the strategies were significantly above the mean value of 4.0 as shown in Table 3. This implies that all the strategies were perceived as strongly effective at motivating or promoting the desired behaviour towards COVID-19 prevention. The *Verifiability* strategy was perceived as the most effective strategy ($t(50) = 13.7$, $p < 0.005$) while the Reminder persuasive strategy was considered as the least effective strategy ($t(50) = 6.317$, $p < .005$). This also validates the effectiveness of the heuristic analysis we carried out on the game before running our user study [4]. We discuss some implications of these strategies in the discussion section.

Table 2. Participants' demographic information

Gender	Female = 45%, Male = 54%
Age	18–25 years old = 19.6%, 26–35 years old = 76.6; 36–45 years old = 1.9%, Above 45 years old = 1.9%
Marital status	Married = 33.33%, Single = 66.67%
Education	Bachelor's degree = 54.9%; College diploma = 5.8%; High School = 11.8%; Master's degree = 27.5%

3.2   The Impact of Personality Traits on the Effectiveness of Persuasive Strategies

The structural model of the relationships between persuasive strategies and personality traits revealed several unique relationships. As shown in Table 3, people high in the Agreeableness trait were significantly motivated by most of the persuasive strategies (p < .05) namely: *Reward* (β = .45), *Competition* (β = .34), *Praise* (β = .33), *Punishment* (β = .26), *Recognition* (β = .40), *Reminder* (β = .30), *Self-monitoring* (β = .32), *Tailoring* (β = .36). People high in conscientiousness were only motivated by *Competition* (β = .34), *Recognition* (β = .33), *Reminders* (β = .30), while people high in Neuroticism were demotivated by the *Self-monitoring* strategy (β = −.23). (All values were significant at p < 0.05).

Table 3. One sample t-test for each persuasive strategy with a test value of 4; and the standardized path coefficients and significance of the models between personality traits and persuasive strategies. Bolded are p < .05 and '–' represents non-significant coefficients.

Factors	Mean	Std. deviation	p-value	Factors	AGR	CON	NEU
Verifiability	6.04	1.14	0.0001	Verifiability	–	–	–
Praise	5.97	1.16	0.0001	Praise	**.33**	–	–
Suggestion	5.96	1.17	0.0001	Suggestion	–	–	–
Punishment	5.88	1.10	0.0001	Punishment	**.26**	–	–
Self-monitoring	5.76	1.29	0.0001	Self-monitoring	**.32**	–	**−.23**
Real world feel	5.76	1.37	0.0001	Real world feel	–	–	–
Reward	5.76	1.07	0.0001	Reward	**.45**	–	–
Liking	5.75	1.32	0.0001	Liking	–	–	–
Competition	5.73	1.44	0.0001	Competition	**.34**	**.34**	–
Tailoring	5.71	1.23	0.0001	Tailoring	**.36**	–	–
Recognition	5.59	1.55	0.0001	Recognition	**.40**	**.33**	–
Reminder	5.41	1.59	0.0001	Reminder	**.30**	**.30**	–
All values were significant at p < 0.005				AGR = Agreeableness, NEU = Neuroticism, CON = Conscientiousness			

4   Discussion

4.1   Designing Persuasive Technologies Targeted at Africans of Various Personality Types

In this section, we discuss some implications of the relationships uncovered between the personality traits and some of the persuasive strategies and provide design suggestions for implementing these persuasive strategies for various personality traits among African audiences.

Reward Strategy and Agreeableness Personality Trait. The *Reward* strategy had a strong positive relationship with the Agreeableness trait and hence would likely be effective for motivating people high in agreeableness. In the COVID Dodge game, *rewards* were implemented by awarding points to players for observing the COVID-19 precautionary measures and awarding badges for achieving various milestones in the game. Research reveals that people high in agreeableness tend to be tender-minded [5]. Therefore, since tender-minded people are mostly guided by feelings and emotions, and *rewards* mostly elicit positive emotions (happiness or excitement) and positive motivational values [2], hence *reward* implementations can capitalize on these feelings to create an avenue for behaviour change. This is evident from comments by two participants that were high in agreeableness: *"The rewards motivated me to play more." – P3; "It's always fun to win rewards ..." – P5.*

Although game *rewards* are not tangible, it is important to develop *rewards* that represent some emotional, personal or social meaning for the players, to elicit more positive emotions from them. When implementing rewards in persuasive gamified designs targeted at the African population, it is important to also reflect their unique culture to make it more relatable. For example, an achievement badge designed in the likeness of a popular fruit in African countries (for example, an African Star Apple or Garden eggs or Kolanuts) may be more relatable than a badge designed to look like cranberries or peaches. In situations where tailoring of these *rewards* cannot be achieved, badges can be designed to resemble generally accepted abstract items, irrespective of cultural norms.

Reminding the Conscientious and Agreeable. Although *reminders* are among the widely used persuasive strategies in persuasive games and gamified systems design, it emerged as the least effective of all the strategies implemented overall for the African audience. It may be because of the bad reputation that *reminder* strategy implementations have with mobile phone users. *Reminders* implemented as push notifications are perceived by many users as either annoying, distracting, or unimportant [28]. They can be annoying when the notifications are reoccurring too frequently and they can be unimportant if the notification is random and has no personal significance to the users of the system. This is evident from this participant's comment: *"I played when I had time, wasn't influenced by reminders." – P28.* We implemented *reminders* in COVID Dodge as push notifications of COVID-19 tips and notifications to play the game.

With respect to the personality types, our results showed that *Reminders* motivate people high in agreeableness and conscientiousness significantly. Conscientious people tend to be very organized and orderly [8], therefore *reminders* would ultimately be significant to them since *reminders* are one of the tools for self-organization and personal information management [14].

Reminders are often used by persuasive game designers to achieve two major goals: to remind and keep users aware of the target behaviours and to remind users to play the persuasive game to get exposure to the intervention. While implementing these *reminders*, designers are advised to moderate the persistency of the notifications to limit interference with users' other mobile phone activity, since persuasive interventions should never be obtrusive [19]. This is especially important for African users in rural areas, where the power supply is limited. Users are likely to delete apps or games that are seemingly power-intensive [16] and a game with frequently persistent reminders would likely be seen as such. Therefore, persuasive games designed for African populations should only implement meaningful and moderately persistent reminders and notifications of the target behaviours in their intervention.

Tailoring Strategy for the Agreeableness Personality Trait. The *Tailoring* strategy, which involves designing systems to suit the needs and preferences of a particular user group, had a positive appeal to people with the Agreeableness personality trait as seen in Table 3. Tailoring is a unique strategy for persuasion because it creates a feeling of inclusiveness for the user of the persuasive gamified system.

An attribute of people high in Agreeableness is their tendency to be compliant and cooperative [5]. Since the game was tailored to the African culture, which complies with the norms of Africans in general, it will more likely influence people high in agreeableness and promote the desired behaviour change. This is evident by the following comments from participants high in agreeableness: *"The African setting made it relatable."* - *P21. "I am influenced by the music"* - *P28.* Although the African culture is diverse, it is characterised by similarities in music style (use of percussion and upbeat sounds) [12], colourful representations [18] and communal values [26]. All these characteristics can be utilized by persuasive game designers to create a sense of inclusiveness and make games relatable to the African audience, especially for those with the Agreeableness personality trait.

Overall, Agreeableness and Conscientiousness emerged as the personality traits that predicted most of the variability in the effectiveness of the persuasive strategies implemented in the game. We found no significant relationships between the 12 persuasive strategies implemented and the Extraversion and the Openness personality trait. Research should therefore investigate for more Extraversion and Openness-oriented persuasive strategies.

4.2 Limitations

One limitation of this study is the relatively small sample size. In future investigations, a larger sample size would be used and the game would be played over a longer term to enable detailed exposure to the intervention and analysis.

The effectiveness of the persuasive strategies implemented in COVID Dodge was self-reported. There is always a possibility for participant bias, although, self-report is still one of the predominant ways of assessing belief, we acknowledge the actual effectiveness with respect to motivating the desired behaviour may differ. In future, we will also gather some behaviour data using techniques such as diary study to investigate impact in actual behaviours such as how many times users complied or failed to comply with the COVID-19 precautionary measures.

4.3 Conclusion

This paper investigated the impact of personality traits on the effectiveness of 12 persuasive strategies implemented in a persuasive game for disease awareness and prevention

(COVID-19) targeted at the African population. In a one-week in-the-wild study of 51 African participants, we uncovered that all the persuasive strategies were perceived as effective at promoting COVID-19 safety awareness. We also uncovered that personality influences the effectiveness of the strategies. People high in Agreeableness were motivated by eight of the persuasive strategies, while people high in Neuroticism were demotivated by the *Self-Monitoring* strategy. Agreeableness and Conscientiousness emerged as the personality traits that predict most of the variability in the effectiveness of the persuasive strategies implemented in the game. We concluded by providing design suggestions on implementing the persuasive strategies in games and gamified systems for different personality traits in the African population.

Acknowledgement. This research was undertaken, in part, thanks to funding from the Canada Research Chairs Program. We acknowledge the support of the Natural Sciences and Engineering Research Council of Canada (NSERC) through the Discovery Grant.

References

1. Alqahtani, F., et al.: Personality-based approach for tailoring persuasive mental health applications. User Model. User-Adapt. Interact., 1–43 (2021)
2. Banich, M.T., Floresco, S.: Reward systems, cognition, and emotion: introduction to the special issue (2019). https://doi.org/10.3758/s13415-019-00725-z
3. Busch, M., Mattheiss, E., Reisinger, M., Orji, R., Fröhlich, P., Tscheligi, M.: More than sex: the role of femininity and masculinity in the design of personalized persuasive games. In: Meschtscherjakov, A., De Ruyter, B., Fuchsberger, V., Murer, M., Tscheligi, M. (eds.) PERSUASIVE 2016. LNCS, vol. 9638, pp. 219–229. Springer, Cham (2016). https://doi.org/10.1007/978-3-319-31510-2_19
4. Ndulue, C., Orji, R.: Heuristic evaluation of an African-centric mobile persuasive game for promoting safety measures against COVID-19. In: 3rd African Human-Computer Interaction Conference (AfriCHI 2021), 10 pages (2021). https://doi.org/10.1145/3448696.3448706
5. Costa, P., McCrae, R., Dye, D.: Facet scales for agreeableness and conscientiousness: a revision of the NEO personality inventory. Pers. Individ. Differ. 12(9), 887–898 (1991). https://doi.org/10.1016/0191-8869(91)90177-D
6. Drozd, F., Lehto, T., Oinas-Kukkonen, H.: Exploring perceived persuasiveness of a behavior change support system: a structural model. In: Bang, M., Ragnemalm, E.L. (eds.) PERSUASIVE 2012. LNCS, vol. 7284, pp. 157–168. Springer, Heidelberg (2012). https://doi.org/10.1007/978-3-642-31037-9_14
7. Gamberini, L., et al.: Saving is fun. In: Proceedings of the 8th International Conference on Advances in Computer Entertainment Technology - ACE 2011, p. 1. ACM Press, New York (2011). https://doi.org/10.1145/2071423.2071443
8. Goldberg, L.R.: The structure of phenotypic personality traits. Am. Psychol. (1993). https://doi.org/10.1037/0003-066X.48.1.26
9. Hair, J.F. et al.: When to use and how to report the results of PLS-SEM (2019). https://doi.org/10.1108/EBR-11-2018-0203
10. Hamari, J., Koivisto, J., Pakkanen, T.: Do persuasive technologies persuade? - a review of empirical studies. In: Spagnolli, A., Chittaro, L., Gamberini, L. (eds.) PERSUASIVE 2014. LNCS, vol. 8462, pp. 118–136. Springer, Cham (2014). https://doi.org/10.1007/978-3-319-07127-5_11

11. John, O.P., Srivastava, S.: Big five inventory (Bfi). Handb. Personal Theory Res. (1999). https://doi.org/10.1525/fq.1998.51.4.04a00260
12. Jones, A.M.: African Music: A People's Art. By Francis Bebey (trs. Josephine Bennett). Harrap, London (1975). p. 184. £4.50. Africa (Lond). 46, 3, 300–300 (1976). https://doi.org/10.2307/1159409
13. Kreuter, M.W., McClure, S.M.: The role of culture in health communication. Annu. Rev. Public Health 25(1), 439–455 (2004). https://doi.org/10.1146/annurev.publhealth.25.101802.123000
14. Lansdale, M.W.: The psychology of personal information management. Appl. Ergon. 19(1), 55–66 (1988). https://doi.org/10.1016/0003-6870(88)90199-8
15. Ndulue, C., Oyebode, O., Orji, R.: PHISHER CRUSH: a mobile persuasive game for promoting online security. In: Gram-Hansen, S.B., Jonasen, T.S., Midden, C. (eds.) PERSUASIVE 2020. LNCS, vol. 12064, pp. 223–233. Springer, Cham (2020). https://doi.org/10.1007/978-3-030-45712-9_17
16. Ndulue, C., Orji, R.: Developing persuasive mobile games for African rural audiences. In: Adjunct Publication of the 27th Conference on User Modeling, Adaptation and Personalization – UMAP 2019 Adjunct, pp. 179–184. ACM Press, New York (2019). https://doi.org/10.1145/3314183.3323857
17. Ndulue, C., Orji, R.: Heuristic evaluation of an African-centric mobile persuasive game for promoting safety measures against COVID-19. In: ACM International Conference Proceeding Series, pp. 43–51 (2021). https://doi.org/10.1145/3448696.3448706
18. Ndulue, C., Orji, R.: STD Pong: changing risky sexual behaviours in Africa through persuasive games. In: Proceedings of the Second African Conference for Human Computer Interaction on Thriving Communities - AfriCHI 2018, pp. 1–5. ACM Press, New York (2018). https://doi.org/10.1145/3283458.3283463
19. Oinas-Kukkonen, H., Harjumaa, M.: Persuasive systems design: key issues, process model, and system features. Commun. Assoc. Inf. Syst. 24(1), 485–500 (2009)
20. Orji, R., et al.: LunchTime: a slow-casual game for long-term dietary behavior change. Pers. Ubiquitous Comput. 17(6), 1211–1221 (2013). https://doi.org/10.1007/s00779-012-0590-6
21. Orji, R., Vassileva, J., Mandryk, R.L.: Modeling the efficacy of persuasive strategies for different gamer types in serious games for health. User Model. User-Adap. Inter. 24(5), 453–498 (2014). https://doi.org/10.1007/s11257-014-9149-8
22. Orji, R., et al.: Tailoring persuasive health games to gamer type. In: Proceedings of the SIGCHI Conference on Human Factors in Computing Systems - CHI 2013, p. 2467. ACM Press, New York (2013). https://doi.org/10.1145/2470654.2481341
23. Orji, R., et al.: Towards personality-driven persuasive health games and gamified systems. In: Conference on Human Factors in Computing Systems - Proceedings (2017). https://doi.org/10.1145/3025453.3025577
24. Orji, R., Moffatt, K.: Persuasive technology for health and wellness: state-of-the-art and emerging trends. Health Inform. J. (2018). https://doi.org/10.1177/1460458216650979
25. Oyebode, O., et al.: Nourish your tree! Developing a persuasive exergame for promoting physical activity among adults. In: 2020 IEEE 8th International Conference on Serious Games and Applications for Health (SeGAH), pp. 1–7. IEEE (2020). https://doi.org/10.1109/SeGAH49190.2020.9201637
26. Oyeshile, O.A.: Communal Values, Cultural Identity and the Challenge of Development in Contemporary Africa
27. Oyibo, K., et al.: Investigation of the persuasiveness of social influence in persuasive technology and the effect of age and gender. In: CEUR Workshop Proceedings (2017)
28. Shirazi, A.S., et al.: Large-Scale Assessment of Mobile Notifications. https://doi.org/10.1145/2556288.2557189

29. Thomas, R.J. et al.: Can i influence you? development of a scale to measure perceived persuasiveness and two studies showing the use of the scale. Front. Artif. Intell. (2019). https://doi.org/10.3389/frai.2019.00024
30. van Velsen, L., et al.: Tailoring persuasive electronic health strategies for older adults on the basis of personal motivation: web-based survey study. J. Med. Internet Res. (2019). https://doi.org/10.2196/11759

Exploring for Possible Effect of Persuasive Strategy Implementation Choices: Towards Tailoring Persuasive Technologies

Oladapo Oyebode[1]([✉]) [ID], Felwah Alqahtani[1,2] [ID], and Rita Orji[1] [ID]

[1] Faculty of Computer Science, Dalhousie University, NS B3H 4R2 Halifax, Canada
{oladapo.oyebode,felwah.alqahtani,rita.orji}@dal.ca
[2] Faculty of Computer Science, King Khalid University, Abha, Saudi Arabia

Abstract. Persuasive strategies have been implemented in various ways in persuasive systems to motivate behaviour change. However, there is no empirical evidence regarding whether or not the effectiveness of persuasive systems varies based on implementation choices and why. To address this gap, we conduct a large-scale study involving 568 participants to investigate the perceived persuasiveness or effectiveness of different implementations of each strategy in the same system. We focused on six (6) popular strategies from the Persuasive Systems Design (PSD) model: *self-monitoring, suggestion, reward, cooperation, social role*, and *normative influence*. Our results show that the perceived persuasiveness of distinct implementations of the same strategy varies. For instance, people perceive Social Role strategy implemented as *communication between a user and a "human" therapist* as significantly more persuasive than implementing the strategy as *communication between a user and a "non-human" therapist*. Also, implementing Suggestion strategy as a *list of suggestions/tips accessible via a menu* is perceived as significantly more persuasive than *contextual pop-up tips*. We perform thematic analysis of qualitative comments from participants to examine the reasons for their implementation choices (*why*). We also offer practical design guidelines for tailoring persuasive systems based on our findings.

Keywords: Persuasive strategy · Implementation choices · Persuasive system · Behaviour change · Personalization · Tailoring · Design implications

1 Introduction

Over the years, persuasive technology (PT) researchers have developed frameworks including Persuasive Technology Tools [1], Principles of Persuasion [2], and the Persuasive Systems Design (PSD) Model [3] comprising various persuasive strategies (PS) that could be employed in applications design to promote behaviour change. However, decisions regarding which PS to employ and how to implement them in persuasive applications are usually based on designer's discretion. Research has shown that the effectiveness of PS varies depending on user characteristics since different users or user groups are motivated by different PS [4–7] and may not be motivated by the same PS

© Springer Nature Switzerland AG 2022
N. Baghaei et al. (Eds.): PERSUASIVE 2022, LNCS 13213, pp. 145–163, 2022.
https://doi.org/10.1007/978-3-030-98438-0_12

[8–12]. While the need to explore the implementation effect of PS on behaviour change has been suggested in the literature [13, 14], whether or not the effectiveness of PS varies depending on how each strategy is implemented in a system is yet to be investigated through an empirical study.

To address this gap, we conducted a large-scale study of 568 participants to examine and compare the perceived persuasiveness or effectiveness of distinct implementations of each strategy in the same system. We focused on six (6) popular PSD strategies [15–20]: *self-monitoring, suggestion, reward, cooperation, social role,* and *normative influence.* To collect data from participants, we iteratively developed and presented high-fidelity prototype illustrating each strategy implementation within the domain of smoking cessation, followed by a validated scale measuring perceived persuasiveness [21] of each implementation. We also collected qualitative data from participants to understand the reasons for their implementation choices (*why*). Our results show that the persuasiveness of different implementations of the same strategy varies and that the implementations motivate for different reasons.

Our work offers four contributions in the field of PT design in Human-Computer Interaction (HCI). First, we explore distinct implementations of each strategy and underpin the importance of selecting the appropriate implementations to improve the effectiveness of persuasive systems. Second, we provide qualitative insights to explain the reasons for participants' implementation choices. Third, we deconstruct various implementations of strategies in persuasive systems across various domains from the literature. Fourth, we reflect on the implications of our findings and offer practical design guidelines for tailoring persuasive systems.

2   Related Work

Persuasive strategies (PS) motivate behaviour change without using coercion or deception. Over the years, several persuasion frameworks including Fogg's Persuasive Technology Tools [1], Cialdini's Principles of Persuasion [2], and the Persuasive Systems Design (PSD) model by Oinas-Kukkonen et al. [3] proposed many PS that have been employed in practice to design persuasive technologies. For our study, we focus on six popular PS [15–20] from the PSD model: *self-monitoring, suggestion, reward, cooperation, normative influence,* and *social role* (see Table 1).

PS have been implemented in a number of ways in the literature, however, implementation choices are usually based on designer's discretion. We explore the various implementations of the PS in Table 1 in subsequent subsections and present a summary in Table 2 while highlighting popular implementations per strategy.

2.1   Self-monitoring Strategy

To encourage physical activity, Hosseini et al. [22] employed self-monitoring by showing the distance covered for the current day, the previous day, and current week in *textual format* on a separate display, as well as a circular *progress bar* that reflects how much of a user's daily goal has been reached. Similarly, users' progress or performance was presented using *textual representations* in [23–29] and via *progress bars* in [23, 30–33].

Table 1. Six persuasive strategies and corresponding descriptions.

Strategy	Description
Self-monitoring	Provides means for users to track progress toward their target behaviour or goal
Suggestion	Provides tailored suggestions or tips for achieving the desired behaviour during system use
Reward	Incentivizes users for achieving specific milestones using virtual rewards
Cooperation	Provides means for users to work together to achieve their intended behaviour
Normative influence	Provides means of gathering users with similar goals to facilitate behaviour change or reinforcement
Social role	System assumes the role of a respected person (e.g., a health authority or expert) to support users through the behaviour change process

Also, self-monitoring was implemented using *charts* [23, 32–34] such as color-coded *bar charts* used by [34] to show healthy and unhealthy levels of users' vital signs. Another implementation of self-monitoring strategy is the *calendar* feature used in [35] that allows users to track number of days exercised.

2.2 Suggestion Strategy

The suggestion strategy was implemented in a number of ways in the literature. For instance, the BlueWatch application by [36] provided a *list of recommendations* accessible through the "My Tasks" tab/menu to improve the well-being of adults experiencing depressive symptoms. Similarly, through dedicated in-app menu items or tabs, users can access a *list of suitable menus or foods* [37], a *list of personalized dietary suggestions* [38], *a list of recommended heart-friendly foods* [39], and *personalized list of activity suggestions* to manage cigarette cravings [40]. Rather than using menu-driven suggestions or tips, [41] presented *pop-up messages containing suggestions* of other healthy food items to buy and [42] offered transport suggestions in form of *pop-up alerts* to promote sustainable travel choices. Another implementation of the strategy is the *delivery of motivational tips or suggestions via short messaging service (SMS)* [43].

2.3 Reward Strategy

The reward strategy was implemented as *badges* and *points* earned by users for achieving smoking cessation milestones [44]. Likewise, [45] awarded *points* for every healthy meal choice made by users. *Point-based* reward system was also utilized in [22, 46–50], while *badges* were used in [47, 49, 51] to incentivize users. Conversely, *ribbons* and *trophies* were employed as virtual rewards as users progress and achieve their goals [52]. Similarly, [53] offered *trophies* to encourage users to be physically active. Other implementations of the reward strategy include *streak coins* [53] and *animated graphics* (such as virtual rose [54], butterflies [55, 56], e-postcard [57], etc.).

2.4 Social Role Strategy

The strategy was implemented as an interactive *online chat* feature used by a *human expert* for offering lifestyle and fitness advice to users [24]. Similarly, [58] facilitated personal counselling on smoking by providing a means of contacting *human counsellors* directly for advice. On the other hand, [59] utilized a non-human *avatar*, named Brigitte, to inform users on different nutritional choices. Likewise, [60] used an *animated character* in the form of a *blob* to present age-appropriate and gender-neutral guidance and feedback to address childhood anxiety. Also, [61] designed a *virtual specialist* acting as an exercise trainer and nutritionist to support interaction between users and health specialists. Social Role strategy was also operationalized using *chatbot* to facilitate communication with users on their smoking habits [62] and physical and mental health [63].

2.5 Cooperation Strategy

The cooperation strategy was implemented in [64] by allowing a user to team up with a partner (who may be a friend or stranger) to compete with other teams in an exergame. Similarly, [65] allowed users to connect with nearby users (e.g., roommates and friends) to work together toward a common goal (e.g., sleep goal). Users were randomly assigned to groups in [66] while friends collaborate to exercise in [67, 68]. Other works allow users who reside in the same geolocation [69] or work in same office [70] to team up toward achieving a behaviour change goal.

2.6 Normative Influence Strategy

In [71], Pollak et al. implemented the strategy in form of a *discussion forum* through which kids share picture of their healthy meals to showcase their balanced diet. A similar feature that allows users to share posts about their weight loss and sleep habits was utilized in [72] and [73] respectively. Also, [74] provided an in-app *blogging* feature to allow users to share their smoking-related success stories via blog posts. *Group chat* is another implementation of normative influence strategy where users with similar interests can discuss various topics including relaxation exercises, sleep habits, cancer screening experiences, etc. [65, 75, 76].

Table 2. Summary of strategy implementations. Popular implementations are bolded for emphasis.

Strategy	Implementations	Sources
Self-monitoring	**Textual representation of user progress, graphs/charts with or without progress bars**, calendar feature	[22–35]
Suggestion	**List of suggestions/tips accessible via a menu/tab, contextual pop-up tips**, suggestions delivered via SMS	[36–43]

(continued)

Table 2. (*continued*)

Strategy	Implementations	Sources
Reward	**Points**, **badges**, trophies, ribbons, coins, animated graphics	[22, 44–57]
Cooperation	**Teaming up with known people** (e.g., friends, co-workers, etc.), **teaming up with strangers**	[64–70]
Normative influence	**Group chats**, **forums**, blogs	[65, 71–76]
Social role	**Chat with human**, **chat with non-human** (e.g., virtual agents or chatbots)	[24, 58–63]

3   Methodology

The goal of our work is to investigate whether or not the perceived persuasiveness of distinct implementations of a strategy in the same system varies. To achieve this, we conducted an empirical study using a within-subject design and employing the following well-established procedure:

1. We selected six (6) strategies commonly used in persuasive systems design [15–20]: *self-monitoring, suggestion, reward, cooperation, normative influence,* and *social role* (see Table 1).
2. We identified various implementations of each strategy after a comprehensive literature search (see Table 2).
3. We chose two popular implementations per strategy (see the bolded implementations in Table 2) and then created high-fidelity prototype of each implementation in the context of smoking cessation.
4. We conducted a large-scale study to assess the perceived persuasiveness of each prototype/implementation.
5. We analyzed the data using statistical techniques/tools and presented our findings.

3.1   Prototype Design

To assess the perceived persuasiveness or effectiveness of distinct implementations of each strategy, we first created a low-fidelity prototype (LFP) to illustrate each implementation as a feature in a persuasive app for discouraging smoking behaviour. Each prototype was iteratively designed and refined based on evaluation feedback from fifteen (15) HCI and persuasive technology experts. Next, we created a high-fidelity version of each LFP which was evaluated by the same group of evaluators and refined based on their feedback. The prototypes were designed in such a way that target audience from diverse backgrounds can understand them easily. Figure 1 shows high-fidelity prototypes illustrating the *Suggestion* strategy: first implementation (*contextual pop-up tips*) and second implementation (*list of suggestions/tips accessible via a menu*), respectively. We created our prototypes using the Balsamiq [77] and proto.io [78] tools for low-fidelity and high-fidelity prototyping respectively.

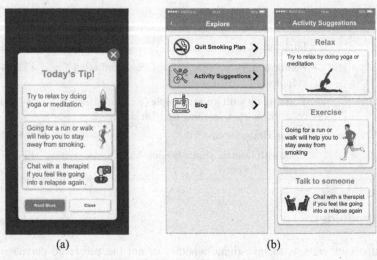

(a)   (b)

Fig. 1. (a) **Contextual pop-up tips** (first implementation of *Suggestion* strategy), and (b) **List of suggestions/tips accessible via a menu** (second implementation of *Suggestion* strategy).

3.2 Data Collection: Online Study

We conducted a large-scale study involving participants recruited using Amazon Mechanical Turk (MTurk). MTurk was chosen because it is an acceptable and reliable method of recruiting large and diverse participants and has been used in many HCI research including [9, 79–82]. Additionally, MTurk distributes surveys to the global audience in an efficient, secure, and cost-effective manner with high quality [83, 84]. The first part of the study comprises demographic questions such as age group, gender, marital status, educational qualification, and job category. In the second part, we presented the high-fidelity prototype illustrating each implementation of a strategy to participants, followed by questions that assess the perceived persuasiveness (or perceived effectiveness) of each prototype using the Perceived Persuasiveness Questionnaire (PPQ). The PPQ, adapted from [21], has been used in many persuasive technology research including [4, 9, 10, 82, 85] and consists of the following items measured using a 7-point Likert scale ranging from "1 – Strongly Disagree" to "7 – Strongly Agree":

1. This app would influence me to stop smoking
2. This app would convince me to stop smoking
3. This app would be personally relevant for me
4. This app would make me reconsider my smoking habits
5. The strategy would make or motivate me to use the app

Participants were also asked to provide qualitative comments about each prototype or implementation to justify their ratings.

Participants. To be eligible, participants must meet the following inclusion criteria: (i) 18 years or older, (ii) presently smoking or have smoked in the past, and (iii) proficient in

English. As shown in Table 3, our participants were diverse in terms of age group, marital status, educational qualification, and job category. This aligns with research evidence that more than 50% of MTurk users are between 18 to 35 years of age and that the same proportion (>50%) holds a minimum of Bachelor's degree, while a greater percentage are married [86, 87]. Also, a greater percentage of smokers have been shown to be males [88], in line with our participants' gender distribution (see Table 3). To prevent possible bias due to prototypes ordering, we used the randomization feature of the survey tool to change the order of the prototypes' presentation for each participant. Moreover, we conducted a pilot study involving 50 participants recruited from a university and MTurk to test the validity of our study instruments, prior to conducting the actual study.

We included 568 responses in our analysis, after removing incomplete responses and incorrect responses to comprehension and attention-based questions [83].

Table 3. Demographic distribution of participants.

Age	18–25 (12.7%), 26–35 (47.2%), 36–45 (20.8%), Above 45 (19.4%)
Gender	Male (65.5%), Female (33.4%), Other (1.1%)
Marital status	Single (20.2%), Married (76.2%), Divorced (0.7%), Separated (0.7%), Registered Partnership (1.1%), Widowed (0.4%); Other (0.7%)
Educational qualification	Bachelor's degree (52.5%), Master's degree (34.3%), Doctoral degree (1.1%), College diploma (3.3%), High school diploma or equivalent (7.2%), Less than high school diploma (0.4%), Other (1.2%)
Job category	Technology (26.8%), Finance (18.8%), Manufacturing (13.0%), Healthcare (10.2%), Education (5.1%), Construction (4.8%), Hospitality (2.8%), Others (18.5%)

3.3 Data Analysis

To analyze our data, we utilized well-established analytical methods and tools which are summarized below:

1. We computed the Kaiser-Meyer-Olkin (KMO) Measure of Sampling Adequacy and the Bartlett Test of Sphericity (BTS). Using SPSS version 27, our results showed that the KMO value was **0.948** (well above the recommended value of 0.6 [89]) which means that sampling is strongly adequate, while the BTS was statistically significant ($\chi^2(2145) = 29765.080$, $p < .0001$). These tests are necessary prior to multi-variable analysis.

2. To determine the persuasiveness score for each implementation of a strategy, we calculated the average rating of the five PPQ items per participant. Next, we conducted a One-Sample T-Test to examine the persuasiveness of individual implementations using neutral rating of 4 as the test value.

3. Next, we conducted a Paired-Samples T-Test with the two distinct implementations of each strategy as paired variables to compare their persuasiveness.
4. Finally, we performed thematic analysis of participants' qualitative comments to support their quantitative ratings.

4   Results

In this section, we present the results of our comparative analysis of distinct implementations of each strategy employed in the same system (smoking cessation app). We also support our findings with participants' qualitative feedback after conducting thematic analysis.

4.1   Comparing the Persuasiveness of Distinct Implementations of Each Strategy

The results of the One-Sample T-Test showed that the persuasiveness scores of the various implementations are significantly higher than the neutral rating of 4 ($p < .0001$), indicated by the horizontal line in Fig. 2. This means that participants perceived the implementations as persuasive; however, the persuasiveness of the first implementation (IMP-1) and second implementation (IMP-2) of each strategy varies, as shown in Fig. 2. To determine if the implementations are significantly different in their persuasiveness per strategy, we conducted a Paired-Samples T-Test.

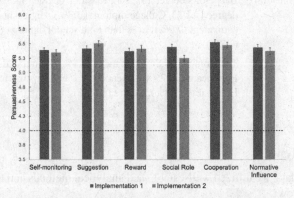

Fig. 2. A clustered bar chart showing the overall persuasiveness of two (2) distinct implementations of individual strategies. The horizontal line indicates the neutral rating of 4 (based on the 7-point Likert scale used in rating the PPQ items).

Suggestion Strategy. The results of the Paired-Samples T-Test revealed that IMP-2 (*Mean* = 5.507, *SD* = 1.078) of the strategy is perceived as significantly more persuasive ($p < .001$) than IMP-1 (*Mean* = 5.415, *SD* = 1.179). Findings from thematic analysis of qualitative comments showed that participants preferred IMP-2 (i.e., list of suggestions/tips accessible via a menu) because it offers *flexibility* to view recommendations or tips whenever required which in turn builds *confidence* in their ability to follow them. Conversely, participants who disliked IMP-1 (i.e., contextual pop-up tips) found the implementation to be *annoying, discouraging,* and *intrusive.* Below are sample comments from participants:

> *"Having the choice to seek out suggestions makes it more likely that they **will be followed**."* [P87] – IMP-2

> *"Pop-up suggestions just **annoy** me, and would make me **less likely to want to keep using the app**"* [P120] – IMP-1

Social Role Strategy. For social role strategy, IMP-1 (*Mean* = 5.442, *SD* = 1.159) is significantly more persuasive ($p < .001$) than IMP-2 (*Mean* = 5.250, *SD* = 1.227). Qualitative findings showed that participants prefer IMP-1 (i.e., chatting with a human therapist) because it: (i) makes them personally *accountable,* (ii) is *more effective,* (iii) promotes *self-awareness,* (iv) offers guaranteed *help and support* when needed, (v) provides *human touch,* (vi) is *encouraging* or *motivating,* (vii) increases *self-confidence,* and (viii) gives room for *expert* opinion. However, IMP-2 which involves chatting with a non-human therapist (virtual agent or chatbot) was perceived as *lacking human touch, non-intuitive, boring,* open to *data breach, hinderance* to achieving set goal (i.e., less effective), and *less satisfying.* Below are some of the comments from participants:

> *"I think having a human interaction would make me feel **personally accountable** for my decisions"* [P39] – IMP-1

> *"This would definitely be really **direct and personal**, it would be **hard to ignore** and a **nice resource**."* [P414] – IMP-1

> *"...I **deeply hate** being advised by a bot. **Impersonal, cold**, and feels being **treated just as another number in a statistic**."* [P192] – IMP-2

Cooperation Strategy. For cooperation strategy, IMP-1 (*Mean* = 5.524, *SD* = 1.105) is perceived as more persuasive than IMP-2 (*Mean* = 5.477, *SD* = 1.140), although the difference in persuasiveness is marginally significant ($p = .062$). Participants' qualitative feedback revealed that teaming up with friends (IMP-1) is *encouraging, motivating, helpful, appropriate,* and a *confidence builder.* However, IMP-2 (i.e., teaming up with strangers) is less preferred because it *lacks interpersonal relationship, reduces confidence,* raises *distrust* and *insecurity,* is *less motivating* as well as *less appealing/satisfying.* Sample comments from participants are shown below:

> *"This time being part of a team, especially with someone whom you can relate to, is a **big help** in stopping smoking process."* [P18] – IMP-1

> *"**No real motivation** when working with strangers. You don't know them and don't know if they'll **cheat** or if they'll even participate..."* [P98] – IMP-2

Normative Influence Strategy. IMP-1 (*Mean* = 5.437, *SD* = 1.232) of the strategy is perceived as more persuasive than IMP-2 (*Mean* = 5.374, *SD* = 1.313) but the difference in persuasiveness between both implementations is marginally significant ($p = .088$). Based on participants' qualitative feedback, IMP-1 (i.e., group chat) is preferred by participants because it: (i) increases *motivation*, (ii) offers *sense of belonging*, (iii) fosters *help and support* from peers, (iv) increases *self-confidence*, (v) acts as a *source of encouragement*, and (vii) promotes *openness in sharing personal experiences*. IMP-2 (i.e., discussion forum), however, was less preferred due to its susceptibility to *unsolicited ads*, *long posts* which could be *intimidating* and *boring*, and *misinformation*. Below are sample comments from participants:

> *"Being able to chat with others on the same journey would **motivate** me to **stick with my goals**. This app would **help** greatly."* [P287] – IMP-1

> *"Given the choice, I think chatting would be more helpful. **Articles/blogs may be more intimidating and full of bad advice**"* [P116] – IMP-2

Self-monitoring Strategy. For self-monitoring strategy, IMP-1 (*Mean* = 5.389, *SD* = 0.990) is more persuasive than IMP-2 (*Mean* = 5.348, *SD* = 1.126), but the persuasiveness of both implementations is not significantly different ($p = .155$). Based on qualitative findings, participants perceived IMP-1 (graphs/charts) as *visually appealing, easy to read and interpret, promoting self-awareness*, and *increasing self-confidence,* while IMP-2 (textual representation) was perceived as *boring* (not appealing), *less effective/helpful, hard to read/interpret, less intuitive*, and *less engaging*. Yet, some participants think IMP-2 could be as effective as IMP-1 (see [P510] below). Below are sample comments from participants:

> *"...Seeing myself shooting beyond the warning dots would **jolt me into taking precaution** and **avoid reaching the limit at all cost**."* [P152] – IMP-1

> *"I find the way it is displayed (text only) quite **boring** and it **doesn't appeal** to me."* [P60] – IMP-2

> *"Text is less engaging than it was with the charts, but it looks like it would **function the same**"* [P510] – IMP-2

Reward Strategy. Although IMP-2 (*Mean* = 5.414, *SD* = 1.256) of the Reward strategy is perceived as more persuasive than IMP-1 (*Mean* = 5.372, *SD* = 1.232), the difference in persuasiveness of both implementations is not significant ($p = .197$). Qualitative findings revealed that participants tend to have less preference for IMP-1 of the strategy (i.e., points) because it is *boring* and *not motivating enough*, compared to IMP-2 (badges) which they perceived as *motivating/encouraging, fun, attention grabbing*, a *sense of fulfillment*, a *confidence booster*, and *effective*. Also, some participants think points or badges are of no value since they cannot be exchanged for real-world incentives such as cash and gift cards (see [P77] below). Some of the comments from participants are shown below:

*"Badges are **more effective** and **attention grabbing** than points"* [P10] – IMP-2

*"Badges would **make me proud** of my achievements and progress"* [P119] – IMP-2

*"The points system is a little **boring** than a badge one"* [P326] – IMP-1

*"If the points got me a **gift card** it would be cool but **just getting points is useless**"* [P77] – IMP-1

5 Discussion

This work empirically examined and compared the perceived persuasiveness of different implementations of each persuasive strategy in the same system. Our results showed that the persuasiveness of strategy implementations varies which means that people are motivated differently by different implementations of the same strategy in the same system. For example, implementing *suggestion* strategy as a list of tips or suggestions accessible on demand via a menu was perceived as significantly more persuasive than contextual pop-up tips. In other words, people prefer to navigate the system to view suggestions/tips as needed rather than having the system pops them up which could be intrusive, as revealed in this qualitative comment: *"Could be intrusive. I don't know the timer. If the popup is once a week, could be OK"* [P71]. Nevertheless, contextual tips offer timely suggestions which has been shown to be effective in behaviour change interventions [90] but the interval should be adaptive such that the suggestions do not pop-up while the user is actively engaged (e.g., on a phone call or attending an online meeting). Therefore, we recommend that **to appeal to a wider audience, designers of persuasive applications should offer users the flexibility of viewing in-app suggestions/tips whenever required (on demand). They may also offer adaptive contextual tips that are non-intrusive**.

Regarding the *social role* strategy, people prefer to interact with a human rather than a virtual agent or chatbot, based on our findings. Participants were doubtful about a chatbot's ability to be empathetic, respond dynamically to emotions, and provide accurate response to their queries. They were also skeptical about the protection or confidentiality of the sensitive data collected while interacting with the chatbot. These findings align with research evidence on chatbots' limitations in the healthcare domain [91, 92]. Therefore, **to motivate users of persuasive applications, designers should provide a means of interacting with human specialists when necessary. On the other hand, if a chatbot or agent is used, it should be emotionally sensitive and users need to be assured of the confidentiality of their sensitive data**.

Furthermore, as regards the *cooperation* strategy, our findings showed that people found teaming up with friends to be more persuasive or effective than collaborating with strangers. Participants' qualitative feedback revealed "trust" as a major factor for choosing friends over strangers. This agrees with research evidence that people generally trust those they already know (such as friends, relatives, neighbours, colleagues, etc.) [93]. However, some participants still prefer working with strangers probably because it shields them from being judged by friends/family members or due to other personal reasons, as shown in the following comment: *"I would rather work with strangers than friends or family. Motivation from strangers would be more beneficial to me personally."* [P54]. Therefore, **to motivate a wider audience, persuasive systems designers should** allow users to choose who they would like to collaborate with – a friend or stranger or both.

As regards *normative influence* strategy, people prefer group chats to discussion forums or blogs, according to our findings. The social interaction and connectedness with peers in a group is the main motivating factor for participants, while reading random and possibly long posts in forums/blogs was found to be intimidating and demotivating. Therefore, **designers of persuasive systems should provide chat rooms in which people can communicate interactively and openly with peers**.

Moreover, implementing *self-monitoring* strategy in form of graphs or charts (IMP-1) was perceived as more persuasive than a textual representation (IMP-2) of users' progress/performance. This is because participants found the progress charts to be easy to read/interpret and better at grabbing their attention than the text-only equivalent, based on our findings. This confirms existing research in that people generally perceive visuals as more effective, helpful, and trustworthy than texts [94, 95]. Interestingly, the use of appropriate colors to indicate progress levels (e.g., green for "good" progress and red for "not good") in both IMP-1 and IMP-2 made some participants to perceive both implementations as equally effective, as shown in the following comment: *"The red and green numbers are as effective as the graph" [P43]*. Therefore, **designers of persuasive applications should prioritize the use of visuals such as graphs or charts to show users' progress/performance. In cases where texts are utilized, appropriate use of colours to indicate performance level could increase motivation.**

As regards *reward* strategy, our results showed that participants perceived badges as more persuasive than points. Also, participants want to exchange accumulated badges or points for tangible items including money, gift cards, goods, etc. While tangible rewards could improve user engagement [96], offering tangible rewards to people who are already motivated could confuse them about the real motives [97] and benefits of adopting a healthy behaviour [10]. Therefore, **we suggest that although designers of persuasive systems could consider exchanging virtual rewards with tangible items to increase user motivation, they should apply caution to avoid redirecting the actual benefit of adopting a desired behaviour to something external. Designers should choose badges over points as reward implementation.**

Finally, this study utilized a large sample size distributed across diverse population; hence, our findings would be stable. However, future research is needed to examine whether changes in sample size and personal/social characteristics of participants will have little or no effect on study findings.

6 Conclusion and Future Work

In this paper, we conducted a large-scale study of 568 participants to investigate and compare the perceived persuasiveness/effectiveness of distinct implementations of each strategy in the same system. Our work makes novel contributions to PT research in HCI by showing that the perceived persuasiveness of distinct implementations of the same strategy varies and that the implementations motivate for different reasons. Based on these findings, we offer practical guidelines on how to tailor persuasive systems by selecting appropriate strategy implementations. Future research will conduct further studies to investigate how to adapt strategy implementations to individuals based on certain characteristics such as personality traits and stages of behaviour change.

Acknowledgement. This research was undertaken, in part, thanks to funding from the Canada Research Chairs Program. We acknowledge the support of the Natural Sciences and Engineering Research Council of Canada (NSERC) through the Discovery Grant.

References

1. Fogg, B.J., Fogg, G.E.: Persuasive Technology: Using Computers to Change What We Think and Do. Morgan Kaufmann, San Francisco (2003)
2. Cialdini, R.B.: Harnessing the science of persuasion. Harv. Bus. Rev. **79**, 72–81 (2001)
3. Oinas-Kukkonen, H., Harjumaa, M.: Persuasive systems design: key issues, process model, and system features. Commun. Assoc. Inf. Syst. **24**, 96 (2009)
4. Orji, R., Nacke, L.E., Di Marco, C.: Towards personality-driven persuasive health games and gamified systems. In: Proceedings of the 2017 CHI Conference on Human Factors in Computing Systems - CHI 2017, pp. 1015–1027 (2017)
5. Orji, R., Mandryk, R.L., Vassileva, J.: Gender, age, and responsiveness to cialdini's persuasion strategies. In: MacTavish, T., Basápur, S. (eds.) PERSUASIVE 2015. LNCS, vol. 9072, pp. 147–159. Springer, Cham (2015). https://doi.org/10.1007/978-3-319-20306-5_14
6. Orji, R., Abdullahi, A.M., Oyibo, K.: Personalizing persuasive technologies: do gender and age affect susceptibility to persuasive strategies? In: Adjunct Publication of the 26th Conference on User Modeling, Adaptation and Personalization, Singapore, Singapore, pp. 329–334. Association for Computing Machinery, Inc. (2018)
7. Noorbehbahani, F., Zarein, Z.: The impact of demographic factors on persuasion strategies in personalized recommender system. In: 2018 8th International Conference on Computer and Knowledge Engineering, ICCKE 2018, pp. 104–109. Institute of Electrical and Electronics Engineers Inc. (2018)
8. Kaptein, M., Duplinsky, S., Markopoulos, P.: Means based adaptive persuasive systems. In: Proceedings of the SIGCHI Conference on Human Factors in Computing Systems, Vancouver, BC, Canada, pp. 335–344 (2011)
9. Orji, R., Tondello, G.F., Nacke, L.E.: Personalizing persuasive strategies in gameful systems to gamification user types. In: Proceedings of the 2018 CHI Conference on Human Factors in Computing Systems - CHI 2018, pp. 1–14 (2018)
10. Orji, R., Vassileva, J., Mandryk, R.L.: Modeling the efficacy of persuasive strategies for different gamer types in serious games for health. User Model. User-Adap. Inter. **24**(5), 453–498 (2014). https://doi.org/10.1007/s11257-014-9149-8
11. Busch, M., et al.: Using player type models for personalized game design - an empirical investigation. Interact. Des. Archit. **28**, 145–163 (2016)
12. Oyebode, O., Orji, R.: Deconstructing persuasive strategies in mental health apps based on user reviews using natural language processing. In: Proceedings of the Eighth International Workshop on Behavior Change Support Systems co-located with the 15th International Conference on Persuasive Technology (PERSUASIVE 2020), pp. 1–13. CEUR-WS (2020)
13. Karlijn, S., Nibbeling, N., Wang, S., Ettema, D., Simons, M.: Unraveling mobile health exercise interventions for adults: scoping review on the implementations and designs of persuasive strategies. JMIR Mhealth Uhealth **9**, e16282 (2021). https://doi.org/10.2196/16282
14. Alqahtani, F., Meier, S., Orji, R.: Personality-based approach for tailoring persuasive mental health applications. User Model. User-Adapted Interact. **2021**, 1–43 (2021). https://doi.org/10.1007/S11257-021-09289-5

15. Orji, R., Moffatt, K.: Persuasive technology for health and wellness: state-of-the-art and emerging trends. Health Inform. J. **24**, 66–91 (2018). https://doi.org/10.1177/1460458216650979

16. Wiafe, I., Nakata, K.: Bibliographic analysis of persuasive systems: techniques, methods and domains of application. In: 7th International Conference on Persuasive Technology (PERSUASIVE 2012), Linköping, Sweden, pp. 61–64 (2012)

17. Oyebode, O., Alqahtani, F., Orji, R.: Using machine learning and thematic analysis methods to evaluate mental health apps based on user reviews. IEEE Access. **8**, 111141–111158 (2020). https://doi.org/10.1109/ACCESS.2020.3002176

18. Portz, J.D., Miller, A., Foster, B., Laudeman, L.: Persuasive features in health information technology interventions for older adults with chronic diseases: a systematic review. Heal. Technol. **6**(2), 89–99 (2016). https://doi.org/10.1007/s12553-016-0130-x

19. Almutari, N., Orji, R.: How effective are social influence strategies in persuasive apps for promoting physical activity? A systematic review. In: ACM UMAP 2019 Adjunct - Adjunct Publication of the 27th Conference on User Modeling, Adaptation and Personalization, pp. 167–172. Association for Computing Machinery, Inc (2019)

20. Orji, R., Oyibo, K., Lomotey, R.K., Orji, F.A.: Socially-driven persuasive health intervention design: competition, social comparison, and cooperation. Health Inform. J. **25**, 1451–1484 (2019). https://doi.org/10.1177/1460458218766570

21. Thomas, R.J., Masthoff, J., Oren, N.: Can i influence you? Development of a scale to measure perceived persuasiveness and two studies showing the use of the scale. Front. Artif. Intell. **2**, 1–14 (2019). https://doi.org/10.3389/FRAI.2019.00024

22. Hosseini, S., Krüger, A., Altmeyer, M., Lessel, P.: SilverCycling: evaluating persuasive strategies to promote physical activity among older adults. In: Proceedings of the 2018 ACM Conference Companion Publication on Designing Interactive Systems, Hong Kong, China, pp. 45–50. Association for Computing Machinery, Inc (2018)

23. Muneer, A., Fati, S.M., Fuddah, S.: Smart health monitoring system using IoT based smart fitness mirror. Telkomnika (Telecommunication Comput. Electron. Control), 317–331 (2020). https://doi.org/10.12928/TELKOMNIKA.v18i1.12434

24. Ganesan, A.N., et al.: International mobile-health intervention on physical activity, sitting, and weight: the Stepathlon cardiovascular health study. J. Am. Coll. Cardiol. **67**, 2453–2463 (2016). https://doi.org/10.1016/j.jacc.2016.03.472

25. Consolvo, S., Everitt, K., Smith, I., Landay, J.A.: Design requirements for technologies that encourage physical activity. In: Proceedings of the SIGCHI Conference on Human Factors in Computing Systems, Montreal, Quebec, Canada, pp. 457–466. Association for Computing Machinery (2006)

26. Toscos, T., Faber, A., Connelly, K., Upoma, A.M.: Encouraging Physical Activity in Teens: can technology help reduce barriers to physical activity in adolescent girls? In: 2nd International Conference on Pervasive Computing Technologies for Healthcare (PervasiveHealthcare), pp. 218–221 (2008)

27. Miller, A.D., Mynatt, E.D.: StepStream: a school-based pervasive social fitness system for everyday adolescent health. In: Proceedings of the SIGCHI Conference on Human Factors in Computing Systems, Toronto, Ontario, Canada, pp. 2823–2832. Association for Computing Machinery (2014)

28. Paay, J., Kjeldskov, J., Skov, M.B., Lichon, L., Rasmussen, S.: Understanding individual differences for tailored smoking cessation apps. In: Proceedings of the 33rd Annual ACM Conference on Human Factors in Computing Systems, Seoul, Republic of Korea, pp. 1699–1708. Association for Computing Machinery (2015)

29. Duan, H., et al.: Using goal-directed design to create a mobile health app to improve patient compliance with hypertension self-management: development and deployment. JMIR mHealth uHealth. **8**, e14466 (2020). https://doi.org/10.2196/14466

30. Hendrie, G.A., James-Martin, G., Williams, G., Brindal, E., Whyte, B., Crook, A.: The development of VegEze: smartphone app to increase vegetable consumption in Australian adults. JMIR Form. Res. **3**, e10731 (2019). https://doi.org/10.2196/10731

31. Rapeepisarn, T., Tatiyanupanwong, S., Kornvisitvatin, B., Tangsripairoj, S.: IRelief: an Android application for smartphone syndrome prevention and treatment. In: Proceedings of the 2016 5th ICT International Student Project Conference, ICT-ISPC 2016, pp. 121–124 (2016). https://doi.org/10.1109/ICT-ISPC.2016.7519251

32. Altmeyer, M., Lessel, P., Sander, T., Krüger, A.: Extending a gamified mobile app with a public display to encourage walking. In: Proceedings of the 22nd International Academic Mindtrek Conference, New York, NY, USA, pp. 20–29. ACM (2018)

33. Patterson, T., et al.: KeepWell: a generic platform for the self-management of chronic conditions. In: Kyriacou, E., Christofides, S., Pattichis, C.S. (eds.) XIV Mediterranean Conference on Medical and Biological Engineering and Computing 2016. IP, vol. 57, pp. 891–896. Springer, Cham (2016). https://doi.org/10.1007/978-3-319-32703-7_174

34. Zan, S., Agboola, S., Moore, S.A., Parks, K.A., Kvedar, J.C., Jethwani, K.: Patient engagement with a mobile web-based telemonitoring system for heart failure self-management: a pilot study. JMIR mHealth uHealth. **3**, e33 (2015). https://doi.org/10.2196/mhealth.3789

35. Hong, Y.A., et al.: Efficacy of a mobile-enabled web app (iCanFit) in promoting physical activity among older cancer survivors: a pilot study. JMIR Cancer **1**, e7 (2015). https://doi.org/10.2196/CANCER.4389

36. Fuller-Tyszkiewicz, M., et al.: A mobile app-based intervention for depression: end-user and expert usability testing study. JMIR Ment. Heal. **5**, e54 (2018). https://doi.org/10.2196/mental.9445

37. Salim, M.H.M., Ali, N.M., Noah, S.A.M.: Mobile application on healthy diet for elderly based on persuasive design. Int. J. Adv. Sci. Eng. Inf. Technol. **7**, 222–227 (2017)

38. de la TorreDíez, I., Garcia-Zapirain, B., López-Coronado, M., Rodrigues, J.J.P.C., del Pozo Vegas, C.: A new mHealth app for monitoring and awareness of healthy eating: development and user evaluation by Spanish users. J. Med. Syst. **41**(7), 1–7 (2017). https://doi.org/10.1007/s10916-017-0753-0

39. Oyebode, O., Graham-Kalio, B., Orji, R.: HeartHealth: a persuasive mobile app for mitigating the risk of ischemic heart disease. In: Gram-Hansen, S.B., Jonasen, T.S., Midden, C. (eds.) PERSUASIVE 2020. LNCS, vol. 12064, pp. 126–138. Springer, Cham (2020). https://doi.org/10.1007/978-3-030-45712-9_10

40. Hassandra, M., et al.: Effectiveness of a mobile phone app for adults that uses physical activity as a tool to manage cigarette craving after smoking cessation: a study protocol for a randomized controlled trial. JMIR Res. Protoc. **4**, e125 (2015). https://doi.org/10.2196/resprot.4600

41. Siawsolit, C., Seepun, S., Choi, J., Do, A., Kao, Y.: Personalized assistant for health-conscious grocery shoppers. In: de Vries, P.W., Oinas-Kukkonen, H., Siemons, L., Beerlage-de Jong, N., van Gemert-Pijnen, L. (eds.) PERSUASIVE 2017. LNCS, vol. 10171, pp. 95–106. Springer, Cham (2017). https://doi.org/10.1007/978-3-319-55134-0_8

42. Anagnostopoulou, E., Bothos, E., Magoutas, B., Schrammel, J., Mentzas, G.: Persuasive interventions for sustainable travel choices leveraging users' personality and mobility type. In: Ham, J., Karapanos, E., Morita, P.P., Burns, C.M. (eds.) PERSUASIVE 2018. LNCS, vol. 10809, pp. 229–241. Springer, Cham (2018). https://doi.org/10.1007/978-3-319-78978-1_19

43. Chen, T., et al.: Are you smoking? Automatic alert system helping people keep away from cigarettes. Smart Heal. **9–10**, 158–169 (2018). https://doi.org/10.1016/j.smhl.2018.07.008

44. Bascur, A., Rossel, P., Herskovic, V., Martínez-Carrasco, C.: Evitapp: persuasive application for physical activity and smoking cessation. In: Proceedings (2018). https://doi.org/10.3390/proceedings2191208

45. Orji, R., Vassileva, J., Mandryk, R.L.: LunchTime: a slow-casual game for long-term dietary behavior change. Pers. Ubiquitous Comput. **17**, 1211–1221 (2013). https://doi.org/10.1007/s00779-012-0590-6

46. Almonani, E., Husain, W., San, O.Y., Almomani, A., Al-Betar, M.: Mobile game approach to prevent childhood obesity using persuasive technology. In: 2014 International Conference on Computer and Information Sciences, ICCOINS 2014 - A Conference of World Engineering, Science and Technology Congress, ESTCON 2014 – Proceedings, pp. 1–5 (2014). https://doi.org/10.1109/ICCOINS.2014.6868418

47. Fanning, J., Roberts, S., Hillman, C.H., Mullen, S.P., Ritterband, L., McAuley, E.: A smartphone "app"-delivered randomized factorial trial targeting physical activity in adults. J. Behav. Med. **40**(5), 712–729 (2017). https://doi.org/10.1007/s10865-017-9838-y

48. Zuckerman, O., Gal-Oz, A.: Deconstructing gamification: evaluating the effectiveness of continuous measurement, virtual rewards, and social comparison for promoting physical activity. Pers. Ubiquit. Comput. **18**(7), 1705–1719 (2014). https://doi.org/10.1007/s00779-014-0783-2

49. Haque, S., Isomursu, M., Kangas, M., Jämsä, T.: Measuring the influence of a persuasive application to promote physical activity. In: Personalizing Persuasive Technologies (PPT) Workshop at PERSUASIVE 2018 Conference, pp. 43–57 (2018)

50. De Oliveira, R., Cherubini, M., Oliver, N.: MoviPill: improving medication compliance for elders using a mobile persuasive social game. In: UbiComp 2010 - Proceedings of the 2010 ACM Conference on Ubiquitous Computing, pp. 251–260 (2010)

51. Ganesh, S., Marshall, P., Rogers, Y., O'Hara, K.: FoodWorks: tackling fussy eating by digitally augmenting children's meals. In: Proceedings of the NordiCHI 2014: The 8th Nordic Conference on Human-Computer Interaction: Fun, Fast, Foundational, New York, New York, USA, pp. 147–156. Association for Computing Machinery, Inc (2014)

52. Munson, S.A., Consolvo, S.: Exploring goal-setting, rewards, self-monitoring, and sharing to motivate physical activity. In: 2012 6th International Conference on Pervasive Computing Technologies for Healthcare Workshop, PervasiveHealth 2012, pp. 25–32 (2012). https://doi.org/10.4108/ICST.PERVASIVEHEALTH.2012.248691

53. Oyebode, O., Maurya, D., Orji, R.: Nourish your tree! Developing a persuasive exergame for promoting physical activity among adults. In: 2020 IEEE 8th International Conference on Serious Games and Applications for Health, SeGAH 2020, pp. 1–7. Institute of Electrical and Electronics Engineers Inc. (2020)

54. Aino, A., et al.: Mobile mental wellness training for stress management: feasibility and design implications based on a one-month field study. JMIR Mhealth Uhealth **1**(2), e11, e2596 (2013). https://doi.org/10.2196/MHEALTH.2596. https://mhealth.jmir.org/2013/2/e11

55. Consolvo, S., et al.: Activity sensing in the wild: a field trial of UbiFit Garden. In: Conference on Human Factors in Computing Systems – Proceedings, pp. 1797–1806 (2008). https://doi.org/10.1145/1357054.1357335

56. Consolvo, S., et al.: Flowers or a robot army?: Encouraging awareness & activity with personal, mobile displays. In: Proceedings of the 10th International Conference on Ubiquitous Computing - UbiComp 2008, pp. 54–63 (2008)

57. Ahtinen, A., Huuskonen, P., Häkkilä, J.: Let's all get up and walk to the north pole: design and evaluation of a mobile wellness application. In: Proceedings of the 6th Nordic Conference on Human-Computer Interaction Extending Boundaries - NordiCHI 2010, New York, New York, USA, pp. 3–12. ACM Press (2010)

58. Paay, J., Kjeldskov, J., Skov, M.B., Srikandarajah, N., Brinthaparan, U.: Personal counseling on smart phones for smoking cessation. In: Proceedings of the 33rd Annual ACM Conference Extended Abstracts on Human Factors in Computing Systems, Seoul, Republic of Korea, pp. 1427–1432. Association for Computing Machinery (2015)

59. Bomfim, M.C.C., Wallace, J.R.: Pirate Bri's grocery adventure: teaching food literacy through shopping. In: Extended Abstracts of the 2018 CHI Conference on Human Factors in Computing Systems, Montreal QC, Canada, pp. 1–6. Association for Computing Machinery (2018)

60. Patwardhan, M., Amresh, A., Stoll, R., Gary, K.A., Hamel, D.B., Pina, A.: Designing a mobile application to support the indicated prevention and early intervention of childhood anxiety. In: Proceedings of the conference on Wireless Health, Bethesda, Maryland, pp. 1–8. Association for Computing Machinery, Inc (2015)

61. Silva, J.M., Zamarripa, S., Moran, E.B., Tentori, M., Galicia, L.: Promoting a healthy lifestyle through a Virtual Specialist solution. In: CHI 2006 Extended Abstracts on Human Factors in Computing Systems, Montreal, Quebec, Canada, pp. 1867–1872. ACM Press (2006)

62. Calvaresi, D., Calbimonte, J.P., Dubosson, F., Najjar, A., Schumacher, M.: Social network chatbots for smoking cessation: agent and multi-agent frameworks. In: 2019 IEEE/WIC/ACM International Conference on Web Intelligence (WI), Thessaloniki, Greece, pp. 286–292. Association for Computing Machinery, Inc (2019)

63. Chung, K., Cho, H.Y., Park, J.Y.: A chatbot for perinatal women's and partners' obstetric and mental health care: development and usability evaluation study. JMIR Med. Inf. **9**, e18607 (2021). https://doi.org/10.2196/18607

64. Staiano, A., Kihm, H.S., Sandoval, P.: The use of competition to elicit vigorous intensity physical activity during children's exergame play. J. Fam. Consum. Sci. **110**, 39–47 (2018). https://doi.org/10.14307/jfcs110.3.39

65. Horsch, C., Brinkman, W.-P., van Eijk, R., Neerincx, M.: Towards the usage of persuasive strategies in a virtual sleep coach. In: 26th BCS Conference on Human Computer Interaction (HCI), pp. 1–4. BCS Learning & Development (2012)

66. Liew, S.J., Gorny, A.W., Tan, C.S., Müller-Riemenschneider, F.: A mobile health team challenge to promote stepping and stair climbing activities: exploratory feasibility study. JMIR Mhealth Uhealth **8**(2), e12665 (2020). https://doi.org/10.2196/12665. https://mhealth.jmir.org/2020/2/e12665

67. Edney, S., et al.: "Active Team" a social and gamified app-based physical activity intervention: randomised controlled trial study protocol. BMC Public Health **17**, 859 (2017). https://doi.org/10.1186/s12889-017-4882-7

68. Kernot, J., Olds, T., Lewis, L.K., Maher, C.: Usability testing and piloting of the mums step it up program - a team-based social networking physical activity intervention for women with young children. PLoS One **9**, e108842 (2014). https://doi.org/10.1371/JOURNAL.PONE.0108842

69. Kanstrup, A.M., Bertelsen, P.S., Knudsen, C.: Changing health behavior with social technology? A pilot test of a mobile app designed for social support of physical activity. Int. J. Environ. Res. Public Heal. **17**, 8383 (2020). https://doi.org/10.3390/IJERPH17228383

70. Ren, X., Yu, B., Lu, Y., Brombacher, A.: Exploring cooperative fitness tracking to encourage physical activity among office workers. Proc. ACM Hum.-Comput. Interact. **2**, 20 (2018). https://doi.org/10.1145/3274415

71. Pollak, J.P., Gay, G., Byrne, S., Wagner, E., Retelny, D., Humphreys, L.: It's time to Eat! Using mobile games to promote healthy eating. IEEE Pervasive Comput. **9**, 21–27 (2010). https://doi.org/10.1109/MPRV.2010.41

72. Eikey, E.V., et al.: Desire to be underweight: exploratory study on a weight loss app community and user perceptions of the impact on disordered eating behaviors. JMIR Mhealth Uhealth **5**, e6683 (2017). https://doi.org/10.2196/MHEALTH.6683

73. Oyebode, O., Alhasani, M., Mulchandani, D., Olagunju, T., Orji, R.: SleepFit: a persuasive mobile app for improving sleep habits in young adults. In: SeGAH 2021 - 2021 IEEE 9th International Conference on Serious Games and Applications for Health, pp. 1–8 (2021). https://doi.org/10.1109/SEGAH52098.2021.9551907

74. Graham, C., Rouncefield, M., Satchell, C.: Blogging as "therapy"? Exploring personal technologies for smoking cessation. Health Inform. J. **15**, 267–281 (2009). https://doi.org/10.1177/1460458209345897

75. Mukhtar, H., Ali, A., Belaid, D., Lee, S.: Persuasive healthcare self-management in intelligent environments. In: Proceedings - 8th International Conference on Intelligent Environments, IE 2012, pp. 190–197 (2012)

76. Duong, H.T., Hopfer, S.: Let's chat: development of a family group chat cancer prevention intervention for vietnamese families. Heal. Educ. Behav. **48**, 208–219 (2021). https://doi.org/10.1177/1090198121990389

77. Balsamiq: Balsamiq. Rapid, effective and fun wireframing software. https://balsamiq.com/

78. Protoio Inc.: Proto.io - Prototypes that feel real. https://proto.io/

79. Jia, Y., Xu, B., Karanam, Y., Voida, S.: Personality-targeted gamification: a survey study on personality traits and motivational affordances. In: Proceedings of the 2016 CHI Conference on Human Factors in Computing Systems, San Jose, California, USA, pp. 2001–2013. Association for Computing Machinery (2016)

80. Koshy, V., Park, J.S.: We just use what they give us: understanding passenger user perspectives in smart homes. In: Conference on Human Factors in Computing Systems (2021). https://doi.org/10.1145/3411764.3445598

81. Hasan, R., Bertenthal, B.I., Hugenberg, K., Kapadia, A.: Your photo is so funny that i don't mind violating your privacy by sharing it: effects of individual humor styles on online photo-sharing behaviors. In: Conference on Human Factors in Computing Systems (2021). https://doi.org/10.1145/3411764.3445258

82. Oyebode, O., Ndulue, C., Mulchandani, D., Adib, A.A.Z., Alhasani, M., Orji, R.: Tailoring persuasive and behaviour change systems based on stages of change and motivation. In: CHI Conference on Human Factors in Computing Systems (CHI 2021), Yokohama, Japan, 19 pages. ACM, New York (2021)

83. Mason, W., Suri, S.: Conducting behavioral research on Amazon's Mechanical Turk. Behav. Res. Methods. **44**, 1–23 (2012). https://doi.org/10.3758/s13428-011-0124-6

84. Buhrmester, M., Kwang, T., Gosling, S.D.: Amazon's Mechanical Turk: a new source of inexpensive, yet high-quality data? In: Kazdin, A.E. (ed.) Methodological Issues and Strategies in Clinical Research, 4th edn., pp. 133–139. American Psychological Association (2015)

85. Wais-Zechmann, B., Gattol, V., Neureiter, K., Orji, R., Tscheligi, M.: Persuasive technology to support chronic health conditions: investigating the optimal persuasive strategies for persons with COPD. In: Ham, J., Karapanos, E., Morita, P.P., Burns, C.M. (eds.) PERSUASIVE 2018. LNCS, vol. 10809, pp. 255–266. Springer, Cham (2018). https://doi.org/10.1007/978-3-319-78978-1_21

86. Ross, J., Zaldivar, A., Irani, L., Tomlinson, B.: Who are the turkers? Worker demographics in amazon mechanical turk. Technical report (2009)

87. Difallah, D., Filatova, E., Ipeirotis, P.: Demographics and dynamics of Mechanical Turk workers. In: WSDM 2018 - Proceedings of the 11th ACM International Conference on Web Search and Data Mining, pp. 135–143. Association for Computing Machinery, Inc (2018)

88. Higgins, S.T., et al.: A literature review on prevalence of gender differences and intersections with other vulnerabilities to tobacco use in the United States, 2004–2014. Prev. Med. (Baltim) **80**, 89–100 (2015). https://doi.org/10.1016/j.ypmed.2015.06.009

89. Kaiser, H.F.: A second generation little jiffy. Psychometrika **35**, 401–415 (1970)

90. Fry, J.P., Neff, R.A.: Periodic prompts and reminders in health promotion and health behavior interventions: Systematic review. J. Med. Internet Res. **11**, e16 (2009). https://doi.org/10.2196/jmir.1138

91. Palanica, A., Flaschner, P., Thommandram, A., Li, M., Fossat, Y.: Physicians' perceptions of chatbots in health care: cross-sectional web-based survey. J. Med. Internet Res. **21**, e12887 (2019). https://doi.org/10.2196/12887

92. Powell, J.: Trust me, i'm a chatbot: how artificial intelligence in health care fails the turing test. J. Med. Internet Res. **21**, e16222 (2019). https://doi.org/10.2196/16222

93. Bauer, P.C., Freitag, M.: Measuring Trust. The Oxford Handbook of Social and Political Trust, pp. 15–36 (2018). https://doi.org/10.1093/OXFORDHB/9780190274801.013.1

94. Hall, M.G., Grummon, A.H., Lazard, A.J., Maynard, O.M., Taillie, L.S.: Reactions to graphic and text health warnings for cigarettes, sugar-sweetened beverages, and alcohol: an online randomized experiment of US adults. Prev. Med. (Baltim) **137**, 106120 (2020). https://doi.org/10.1016/J.YPMED.2020.106120

95. Tait, A.R., Voepel-Lewis, T., Zikmund-Fisher, B.J., Fagerlin, A.: The effect of format on parents' understanding of the risks and benefits of clinical research: a comparison between text, tables, and graphics **15**, 487–501 (2010). https://doi.org/10.1080/10810730.2010.492560. http://dx.doi.org/10.1080/10810730.2010.492560

96. Lemola, S., et al.: Can a 'rewards-for-exercise app' increase physical activity, subjective well-being and sleep quality? An open-label single-arm trial among university staff with low to moderate physical activity levels. BMC Public Heal. **211**, 21, 1–10 (2021). https://doi.org/10.1186/S12889-021-10794-W

97. Cherubini, M., Villalobos-Zuñiga, G., Boldi, M.-O., Bonazzi, R.: The unexpected downside of paying or sending messages to people to make them walk. ACM Trans. Comput. Interact. **27**, 1–44 (2020). https://doi.org/10.1145/3365665

Player Matching in a Persuasive Mobile Exergame: Towards Performance-Driven Collaboration and Adaptivity

Oladapo Oyebode(✉) and Rita Orji

Faculty of Computer Science, Dalhousie University, Halifax, NS B3H 4R2, Canada
{oladapo.oyebode,rita.orji}@dal.ca

Abstract. Persuasive technologies (PTs) for promoting physical activity (PA) have experienced widespread attention over the years. However, limited knowledge exists on how best to design and match individuals in cooperative or social-based physical activity PTs to achieve the best outcome. It is established that people in the same group influence each other's behaviours. Although few group formation techniques have been proposed in the literature, none of these techniques consider individuals' normal PA levels in the real-world prior to assigning them to groups as a dimension to inform group formation. In this paper, we propose a group formation approach called *Performance-based User Matching* (PUM) which is based on the hypothesis that assigning users with similar PA levels to the same group (SG) will increase motivation and collective performance, compared to grouping users with dissimilar or mixed PA levels (MG). We empirically validated this approach in an exergaming context by conducting a 6-week field study using a persuasive exergame we developed to investigate and compare the SG and MG paradigms in terms of PA performance (step counts). Our findings show that players in the SG groups significantly increased their PA levels compared to those in the MG groups. Also, players in the SG groups individually and collectively exceeded their baseline steps during the intervention period, compared to those in the MG groups. Our findings hold promises for adaptive user matching and socially-driven persuasive applications design.

Keywords: Player matching · Physical activity · Cooperative work · Persuasive exergaming · User matching · Group formation · Group-based competition · Performance-based user matching

1 Introduction

Physical activity (PA) is a contributor to quality health and well-being. However, most people do not engage in consistent PA needed to achieve their health and wellness goals [1]. For instance, research has shown that up to 65% of US adults engage in sedentary behaviour (SB), such as watching TV, videos, or computer use outside school/work [2]. Consequently, SB and physical inactivity/low PA contribute to disease burden [3–15] and mortality [4, 16, 17]. Hence, increasing PA and reducing SB will practically improve physical and mental well-being [18–20].

© Springer Nature Switzerland AG 2022
N. Baghaei et al. (Eds.): PERSUASIVE 2022, LNCS 13213, pp. 164–173, 2022.
https://doi.org/10.1007/978-3-030-98438-0_13

To promote PA, mobile technologies equipped with activity sensors and behaviour change strategies have witnessed widespread use over the years. Majority of existing works in this area, however, target individuals directly and have not explored the possibility of increasing PA levels by grouping users based on commonalities. Cooperation, which is a persuasive strategy that provides the means for people to work together to achieve a shared behaviour goal [21], has been found to provide mutual support, group encouragement, and reinforcement [22]. Research has also shown that cooperative exergaming increases motivation, self-efficacy, and persistence [23]. This presents a challenge on how to group people (or match players to a team) for a better outcome such that individuals in a group are motivated and increase their physical activity levels. Few studies that explore grouping effects on PA adopted various approaches for matching people including physical proximity [24, 25], social connectedness [26], and personality traits [27]. Since people in the same group influence each other's behaviours [28], upward comparison (i.e., comparing oneself with an individual performing better) and downward comparison (i.e., comparing oneself with a worse-performing individual) could occur [29]. Consequently, individuals could be demotivated by either feeling incompetent to contribute meaningfully to overall group performance or perceiving others as not doing enough and hence scale back their commitment to the group (thereby reducing their PA levels). We hypothesize that this issue could be addressed by matching people in groups based on their PA levels in the real-world such that individuals with similar PA levels are assigned to the same group. Hence, the overarching hypothesis guiding this study is that *matching individuals with similar PA level will lead to greater increase in PA.*

Therefore, in this paper, we propose a concept named Performance-based User Matching (PUM). The PUM is based on the premise that assigning players with similar PA levels to the same group (SG) will increase motivation and overall performance, compared to grouping players with dissimilar or mixed PA levels (MG). To the best of our knowledge, this approach is yet to be empirically studied in the literature within the context of persuasive exergaming. We validate the PUM concept by conducting a 6-week field study using our TreeCare persuasive exergame [30–32] to investigate and compare the SG and MG paradigms in terms of players' PA levels and collective performance. The game operationalized PA levels using step counts.

Our work offers four contributions in the area of persuasive technology (PT) for improving PA and discouraging SB: First, we propose the PUM approach to motivate players to increase their activity levels while working cooperatively (in teams). Second, we conducted an empirical study to validate PUM and to show that player matching using PUM plays a significant role in improving players' PA levels and collective performance. Third, we offer qualitative insights to explain observed group variations. Finally, we reflect on the implications of our findings in PTs design and discuss future direction including adaptive user matching in persuasive applications or games.

2 Methodology

The goal of this work is to empirically assess the proposed Performance-based User Matching (PUM) technique for collaborative PTs within the context of persuasive exergaming for promoting physical activity. Specifically, we aim to validate the following research hypotheses:

H1: Cooperative work will improve individual players' PA level overall.
H2: Matching players with similar PA levels to the same group will yield improved individual and collective performance, compared to grouping players with dissimilar or mixed PA levels.

To achieve our research goal, we first developed a group-based multiplayer mode (called *Tournament Mode*) within our TreeCare persuasive exergame [30–32] to allow intra-group cooperation and between-group competition. Second, we created three groups (SG1, SG2, SG3) containing players with similar PA levels and two groups having players with dissimilar or mixed PA levels (MG1, MG2) for the purpose of this study. Third, we conducted a 6-week field study to collect the PA levels (step counts) of players. We collected the baseline (usual) daily steps of players in the first week prior to group assignment, after which players were assigned to groups and allowed to cooperate within group to achieve collective goal while competing with other groups (between-group competition) for the remaining 5 weeks. Fourth, we analyzed our quantitative data using well-known statistical methods and tools to validate H1 and H2. Finally, we analyzed the qualitative data to understand players' opinions and comments for more insights.

2.1 TreeCare Game and the "Tournament Mode"

TreeCare is a persuasive exergame that uses the metaphor of a flourishing tree (in a garden) with green leaves and fruits to represent the performance of a physically active and consistent player in the real-world, while an empty tree with no leaf and fruit represents little or no activity. Thus, the health of the tree is highly dependent on the players' physical activity level in the real-world which, in turn, is operationalized using their step counts. The game provides 14 intervention features based on twelve (12) persuasive strategies to motivate players to be physically active [32].

The *Tournament* mode of the game is a group-based mode where a group of n players cooperate to achieve their collective goal while competing with other groups (between-group competition). Each group has a captain who approves join requests from interested players and can also invite players to join the group. The creator of a group automatically becomes the captain but can re-assign captainship to another member of the group. Once a group joins an active tournament, the group will be assigned an empty tree for that tournament. Group members collaborate to nurture their tree via their combined physical activity (i.e., overall step counts for the group).

The minimum daily goal for each group is 10,000 steps and determined prior to the start of a tournament by its creator. For every 3,000 steps achieved in a day, a group gains a green leaf on its tree. If a group fails to meet its daily goal, it loses the number of leaves that corresponds to the remaining steps required to meet the target goal. However, if a group meets its daily goal consistently for 7 days, its tree gains an extra fruit. Furthermore, each tournament has a leaderboard that ranks groups in descending order of the total steps achieved. Members of a group can track individual and collective step count, and also view the group's tree that shows their performance. The top 3 groups are awarded a trophy that corresponds to their position on the leaderboard.

2.2 Study Procedure and Data Collection

The study commenced with an online survey to collect participants' demographic data, current physical activity behaviour data using the Global Physical Activity Questionnaire (GPAQ) scale [33], and gamification user types data using the Hexad framework [34]. Prior to completing the survey, participants were asked to provide their consent in line with the study ethics approval. Afterwards, each participant was asked to installed a version of TreeCare that has all its intervention features disabled except the step tracking feature which record steps in the background. Participants were then asked to go along with their phone as they perform their usual daily activity for 1 week (baseline period). At the end of the baseline period, participants uninstalled the step counter version, and then installed the intervention version with all game features enabled including group-based collaboration and competition. A simple guide or tutorial was made available to participants on how the game works and we addressed any questions participants might have prior to the commencement of the study. Participants' daily step data were recorded over the next 5 weeks (intervention period), as they work together in a group of four and compete with other groups via the game's Tournament mode. After the intervention period, we administered an online survey to collect quantitative data and qualitative comments related to user experience and usability. We also randomly interviewed 5 participants to collect detailed feedback.

Participants. We recruited participants using university mailing lists and through social media. We also leveraged snowball sampling to recruit additional participants. All participants were screened based on the following inclusion criteria: First, participants should be 18 years of age or older. Second, participants should own an Android smartphone and carry it with them throughout the study. However, people with health conditions that prevent them from actively walking or running were excluded from the study. In total, 26 participants were recruited to participate in the study and were allowed to withdraw at any point. Three (3) participants dropped out in the middle of the study due to their unexpected change in work schedule. Participants were diverse in terms of age, gender, education, profession, geographical location, and physical activity behaviour. For example, the age group of participants were 18–25 (35%), 26–35 (61%), and 36–45 (4%). In addition, 43% of participants were males while 56% were females. Participants were sedentary for 7.41 hours on average daily. Participants received a monetary compensation of $10 for participating in the study in line with the study ethics approval.

Group Assignments. After the baseline period, we manually assigned 20 participants to five groups based on their individual step counts during the baseline period, with each group having four (4) members. Groups SG1, SG2, and SG3 contain members with *similar* PA levels, while the remaining two groups (MG1 and MG2) have members with *dissimilar* or *mixed* PA levels. SG1 members belong to the low-activity category (i.e., average daily steps less than 3000) while SG2 and SG3 members were moderately active (i.e., average daily steps is between 3000 and 7000), in line with step count recommendations in [35]. However, MG1 and MG2 each comprises members from low-activity, moderate-activity, and high-activity (i.e., above 7000 average daily steps) categories, mixed together. The five groups were made to compete in the same active tournament during the 5-week intervention period. The tournament requires each participating group to achieve a collective daily goal of 10,000 steps.

2.3 Data Analysis

We used well-established techniques to analyze the data collected. Specifically, we conducted Repeated-Measure Analysis of Variance (RM-ANOVA) and post-hoc tests to validate H1, as well as ANOVA and Paired Samples T-Test to validate H2. We also leveraged the Hexad gamification user types model [34] to examine players' disposition to teamwork. Finally, we utilized the thematic analysis method to analyze participants' qualitative comments.

3 Results

In this section, we present the results of the 6-week field study, having analyzed the quantitative and qualitative data collected using the methods in Sect. 2.3.

H1: *Cooperative work will improve individual players' PA level overall.*

Using RM-ANOVA and Bonferroni post-hoc tests, we compared participants' baseline with each intervention week and also compared the baseline with intervention overall. Our results showed that there is no significant difference between the baseline step counts and those achieved during each intervention week ($F_{3.008, 57.155} = 1.204$, $p = .317$). Similarly, no significant difference was observed between the baseline and the intervention steps overall ($F_{1, 19} = 1.772$, $p = .199$) probably due to the limited number of participants. Nevertheless, participants' mean daily steps revealed considerably higher PA levels during the intervention period (13%) than the baseline, as shown in Fig. 1. Hence, H1 was somewhat supported.

H2: *Matching players with similar PA levels to the same group will yield improved individual and collective performance, compared to grouping players with dissimilar or mixed PA levels.*

Our ANOVA results revealed a statistically significant difference between the groups ($F_{4, 638} = 41.551$, $p < .001$). A Bonferroni post hoc test revealed that the mean daily step count of individual participants in SG2 is significantly higher than that of the other groups ($p < .001$). Similarly, the mean daily step count of participants in SG3 is significantly higher than that of SG1 ($p < .001$), MG1 ($p = .012$), and MG2 ($p = .002$). There was no significant difference between the mean daily step count of participants in SG1 and MG1 ($p = .424$). Likewise, no significant difference exists between the mean daily step count of participants in SG1 and MG2 ($p = .646$). This shows that MG1 and MG2 could not significantly outperform SG1 despite SG1 comprising players with low activity. Our

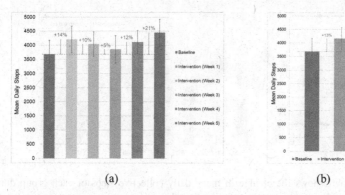

(a)   (b)

Fig. 1. (a) Comparing participants' mean daily step count during the baseline period (*baseline*) with that of each intervention week, and (b) Comparing participants' baseline with the mean daily step count achieved during the entire intervention period.

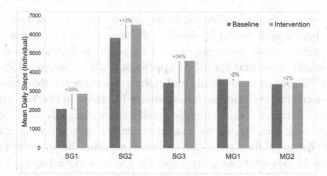

Fig. 2. The chart shows the change in mean daily step count of individual participants per group during the intervention period, compared to the baseline period.

results also showed that the mean daily step counts of participants in MG1 and MG2 are not significantly different ($p = 1.000$). In general, matching players with similar PA levels to the same group leads to improved individual performance (an average of 28.3% increase), compared to groups containing players with mixed or dissimilar PA levels (an average of 0% increase), as shown in Fig. 2.

As regards collective performance, Fig. 3 shows that SG1 recorded the most increase in collective step count from baseline to intervention (43%) which is statistically significant ($p = .015$) according to the Paired-Samples T-Test results. SG3 is next in line to achieve a better performance with a 34% increase in the collective steps from baseline to intervention, followed by SG2 with an 11% increase. However, MG1 showed an 11% decline in collective performance from baseline to intervention, while MG2 has only 2% marginal increase from baseline to intervention. Overall, groups comprising players with similar PA levels achieved a 29.3% increase in collective performance on average from baseline to intervention, compared to groups consisting of players with dissimilar or mixed PA levels (an average decline of 4.5%). Therefore, our findings support H2.

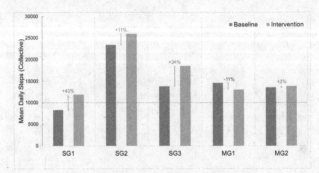

Fig. 3. The chart shows the change in mean daily collective steps of each group during the intervention period, compared to the baseline period.

4 Discussion

In this work, we empirically studied the PUM concept which is based on the premise that assigning people with similar PA levels to the same group will increase individual and collective performance, compared to grouping people with dissimilar or mixed PA levels. **Our results show that the PUM approach leads to increased PA levels, as players in the SG groups individually and collectively exceeded their baseline steps during the 5-week intervention period, compared to those in the MG groups.**

To understand players' behaviours, we conducted further analysis of the pre-study and post-study data. Specifically, we examined players' disposition to teamwork by analyzing their ratings of the four *Socialiser* items (measured on a 7-point Likert scale) in the Hexad model [34] across the five groups. The results of a One-Sample T-Test (using neutral rating of 4 as the test value) showed that players in each group are significantly open to teamwork: SG1 ($p < .001$), SG2 ($p = .008$), SG3 ($p = .010$), MG1 ($p = .033$), and MG2 ($p = .048$). This means that players in individual groups have relatively equal chance of achieving cooperative success. However, this is not the case considering the less-impressive performance of the two MG groups. The main reason for this shortfall, as evident in participants' qualitative comments when asked how they feel about their group's performance, is the unequal ability of players in the MG groups with respect to their PA level. In other words, some players were more physically active (i.e., contributing more step counts) than others in the group which, in turn, led to downward comparison that eventually triggered irritation and demotivation. The following comments from two participants in MG1 and MG2, respectively, support this finding: *"The team ranking made me push myself to get more steps so as to improve my team. I was angry when my teammates did not work enough to climb higher ranks."* [P7], *"I do not get discouraged personally, but I lost interest in that team."* [P10]. Conversely, most players in the SG groups highlighted their efforts in contributing towards higher group ranking and even got more motivated as their group collectively improves, as revealed in the following sample comments: *"I was motivated to increase my physical activity because I wouldn't want my team to have a low performance."* [P3], *"I always get more motivated when my team performs good in the team competition."* [P12].

Our findings have implications for socially-oriented persuasive applications design that assign people to work together to improve overall effectiveness via social influence. Specifically, **we suggest that users with similar ability levels should be matched to the same group**, as users in mixed groups are more prone to the adverse effects of upward and downward comparisons which in turn could demotivate them. To achieve this, designers/developers should **provide in-app features that match users to groups/teams based on their current PA levels (low, moderate, high activity level) and continuously recommend other groups they could join as their PA levels change**. This adaptive matching approach could be achieved using machine learning techniques, hence an interesting direction for future research.

5   Conclusion and Future Work

To improve the effectiveness of group-based PA interventions, we propose a group formation approach called *Performance-based User Matching (PUM)* which is based on the premise that assigning users with similar PA levels to the same group (SG) will increase motivation and collective performance, compared to grouping users with dissimilar or mixed PA levels (MG). We empirically validated this approach in an exergaming context by conducting a 6-week field study using our TreeCare persuasive exergame to investigate and compare SG and MG paradigms in terms of players' PA levels and collective performance. The game operationalized PA levels using step counts.

Our findings showed that players in the SG groups significantly increased their PA levels, compared to those in the MG groups. Also, players in the SG groups individually and collectively exceeded their baseline steps during the 5-week intervention period, compared to those in the MG groups. Hence, the PUM technique improved the overall effectiveness of the TreeCare game with regard to motivating players to be more physically active while working cooperatively.

Future work will build upon our findings to adaptively match users to groups based on their current step counts within the game using machine learning (ML) techniques. In addition, users' individual preferences will be collected as part of the feedback loop to further improve the game's overall effectiveness and user engagement.

Acknowledgement. This research was undertaken, in part, thanks to funding from the Canada Research Chairs Program. We acknowledge the support of the Natural Sciences and Engineering Research Council of Canada (NSERC) through the Discovery Grant.

References

1. Lavie, C.J., Ozemek, C., Carbone, S., Katzmarzyk, P.T., Blair, S.N.: Sedentary behavior, exercise, and cardiovascular health. Circ. Res. **124**, 799–815 (2019). https://doi.org/10.1161/CIRCRESAHA.118.312669
2. Yang, L., et al.: Trends in sedentary behavior among the US population, 2001–2016. JAMA **321**, 1587–1597 (2019). https://doi.org/10.1001/JAMA.2019.3636

3. González, K., Fuentes, J., Márquez, J.L.: Physical inactivity, sedentary behavior and chronic diseases. Korean J. Fam. Med. **38**, 111–115 (2017). https://doi.org/10.4082/kjfm.2017.38.3.111
4. Katzmarzyk, P.T., Powell, K.E., Jakicic, J.M., Troiano, R.P., Piercy, K., Tennant, B.: Sedentary behavior and health: update from the 2018 physical activity guidelines advisory committee. Med. Sci. Sports Exerc. **51**, 1241 (2019). https://doi.org/10.1249/MSS.0000000000001935
5. Furlanetto, K.C., et al.: Sedentary behavior is an independent predictor of mortality in subjects with COPD. Respir. Care. **62**, 579–587 (2017). https://doi.org/10.4187/RESPCARE.05306
6. Kim, D., Vazquez-Montesino, L.M., Li, A.A., Cholankeril, G., Ahmed, A.: Inadequate physical activity and sedentary behavior are independent predictors of nonalcoholic fatty liver disease. Hepatology **72**, 1556–1568 (2020). https://doi.org/10.1002/HEP.31158
7. Lemes, I.R., et al.: Association of sedentary behavior and metabolic syndrome. Public Health **167**, 96–102 (2019). https://doi.org/10.1016/J.PUHE.2018.11.007
8. Bellettiere, J., et al.: Sedentary behavior and cardiovascular disease in older women: the OPACH study. Circulation **139**, 1036–1046 (2019). https://doi.org/10.1161/CIRCULATIONAHA.118.035312
9. Vancampfort, D., et al.: Sedentary behavior and physical activity levels in people with schizophrenia, bipolar disorder and major depressive disorder: a global systematic review and meta-analysis. World Psychiatry **16**, 308–315 (2017). https://doi.org/10.1002/WPS.20458
10. Lee, E., Kim, Y.: Effect of university students' sedentary behavior on stress, anxiety, and depression. Perspect. Psychiatr. Care **55**, 169 (2019). https://doi.org/10.1111/PPC.12296
11. Wheeler, M.J., et al.: Sedentary behavior as a risk factor for cognitive decline? A focus on the influence of glycemic control in brain health. Alzheimer's Dement. Transl. Res. Clin. Interv. **3**, 291–300 (2017). https://doi.org/10.1016/J.TRCI.2017.04.001
12. Falck, R.S., Landry, G.J., Best, J.R., Davis, J.C., Chiu, B.K., Liu-Ambrose, T.: Cross-sectional relationships of physical activity and sedentary behavior with cognitive function in older adults with probable mild cognitive impairment. Phys. Ther. **97**, 975–984 (2017). https://doi.org/10.1093/PTJ/PZX074
13. Stubbs, B., et al.: Relationship between sedentary behavior and depression: a mediation analysis of influential factors across the lifespan among 42,469 people in low- and middle-income countries. J. Affect. Disord. **229**, 231–238 (2018). https://doi.org/10.1016/J.JAD.2017.12.104
14. Friedenreich, C.M., Ryder-Burbidge, C., McNeil, J.: Physical activity, obesity and sedentary behavior in cancer etiology: epidemiologic evidence and biologic mechanisms. Mol. Oncol. **15**, 790–800 (2021). https://doi.org/10.1002/1878-0261.12772
15. Jochem, C., Wallmann-Sperlich, B., Leitzmann, M.F.: The influence of sedentary behavior on cancer risk: epidemiologic evidence and potential molecular mechanisms. Curr. Nutr. Rep. **8**, 167–174 (2019). https://doi.org/10.1007/S13668-019-0263-4/FIGURES/1
16. Diaz, K.M., et al.: Patterns of sedentary behavior and mortality in U.S. middle-aged and older adults a national cohort study. Ann. Intern. Med. **167**, 465–475 (2017). https://doi.org/10.7326/M17-0212/SUPPL_FILE/M17-0212_SUPPLEMENT.PDF
17. Gilchrist, S.C., et al.: Association of sedentary behavior with cancer mortality in middle-aged and older US adults. JAMA Oncol. **6**, 1210–1217 (2020). https://doi.org/10.1001/JAMAONCOL.2020.2045
18. Dempsey, P.C., et al.: Global public health guidelines on physical activity and sedentary behavior for people living with chronic conditions: a call to action. J. Phys. Act. Health **18**, 76–85 (2020). https://doi.org/10.1123/JPAH.2020-0525
19. Aguirre-Betolaza, A.M., Mujika, I., Loprinzi, P., Corres, P., Gorostegi-Anduaga, I., Maldonado-Martín, S.: Physical activity, sedentary behavior, and sleep quality in adults with primary hypertension and obesity before and after an aerobic exercise program: EXERDIET-HTA study. Life **10**, 153 (2020). https://doi.org/10.3390/LIFE10080153

20. Schuch, F.B., et al.: Associations of moderate to vigorous physical activity and sedentary behavior with depressive and anxiety symptoms in self-isolating people during the COVID-19 pandemic: a cross-sectional survey in Brazil. Psychiatry Res. **292**, 113339 (2020). https://doi.org/10.1016/J.PSYCHRES.2020.113339

21. Oinas-Kukkonen, H., Harjumaa, M.: Persuasive systems design: key issues, process model, and system features. Commun. Assoc. Inf. Syst. **24**, 96 (2009)

22. Orji, R., Oyibo, K., Lomotey, R.K., Orji, F.A.: Socially-driven persuasive health intervention design: competition, social comparison, and cooperation. Health Inform. J. **25**, 1451–1484 (2019). https://doi.org/10.1177/1460458218766570

23. Marker, A.M., Staiano, A.E.: Better together: outcomes of cooperation versus competition in social exergaming. Games Health J. **4**, 25–30 (2015). https://doi.org/10.1089/G4H.2014.0066

24. Ren, X., Yu, B., Lu, Y., Brombacher, A.: Exploring cooperative fitness tracking to encourage physical activity among office workers. Proc. ACM Hum.-Comput. Interact. **2**, 20 (2018). https://doi.org/10.1145/3274415

25. Kanstrup, A.M., Bertelsen, P.S., Knudsen, C.: Changing health behavior with social technology? A pilot test of a mobile app designed for social support of physical activity. Int. J. Environ. Res. Public Health **17**, 8383 (2020). https://doi.org/10.3390/IJERPH17228383

26. Esakia, A., McCrickard, D.S., Harden, S.M., Horning, M.: FitAware: channeling group dynamics strategies with smartwatches in a physical activity intervention. In: CHI EA 2017: Proceedings of the 2017 CHI Conference Extended Abstracts on Human Factors in Computing Systems, pp. 2551–2559. Association for Computing Machinery (2017)

27. Chan, G., Arya, A., Orji, R., Zhao, Z., Stojmenovic, M., Whitehead, A.: Player matching for social exergame retention: a group personality composition approach. In: CHI PLAY 2020 - Extended Abstracts of the 2020 Annual Symposium on Computer-Human Interaction in Play, pp. 198–203. Association for Computing Machinery, Inc. (2020)

28. Brown, R., Pehrson, S.: Group Processes: Dynamics Within and Between Groups. Wiley, Hoboken (2019)

29. Suls, J., Martin, R., Wheeler, L.: Social comparison: why, with whom, and with what effect? Curr. Dir. Psychol. Sci. **11**, 159–163 (2002). https://doi.org/10.1111/1467-8721.00191

30. Oyebode, O., Maurya, D., Orji, R.: Nourish your tree! Developing a persuasive exergame for promoting physical activity among adults. In: 2020 IEEE 8th International Conference on Serious Games and Applications for Health, SeGAH 2020, pp. 1–7. Institute of Electrical and Electronics Engineers Inc. (2020)

31. Oyebode, O., Orji, R.: A persuasive mobile game for reducing sedentary behaviour and promoting physical activity. In: Adjunct Proceedings of the 15th International Conference on Persuasive Technology (Persuasive 2020), pp. 1–4 (2020)

32. Oyebode, O., Ganesh, A., Orji, R.: TreeCare: development and evaluation of a persuasive mobile game for promoting physical activity. In: 2021 IEEE Conference on Games (CoG), pp. 1–8. IEEE (2021)

33. Armstrong, T., Bull, F.: Development of the World Health Organization Global Physical Activity Questionnaire (GPAQ). J Public Health **14**, 66–70 (2006). https://doi.org/10.1007/s10389-006-0024-x

34. Tondello, G.F., Wehbe, R.R., Diamond, L., Busch, M., Marczewski, A., Nacke, L.E.: The gamification user types Hexad scale. In: CHI PLAY 2016 - Proceedings of the 2016 Annual Symposium on Computer-Human Interaction in Play, pp. 229–243. Association for Computing Machinery, Inc. (2016)

35. Kraus, W.E., et al.: Daily step counts for measuring physical activity exposure and its relation to health. Med. Sci. Sports Exerc. **51**, 1206–1212 (2019). https://doi.org/10.1249/MSS.0000000000001932

Coaxing: An Empirical Exploration of a Novel Way to Nudge Athletic Performance in Sports

Dees Postma[✉], Sander ten Brinke, Robby van Delden, and Dennis Reidsma

University of Twente, P.O. Box 217, Enschede, The Netherlands
d.b.w.postma@utwente.nl
https://www.utwente.nl/en/eemcs/hmi/

Abstract. This paper presents design work and empirical work, exploring a novel way of steering player behaviour and performance in sports, called 'coaxing'. We propose that athletic performance might be influenced by tricking players into thinking that their athletic abilities are different from what they really are. We approach this proposition from three different angles. First, we use related work to theoretically ground the concept of coaxing in literature. Second, we take a research-through-design approach to illustrate the potential of coaxing for sports practice, specifically volleyball. Third, we carried out an experimental study to shed light on the effectiveness of coaxing, also in the context of volleyball. For the experimental study, we explored the idea of coaxing by means of an augmented ball-catching task. For every participant, we quantified their ability to intercept fly balls and presented them with visualisations that either overstated or understated this ability; in the expectation that this would impact how they acted in the ball-catching task. While the effects of coaxing failed to reach significance, data suggest that coaxing might yet be a viable form of steering player behaviour. Contrary to our hypothesis, participants whose abilities had been understated mostly outperformed their counterparts. We discuss the particularities of the current findings and their implications for sports practice. We conclude with practical and theoretical recommendations to further develop the concept of coaxing.

Keywords: Steering behaviour · Coaxing · Perceptual-motor training · Augmentation · Sports interaction technology · Sports · Volleyball · Nudging

1 Introduction

Sports and technology are getting ever-more intricately linked: activity trackers are standard issue when going for a run; augmented reality is within reach when shooting ball, and sports apparel ensures optimal thermal-regulation when exercising. Technology is omnipresent and shapes the way athletes train and perform.

© Springer Nature Switzerland AG 2022
N. Baghaei et al. (Eds.): PERSUASIVE 2022, LNCS 13213, pp. 174–189, 2022.
https://doi.org/10.1007/978-3-030-98438-0_14

It is even contended that technology might be the main driving factor behind athletic performance in the future [38].

The Olympic motto taps into this focus on athletic performance: with *'Faster, Higher, Stronger - Together'* the Olympic founder Pierre de Coubertin wanted a slogan to emphasise excellence [5]. Recognising the apparently important role that recorded performance plays, in this paper we start with looking into a possible strategy to improve athlete's performance using 'persuasive' technology.

The field of SportsHCI not only aims to perfect performance; the unbridled potential of interaction technology for sports comes to light when also considering the many other application domains that it caters to, for example: entertainment [13,15,33,62], refereeing [3,4,10]; safety [1,2]; training [22,27,31,32,39,40,51,59] and research [11,59,64]. And this is just painting the picture in broad strokes. Zooming in on 'training' for example, systems have been developed that foster engagement [35,47,49,73], and accelerate learning [8,14,26,29,39,40,60], with even finer distinctions made for the different skill domains, such as physical [50], technical [54,65], tactical [22] and perceptual-cognitive [16,22,31,40,60,61].

For the current contribution, we capitalise on the visual nature of an interactive floor [56] to explore a novel game mechanic for steering player behaviour and performance in sports, which we call 'coaxing'. In this regard coaxing is tricking athletes to perform better by misrepresenting their capabilities. In Sect. 2, we present an investigation of how the concept of coaxing is theoretically situated within the fields of ecological psychology and persuasion. In Sect. 3 we present design work to illustrate the various applications of coaxing for (volleyball) practice. Specifically, we present four training game concepts that make use of coaxing to support volleyball players in their practice. In Sect. 4 we present empirical work to investigate the effectiveness of coaxing. Together, these sections investigate the potential of coaxing for sports.

For our experimental study, we present players with an altered visual representation of their motor abilities to trick them ('coax' them) into thinking their action capabilities are either greater or poorer than they actually are, causing them to over or underestimate their abilities. We tested this idea with a ball catching task, derived from the serve-reception task in volleyball. Players were presented with a range of ball trajectories, pitched towards them at various angles. For each ball angle, we determined the greatest distance that the player could cover within the flight time of the ball (their factual action boundary) and manipulated this area in order to visually represent either a smaller-than-actual 'action boundary' (0.75x) or a greater-than-actual 'action boundary' (1.25x) to the player, under the guise of showing them their factual 'action boundary' for catching fly balls (see Fig. 3). We hypothesised that participants in the 1.25x-group would intercept more balls than their counterparts in the 0.75x-group.

2   Related Work

To explore coaxing, we ground the concept in related work in two ways. First, we develop the concept by considering the fundamental principles of Ecological Psychology, specifically focusing on the concept of *affordances* [24]. Second, we situate the concept of coaxing within its broader theoretical framework of steering and persuasion.

2.1 Affordances

From the perspective of Ecological Psychology, it is contended that people perceive the world in terms of what they can or cannot do. That is, people perceive the world in terms of their action possibilities, known as affordances [24]. Which action possibilities are manifest in any given situation depends on the relationship between the behaviourally relevant properties of the athlete's action system on the one hand and the behaviourally relevant properties of the environment on the other hand [69]. Put into concrete terms: a ball affords catching to a player whose abilities are such that the demands imposed by the flight-trajectory of the ball can be met (e.g. in terms of speed and direction) [57]. In the present study we aim to influence catching performance by providing players with an altered representation of their own locomotor abilities, thereby subtly adding to the extant agent-environment factors that relate to form the affordance of catchability.

Many studies have set out to examine how people respond to changes in the agent-environment system [17–21, 24, 28, 36, 43, 45, 52, 57, 69, 70]. People can adapt quickly when imposing changes on their (motor) abilities. In braking a car to a safe stop for example, people quickly recalibrated when their brake-strength had been adjusted [17–19]. The same phenomenon has been shown to occur for instance in sitting and stair climbing [43]. Though, in all of these studies, *actual changes* had been made to the (motor) abilities of the agent. The present study is unique in the sense that it presents participants with *feigned, covert changes* to their motor abilities. Here, we investigate the influence that such changes might have on motor performance and how such changes might be leveraged for training purposes.

2.2 Approaches to Steering Behaviour

Steering can be considered to fall under the umbrella of 'Procedural Persuasion'. With procedural persuasion referring to "...*the interpretations addressed by the rules of the persuasive game between visual, haptic, sonic and linguistic representations which guide players' interpretation.*" [12]. Steering differentiates itself from many forms of persuasion in the approach that is taken to influence behaviour. Whereas truly persuasive technologies set out to willingly and transparently persuade the user [63], steering can involve users to be deceived, coerced or unknowingly influenced in their behaviour (all supposedly with benevolent intentions). Building on the conceptual model of de la Hera Conde-Pumpido on persuasive game structures, Fig. 1 presents a high-level conceptual overview of how steering in general and coaxing in particular relates to persuasion.

'Coaxing' as a method to interactively steer behaviour adds to a family of existing approaches that include 'require', 'insist' and 'entice' [68]. Whereas coaxing takes a gentle yet persistent approach to steering behaviour, 'require' is much more forceful. In the latter, an agent is literally *required* to take a certain course of action in order for the game to work as intended. 'Insist' is more lenient in the sense that the game works as intended even if the player does not act as insisted, however not doing so might give the player distinct disadvantages. An archetypal example of the 'insist' approach is to provide players with game outcome related rewards in the form of 'power-ups'. The final and least forceful of the three approaches is to 'entice' players to act in a certain way [68]. Typically, enticement is done by providing players with rewards that have intrinsic value, but no game-outcome related value, for example by providing players with upgrades in the appearance of their avatar. 'Coaxing', as explored in this study, adds to these approaches. Arguably, coaxing is the most subtle and covert way to steer behaviour which might be an advantageous trait in the context of skill balancing cf. [23].

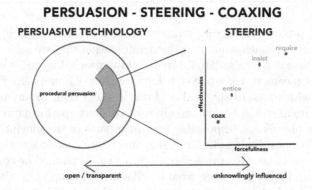

Fig. 1. Coaxing embedded in its broader theoretical context of steering and persuasion.

3   Illustrating Coaxing Through Concept Designs

To investigate the potential value of coaxing for sports practice, we adopted a research-through-design approach. We designed four distinct implementations of the coaxing concept for volleyball practice (see Fig. 2) and evaluated their potential benefits by means of formative user testing. Specifically, we used Design Thinking [37], iteratively cycling through its various stages, to arrive at fruitful applications for volleyball training. In doing so, we consulted 8 trainers and 15 players from 4 different sports clubs. In earlier stages of design, we presented our target-audience with lo-fi digital prototypes with which they could (digitally) interact while in later stages we also tested hi-fi prototypes using an interactive LED floor, see: [56]. Not all participants were confronted with all prototypes. Below, we briefly describe four of the most promising concepts that emerged from our design process to illustrate how the theory behind coaxing might find its way to practice.

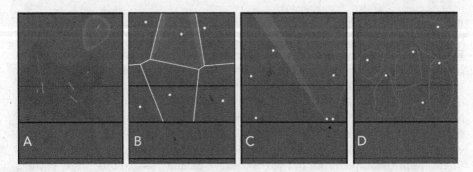

Fig. 2. Four different implementations of coaxing through visual manipulation in the context of volleyball. Blue surface areas represent players' factual motor abilities; green surface areas represent how such abilities might be (visually) overstated - coaxing players to perform differently. (Color figure online)

Figure 2A presents a coaxing strategy around '(mis)representing a player's action boundaries', much similar to the manipulation that we set out to empirically test in Sect. 4 (see also [56] for more information). Figure 2B uses Voronoi diagrams as a means to coax player behaviour. The Voronoi cells show for any given player which area of the field is closer to them than to any other player. The mathematical concept is commonly used in sports performance analysis to indicate what players are responsible for which parts of the playing field, based on their relative positioning [42,53]. Using this to our advantage, the individual Voronoi cells could be misrepresented visually (i.e., expanded or contracted) to steer behaviour. Figure 2C shows, what is colloquially known as, a 'block shadow'. The block shadow is that part of the field that is shielded off from a direct hit from a spike by 'the block' (involving up to three players). Visualising the block shadow might help players cover the field more effectively. This effect might be enhanced by expanding or contracting the factual block shadow, coaxing players to veer from or move towards the block shadow. Finally, Fig. 2D illustrates a variant of coaxing wherein the trainer or coach is free to draw (misrepresented) shapes on the floor. These custom shapes might be pinned to individual players and are scaled proportionally relative to their kinematic characteristics. This variant is especially useful to capture the many idiosyncrasies that come with defensive tactics in volleyball. From user tests with this prototype it was learned that (expert) players have very outspoken notions of accountability and positioning when it comes to defending certain parts of the field.

Both players and trainers were enthusiastic about these four training concepts. They affirmed that the concepts were relevant for volleyball practice and that they might have merit for training. Players and coaches considered the coaxing elements interesting, however they were uncertain whether the coaxing approach would lead to notable training effects. In what follows, we present an experimental study to investigate the effectiveness of coaxing in nudging athletic performance.

4 Investigating Coaxing in an Experimental Task

To study the effects of coaxing on athletic performance, we designed a ball-catching task. We aimed to influence catching performance by visually misrepresenting participants' abilities to make a catch, see Fig. 3.

4.1 Methods

Participants. Twenty-six participants were recruited for a ball-catching task. Participants were between 19 and 59 years of age (M = 27.9 years; SD = 10.3) and were experienced in playing ball sports (*M = 8.8 years; SD = 8.0*). The experiment was approved by the ethical committee of Electrical Engineering Mathematics and Computer Science (EEMCS) of the University of Twente (RP 2019-16).

Setup and Apparatus. An interactive installation was built to systematically test and manipulate participants' performance in a fly-ball catching task. Using digital image projection in combination with motion capture, an interactive ground surface was created with visualisations responsive to player motion. The visualisation showed a boundary at a certain distance around the participants, of which they were told that this represented their 'action boundary' (i.e. the maximum distance at which they supposedly could catch a ball thrown at them).

A ball projection machine (Lobster Elite Liberty) was used for consistent ball delivery. Vertical ball projection angle and release velocity were kept constant, resulting in ball trajectories with a flight time of 1.40 s, with the ball travelling 6.65 m. The positioning of the ball pitching machine and the horizontal ball projection angle were varied to hit different targets (see Fig. 3). The pitching machine proved to be consistent in ball delivery (*SD = 0.09* m). The pitching machine was hidden from sight.

We used the software and the setup from [46], using four top-down Kinects, two PCs, and two high-end projectors to track players in a 5.3 m by 5.3 m interactive projection field.

Quantifying Action Boundaries. In order to present players with an *altered* visualisation of their ability to intercept fly balls, their *factual* ability had to be quantified first. To quantify the *size* of a player's locomotor range, a macro-dynamical model on sprint running was instigated [55]. The model, specifically developed for the case of catching fly balls, calculates locomotor range based on the maximal running speed and acceleration of the player and the time that is available for ball interception. Players' maximal running speed and acceleration were obtained with the help of the playground's trackers.

To quantify the *shape* of a player's locomotor range, a pilot study was performed. We measured for one participant the greatest distance that he could cover in 1.40 s for targets placed at various angles (i.e. −90° to +90°). Performance was sampled multiple times, in steps of 15°. It was found that, by and

Fig. 3. Illustration of the experimental setup. From left to right: the participant, kinects and projectors, occlusion screen and ball projection machine. The white semi-circle represents the participant's factual locomotor range; the blue semi-circle the smaller-than-actual locomotor range (−25%) and the red semi-circle the greater-than-actual locomotor range (+25%). All fly balls were projected *at* the boundary of a participant's locomotor range (black cross marks). (Color figure online)

large, target angle had no effect on locomotor range. The greatest distance that could be covered was roughly the same for all targets. As such, we decided to represent players' action boundaries as semi-circles, with a radius that reflected their locomotor abilities (Fig. 3, white semi-circle).

Manipulating Action Boundaries. To provide players with an altered representation of their locomotor abilities, we applied a linear transformation to their quantified locomotor range. Participants were provided with a 25% smaller-than-actual locomotor range (in Fig. 3 the blue semi-circle) or a 25% greater-than-actual locomotor range (in Fig. 3 the red semi-circle).

Experimental Design and Procedure. To examine the effects of coaxing on performance, participants were tested in a two-group between-subjects design. Participants were randomly yet evenly divided between two groups: a 0.75x-group and a 1.25x-group. The altered visualisations were presented to the participants throughout the experiment, but not *during* a trial. This was done to minimise the risk of participants finding out that the projected action boundary in actuality did not represent their *true* action boundary.

It is important to note that for every participant, regardless of which group they were in, fly balls were projected *at* the border of their *factual* action boundary, not at the border of their *altered* action boundary. Participants received a total of 21 trials (7 targets, 3 repetitions). The targets varied in projection angle, ranging from −60° to 60°, in steps of 20° (indicated by the black cross marks in Fig. 3). Trials were presented in a block-randomised order.

Right before the start of a trial, the experimenter verbally cued the participant to get ready. Participants were emphatically instructed to intercept as many fly balls as possible. Interception was considered successful whenever a participant caught or touched the ball before it hit the ground (participants were not made aware of this definition). After the experiment, participants completed a questionnaire inquiring about their experiences with the experiment

Data Analysis. A number of measures were obtained to investigate the effects of coaxing on player behaviour. At the start of the experiment, maximal running speed, maximal running acceleration and locomotor range were determined from the tracker data. Besides these kinematic qualities, 'running distance' was determined from the tracker data for every trial. Running distance was the distance that a participant had covered during a single trial while running to make a catch[1]. To make 'running distance' more meaningful, we normalised running distance by dividing it by locomotor range. With values smaller than 1 signifying that the distance travelled was smaller than the locomotor range of the participant and values greater than 1 signifying the opposite. We call this variable *'normalised running distance'*. In addition, we measured participants' response time on the basis of off-line, post-hoc video analysis.

For this study, we set out to examine whether 'coaxing' would influence player behaviour and performance. Specifically, we were interested to know a) whether coaxing would influence catching performance and b) whether coaxing would influence (normalised) running distance. To address these issues, we performed *mixed effects regression* analysis, see: [34, 66, 71, 72]. The data were analysed using the lme4-package [9] of the R-software package [58]. We modelled the random-effects structure and started out with an intercept-only model. A step-wise forward selection approach was used to add predictors to the model. Two separate models were constructed to investigate the effects of *condition* (0.75x vs 1.25x) on 'normalised running distance' and 'catching performance', respectively. A Bonferroni correction was applied to mitigate the effects of multiple testing.

4.2   Results

Normalised running distance was modelled using *Linear* Mixed Effects Regression. It was found that the best possible model to explain the variance in 'normalised running distance' did not include 'condition' as a significant predictor. Since our primary motive is to investigate the effects of coaxing and not to characterise 'normalised running distance' per se, we will dispense any further discussion about the modelling of 'normalised running distance'.

Catching performance was modelled using GLMER. It was found that the best possible model to explain the variance in 'catching performance' involved 'condition' as a significant predictor (though see Sect. 4.2). Table 1 presents a list of the significant (interaction) effects involved in our final model specification.

Because our main focus is on understanding the effects of coaxing, and not on modelling 'catchability' per se, we will limit our discussion of the model specification to the effects relevant to coaxing (that is, the first-order interaction effect of *manipulation* × *normalised running distance*, see Fig. 4).

Condition, moderated by *normalised running distance*, showed to be a significant predictor for 'catching performance' in running to catch fly balls. Figure 4

---

[1] The measurement of *running distance* required manual operation of the Playground trackers. Data recording from the trackers was initiated right before ball projection and manually stopped when either the ball hit the floor or when the participant contacted the ball.

Table 1. Fixed effects structure (top) and random effects structure (bottom) of the mixed effects regression model for predicting ball contact

fixed effects (z-transformed)	est. (log odds)	SE	Z	p¹	95% CI	random effects	var.	95% CI
intercept	2.804	1.169	2.399	0.016	0.614 – 5.346	participant	0.75	0.314 – 1.127
trial number	0.250	0.121	2.076	0.038	-0.012 – 0.513	trail id	0.22	0.000 – 0.750
max velocity (m/s)	0.750	0.254	2.951	0.003	0.237 – 1.264			
ball angle (deg)	0.132	0.285	0.463	0.643	-0.412 – 0.751			
distance (dist / AB)	2.097	0.765	2.742	0.006	0.658 – 3.942			
manipulation (type 1.25)	-1.292	0.891	-1.451	0.146	-3.168 – 0.486			
experience (experienced)	-0.185	0.598	-0.309	0.757	-1.502 – 0.920			
trial number × max velocity	-0.391	0.121	-3.229	0.001	-0.661– -0.157			
ball angle × distance	0.376	0.140	2.682	0.007	0.092 – 0.688			
distance × manipulation	-1.639	0.683	-2.399	0.016	-3.229 – -0.299			
ball angle × experience	-0.680	0.259	-2.625	0.009	-1.316 – -0.179			

¹p-values smaller than 0.025 are considered significant (p=0.05, Bonferroni n=2)

shows that the odds of making a successful catch increase with normalised running distance, but differently so for the 0.75x-group and the 1.25x-group. Participants that were presented a smaller-than-actual action boundary performed worse than their counterparts when the distance covered was relatively short (i.e. a distance shorter than 0.65× their locomotor range). Conversely, participants that were presented with a smaller-than-actual action boundary performed better than their counterparts when the distance covered was relatively great (greater than 0.65×). On average, the 0.75x-group successfully intercepted the ball 76.9% of the times while the 1.25x-group intercepted the ball successfully 69.9% of the times. Overall, the model captured 79.08% of the variability in catching performance (sensitivity = 80.82%; specificity = 69.88%).

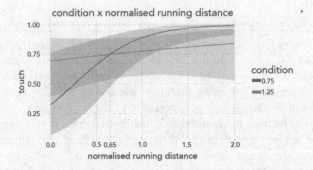

Fig. 4. Partial effect condition x normalised running distance

Model Criticism. We performed outlier-analysis on the basis of Z-transformations to investigate the influence of potential outliers on the fit of the model. It was found that a small group of outliers for normalised running distance (with absolute Z-values greater than 3) might have impacted the fit of the model. Although there is no strong theoretical reason to not allow for extreme values in normalised running distance, it seems fair to assume that participants would not have been able to cover distances thrice their measured locomotor range or more. As such, we investigated how the removal of such extreme values would influence our findings. It was found that the effect of *condition × normalised running distance* was no longer significant ($p = 0.222$) when values with an absolute Z-score greater than 3 were removed. So, at least in part, the significant effect for normalised running distance × condition seemed to be carried by this group of outliers.

Finding that the present results are not unambiguously significant prompts further inquiry. To make the data more tangible, we calculated the *Average Marginal Effects* and the marginal effect of condition (i.e. *discrete change*) on catching performance as a function of normalised running distance for the trimmed model.

Marginal Effects. Average Marginal Effects, or AMEs, specify how a one-unit change in one of the independent variables affects the dependent variable on average [41]. Figure 5 provides the Average Marginal Effects with 95% confidence intervals for the trimmed model. From the confidence intervals it can be observed that the estimated AME falls between -19.32% and $+4.70\%$. While helpful, AMEs tell a limited story as they represent an average. To further unpack the Average Marginal Effect for condition, we plot the marginal effect of condition (i.e. *discrete change*) on catching performance as a function of normalised running distance (Fig. 5) with 90% confidence intervals. This figure shows the discrete difference between the 0.75x-group and the 1.25x-group for increasing values of normalised running distance on the predicted probability of making a successful catch. Regions where the confidence bands do not include the null-line represent the range of values for 'normalised running distance' where 'condition' has a marginal significant effect on 'catching performance' (i.e. $p < .10$) [41]. From Fig. 5, it can be seen that the effect of 'condition' is indeed *marginally* significant for values of normalised running distance greater than 0.65 and smaller than 2.5 (i.e. the 90% CI, does not include the null-line for that value range).

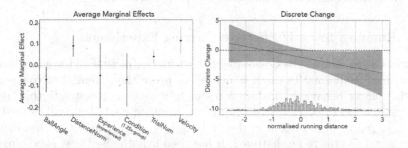

Fig. 5. Plot showing the Average Marginal Effects (right) and a plot showing the marginal effect of condition (i.e. *discrete change*) on catching performance as a function of normalised running distance (left). Both graphs are based on the trimmed model.

5 Discussion

The results of the present study show that coaxing is versatile in its application and that coaxing might potentially be a fruitful way to influence player performance in sports. The results from the experimental study however are not unambiguous. In this section, we will discuss and interpret the particularities of our empirical findings; reflect on the value of coaxing for balancing game play; and make suggestions for further research.

5.1 Interpreting the Results of Coaxing

The most important finding in the present study was that the effect of condition on catching performance was marginally significant when participants had reached or exceeded approximately half their locomotor range. Interestingly, the effect of coaxing favoured the 0.75x-group. Participants in the 0.75x-group intercepted more fly balls than their counterparts in the 1.25x-group. This was different from what we had hypothesised. Our initial hypothesis was that participants that were shown a greater-than-actual action boundary would perform better than participants that were shown a smaller-than-actual action boundary. However, the reverse appeared to be the case. To understand why this might be; we turned to the results from the post-experimental interviews.

Based on the semi-structured interviews, participants generally thought that the action boundaries nicely represented their actual capabilities. However, when prompted, most participants were able to indicate whether their action boundary had been reduced or extended. Interestingly, one participant from the 0.75x-group indicated that his action boundary motivated him to push further *"I tried to reach past the [action] boundary, this motivated me to push myself harder"* (P04). He added: *"though I do think that it really depends on the person, some people might be challenged by the visualisations, whereas other might take them for fact"*. This is an interesting statement – coaxing might potentially act on players' motivation, thereby influencing their performance.

5.2 Running Towards Effective Coaxing Experiments

Clearly, the present results do not paint the definitive picture on the effectiveness of coaxing. Additional research is needed to prove the potential of coaxing in steering player behaviour. In future research, we aim to investigate the role of coaxing in a less complex task environment. Running might be ideally suited for this. The recent introduction of the WaveLight system in athletics[2] has caused many world records to be shattered. It has been hypothesised that psychological factors such as motivation might have had a role to play in that (besides better pacing) [44]. As such, focusing on running in combination with the WaveLight system might provide us with a simpler yet more relevant experimental setting to investigate the effects of (and the mechanisms behind) coaxing.

---

[2] https://www.wavelight-technologies.com.

5.3   Hidden Balancing

The results from our empirical study suggest that coaxing might potentially be interesting in the context of *hidden balancing*. Balancing techniques in (interactive) games and sports have been studied extensively [6,7,23,25,30,48,67], and with good reason. Besides the apparent effects on game-outcome, proper game balancing has been associated with increased levels of fun, engagement and self-esteem (ibid.). The experiences with *implicit* balancing have been positive in that regard. Gerling and colleagues for example, explored hidden balancing strategies (i.e. time balancing and score balancing) [23]. They showed these hidden balancing techniques to promote self-esteem while decreasing the score differential. Coaxing adds to these techniques, potentially enabling interaction designers to promote game balance through the way players perceive their own abilities.

5.4   The Ethics of Coaxing

As we put it before, coaxing is about 'tricking' people into believing their abilities are different from what they truly are. As such, coaxing might potentially impact the way athletes perceive and value their own abilities. When applying coaxing, designers should be careful not to hurt athletes' self esteem and body image. Also, coaxing, once uncovered, might undermine the authority of the trainer/coach. So, even with benevolent intentions, coaxing should be used with care.

6   Conclusion

In the present contribution, we introduced the concept of 'coaxing' as a novel form of behaviour steering; defined it in relation to existing forms of persuasion; designed implementations for volleyball practice; and explored its effects empirically. While the empirical results came out inconclusive, the results hinted towards its possible effectiveness. Furthermore, from post-experimental interviews, it was found that coaxing might influence player motivation: Players might feel challenged by what the technology is telling them about their abilities. In future research, the effects of coaxing need to be investigated further to shed light on its potential for training.

Acknowledgements. This research was partially made possible in the context of the national funded ZonMW *Smart Sports Exercises project* - grant number 546001004, and would not have been possible without the support of all athletes, trainers, and experts who contributed to our activities. We would like to thank the DreamTeam of the DesignLab at the University of Twente who facilitated our experimental work.

References

1. Poseidon (2008). https://poseidon-tech.com/technology/
2. Linx impact assessment system (2015). https://linxias.com
3. Hawk-eye (2018). https://www.hawkeyeinnovations.com/index.html

4. Video assistant referees (VAR) (2020). https://football-technology.fifa.com/en/media-tiles/video-assistant-referee-var/

5. "faster, higher, stronger - together" - IOC session approves historic change in Olympic motto (2021). https://olympics.com/ioc/news/-faster-higher-stronger-together-ioc-session-approves-historic-change-in-olympic-motto

6. Altimira, D., Billinghurst, M., Mueller, F.F.: Understanding handicapping for balancing exertion games. In: CHI 2013 Extended Abstracts on Human Factors in Computing Systems, pp. 1125–1130 (2013)

7. Altimira, D., Mueller, F.F., Clarke, J., Lee, G., Billinghurst, M., Bartneck, C.: Digitally augmenting sports: an opportunity for exploring and understanding novel balancing techniques. In: Proceedings of the 2016 CHI Conference on Human Factors in Computing Systems, pp. 1681–1691 (2016)

8. Anderson, F., Grossman, T., Matejka, J., Fitzmaurice, G.: YouMove: enhancing movement training with an augmented reality mirror. In: Proceedings of the 26th Annual ACM Symposium on User Interface Software and Technology, pp. 311–320 (2013)

9. Bates, D., Mächler, M., Bolker, B., Walker, S.: Fitting linear mixed-effects models using lme4. J. Stat. Softw. **67**(1), 1–48 (2015). https://doi.org/10.18637/jss.v067.i01

10. Chi, E.H., Song, J., Corbin, G.: "Killer App" of wearable computing: wireless force sensing body protectors for martial arts. In: Proceedings of the 17th Annual ACM Symposium on User Interface Software and Technology, pp. 277–285 (2004)

11. Creagh, H.: Cave automatic virtual environment. In: Proceedings: Electrical Insulation Conference and Electrical Manufacturing and Coil Winding Technology Conference (Cat. No. 03CH37480), pp. 499–504. IEEE (2003)

12. de la Hera Conde-Pumpido, T.: A conceptual model for the study of persuasive games. In: DiGRA 2013 - Proceedings of the 2013 DiGRA International Conference: DeFragging Game Studies, August 2014

13. Div, J.: Sony high definition, new jumbotron. Transmission Technology, pp. 78–84 (1986)

14. Drobny, D., Borchers, J.: Learning basic dance choreographies with different augmented feedback modalities. In: CHI 2010 Extended Abstracts on Human Factors in Computing Systems, pp. 3793–3798 (2010)

15. EVS: Secondspectrum - leagues and media. Website (2020). https://evs.com/en

16. Fadde, P.J.: Interactive video training of perceptual decision-making in the sport of baseball. Technol. Instr. Cogn. Learn. **4**(3), 265–285 (2006)

17. Fajen, B.R.: Calibration, information, and control strategies for braking to avoid a collision. J. Exp. Psychol. Hum. Percept. Perform. **31**(3), 480 (2005)

18. Fajen, B.R.: Perceiving possibilities for action: on the necessity of calibration and perceptual learning for the visual guidance of action. Perception **34**(6), 717–740 (2005)

19. Fajen, B.R.: The scaling of information to action in visually guided braking. J. Exp. Psychol. Hum. Percept. Perform. **31**(5), 1107 (2005)

20. Fajen, B.R.: Affordance-based control of visually guided action. Ecol. Psychol. **19**(4), 383–410 (2007)

21. Fajen, B.R., Riley, M.A., Turvey, M.T.: Information, affordances, and the control of action in sport. Int. J. Sport Psychol. **40**(1), 79–107 (2008)

22. Fogtmann, M.H., Grønbæk, K., Ludvigsen, M.K.: Interaction technology for collective and psychomotor training in sports. In: Proceedings of the 8th International Conference on Advances in Computer Entertainment Technology, pp. 1–8 (2011)

23. Gerling, K.M., Miller, M., Mandryk, R.L., Birk, M.V., Smeddinck, J.D.: Effects of balancing for physical abilities on player performance, experience and self-esteem in exergames. In: Proceedings of the SIGCHI Conference on Human Factors in Computing Systems, pp. 2201–2210 (2014)
24. Gibson, J.J.: The theory of affordances. The ecological approach to visual perception (1979)
25. Graf, R., Park, S.Y., Shpiz, E., Kim, H.S.: iGYM: a wheelchair-accessible interactive floor projection system for co-located physical play. In: Extended Abstracts of the 2019 CHI Conference on Human Factors in Computing Systems, pp. 1–6 (2019)
26. Hämäläinen, P.: Interactive video mirrors for sports training. In: Proceedings of the Third Nordic Conference on Human-Computer Interaction, pp. 199–202 (2004)
27. Hämäläinen, P., Ilmonen, T., Höysniemi, J., Lindholm, M., Nykänen, A.: Martial arts in artificial reality. In: Proceedings of the SIGCHI Conference on Human Factors in Computing Systems, pp. 781–790 (2005)
28. Harrison, H.S., Turvey, M.T., Frank, T.D.: Affordance-based perception-action dynamics: a model of visually guided braking. Psychol. Rev. **123**(3), 305 (2016)
29. Helmer, R.J., Farrow, D., Lucas, S., Higgerson, G., Blanchonette, I.: Can interactive textiles influence a novice's throwing technique? Procedia Eng. **2**(2), 2985–2990 (2010)
30. Jensen, M.M., Grønbæk, K.: Design strategies for balancing exertion games: a study of three approaches. In: Proceedings of the 2016 ACM Conference on Designing Interactive Systems, pp. 936–946 (2016)
31. Jensen, M.M., Grønbæk, K., Thomassen, N., Andersen, J., Nielsen, J.: Interactive football-training based on rebounders with hit position sensing and audio-visual feedback. Int. J. Comput. Sci. Sport **13**(1), 57–68 (2014)
32. Jensen, M.M., Rasmussen, M.K., Mueller, F.F., Grønbæk, K.: Keepin' it real: challenges when designing sports-training games. In: Proceedings of the 33rd Annual ACM Conference on Human Factors in Computing Systems, pp. 2003–2012 (2015)
33. Johansen, D., et al.: DAVVI: a prototype for the next generation multimedia entertainment platform. In: Proceedings of the 17th ACM International Conference on Multimedia, pp. 989–990 (2009)
34. Judd, C.M., Westfall, J., Kenny, D.A.: Experiments with more than one random factor: designs, analytic models, and statistical power. Ann. Rev. Psychol. **68**, 601–625 (2017)
35. Kajastila, R., Hämäläinen, P.: Motion games in real sports environments. Interactions **22**(2), 44–47 (2015)
36. van der Kamp, J., Dicks, M., Navia, J.A., Noël, B.: Goalkeeping in the soccer penalty kick. Ger. J. Exerc. Sport Res. **48**(2), 169–175 (2018)
37. Kelley, T., Kelley, D.: Creative confidence: unleashing the creative potential within us all. Currency (2013)
38. de Koning, J.J.: World records: how much athlete? How much technology? Int. J. Sports Physiol. Perform. **5**(2), 262–267 (2010)
39. Kosmalla, F., Daiber, F., Wiehr, F., Krüger, A.: ClimbVis: investigating in-situ visualizations for understanding climbing movements by demonstration. In: Proceedings of the 2017 ACM International Conference on Interactive Surfaces and Spaces, pp. 270–279 (2017)
40. Kosmalla, F., Murlowski, C., Daiber, F., Krüger, A.: Slackliner-an interactive slackline training assistant. In: Proceedings of the 26th ACM International Conference on Multimedia, pp. 154–162 (2018)

41. Long, J.S., Freese, J.: Regression Models for Categorical Dependent Variables Using Stata. Stata Press, College Station (2006)
42. Lopes, A., Fonseca, S., Lese, R., Baca, A.: Using voronoi diagrams to describe tactical behaviour in invasive team sports: an application in basketball. Cuadernos de Psicologia del Deporte **15**(1), 123–130 (2015)
43. Mark, L.S.: Eyeheight-scaled information about affordances: a study of sitting and stair climbing. J. Exp. Psychol. Hum. Percept. Perform. **13**(3), 361 (1987)
44. Mercier, Q., Aftalion, A., Hanley, B.: A model for world-class 10,000 m running performances: strategy and optimization. Front. Sports Act. Living **2**, 226 (2021)
45. Michaels, C.F., Carello, C.: Direct Perception. Prentice-Hall, Englewood Cliffs (1981)
46. Moreno, A., Van Delden, R., Poppe, R., Reidsma, D., Heylen, D.: Augmenting playspaces to enhance the game experience: a tag game case study. Entertain. Comput. **16**, 67–79 (2016)
47. Mueller, F., Agamanolis, S., Picard, R.: Exertion interfaces: sports over a distance for social bonding and fun. In: Proceedings of the SIGCHI Conference on Human Factors in Computing Systems, pp. 561–568 (2003)
48. Mueller, F.F., et al.: Balancing exertion experiences. In: Proceedings of the SIGCHI Conference on Human Factors in Computing Systems, pp. 1853–1862 (2012). https://doi.org/10.1145/2207676.2208322
49. Mueller, F., Cole, L., O'Brien, S., Walmink, W.: Airhockey over a distance: a networked physical game to support social interactions. In: Proceedings of the 2006 ACM SIGCHI International Conference on Advances in Computer Entertainment Technology, pp. 70-es (2006)
50. Mueller, F., et al.: Designing sports: a framework for exertion games. In: Proceedings of the SIGCHI Conference on Human Factors in Computing Systems, pp. 2651–2660 (2011)
51. Mueller, F., Vetere, F., Gibbs, M.R., Agamanolis, S., Sheridan, J.: Jogging over a distance: the influence of design in parallel exertion games. In: Proceedings of the 5th ACM SIGGRAPH Symposium on Video Games, pp. 63–68 (2010)
52. Oudejans, R.R., Michaels, C.F., Bakker, F.C., Davids, K.: Shedding some light on catching in the dark: perceptual mechanisms for catching fly balls. J. Exp. Psychol. Hum. Percept. Perform. **25**(2), 531 (1999)
53. Paulo, A., Zaal, F.T., Seifert, L., Fonseca, S., Araújo, D.: Predicting volleyball serve-reception at group level. J. Sports Sci. **36**(22), 2621–2630 (2018)
54. Pijnappel, S., Mueller, F.: Designing interactive technology for skateboarding. In: Proceedings of the 8th International Conference on Tangible, Embedded and Embodied Interaction, pp. 141–148 (2014)
55. Postma, D.: Affordance based control in running to catch fly balls. NA (2019). https://doi.org/10.1136/bjsports-2014-093968
56. Postma, D., et al.: Towards smart sports exercises: first designs. In: Extended Abstracts of the Annual Symposium on Computer-Human Interaction in Play Companion Extended Abstracts, pp. 619–630 (2019)
57. Postma, D.B., Lemmink, K.A., Zaal, F.T.: The affordance of catchability in running to intercept fly balls. J. Exp. Psychol. Hum. Percept. Perform. **44**(9), 1336 (2018)
58. R Core Team: R: A Language and Environment for Statistical Computing. R Foundation for Statistical Computing, Vienna, Austria (2019). https://www.R-project.org/
59. Ruffaldi, E., Filippeschi, A.: Structuring a virtual environment for sport training: a case study on rowing technique. Robot. Auton. Syst. **61**(4), 390–397 (2013)

60. Sato, K., Sano, Y., Otsuki, M., Oka, M., Kato, K.: Augmented recreational volleyball court: supporting the beginners' landing position prediction skill by providing peripheral visual feedback. In: Proceedings of the 10th Augmented Human International Conference 2019, pp. 1–9 (2019)
61. Savelsbergh, G.: Football IntelliGym efficacy analysis: PSV eindhoven and AZ Alkmaar football academies. Zenodo, Genève (2017). https://doi.org/10.5281/zenodo.268696
62. SecondSpectrum: SecondSpectrum - leagues and media. Website (2020). https://www.secondspectrum.com/ourwork/leagues-media.html
63. Smids, J.: The voluntariness of persuasive technology. In: Bang, M., Ragnemalm, E.L. (eds.) PERSUASIVE 2012. LNCS, vol. 7284, pp. 123–132. Springer, Heidelberg (2012). https://doi.org/10.1007/978-3-642-31037-9_11
64. Stelzer, A., Pourvoyeur, K., Fischer, A.: Concept and application of LPM-a novel 3-D local position measurement system. IEEE Trans. Microw. Theory Tech. **52**(12), 2664–2669 (2004)
65. Stienstra, J., Overbeeke, K., Wensveen, S.: Embodying complexity through movement sonification: case study on empowering the speed-skater. In: Proceedings of the 9th ACM SIGCHI Italian Chapter International Conference on Computer-Human Interaction: Facing Complexity, pp. 39–44 (2011)
66. Tagliamonte, S.A., Baayen, R.H.: Models, forests, and trees of York English: was/were variation as a case study for statistical practice. Lang. Var. Chang. **24**(2), 135–178 (2012)
67. Van Delden, R., Moreno, A., Poppe, R., Reidsma, D., Heylen, D.: Steering gameplay behavior in the interactive tag playground. In: Aarts, E., et al. (eds.) AmI 2014. LNCS, vol. 8850, pp. 145–157. Springer, Cham (2014). https://doi.org/10.1007/978-3-319-14112-1_13
68. Van Delden, R., Moreno, A., Poppe, R., Reidsma, D., Heylen, D.: A thing of beauty: steering behavior in an interactive playground. In: Proceedings of the 2017 CHI Conference on Human Factors in Computing Systems, pp. 2462–2472 (2017)
69. Warren, W.H.: Perceiving affordances: visual guidance of stair climbing. J. Exp. Psychol. Hum. Percept. Perform. **10**(5), 683 (1984)
70. Warren Jr., W.H., Whang, S.: Visual guidance of walking through apertures: body-scaled information for affordances. J. Exp. Psychol. Hum. Percept. Perform. **13**(3), 371 (1987)
71. Winter, B.: Linear models and linear mixed effects models in R with linguistic applications. arXiv preprint arxiv:1308.5499 (2013)
72. Winter, B., Wieling, M.: How to analyze linguistic change using mixed models, growth curve analysis and generalized additive modeling. J. Lang. Evol. **1**(1), 7–18 (2016)
73. Woźniak, P., Knaving, K., Björk, S., Fjeld, M.: Untangling running: designing for real-life runner experiences. Interactions **22**(2), 40–43 (2015)

Saving Life and Keeping Privacy: A Study on Mobile Apps for Suicide Prevention and Privacy Policies

Jaisheen Reen[✉] [iD], Aniefiok Friday [iD], and Rita Orji

Faculty of Computer Science, Dalhousie University, Halifax, NS, Canada
js346515@dal.ca

Abstract. Suicide is a severe public health issue that impacts the lives of many individuals. Mobile health applications (apps) open new possibilities for safety by daily self-monitoring of suicide-related symptoms, which can help with safety planning. These mobile apps can help health professionals and specialists by providing follow-up and care throughout the treatment of patients with suicidal intents. A rising variety of suicide prevention measures based on the usage of new technologies are being developed now. In this paper, we reviewed literature on suicide prevention and also reviewed apps on the Apple App Store (App Store) and the Google Play Store (Play Store) focusing on the persuasive strategies used and the importance given to the privacy of the user. Our findings show that while most apps operationalize persuasive strategies, there is a lack of research on how users' privacy is managed. We also found a lack in adopting an evidence-based approach in preventing suicide. Based on our findings, we recommend designers adopt more evidence-based approaches in helping individuals who are struggling with suicide and use technology to enforce privacy and data protection. Also, developers of suicide mobile intervention should design more interactive apps rather than passive apps and apply a user-center design approach. From our analysis, we offer some design recommendations and propose a communication protocol to enforce privacy when sharing sensitive data for suicide apps.

Keywords: Persuasive strategies · User-centric design approach · Suicide prevention · Evidence-based approach · Privacy

1 Introduction

According to the World Health Organization (WHO), over 700,000 people commit suicide annually [9, 18, 28, 35]. Juan et al. [18] stated "... *for each individual who commits suicide, others 20 could be attempting it*" [18]. There are also indications that a previous suicide attempt is the most powerful risk factor for suicide [16]. Given the social and psychological costs of suicide attempts, the implementation of preventative suicide techniques should remain a top priority [18]. Although conventional interventions help in controlling suicide cases to some extent, they have some limitations, including, the lack of therapists [12], the effect of societal factors such as marginalization, stigma,

© Springer Nature Switzerland AG 2022
N. Baghaei et al. (Eds.): PERSUASIVE 2022, LNCS 13213, pp. 190–207, 2022.
https://doi.org/10.1007/978-3-030-98438-0_15

and oppression on the pathway for an individual to access mental health [1, 5, 11, 29], and privacy concerns [11]. Patrik et al. [31] noted that privacy is one of the six factors that impact suicide risk assessment in emergency department and Robinson et al. [6] discussed ethical challenges around privacy, clinical judgement, and informed consent in their study of social media and suicide prevention. According to O'Grady et al. [24] *"Mobile devices have the potential to deliver evidence-based interventions with greater customization to the individual and at the time when the intervention is required".* However, there are not enough apps that take a comprehensive approach to prevent suicide [13] while effectively managing privacy. Worst of all, some apps disguise potentially harmful content as useful [7].

This motivated our research for studying literature on preventing suicide and investigating the quality of suicide apps. We evaluated mobile suicide apps in terms of Persuasive strategies and privacy management employed in apps interpreted to be effective by the target users. Persuasive strategies are techniques employed in Persuasive Technology to encourage the desired behavior or attitude [26]. For our review we adopted strategies defined in Persuasive System Design (PSD) [25]. Privacy is a state of being free from unwanted intrusion [36]. We adopted the Control and Limitation Theories of privacy [32] which emphasizes the level of privacy as users' ability to control access to their information.

Some parameters we considered in measuring the quality of an app were the interpretation of the effectiveness of the app as shown by users' comments, observations from a full review of the app, combination of Persuasive strategies employed, the privacy policy of the app, and the use of evidence-based approaches in preventing or managing suicide.

2   Related Works

According to Franklin et al. [12], for every 100 mentally ill people, there is approximately one therapist. Patients have varying demands and clinical and digital characteristics, necessitating the development of highly scalable, engaging, and customized software [22] that relies on user data. O'Brien et al. [19] created the "Crisis care" app that enables parents and guardians of outpatient adolescents to access the coping abilities that children have added to the app. While the app was interpreted to be effective in showing acceptability and usability, there was limited information on the combination of persuasive strategies [25] used and other technology adopted in enforcing privacy. O'Grady et al. [24] devised "SafePlan" which adopts safety plans, diaries, and other evidence-based therapeutic interventions (Dialectical Behavior Therapy which is a comprehensive cognitive-behavioral treatment for mental diseases that are complex and difficult to treat [11]) in managing suicide. Being adjunct to face-to-face therapy, apps like SafePlan need to provide a safe means for clinicians to share patients' data. The researchers made the user-entered data stored locally on the user's device rather than on an external server as a measure of enforcing privacy. We considered this limited as users can only print safety plans, diaries, and other content from mobile apps wirelessly to share data with clinicians. While this approach was considered safe by the designers, it demands physical proximity and access to a printer. Furthermore, there is not enough evidence that shows wireless printing provides maximum security, as printers or Wi-Fi can be susceptible to man-in-the-middle-attacks or other exploitations [34].

Tighe et al. [33] discovered from their study on the ibobbly app that an acceptance-based therapy app reduced depression symptoms and psychological distress in the target population but did not affect suicidality or impulsivity. Despite this limitation, their work showed that suicide apps can be an effective self-help tool even for patients with severe cases of suicide ideation and other psychological conditions. Furthermore, although users can access information without the need for live data, there was no discussion of measures taken to secure users' data or verify data downloaded online.

Castillo-Sánchez et al. [7] suggest that health professionals should significantly encourage the development of easy-to-use apps that promote suicide prevention and improve the effectiveness of the therapies they support. Based on their study, 20 mobile apps sampled showed the following main findings: "(1) a high percentage of the apps analyzed in the study (82%) are provided in the English language; (2) the sampled apps were last updated in 2017 when only 45% of them received an update, but the constant and progressive update of treatments should be reflected in the apps; and (3) it is impossible to accurately determine the technical quality of these apps based on the distribution of scores". However, there was limited information as to how these therapies can be implemented with Persuasive Strategies to make them seem more effective. Furthermore, the privacy of sensitive suicide data was not fully elaborated in this study. Other researchers have also explored the usability of mental health (including suicide). For example, Alqahtani et al. [2] classified usability issues into six major categories: (1) bugs, (2) poor user interface (UI) design, (3) data loss, (4) battery, and memory usage issue; (5) lack of guidance, and explanation, and (6) internet connectivity issue. The researchers identified the need to manage health data without violating privacy.

According to Larsen et al. [17], content assessment is critical for suicide prevention apps because the Android and iOS app stores do not have criteria on the restriction of pro-suicidal content or the quality of app content. Gaur et al. [14] were also proponents of early detection and prevention of suicide and proposed using apps that are integrated with medical records thereby enabling predictive measures while also analyzing the history of patients. They proposed different improvements to suicide apps including the use of lexicon and other labels defined by authorities, such as the Columbia Suicide Severity Rating Scale (C-SSRS) and use of Artificial Intelligence (AI) for identifying people who are at high risk of suicide. However, the usability, Persuasive Strategies, and possible privacy concerns in sharing data across various medical apps were not discussed in detail. These facts prompted our study towards investigating persuasive strategies and privacy use in suicide apps as we uncovered that limited works are addressing the persuasive strategies and privacy concerns used in suicide mobile apps.

3   Method

This section outlines the review method we followed for this review to reach our objective. We highlight the inclusion criteria and process by which data was extracted for the reviewed apps. Our primary objective was to ascertain the efficacy of the mobile intervention in preventing suicide by investigating the design patterns, treatment approaches, and privacy strategies employed for mobile technology-based suicide intervention. Our approach followed a similar process of a full review as employed by Orji et al. [26].

3.1 Selection Process

To achieve our objective, we conducted two reviews. First, we reviewed mobile apps available to the public. We reviewed apps from the Apple App Store (n = 5) and the Google Play Store (n = 12), and multi-homing apps (apps deployed on both the AppStore and the Google Play Store) (n = 18) and apps from the literature (n = 4). This review emphasizes existing mobile apps published on mobile app platforms like Apple's App Store and Google's Play Store. We considered these two platforms as they are dominant mobile app platforms. We excluded other platforms (example, the Amazon App store, Huawei AppGallery, Aptoide) as they have a lower market share, are strongly affiliated to a private company, or are restricted to a geopolitical region [37]. To perform our review, both coders downloaded and installed apps from the Google Play Store. For the five apps on App Store, one coder reviewed the installed app. Each coder labeled different strategies used in the installed apps separately in a coding sheet (Microsoft Excel). Most of the categories in the coding sheet were adapted from Alqahtani et al. [1] and the rest were agreed upon by two coders after going through different apps. This coding sheet was then reviewed together to highlight areas in which two coders agree or disagree before calculating the Cohen Kappa coefficient [13].

We included apps that satisfy the following inclusion criteria:

- Designed for an English-speaking population.
- The app is mainly designed for suicide prevention or is focused on mental issues related to suicide prevention. As an example the app Better Stop Suicide app [38], did not provide direct remedies in preventing suicide but focused on informing the end-user on how to assist their social network in preventing suicide. DMHS: Interactive Suicide Prevention App [39] on the other hand was designed to enable the end-user access resource that can assist them during their journey in overcoming suicidal risks.
- The app is publicly available as a free app.

The second review concerns suicide apps studied in the academic literature academic literature. We searched three digital resources: PubMed, Google Scholar, and the ACM digital library. This review included papers that meet the following criteria:

- The paper should be focused on prevention, detection, or managing suicide with the possible use of mobile technology or computer algorithms that can be deployed on mobile devices.
- The paper should be in English.
- The papers should be published in the last five years (2016–2021).

The search query included a combination of the following search terms: "Suicide prevention", "Suicide", "Safety plan" "Mobile apps for suicide prevention", "Suicide mobile intervention", "Suicide factors". To refine our search results, a combination of special characters (+, −) and words (AND, OR) were used as Boolean operators across digital libraries (ACM, Google Scholar, PubMed) and app stores (AppStore and Play Store). The collated results from both app and literature searches were then analyzed to identify trends adopted by developers targeting mobile intervention for suicide prevention [27].

From our search, a total of 35 apps were selected from the target platforms: App Store (n = 5), Play Store (n = 12), and both platforms (n = 18) as shown in Fig. 1. We then proceeded by visiting the app web page, user's reviews, and general description made available by AppStore or Play Store. Lastly, each included app was then installed on a mobile device running Andriod (Nokia 5.1 Plus running Android 10; Oneplus 6T running Andriod 10, OxygenOS version 10.3.12) and iPhone running iOS 15.1.1. We excluded apps that could not be installed, needed identifiable information (for example a user's full name), failed to launch after successful installation. We proceeded to investigate apps published in academic journals. From our initial search of 80 papers, we obtained 62 papers focused on suicide and reviewed 35 papers that met all criteria. Papers focused only on depression and mental health were excluded (see Fig. 2).

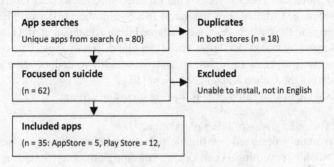

Fig. 1. Apps selection process.

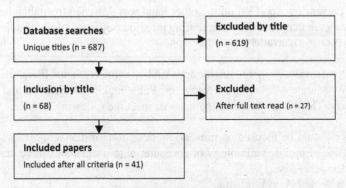

Fig. 2. Paper selection process

3.2 Data Analysis

We proceeded to code the collated literature and apps following our inclusion and exclusion criteria. Afterward, we examined the selected apps against the following information (see Table 1).

Table 1. Evaluation criteria selected for suicide mobile app review

Analysis	Description
App name; rating; platform, developer, last update	Name of the app, the rating, and target platform the app was designed for, the name of the developer, and the last update for the app
Persuasive strategies	Set of Persuasive Strategies based on Persuasive System Design (PSD) [25] model
Suicide prevention approach	The approach adopted by the app developers in preventing suicide. For example, did the user develop an emergency plan, apply meditation, or call a resource person as a means of preventing suicide?
Phase	The actual or perceived phase of suicidal patients the app was designed to assist. Suicide phase labels were adopted from the works of Gaur et al. [5] (see Table 2 for details)
Privacy policy and data security	Indicator whether data protection and privacy policy in place that guides the use of patient's data and protects patients from a possible data breach or other privacy concerns
Downloads	Total number of downloads recorded for an app in view
Psychology framework	Any psychological framework for managing suicide adopted by the app developers; for example, the use of Cognitive Behavior Therapy in managing suicidal thoughts
Teams with medical professional/consultants	Indicator whether the app was built in collaboration with mental health professionals or by consulting mental health professionals
Psychoeducation	Indicator whether the app provided psychoeducational materials to help patients deal with suicide

Similarly, collated literature was analyzed to identify approaches used by researchers and mental health professionals in designing a mobile intervention. This literature review was performed to better understand how publicly available apps adopted research-based approaches in end-user products for managing suicide. For the literature review, the following information was considered: Title, Year, Audience, Venue, Abstract, Findings, Recommendations, or Suggestions.

Table 2. Suicide phase definition adapted from [14]

Term	Description and example
Indicator	The patient shows a pessimistic character, may exhibit signs of depression and may have a family history of suicide
Ideation	The patient has suicidal thoughts, is feeling suicidal, or needs suicide care
Behavior	The patient is exhibiting suicidal behaviors or self-harm, is planning or having an actual plan on committing suicide, is verbally threatening to commit suicide, or is involved with dangerous behavior like drug abuse and drunk driving
Attempt	The patient has previous or known suicide attempts, suicidal or attempted deliberate poisoning, attempted suicide by self-administered drug, or attempted suicide while incarcerated
Supportive	Uses suicidal terms but does not show risk or past suicide attempts

4   Result

We analyzed our data to gain insights into three key areas: (1) the persuasive strategies used in mobile apps for suicide, (2) the approaches used in suicide apps in managing suicide, and (3) the privacy policy trends in suicide apps.

4.1   Persuasive Strategies Used in Mobile Apps for Suicide Prevention

From the collated apps, we performed an independent evaluation of the various persuasive strategies employed across the apps. After the individual evaluation, the generated coding sheets were compared to ascertain the level of agreement between the two researchers. We obtained a relative observed agreement of 1.0 and a hypothetical probability of chance agreement of 0.69. Calculating the Cohen Kappa's coefficient gave a value of one (1.0), which shows total agreement between the rating of both researchers.

Our results show that the considered apps employ a combination of persuasive strategies (max $= 5$, min $= 1$, M $= 2.74$, SD $= 5.67$) as depicted in Fig. 3. The most common persuasive strategies were: Expertise ($n = 6$), Suggestion ($n = 13$), Tunnelling ($n = 15$), Self-monitoring ($n = 16$) and Personalization ($n = 18$). Other strategies together had an average adoption rate of 2.2, with strategies like Reduction, Simulation, Social Comparison, Social Role, Surface Credibility, Tailoring, Trustworthiness, and Verifiability having the lowest adoption ($n = 1$). We believe the complex and very personal nature of suicide [8, 20, 30] accounts for the high adoption rate of the Personalization strategy when compared to other persuasive strategies.

Every persuasive strategy can be operationalized in different ways. Table 3 shows the most common persuasive strategies along with their different implementations. In Table 4 we show the summary of other criteria on reviewed apps.

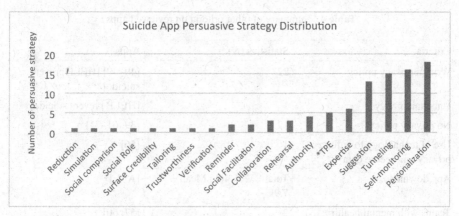

Fig. 3. Persuasive strategy distribution across apps reviewed. *TPE is third party endorsement

Table 3. Implementation of the five most-used persuasive strategies across suicide apps.

Strategy	How persuasive strategies were implemented
Personalization	Users can create a safety plan (18 apps), set alarms (2 apps), Create a personal wellness plan (3 apps), Creation of good memories box (2 apps), allows users to customize the appearance of the app, for example, color (3 apps), writing your distractions (1 app)
Self-monitoring	Mood tracker (9 apps), Write your triggers (2 apps), Journal (7 apps), Self-assessment questionnaire (4 apps), Recording voice memo (2 apps)
Tunneling	User-guided through a process example, selecting calming audio (3 apps), Users follow series of steps to manage suicide (3 apps), Users are guided through steps to take breathing exercises (5 apps), Users are guided through 5-4-3-2-1 sensory grounding strategy (3 apps), Users are guided through steps to take the daily pledge (2 apps)
Suggestion	Users are prompted to apply Stressbusters (1 app), Users are prompted to seek guidance (1 app), Users are prompted on things to consider before attempting suicide (2 apps), Advice about what to do (3 apps), Users can view tips on handling situations (3 apps), Suggestions based on results (1 app), Life tips are displayed to the user (1 app)
Expertise	App uses crises support helpline number (2 apps), App uses human or machine counselors (2 apps), Local services (1 app), Psychologist's video speaking about suicide (2 apps)

Table 4. Summary of other criteria on reviewed apps

Criteria	Statistics (N)	Apps
Written privacy policy	22	[40–60] [HELP prevent suicide]***
Uncertain policy	1	[HELP prevent suicide]***
No privacy policy	12	[39, 61–71]
Use of technology to enforce privacy and secure data*	1	[56]
App downloads	Total = 266.46k; Mean = 7.9k	[ALL]**
Teams with mental health staff/consultant	2	[57, 60]
Teams without mental health staff/consultant	33	[ALL]** excluding [57, 60]
User data stored locally	1	[58]
Uncertain data security measure	33	[ALL]** excluding [56, 58]
Gender-specific suicide app	1	[63]
Evidence-based treatment approach	2	[50, 60]

*The app in view does not store data on the mobile device but remotely on their server using commercial grade data security technology. **Applicable to all apps reviewed. ***App no longer available in AppStore at time of writing.

4.2 The Approach Used in Suicide Apps in Managing Suicide

The apps reviewed did not explicitly state what phase of suicide they were focused on except for "Crisis Care" [13] which was described as an app for adolescents who had recently left care facilities. In addition, the psychological or evidence-based approach that drove the design of these apps was not stated by the developers except for three apps (Better Stop Suicide [38], ReMinder Suicide Safety Plan [43], Hope by CAMH [72]). Furthermore, there was also no public listing of apps mentioned in the literature reviewed in both the AppStore and the Play Store. We identify this as a gap in the literature on suicide prevention apps as the number of techniques did not translate to actual mobile apps publicly available (see Table 5). We summarize our review of the various approaches used across the apps in Table 5.

Table 5. The approach used in managing suicide across reviewed apps.

App name	Suicide Prevention Approach as observed in apps
[38, 47, 61]	Meditation techniques (users are asked to think about a pleasant event), breathing exercises (users are asked to take a controlled breath for relaxation), and mindfulness (like maintaining a moment-by-moment awareness of our thoughts, feelings, bodily sensations, and surrounding environment) [10]
[39, 42, 53, 54, 62, 64–66, 69, 70, 73, 74]	Self-management tool (users can track their progress daily using a diary, journals, videos, or audio to record their thoughts), goal settings (users can set goals on their emotional health and make commitments to stay alive)
[61]	Gratitude (users are prompted to list things, events, or people they are grateful for)
[42, 51, 57, 61, 75]	Emergency Safety Plan (users can draft plans on how to manage suicide thoughts or crisis. Plans can include places to visit, contacts to call, or things to do to keep a user from suicidal thoughts)
[55–57]	Psychoeducational contents (materials are made available for users to get informed on different topics on suicide)
All apps reviewed	Psychoeducational materials (materials are made available for users to get informed on different topics on suicide) and Help Lines (users can call helplines of publicly approved health centers, organizations, or professionals dealing with suicide)
[42, 48, 62, 63, 71]	Suggestions on staying alive (users get periodic suggestions on various topics that encourage healthy mental habits or encouragement to stay positive and alive)
[50, 60]	Adopts the 5-4-3-2-1 [3] sensory grounding strategy, PHQ-9 test [21] for self-administration
[67]	Uses comparison of life scenarios
[41, 50, 56, 59, 65, 75]	App uses social network or connection

4.3 Transparency of Privacy Policy

A predominant issue mentioned by several researchers in investigating interventions for suicide is the need for privacy [5, 8]. Due to societal stigmatization, patients who have suicidal thoughts, find it challenging to communicate their emotional state and thoughts with family, friends, and even clinicians [5]. From the apps that were reviewed,

13 developers failed to provide a detailed privacy statement (no policy = 12; unclear or uncertain = 1) on the data collected and how it is used, while 22 apps provided links to their privacy policy (see Fig. 4). Of the 22 apps with the privacy statement, only one app stated commercial level data security was used in protecting users' data while another app saves users' data locally in the device. Our analysis shows interesting trends that are being implemented for designing suicide apps and raises questions on the quality and interpreted effectiveness of suicide apps.

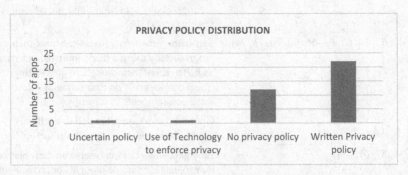

Fig. 4. Privacy Policy distribution across suicide apps.

5 Discussion

Our results show that several mobile apps targeting suicide do not employ evidence-based treatment approaches in helping people suffering from suicidal tendencies (see Table 6). This observation is consistent with Larsen et al.'s [17] research.

These comments raise questions about the overall quality and safety of publicly available apps for a very sensitive health concern, like suicide. Furthermore, developers should adopt well-established design patterns and best practices to improve the overall usability and effectiveness of an app. Therefore, in our review, we considered the current trend of these apps in addressing data security, and the approach adopted for treatment. Furthermore, there was limited knowledge of apps being developed with contributions of professional mental health professionals or in partnership with primary care centers dealing with mental health (see Table 4 and Table 5). This raises questions regarding the overall quality and safety of publicly available apps for a very sensitive health concern, like suicide. More effort may be needed to encourage developers to adopt design patterns that have been shown to improve the overall usability and effectiveness of an app.

5.1 Design Recommendations

The need for anonymity and access to help were identified as part of the challenges faced by users of mobile apps designed for mental health. The privacy case when dealing with suicide cannot be under-emphasized [1, 5, 8]. While several researchers have mentioned the need for patient data to be safe, there is the need to discuss how privacy can be upheld using technology. Works by Chaum [8] have shown practical ways in which privacy can

Table 6. Poor use of evidence-based treatment for reviewed suicide apps.

Challenge	User's comment or app review
Quick access to help	*"…I just wanted someone to guide me towards helping myself. But I have to wait until 4 pm. That's absolutely garbage. The sites that say they're 24/7 aren't. They run weird hours like 6 pm to 2 am. They expect you to wait until their open hours. As if that's a conversation you can put off and have later…"* *"I tried to reach out for help today. I tried every single number listed and I tried several chats. No one is available or there isn't help available in my area. This just made it worst I feel worse than I did before…"*
Limited information on evidence-based approach for treatment	***"Better Stop Suicide** has been designed to help tackle the growing problem of suicide, which takes the lives of over 800,000 people every year. This is a free app using world-leading psychological techniques and technology to stop people from committing suicide…"* – Here we have no further knowledge of any evidence-based approach used [29] *"Suicidal thoughts can seem like they will last forever – but these thoughts and feelings pass with time. This app is designed to support those dealing with suicidal thoughts and help prevent suicide…"* - **Suicide Safety Plan App** [61] *"A suicide prevention app aimed at users in the northeast of Scotland. Provides helpful info for those affected in any way by suicide, extensive contact details for services in Aberdeen city, Aberdeenshire and Moray as well as allowing users to create their own safety plan"* - **Prevent Suicide App** [44] *"This app empowers you to help yourself to stay safe and to reach out to others when you have thoughts of suicide. It will help you recognize your triggers; things you can do to divert your mind, people you can see or places where you can go to be safe, connected, and distracted; who you can contact when you are struggling, who will help you from a professional perspective, and what you can do to keep your environment safe."* - **Be Safe** [46]

be managed using cryptography. Blockchain technology also provides an invaluable means of managing privacy using anonymous transactions but is considered a poor fit where mental health professionals are required by law to identify their patients. Furthermore, public blockchains are generally not designed for medical use or for enforcing regulatory health policies. These ideas lead us to search for an effective and less costly alternative that can help maintain privacy, especially when using resource-constrained devices like a mobile phone over a large network of caregivers. We propose a communication protocol that uses cryptography to mask the identities of parties involved in a communication channel. We consider the proposed protocol suitable for two use cases.

The first use case allows for a patient's identity to be masked from the caregiver and every other participant on the network. This is ideal where caregivers are volunteer workers and are spread across a wide network of hospitals, public health agencies, and private health service providers. In the second use case, both the identity and message of the patient and the caregiver are known only to both parties in direct communication. Also, we offer a list of recommendations in Table 7 categorized by the following criteria: Privacy, System, Persuasive strategies design and usability, and Health, safety, and quality control.

Table 7. Recommendations for suicide apps based on literature and app reviews

Recommendation	Comments
Privacy and social recommendations	
Privacy policy	There may be a need for both Android and iOS to provide improved privacy policies for health apps, especially those focused on mental health and suicide. In-app advertisements strategy may give users the indication that information about their mental states is being sold to marketers, thus hampering the user's intentions of seeking help
Appropriate use of social networks	We have little or no knowledge of interactive technology that enables suicide patients to build supportive networks that intervene in loneliness, isolation, depression, and self-harm which could be triggering suicide ideation [4, 5]
System recommendations	
Data storage and interoperability	Data tracking and storage features of suicide apps should support users to export data [1] and have access to long-term self-monitoring data
Persuasive strategy design & usability recommendations	
Personalization and Adaptation	Personalization and Adaption strategies should be considered in app design. Allowing users to modify the mobile intervention in ways that best suit their daily activities could improve the user experience and overall user perception of the app in managing suicidal risks [1]. Also, where psychoeducational materials are available, effort should be employed to recommend information based on the current state, context, and preferences of the user [23]
Design for impaired cognitive abilities	App designed for suicide management should be easy to use which contributes to the acceptance of use or even adoption of technology. with minimal barriers for users with impaired cognitive abilities to reach their set goals. Suicide apps should also have clear communication [20]

(*continued*)

Table 7. (*continued*)

Recommendation	Comments
Health, safety & quality control recommendations	
Evidence-based design	Suicide apps should be built using approaches based on research findings or recommendations by World Health Organization, The American Psychology Association (APA), or other approved bodies [22, 23]
Safe content	App dealing with suicide should also consider factors that are closely linked to suicide and follow recommended safe content measures based on research findings. For example, substance abuse should not be directly or indirectly encouraged while dealing with suicide topics
Access to help	Approved public helplines or resources should be readily available in mobile apps designed to manage suicide [1]. Links to resource websites, direct call buttons for emergency calls, and effective chatbots based on expert systems could be adopted [23, 29]. Also being able to determine the current context of a suicidal patient could be necessary for appropriate and timely intervention by sending appropriate messages [15]

6 Conclusions

Setting standards for identifying mobile apps for suicide monitoring, prevention, and intervention is a difficult undertaking. In this review, our goal was to identify various drawbacks and gaps in the design of the apps meant for suicide prevention. The data we gathered from the app reviews allowed us to observe the different patterns and techniques used in these apps and approaches that could have been done differently. We reviewed 35 apps from the App Store and Play Store with 4 apps from the literature selected. Our results showed that there is a poor use of privacy policy and limited use of technology to ensure privacy and implement evidence-based treatment in suicide apps. we highlighted the limitations in these apps, offered a set of design recommendations, and proposed a communication protocol that uses cryptographic keys to enforce privacy allowing users to reveal or mask their identities when needed.

Suicide remains a life-threatening concern in public health and more effort is required to bring the rate of suicide to a very minimal value or near zero. Our proposed communication protocol can further improve the quality of communication for mobile health apps. We plan to further investigate how to implement a workable privacy communication protocol for health services.

Acknowledgment. This research was undertaken, in part, thanks to funding from the Canada Research Chairs Program. We acknowledge the support of the Natural Sciences and Engineering Research Council of Canada (NSERC) through the Discovery Grant.

References

1. Alqahtani, F., Khalifah, G.A., Oyebode, O., Orji, R.: Apps for mental health: an evaluation of behavior change strategies and recommendations for future development. Front. Artif. Intell. **2**, 30 (2019). https://doi.org/10.3389/FRAI.2019.00030/BIBTEX
2. Alqahtani, F., Orji, R.: Usability issues in mental health applications. In: ACM UMAP 2019 Adjunct - Adjunct Publication of the 27th Conference on User Modeling, Adaptation and Personalization, Haapie, pp. 343–348 (2019). https://doi.org/10.1145/3314183.3323676
3. Bakker, K., Moulding, R.: Sensory-processing sensitivity, dispositional mindfulness and negative psychological symptoms. Pers. Individ. Differ. **53**(3), 341–346 (2012). https://doi.org/10.1016/J.PAID.2012.04.006
4. Beltagy, I., Peters, M.E., Cohan, A.: Longformer: the long-document transformer (2020). http://arxiv.org/abs/2004.05150. Accessed 15 Nov 2021
5. Bogunovic, I., Mitrović, S., Scarlett, J., Cevher, V.: Robust submodular maximization: a non-uniform partitioning approach. In: 34th International Conference on Machine Learning, ICML 2017, vol. 1, pp. 783–801 (2017)
6. Buus, N., et al.: Stakeholder perspectives on using and developing the MYPLAN suicide prevention mobile phone application: a focus group study. Arch. Suicide Res. **24**(1), 48–63 (2020). https://doi.org/10.1080/13811118.2018.1489319
7. Castillo-Sánchez, G., Camargo-Henríquez, I., Muñoz-Sánchez, J.L., Franco-Martín, M., de la Torre-Díez, I.: Suicide prevention mobile apps: descriptive analysis of apps from the most popular virtual stores. JMIR Mhealth Uhealth **7**(8), 1–9 (2019). https://doi.org/10.2196/13885
8. Chaum, D.: Achieving electronic privacy. Sci. Am. **267**(2), 96–101 (1992)
9. Choo, C.C., Kuek, J.H.L., Burton, A.A.D.: Smartphone applications for mindfulness interventions with suicidality in Asian older adults: a literature review. Int. J. Environ. Res. Public Health **15**, 12 (2018). https://doi.org/10.3390/ijerph15122810
10. Colzato, L.S., Ozturk, A., Hommel, B.: Meditate to create: the impact of focused-attention and open-monitoring training on convergent and divergent thinking. Front. Psychol. **3**, 116 (2012). https://doi.org/10.3389/FPSYG.2012.00116
11. Dimeff, L., Linehan, M.M.: Dialectical behavior therapy in a nutshell. Calif. Psychol. **34**(3), 10–13 (2001)
12. Franklin, J.C., et al.: A brief mobile app reduces nonsuicidal and suicidal self-injury: evidence from three randomized controlled trials. J. Consult. Clin. Psychol. **84**(6), 544–557 (2016). https://doi.org/10.1037/ccp0000093
13. Franzen, M.: Kappa coefficient. In: Kreutzer, J.S., DeLuca, J., Caplan, B. (eds.) Encyclopedia of Clinical Neuropsychology, pp. 1903–1904. Springer, Cham (2018)
14. Gaur, M., et al.: Knowledge-aware assessment of severity of suicide risk for early intervention. In: The Web Conference 2019 - Proceedings of the World Wide Web Conference, WWW 2019, Cdc, pp. 514–525 (2019). https://doi.org/10.1145/3308558.3313698
15. Honary, M., et al.: Shaping the design of smartphone-based interventions for self-harm. In: Conference on Human Factors in Computing Systems – Proceedings (2020). https://doi.org/10.1145/3313831.3376370
16. Jeong, Y.W., Chang, H.J., Kim, J.A.: Development and feasibility of a safety plan mobile application for adolescent suicide attempt survivors. CIN – Comput. Inform. Nurs. **38**(8), 382–392 (2020). https://doi.org/10.1097/CIN.0000000000000592

17. Larsen, M.E., Nicholas, J., Christensen, H.: A systematic assessment of smartphone tools for suicide prevention. PLoS ONE **11**(4), 1–14 (2016). https://doi.org/10.1371/journal.pone.015 2285

18. Martínez-Miranda, J., et al.: Implementation of a health information system to support the screening and surveillance of suicidal behaviours. In: PervasiveHealth: Pervasive Computing Technologies for Healthcare, pp. 136–144 (2020). https://doi.org/10.1145/3418094.3418108

19. McManama, K.H., O'Brien, M.L., Ross, A., Gironda, C., Wharff, E.A.: A pilot study of the acceptability and usability of a smartphone application intervention for suicidal adolescents and their parents. Arch. Suicide Res. **21**(2), 254–264 (2017). https://doi.org/10.1080/138 11118.2016.1182094

20. Melia, R., et al.: Mobile health technology interventions for suicide prevention: systematic review. JMIR mHealth uHealth **8**(1), e12516 (2020). https://doi.org/10.2196/12516

21. Miller, P., Newby, D., Walkom, E., Schneider, J., Li, S.C., Evans, T.J.: The performance and accuracy of depression screening tools capable of self-administration in primary care: a systematic review and meta-analysis. Eur. J. Psychiatry **35**(1), 1–18 (2021). https://doi.org/ 10.1016/J.EJPSY.2020.10.002

22. Morgiève, M., et al.: A digital companion, the Emma app, for ecological momentary assessment and prevention of suicide: quantitative case series study. JMIR mHealth uHealth **8**(10), e15741 (2020). https://doi.org/10.2196/15741

23. Mouchabac, S., Leray, P., Adrien, V., Gollier-Briant, F., Bonnot, O.: Prevention of suicidal relapses in adolescents with a smartphone application: Bayesian network analysis of a pre-clinical trial using in silico patient simulations. J. Med. Internet Res. **23**(9), 1–14 (2021). https://doi.org/10.2196/24560

24. O'Grady, C., Melia, R., Bogue, J., O'Sullivan, M., Young, K., Duggan, J.: A mobile health approach for improving outcomes in suicide prevention (SafePlan). J. Med. Internet Res. **22**(7), e17481 (2020). https://doi.org/10.2196/17481

25. Oinas-Kukkonen, H., Harjumaa, M.: Persuasive systems design: key issues, process model, and system features. Commun. Assoc. Inf. Syst. **24**(1), 485–500 (2009). https://doi.org/10. 17705/1cais.02428

26. Orji, R.: Why are persuasive strategies effective? Exploring the strengths and weaknesses of socially-oriented persuasive strategies. In: de Vries, P.W., Oinas-Kukkonen, H., Siemons, L., Beerlage-de Jong, N., van Gemert-Pijnen, L. (eds.) PERSUASIVE 2017. LNCS, vol. 10171, pp. 253–266. Springer, Cham (2017). https://doi.org/10.1007/978-3-319-55134-0_20

27. Orji, R., Moffatt, K.: Persuasive technology for health and wellness: state-of-the-art and emerging trends. Health Inform. J. **24**(1), 66–91 (2018). https://doi.org/10.1177/146045821 6650979

28. Pang, N., Lu, H., Qian, L.: The entity analysis of social networks in Weibo with suicidal tendencies based on Bert, pp. 125–130 (2021). https://doi.org/10.1145/3468920.3468938

29. Pendse, S.R., Sharma, A., Vashistha, A.: Can i not be suicidal on a sunday?: Understanding technology-mediated pathways to mental health support. In: Conference on Human Factors in Computing Systems – Proceedings (2021). https://doi.org/10.1145/3411764.3445410

30. Pennou, A., Lecomte, T., Potvin, S., Khazaal, Y.: Mobile intervention for individuals with psychosis, dual disorders, and their common comorbidities: a literature review. Front. Psychiatry **10**, 302 (2019). https://doi.org/10.3389/fpsyt.2019.00302

31. Petrik, M.L., Gutierrez, P.M., Berlin, J.S., Saunders, S.M.: Barriers and facilitators of suicide risk assessment in emergency departments: a qualitative study of provider perspectives. Gen. Hosp. Psychiatry **37**(6), 581–586 (2015). https://doi.org/10.1016/J.GENHOSPPSYCH.2015. 06.018

32. Tavani, H.T.: Philosophical theories of privacy: implications for an adequate online privacy policy. Metaphilosophy **38**(1), 1–22 (2007). https://doi.org/10.1111/J.1467-9973.2006.004 74.X

33. Tighe, J., Shand, F., Ridani, R., MacKinnon, A., De La Mata, N., Christensen, H.: Ibobbly mobile health intervention for suicide prevention in Australian Indigenous youth: a pilot randomised controlled trial. BMJ Open **7**(1), 1–10 (2017). https://doi.org/10.1136/bmjopen-2016-013518

34. Reddy, S.V., Ramani, K.S., Rijutha, K., Ali, S.M., Reddy, C.H.P.: Wireless hacking-a WiFi hack by cracking WEP. In: ICETC 2010 - 2010 2nd International Conference on Education Technology and Computer, vol. 1 (2010). https://doi.org/10.1109/ICETC.2010.5529269

35. Suicide. https://www.who.int/health-topics/suicide#tab=tab_1. Accessed 15 Nov 2021

36. Privacy Definition & Meaning. Dictionary.com. https://www.dictionary.com/browse/privacy. 29 Nov 2021

37. Biggest app stores in the world 2020. Statista. https://www.statista.com/statistics/276623/number-of-apps-available-in-leading-app-stores/. Accessed 29 Nov 2021

38. Better Stop Suicide app - Stop Suicide App. Suicide Prevention. Mental Health app. https://thebetterappcompany.com/better_stop_suicide. Accessed 28 Nov 2021

39. DMHS: Interactive Suicide Prevention en App Store. https://apps.apple.com/us/app/dmhs-interactive-suicide-prevention/id1136542675?l=es. Accessed 16 Jan 2022

40. Better Stop Suicide - Apps on Google Play. https://play.google.com/store/apps/details?id=com.betterappcompany.betterstopsuicide. Accessed 16 Jan 2022

41. The LifeLine on the App Store. https://apps.apple.com/ca/app/the-lifeline/id752509889. Accessed 16 Jan 2022

42. Stay Alive on the App Store. https://apps.apple.com/gb/app/stay-alive/id915458967. Accessed 16 Jan 2022

43. ReMinder Suicide Safety Plan on the App Store. https://apps.apple.com/ca/app/reminder-suicide-safety-plan/id1407116715. Accessed 30 Nov 2021

44. Prevent Suicide - NE Scotland - Apps on Google Play. https://play.google.com/store/apps/details?id=com.faffdigital.PreventSuicide. Accessed 16 Jan 2022

45. R U Suicidal? – Apps on Google Play. https://play.google.com/store/apps/details?id=com.psychappsint.r.u.suicidal&hl=en_CA&gl=US. Accessed 16 Jan 2022

46. Be Safe - Apps on Google Play. https://play.google.com/store/apps/details?id=org.au.keepcalm.keepsafe&hl=en&gl=US. Accessed 28 Nov 2021

47. My Tools – suicide.ca on the App Store. https://apps.apple.com/ca/app/mes-outils-suicide-ca/id1534604841. Accessed 16 Jan 2022

48. distrACT – Apps on Google Play. https://play.google.com/store/apps/details?id=com.expert selfcare.selfharm&hl=en_CA&gl=US. Accessed 16 Jan 2022

49. Suicide? Help! Tayside – Apps on Google Play. https://play.google.com/store/apps/details?id=com.faffdigital.ChooseLife&hl=en_CA&gl=US. Accessed 16 Jan 2022

50. Hope by CAMH on the App Store. https://apps.apple.com/ca/app/hope-by-camh/id1527950198. Accessed 16 Jan 2022

51. Am I? My Safety Plan on the App Store. https://apps.apple.com/ca/app/am-i-my-safety-plan/id1438254077. Accessed 16 Jan 2022

52. Suicide Prevention App – Apps on Google Play. https://play.google.com/store/apps/details?id=com.app.suicideprevention&hl=en_CA&gl=US. Accessed 16 Jan 2022

53. Calm Urge: Self Harm Tracker on the App Store. https://apps.apple.com/us/app/calm-urge-self-harm-tracker/id1551984419. Accessed 16 Jan 2022

54. My Life My Voice Mood Journal on the App Store. https://apps.apple.com/us/app/my-life-my-voice-mood-journal/id626899759. Accessed 16 Jan 2022

55. TUFMINDS – Apps on Google Play. https://play.google.com/store/apps/details?id=com.app_tufminds.layout&hl=en_CA&gl=US. Accessed 16 Jan 2022

56. Suicide Prevention -Ways to Help a Suicidal Friend – Apps on Google Play. https://play.google.com/store/apps/details?id=com.andromo.dev653868.app1026659&hl=en_CA&gl=US. Accessed 16 Jan 2022

57. Prevent Suicide - Highland – Apps on Google Play. https://play.google.com/store/apps/det
ails?id=com.faffdigital.PSHighland&hl=en_CA&gl=US. Accessed 16 Jan 2022

58. Don't panic - Depression and panic help – Apps on Google Play. https://play.google.com/
store/apps/details?id=org.dontpanic&hl=en_CA&gl=US. Accessed 16 Jan 2022

59. Yellow Ribbon – Apps on Google Play. https://play.google.com/store/apps/details?id=com.
app.yellowribbon&hl=en_CA&gl=US. Accessed 16 Jan 2022

60. MoodTools - Depression Aid – Apps on Google Play. https://play.google.com/store/apps/det
ails?id=com.moodtools.moodtools&hl=en_CA&gl=US. Accessed 16 Jan 2022

61. Suicide Safety Plan on the App Store. https://apps.apple.com/ca/app/suicide-safety-plan/id1
003891579. Accessed 28 Nov 2021

62. SafetyNet: Your Suicide Prevention App – Apps on Google Play. https://play.google.com/
store/apps/details?id=com.application.safetynet&hl=en_CA&gl=US. Accessed 16 Jan 2022

63. A Teen Suicide Prevention Anime for Android - APK Download. https://m.apkpure.com/a-
teen-suicide-prevention-anime/zenbrina.com.flutter_app. Accessed 16 Jan 2022

64. Got Your Back - JS Foundation on the App Store. https://apps.apple.com/us/app/got-your-
back-js-foundation/id1512807496. Accessed 16 Jan 2022

65. Be aware of suicide for Android - APK Download. https://m.apkpure.com/be-aware-of-sui
cide/com.app.baosjrf. Accessed 16 Jan 2022

66. Self Harm Tracker - Sober, Be Calm, Harm Reduction – Apps on Google Play. https://play.
google.com/store/apps/details?id=com.sunny.meditationcare&hl=en_CA&gl=US. Accessed
16 Jan 2022

67. Suicide Cliff - Visual Novel – Apps on Google Play. https://play.google.com/store/apps/det
ails?id=com.gamedanteam.GameDan_Team.Suicide_Cliff&hl=en_CA&gl=US. Accessed
16 Jan 2022

68. Operation Reach Out – Apps on Google Play. https://play.google.com/store/apps/details?id=
suicide.prevention.app&hl=en_CA&gl=US. Accessed 16 Jan 2022

69. Self Harm Recovery – Apps on Google Play. https://play.google.com/store/apps/details?id=
com.la.apps.idranktheseawater&hl=en_CA&gl=US. Accessed 16 Jan 2022

70. Days Without Incidents – Apps on Google Play. https://play.google.com/store/apps/details?
id=codingale.cr.dwi&hl=en_CA&gl=US. Accessed 16 Jan 2022

71. Shatter the Silence – Apps on Google Play. https://play.google.com/store/apps/details?id=
com.nicusa.msi.dmh&hl=en_CA&gl=US. Accessed 16 Jan 2022

72. Hope by CAMH. CAMH. https://www.camh.ca/hopebycamhapp. Accessed 30 Nov 2021

73. Be Safe - Apps on Google Play. https://play.google.com/store/apps/details?id=org.au.kee
pcalm.keepsafe&hl=en&gl=US. Accessed 16 Jan 2022

74. Operation Life – Apps on Google Play. https://play.google.com/store/apps/details?id=operat
ionlife.dva.com.operationlife&hl=en_CA&gl=US. Accessed 16 Jan 2022

75. ReMinder Suicide Safety Plan on the App Store. https://apps.apple.com/ca/app/reminder-sui
cide-safety-plan/id1407116715. Accessed 16 Jan 2022

A Psychological Model for Predicting the Smartphone Zombie Phenomenon and Intervention

Tomohiro Sakai(✉) ⓘ, Yuich Kuriki(✉), Wenzhen Xu(✉), Masato Taya(✉),
and Atsunori Minamikawa(✉)

KDDI Research, Inc., Tokyo, Japan
{to-sakai,yi-kuriki,we-xu,ma-taya,
at-minamikawa}@kddi-research.jp

Abstract. Although the smartphone zombie (SZ) has become a social problem, the cognitive processes that underlie it have not been sufficiently examined and the effective intervention methods to suppress it have remained unverified. This study tested the validity of our psychological model in terms of predicting the Smartphone zombie incidence rate and effectively intervening to curtail it. We first developed the interventional materials and initially tested their effectiveness through a questionnaire survey. We then conducted a field experiment in which a smartphone app collected phone usage logs of 194 Japanese participants who were randomly assigned to experimental and control groups. The experimental group was presented with the interventional materials once a week during a one-month period, while the control group did not see any interventional materials. Our experimental results showed that our psychological model can predict the Smartphone zombie incidence rate that we proved positively correlated with the cognitive processes of SZ, specifically, in terms of smartphone addiction and habit, as well as behavioral intention and willingness. Moreover, we found the interventional materials had the possibility of reducing SZ's behavioral willingness.

Keywords: Smartphone zombie · Smartphone addiction · Behavioral willingness · Fear-arousing appeal · Behavior log

1 Introduction

1.1 Social Issue

Smartphone zombie (SZ) has become a social problem worldwide. It is defined as "the pedestrian act of using a smartphone while walking" [1, p. 87]. Some of the most recent studies suggest that SZ can distract and increase the risk of traffic accidents. Masuda and Haga [2] investigated the effects of inputting texts on cell phones in a laboratory experiment and showed that attention decreased when using the phone, and that walking distance became shorter and stride length became smaller. Further, the number of times the user deviated from the usual walking route was found significantly higher with

© Springer Nature Switzerland AG 2022
N. Baghaei et al. (Eds.): PERSUASIVE 2022, LNCS 13213, pp. 208–220, 2022.
https://doi.org/10.1007/978-3-030-98438-0_16

smartphones than with a feature phone (flip-flop phone). Another is that Haga et al. [3] revealed SZ has a negative impact on visual and auditory attention, as well as on gait stability. Based on the results of these previous studies, it goes without saying that SZ is dangerous, which is why SZ is regulated by ordinances in many countries worldwide. For example, Hawaii enacted an ordinance banning smartphones and imposed a fine of up to $35 for first-time offenders. In Japan, areas such as Kanagawa, Tokyo, and Osaka have also enacted ordinances but do not impose fines.

Even though users know that SZ is dangerous, they still find reasons to be so. A survey conducted by the Telecommunication Carriers Association [4] of Japan shows that over 90% of people think SZ is dangerous, but about half of the respondents still use smartphones while walking. The reasons cited for this include 1) timetable and map app usage, 2) communication on social media sites, and 3) smartphone preferences. These findings can be attributed to two factors, one being smartphone addiction. Mourra et al. [5] investigated whether smartphone addiction tendencies increase SZ risk. Their experimental results show that using a smartphone while walking decreased attention and increased the number of missed external stimuli. Moreover, people with higher smartphone addiction tended to miss even more the external stimuli. Another study also shows that smartphone addiction is expected to be associated with SZ [5]. The other factor is smartphone habit. Smartphones have become widespread throughout the world and using them has become habitual. According to a previous study [1], this determines the behavioral intention and behavioral willingness of the SZ. Even though users know that SZ is dangerous, they tend to engage in such behavior because they are habituated to operating their smartphones.

In light of the above, it is necessary to find a persuasive technology that can prevent SZ based on the user's smartphone habit and smartphone addiction. Therefore, the goal of the present study is to provide empirical evidence that will be useful for inhibiting SZ.

1.2 Related Works

Gerrard et al. [6], as well as Gibbons et al. [7], have proposed the prototype/willingness model (Fig. 1). This model helps to understand and explain the psychological mechanism of the SZ phenomenon.

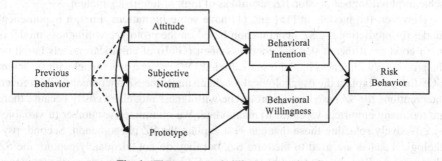

Fig. 1. The prototype/willingness model [6]

The prototype/willingness model focused on the fact that even if one does not intend to take a risky action, the person concerned realizes that he or she is forced by the situation to carry out the action, and thus acts unintentionally [8]. Hence, the model assumes two processes: the reasoned action path, in which individuals act on their own intentions, and the social reaction path, in which behaviors are triggered by social situations regardless of the individual's intentions. In the reasoned action route, it is assumed that attitudes and subjective norms specify behavioral intentions toward acting per the theory of reasoned action [9] and theory of planned behavior [10]. By contrast, the social reaction route assumes that prototypes and subjective norms specify behavioral willingness toward acting. The characteristics of the prototype/willingness model can be summarized in three points. First, when one has acted in the past, positive attitudes toward the risky behaviors [11], positive norms [12], increased behavioral intentions [13], and this is also related to willingness [12]. The less likely an individual perceives the risks and negative consequences associated with the behavior, the more likely he or she will be actively engaged in this behavior [8]. Second, risk behaviors are determined not only by behavioral intention (what one intends to do), but also by behavioral willingness (what one is willing to do). Behavioral willingness is defined as "an openness to risk opportunity–an adolescent or adult's report of what they would consider doing under certain (risk-conducive) circumstances" [7, p. 236]. Third, if we perceive others who are important to us participate in certain social norms in which we are accepted, then behavioral willingness increases as well as our behavioral intentions [14]. In addition, individuals are motivated toward behavioral willingness by a prototype, i.e., the perception (or image) that they associate with a particular behavior.

Few studies have examined the psychological mechanisms of the SZ phenomenon. Among these are Sato and Haga [15] and Sato [1] who have examined the psychological processes that give rise to SZ based on the prototype/willingness model derived from a Japanese population sample. Sato and Haga investigated the processes related to the operation of cell phones while walking on the street. Results from a questionnaire survey conducted among Japanese college students revealed that risk perception negatively influences attitudes toward cell phone service. Results also showed behavioral willingness and behavioral intentions respectively elicit cell phone use behavior. Following the study in [15], Sato [1] investigated the psychological processes of SZ by dividing them into high-risk situations and low-risk situations. Their results revealed that behavioral intention and behavioral willingness inhibit SZ and that behavioral intention mediates behavioral willingness to stop SZ regardless of high or low-risk situation.

However, the models in [15] and [1] have some limitations. First, a hypothetical model for predicting the SZ phenomenon based on the prototype/willingness model is not a good fit. It means that the goodness-of-fit (GOF) of empirical models based on the prototype/willingness model is not sufficient. We create a new model with sufficient GOF that can explain the psychological mechanisms of the SZ phenomenon. Moreover, interventions for SZ based on the prototype/willingness model are costly because there are too many empirical variables to manipulate. We minimize the number of variables by effectively selecting those that can best explain the SZ phenomenon. Second, psychological scales are used to measure SZ, but they do not adequately capture the SZ phenomenon. By contrast, our study focuses on SZ behavior and measures the incidence rate of SZ from smartphone app logs. Third, the generalizability of the psychological model in prior studies [1, 15] is low because it was conducted only among university students. We target people aged 20–69 years.

1.3 Purpose of the Study

Our research has two objectives. First, we aim to validate a new psychological model for predicting the SZ phenomenon in a data-driven manner by using smartphone app log and psychological assessment. We can assume that behavioral intention and behavioral willingness directly predict the SZ phenomenon based on the prototype/willingness model. However, the model omits two important variables to understanding the SZ phenomenon, namely, smartphone addiction and smartphone habit. Therefore, our proposed model predicts the Smartphone zombie incidence rate from log data that could indicate smartphone addiction and smartphone habit, as well as behavioral intention and behavioral willingness. Once this first aim is achieved, we can understand the reasons why people are walking while using their smartphones. We can then determine the psychological variables through which we need to intervene to curtail the SZ phenomenon.

Previous studies, such as [1] and [15], have examined the mechanisms of SZ, but have not used their findings to conduct interventions to regulate them. Hence, our second aim is to validate our proposed model-based intervention effects. We develop the inervention materials before conducting the experiment to determine an effective SZ intervention. The intervention materials are designed to make people aware of the dangers of SZ and to motivate them not to use smartphones while walking. We identify the variables on which the intervention materials have an effect based on our novel psychological model demonstrated in the first aim. Once this second aim is achieved, our findings will suggest persuasive ways to prevent people from becoming SZ.

2 Method

This study consists of two parts, namely, pilot study and main study. Detailed information of each part is described below.

2.1 Developing Intervention Materials in Pilot Study

We conducted a web-based survey of 156 smartphone users in Japan. The survey period was from November 30, 2020 to December 1, 2020. We asked all smartphone users to answer whether they use their phones while walking on a 5-point scale (i.e., 1: never to 5: often) for seven usage behaviors: 1) map and timetable, 2) news app, 3) communication app, 4) social media, 5) game app, 6) habitual use regardless of purpose, and 7) effective use of the most of my time. We gathered the respondents who indeed use their smartphones while walking, randomly divided them into two groups, presented to each group the different intervention materials (Fig. 2), and interviewed them before and after presenting the materials on their intention for using smartphones while walking.

In the pilot study, four images were created to provide an effective intervention on SZ. As shown in Fig. 2, Images 1 and 2 are different illustrations informing that one in 10 people who walked while using a smartphone bumped into others. Image 3 shows the possibility of imprisonment of up to five years if the other person is injured in an accident caused by using a smartphone while walking. Lastly, Image 4 shows that an accident caused by using a smartphone while walking not only injures oneself but also hurt others around. Following Mori et al. [16], respondents were asked about their impressions of each image on a 6-point scale (1: completely disagree to 6: strongly agree).

| Image 1 | Image 2 | Image 3 | Image 4 |

Fig. 2. Intervention materials

2.2 Main Study

Our experimental design is shown in Fig. 3, which begins with Japanese participants being recruited by an online survey company in Japan. There were five screening conditions to recruiting participants: 1) aged 20–69 years, 2) living in Tokyo, Kanagawa, Saitama, Chiba, Aichi, Osaka, Kyoto, or Nara, 3) use Android 8 or higher devices, 4) answered "often" or "sometimes" to SZ behavior, and 5) going out for 10 min on foot at least three to four times a week. After screening, a total of 194 participants consented to participate in the questionnaire experiment.

The participants were then randomly assigned to experimental (n = 97) and control (n = 97) groups. During the one-month intervention period, one of the four intervention materials was presented to the experimental group once a week (and differed per week), whereas no intervention material was presented to the control group. All participants installed the U-Logger, which is an experimental app, but reliable tool, that has been used in previous research on smartphone addiction [17]. We used U-Logger to measure smartphone usage, i.e., it continued to run in the background while obtaining the smartphone operation log. Further, the participants also responded to the psychological scales before and after the intervention (see Sect. 2.3). The number of participants who participated in the experiment until completion is 182 (M_{age} = 39.79 ± 10.38; n = 92 and n = 90 in the experimental and control groups, respectively). The experiment lasted from December 8, 2020 to March 26, 2021.

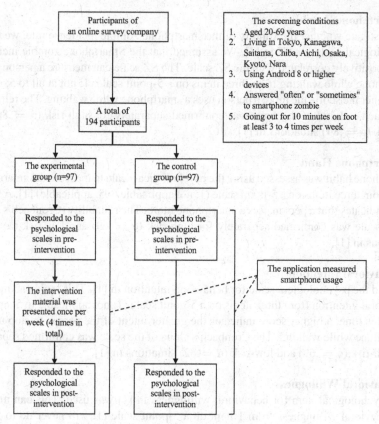

Fig. 3. Experimental design of the main study

2.3 Measurements

We used psychometric measurement and smartphone app log. We used the scales for which reliability and validity from 2 to 6 were confirmed in previous studies [1, 18, 19]. The prior study [1] has developed each scale to assess smartphone zombie, smartphone habit, behavioral intention, and behavioral willingness.

1. Smartphone Zombie Incidence Rate (Smartphone App Log)

We extracted smartphone usage durations based on operation log information that were collected by the U-Logger. Usage duration indicates the time between smartphone screen unlock and screen closure. We used the formula in Eq. (1) to calculate the smartphone zombie incidence rate. The higher the scale score, the more a person uses a smartphone while walking.

$$\text{Smartphone Zombie Incidence Rate} = \frac{\text{smartphone usage durations}}{\text{walking time}} \quad (1)$$

2. Smartphone Zombie

To investigate whether the validity of the smartphone zombie incidence rate, we used a psychological scale for SZ in [1]. We assumed that the Smartphone zombie incidence rate is positively correlated with the SZ scale. The SZ scale can measure a person uses a smartphone while walking from three items on a 5-point scale (1: not at all to 5: often). The higher the score, the more a person uses a smartphone while walking. The reliability (Cronbach's alpha) of the scale was confirmed separately for high-risk ($\alpha = .86$) and low-risk ($\alpha = .84$) situations in [1].

3. Smartphone Habit

Smartphone habit was assessed using the psychological scale to measure the smartphone habit from three items on a 5-point scale (1: not applicable to 5: applicable) [1]. A higher score indicates that a person uses a smartphone more. The reliability (Cronbach's alpha) of the scale was confirmed separately for high-risk ($\alpha = .69$) and low-risk ($\alpha = .69$) situations in [1].

4. Behavioral Intention

We used the psychological scale for behavioral intention in [1]. This scale can measure behavioral intention from three items on a 5-point scale (1: not applicable to 5: applicable). This time, a higher score indicates the greater intent of the person to stop using a smartphone while walking. The Cronbach's alpha of the scale was confirmed separately for high-risk ($\alpha = .69$) and low-risk ($\alpha = .82$) situations in [1].

5. Behavioral Willingness

The psychological item for behavioral willingness in [1] was used. This can measure the behavioral willingness from 1 item on a 5-point scale (1: will never do to 5: will always do). This one item measures the respondent's tendency to use a smartphone while walking and wherein many people around the respondent are SZ. The higher the score is for this item, the more the person is willing to use a smartphone while walking.

6. Smartphone Addiction

Smartphone addiction was measured using the Japanese version [18] of the English scale in [19]. The Japanese version can measure smartphone addiction from 10 items on a 6-point scale (1: completely different to 6: very applicable). The higher the scale score, the more the person is addicted to the smartphone. The scale was confirmed in [19] as demonstrating internal consistency ($\alpha = .82$).

2.4 Data Analysis

We examined the correlation between each variable using correlation analysis. Based on the results, we constructed a hypothetical model for predicting the Smartphone zombie incidence rate. The hypothesized model was tested using structural equation modeling (SEM). In SEM, we assessed model fit by evaluating the overall pattern of the GOF index [20], including the Chi-Square Test, Comparative Fit Index (CFI), the Root-Mean-Square Error of Approximation (RMSEA), and Akaike's Information Criterion (AIC). According to the GOF index [20], the CFI should be .97 or higher, and RMSEA should be less than .08. AIC is used to compare models and the model with the smallest value is the best model. We then determined which models fit the data better.

We calculated the pre-intervention and post-intervention scores for each variable. We then subtracted the pre-intervention scores from the post-intervention scores for each variable. Thus, the amount of change in each variable is calculated. We used the difference in differences (DID) to examine the intervention effects comparing the experimental group with the control group. We then used the effect size by Cohen [21] to evaluate the size of the intervention effects. According to the effect size, values of 0.20, 0.50, and 0.80 for Cohen's d are commonly considered to be indicative of small, medium, and large effects, respectively (.10, .30, and .50, respectively, for Pearson's r).

3 Results

3.1 The Evaluation of Intervention Materials

The number of people who answered "often" or "sometimes" to any of the seven behaviors related to using smartphones while walking was 128 out of 156. These 128 people were randomly divided into two groups, and the changes in SZ before and after presenting the intervention materials and the impression on the intervention materials were examined. When Image 3 was presented, the SZ scores decreased from 2.43 to 2.18 points, indicating a significant difference ($p < .05$). In addition, Image 3 was perceived to be "scary" and "effective in preventing people from becoming SZ". All other images showed no significant difference in change scores of the SZ.

3.2 A New Psychological Model with Behavior Log

We examined the Cronbach's coefficient alpha of smartphone zombie, smartphone habits, behavioral intention, and smartphone addiction at pre-intervention. The Cronbach's coefficient alpha of these psychological scales is as reliable as that of the previous studies. We then examined the correlations between the smartphone zombie incidence rate using log data and the psychological variables at pre-intervention. The correlation coefficients between each variable are shown in Table 1.

The smartphone zombie incidence rate showed a positive correlation with smartphone zombie ($r = .32, p < .01$). In other words, the smartphone zombie incidence rate indicates the actual smartphone zombie. Moreover, the incidence rate was positively correlated with behavioral willingness ($r = .24, p < .05$), suggesting that people who are willing to be in a smartphone zombie state actually use a smartphone while walking. Psychological variables other than the smartphone zombie incidence rate are significantly correlated to each other, as in previous studies.

Following the correlation analysis, we generated a hypothetical model to predict the SZ phenomenon from the pre-intervention data. Our hypothetical model explains smartphone zombie incidence rate from smartphone addiction, smartphone habit, behavioral intention, and behavioral willingness. We tested our hypothetical models with SEM. The results in Table 2 shows sufficient CFI and RMSEA for all models. We determined which model is the best based on each model's AIC. As a result, we determined Model

Table 1. The correlation coefficient between each variable (n = 74)

Variables (Cronbach's coefficient alpha)	2	3	4	5	6
1. Smartphone zombie incidence rate	.32**	.17	−.10	.24*	.03
2. Smartphone zombie (α = .78)	-	.42***	−.53***	.60***	.42***
3. Smartphone habits (α = .75)		-	−.31**	.52***	.35**
4. Behavioral intention (α = .82)			-	−.49***	−.31**
5. Behavioral willingness				-	−.27*
6. Smartphone addiction (α = .82)					-

Note. $^*p < .05$ $^{**}p < .01$ $^{***}p < .001$

2 fits best the data. Model 2 is the model in which the path from smartphone addiction to behavioral willingness is removed from Model 1. The GOF index of Model 2 shows $\chi^2_{(4)} = 0.43, p = .98$; CFI = 1.00; RESEA = 0.00, AIC = 836.31.

Table 2. The GOF index of our hypothetical models (n = 74)

Model	χ^2	df	p-value	CFI	RMSEA	AIC
1	0.40	3	0.94	1.00	0.00	838.28
2	0.43	4	0.98	1.00	0.00	836.31
3	4.29	5	0.51	1.00	0.00	838.16

Model 2 (in Fig. 4) indicated that 1) smartphone addiction positively predicted smartphone habit ($\beta = .35, p < .01$) and negatively predicted behavioral intention ($\beta = −.23, p < .05$), 2) smartphone habit negatively predicted behavioral intention ($\beta = −.23, p < .05$) and positively predicted behavioral willingness ($\beta = .41, p < .001$), 3) behavioral intention negatively predicted behavioral willingness ($\beta = −.36, p < .001$), and 4) behavioral willingness positively predicted the smartphone zombie incidence rate from log data ($\beta = .24, p < .05$).

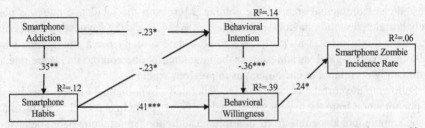

Fig. 4. Model 2 to predicts the smartphone zombie incidence rate from log data. $^*p < .05$ $^{**}p < .01$ $^{***}p < .001$

3.3 Intervention Effects

We examined the intervention effects by comparing the experimental group to the control group using DID. In the analysis, we used the data of 41 participants (experimental group n = 23, control group n = 18) with no missing value for the smartphone zombie incidence rate and used the data of 182 participants (experimental group n = 92, control group n = 90) with no missing value for the other psychological variables. The results presented in Table 3 show that behavioral willingness is more significantly reduced in the experimental group than in the control group ($t_{(178.81)} = 1.98, p < .05, d = 0.29$).

Table 3. Descriptive statistics and T-test for each variable in pre- and post-intervention

Variables	Group	Pre	Post	Difference	t	df	p-value	Effectsize d
Smartphone zombie incidence rate	Experimental	0.19 (0.15)	0.21 (0.20)	0.02 (0.12)	0.62	26.71	ns	0.21
	Control	0.22 (0.24)	0.27 (0.26)	0.05 (0.20)				
Smartphone zombie	Experimental	3.19 (1.08)	2.86 (1.13)	−0.33 (0.79)	1.47	177.13	ns	0.22
	Control	3.02 (1.15)	2.87 (1.08)	−0.15 (0.88)				
Smartphone habits	Experimental	3.47 (1.02)	3.38 (1.00)	−0.09 (0.74)	0.57	179.81	ns	0.08
	Control	3.51 (1.06)	3.48 (1.01)	−0.03 (0.70)				
Behavioral intention	Experimental	4.11 (0.83)	4.30 (0.76)	0.20 (0.79)	0.70	169.85	ns	0.10
	Control	4.26 (0.67)	4.39 (0.74)	0.12 (0.60)				
Behavioral willingness	Experimental	2.76 (1.18)	2.43 (1.08)	−0.33 (1.09)	1.98	178.81	$p < .05$	0.29
	Control	2.56 (1.09)	2.53 (1.14)	−0.02 (0.98)				
Smartphone addiction	Experimental	2.69 (0.90)	2.66 (0.82)	−0.03 (0.60)	1.69	177.38	ns	0.25
	Control	2.73 (0.82)	2.84 (0.99)	0.11 (0.47)				

4   Discussion

We aimed to validate a novel psychological model for predicting the SZ phenomenon from log data. Afterwards, we aimed to validate the intervention effects of the intervention materials in our model.

4.1   Theoretical Insights

Regarding the first aim, we found our psychological model could predict the Smartphone zombie incidence ratee from smartphone addiction, smartphone habit, behavioral intention, and behavioral willingness as shown in Table 3. Our model leveraged the actual behavior logs to measure SZ (contrast to previous studies [1, 15] that did not), which helped understand why people end up as SZ. Moreover, since our model deals with smartphone addiction, which was not assumed in the prototype/willingness model, it can also explain the mechanism that causes people who are addicted to their smartphones to actually use them while walking. Smartphone addiction directly reduces behavioral intention to stop SZ per our model. Also, smartphone addiction mediates smartphone habit and reduces behavioral intention. These results suggest that people who are addicted to their smartphones tend not to stop SZ by themselves. At the same time, they intend to not stop their SZ because they have the habit of using their smartphones. Therefore, they tend to use their smartphones while walking in public where many people are SZ. This indicates the path in our model in which behavioral intention mediates behavioral willingness and increases Smartphone zombie incidence rate. In summary, our model shows people who are addicted to smartphones have the habit of using their smartphones, and they intend to not stop their SZ because they are influenced publicly by many people who are SZ.

Based on our model, we believe that intervening in smartphone addiction, smartphone habit, behavioral intention, and behavioral willingness can reduce SZ. The direct relationship between behavioral willingness and Smartphone zombie incidence rate suggests that SZ is not caused by individual intentions but is influenced by social situations. In terms of behavior change, our model posits how we control behavioral willingness that directly predicts Smartphone zombie incidence rate is particularly important. Thus, as theoretical contribution, we provided a model that can be used for intervention by effectively selecting psychological variables to explain the SZ phenomenon.

4.2 Empirical Insights

When it comes to the second aim of our study, we found that Image 3 (Fig. 2) as intervention material could reduce behavioral willingness. The effect size of the intervention on behavioral willingness was evaluated small with Cohen's d. Image 3 informs users of the penalty. It is conceivable that Image 3 has the effect of loss aversion in SZ. Given the effect of image 3, the ordinances on SZ in many countries mentioned at the beginning would have the effect of loss aversion in SZ. Ordained fines on SZ can be expected to motivate people to avoid financial loss, one with a fear-arousing appeal [22] that has some persuasive effects in preventing people from SZ.

The fear-arousing appeal of Image 3 has a certain effect of reducing behavioral willingness, but care is required on the way it should be used. French and Raven [23] refers to punishment as coercive power in social influence, which generally implies something unpleasant. It is often used to force recipients to do something, which can possibly cause psychological reactance, which is a motivational state directed toward the reestablishment of threatened or eliminated freedom per Brehm's definition [24]. Hence, it is likely to cause a backlash among recipients, and while it may change behavior temporarily, it is unlikely to bring about long-term effects–something that we as researchers should bear in mind.

4.3 Limitations and Future Directions

We obtained a new psychological model for predicting the SZ phenomenon from log data indicating smartphone addiction, smartphone habit, behavioral intention, and behavioral willingness. However, our research focused only on Japanese data. Thus, the generalizability of the results we obtained needs to be considered. It is also important to improve our psychological model to account for socio-cultural factors. Moreover, we measured the Smartphone zombie incidence rate in our psychological model but could not identify the specific apps (e.g., music or gaming app) users interact with. Individual apps may impose different cognitive load and demand varying degrees of attention, whether visual or auditory. Future research will need to consider about the information of the specific apps.

5 Conclusion

Our study demonstrated behavioral willingness directly predicted smartphone zombie incidence rate. We then found that the Image 3 reduced behavioral willingness, but it did not find any direct effects to mitigate the use of smartphones while walking. One reason for this is that walking and using the phone do not necessarily result in accidents. If users observe people who use their smartphones while walking and conclude the risk is not high, they would be willing to do the same. In contrast, if accidents caused by SZ directly affect us, we then become willing to immediately stop SZ.

According to the prototype/willingness model, behavioral willingness for SZ is susceptible to the influence of social norm. We propose to set up environments in which people stop SZ or to prepare alternative ways to replace SZ. For instance, when looking at timetable or map apps, people can stop for a while and look at them, and when playing smartphone games, dedicated spaces can be created where smartphone games can be played. A system that offers rewards (e.g., points that turn into money) if they are not looking at their smartphones while walking could be a way to get them to stop SZ.

References

1. Sato, H.: Psychological process of walking while using a smartphone (in Japanese). Japanese J. Shinshu Stud. Human. **7**(2), 87–98 (2020)
2. Masuda, K., Haga, S.: Effects of cell phone texting on attention, walking, and mental workload: Comparison between the smartphone and the feature phone. Japanese J. Ergon. **51**(1), 52–61 (2015). https://doi.org/10.5100/jje.51.52
3. Haga, S., Sano, A., Sekine, Y., Sato, H., Yamaguchi, S., Masuda, K.: Effects of using a smart phone on pedestrians' attention and walking. Proc. Manuf. **3**, 2574–2580 (2015). https://doi.org/10.1016/j.promfg.2015.07.564
4. https://www.tca.or.jp/press_release/2019/0306_903.html
5. Mourra, G.N., et al.: Using a smartphone while walking: The cost of smartphone-addiction proneness. Addict. Behav. **106**, 106346 (2020). https://doi.org/10.1016/j.addbeh.2020.106346
6. Gerrard, M., Gibbons, F.X., Houlihan, A.E., Stock, M.L., Pomery, E.A.: A dual-process approach to health risk decision making: the prototype willingness model. Dev. Rev. **28**(1), 29–61 (2008). https://doi.org/10.1016/j.dr.2007.10.001
7. Gibbons, F.X., Houlihan, A.E., Gerrard, M.: Reason and reaction: the utility of a dual-focus, dual-processing perspective on promotion and prevention of adolescent health risk behaviour. Br. J. Health. Psychol. **14**(2), 231–248 (2009). https://doi.org/10.1348/135910708X376640
8. Gibbons, F.X., Gerrard, M., Blanton, H., Russell, D.W.: Reasoned action and social reaction: willingness and intention as independent predictors of health risk. J. Pers. Soc. Psychol. **74**(5), 1164–1180 (1998). https://doi.org/10.1037/0022-3514.74.5.1164

9. Fishbein, M., Ajzen, I.: Belief, Attitude, Intention, and Behavior: An introduction to Theory and Research. Addison-Wesley, Reading (1975)

10. Ajzen, I.: The theory of planned behavior. Organ. Behav. Hum. Decis. Process. **50**(2), 179–211 (1991). https://doi.org/10.1016/0749-5978(91)90020-T

11. Bentler, P.M., Speckart, G.: Attitudes "cause" behaviors: a structural equation analysis. J. Pers. Soc. Psychol. **40**(2), 226–238 (1981). https://doi.org/10.1037/0022-3514.40.2.226

12. Gerrard, M., Gibbons, E.X., Benthin, A., Hessling, R.: The reciprocal nature of risk behaviors and cognitions: what you think shapes what you do and vice versa. Health Psychol. **15**(5), 344–354 (1996). https://doi.org/10.1037/0278-6133.15.5.344

13. Bagozzi, R.P.: Attitudes, intentions, and behavior: a test of some key hypotheses. J. Pers. Soc. Psychol. **41**(4), 607–627 (1981). https://doi.org/10.1037/0022-3514.41.4.607

14. Gibbons, F.X., Helweg-Larsen, M., Gerrard, M.: Prevalence estimates and adolescent risk behavior: cross-cultural differences in social influence. J. Appl. Psychol. **80**(1), 107–121 (1995). https://doi.org/10.1037/0021-9010.80.1.107

15. Sato, H., Haga, S.: Factors affecting pedestrians' risk behavior (in Japanese). Japanese J. Rikkyo Psychol, Res. **57**, 37–50 (2015)

16. Mori, K., Hirota, S., Ohyama, K., Onodera, J., Koshikawa, M., Shirai, I.: Fear appeals in no-texting-while-walking posters: evaluation of the fear levels using the implicit positive and negative affect test (in Japanese). In: 82nd, Proceedings on The Japanese Psychological Association, p. 79. The Japanese Psychological Association, Japan (2018)

17. Kurokawa, M., Honjo, M., Mishima, K.: Development of the smartphone-based internet addiction tendency Scale for high school students and technical college students (in Japanese). Japanese J. Exp. Soc. Psychology **60**(1), 37–49 (2020). https://doi.org/10.2130/jjesp.1907

18. Higuchi, S.: Smartphone game addiction (in Japanese). Naigai Publishing, Japan (2018)

19. Kwon, M., Kim, D.J., Cho, H., Yang, S.: The smartphone addiction scale: development and validation of a short version for adolescents. PLoS ONE **8**(12), e83558 (2013). https://doi.org/10.1371/journal.pone.0083558

20. Hair, J.F., Black, W.C., Babin, B.J., Anderson, R.E.: Multivariate Data Analysis, 7th edn. Prentice Hall, London (2010)

21. Cohen, J.: A power primer. Psychol. Bull. **112**(1), 155–159 (1992). https://doi.org/10.1037/0033-2909.112.1.155

22. Higbee, K.L.: What is the "Fear" in a Fear-Arousing Appeal ? Psychol. Rep. **35**(3), 1161–1162 (1974). https://doi.org/10.2466/pr0.1974.35.3.1161

23. French, J.R., Raven, B.H.: The bases of social power. In: D. Cartwright (Ed.) Studies in Social Power. Institute for Social Research, Ann Arbor (1959)

24. Brehm, J.W.: A Theory of Psychological Reactance. Academic Press, New York (1966)

A Blueprint for an AI & AR-Based Eye Tracking System to Train Cardiology Professionals Better Interpret Electrocardiograms

Mohammed Tahri Sqalli[1](✉) iD, Dena Al-Thani[1] iD, Mohamed B. Elshazly[2] iD, and Mohammed Al-Hijji[3] iD

[1] Information and Computing Division, College of Science at Hamad Bin Khalifa University, Doha, Qatar
mtahrisqalli@hbku.edu.qa

[2] Department of Cardiac Electrophysiology, Cleveland Clinic, Cleveland, OH, USA

[3] Interventional and Structural Cardiology Division, Hamad Medical Corporation, Doha, Qatar

Abstract. The electrocardiogram is one of the most used medical tests worldwide. Despite its prevalent use in the healthcare sector, there exists a limited understanding in how medical practitioners interpret it. This is mainly due to the scarcity of international guidelines that unify its interpretation across different health institutions. This leads to a lack of training and unpreparedness by medical students who are about to join the medical workforce. In this paper, we propose a blueprint for a proactive artificial intelligence and augmented reality-based eye tracking system to train cardiology professionals for a better electrocardiogram interpretation. The proposed blueprint is inspired from extensive interviews with cardiology medical practitioners as well as students who interpret electrocardiograms as part of their daily practice. The interviews contributed to identifying the major pain-points within the process of electrocardiogram interpretation. The interviews were also critical in conceptualizing the persuasive components of the training system for a guided correct electrocardiogram interpretation. Throughout the presented blueprint, we detail the three components that constitute the system. These are the augmented reality-based interactive training interface, the artificial intelligence-based processing sub-system, and finally the adaptive electrocardiogram dataset.

Keywords: Electrocardiogram · ECG · Artificial intelligence · Persuasive technology · Eye-tracking · Augmented reality

1 Introduction

The electrocardiogram (ECG) is one of the most used medical tests globally. It is estimated that more than 300 million ECG tests are performed annually [1]. The electrocardiogram is a graph that represents the electrical activity of the human heart. The 12-lead ECG showcases this activity from 12 different viewpoints called leads. Accurate ECG interpretation is a rare skill that is sought after due to its complexity.

© Springer Nature Switzerland AG 2022
N. Baghaei et al. (Eds.): PERSUASIVE 2022, LNCS 13213, pp. 221–229, 2022.
https://doi.org/10.1007/978-3-030-98438-0_17

Yet, there exists a restricted understanding in how expert interpreters reach a correct ECG diagnosis [2]. This causes a chasm between skilled interpreters and novice ones who are just beginning to develop this skill. Studies assessing ECG interpretation competency in cardiology residents reveal that 58% of imminent potential life-threatening ECGs are missed by medical residents [3]. 60% of those residents claim to be convinced that they perform a correct interpretation [3].

As the field of medicine is heading towards the digitalization of most of its aspects [4, 5], we propose a proactive Artificial Intelligence (AI) and Augmented Reality (AR) based eye tracking system to train cardiology professionals to better interpret electrocardiograms. The system's aim is to innovate in terms of how training for ECG interpretation is provided to medical practitioners. The proposal for the development of this system comes in light of the severity of the threat it aims to respond to. The threat lies in the detrimental repercussions of a failed ECG interpretation, ranging from avoidable cardiac deaths to inefficient treatment costing the health, time and money from the patient and the system [6]. The threat also lies in a raise in cardio-vascular diseases specifically, and chronic diseases generally, over the past two decades [7]. During these two decades the prevalence of chronic diseases has risen to 57% as of the year 2020 [8].

In the forthcoming sections of the paper, we start by presenting the related works where we examine existing research and systems using eye-tracking technology to train and to understand ECG interpretations by medical practitioners. The second section details the investigative study by going through the interview process as well as its major results. We then look at the problem the system aims to address, as well as the three components of the system. These components are namely the AR-based training interface, the AI-based processing sub-system, and finally the adaptive ECGs dataset. We finally conclude the paper by discussing its limitations and future works.

2   Related Works

While the use of eye tracking in ECG interpretation is recent, the use of augmented reality in medicine and medical education is in the rise [9]. The first study to use eye tracking in understanding how medical experts interpret an ECG dates back to 2014 [10]. Prior to conducting this initial study [10], the authors [2, 10–12] observed that there are nuances in terms of accuracy of interpretation and the way the ECG interpretation is carried among experts. Moreover, conducting those eye tracking studies also stemmed from the lack of universal best-practices or guidelines for the general ECG interpretation process [6]. Thus, there came a proposal for the adoption of eye tracking in order to understand how medical practitioners proceed into interpreting an ECG. The results of the studies proved that the collected eye-gaze data may be used to unveil insights about how expert annotators proceed with an ECG interpretation. Pioneering eye tracking experiments of both Bond et al. [10] as well as Davies et al. [2] collected the eye-gaze data of over 250 expert ECG interpretations and applied an objective quantitative approach to analyzing it. The authors' major findings resided in quantifying the eye fixation duration over each lead of the 12-lead ECG. This opened doors to comparing the time spent fixating over leads in the frontal plane compared to leads in the transverse plane. This enabled the possibility of ranking the leads that are looked at the most versus the least looked at leads. The conducted eye tracking studies [2, 10–12] were insightful in facilitating the quantification of experts' interpretation of an ECG.

Attempts to develop augmented reality systems for medical education were done mostly in the fields of surgery and anatomy [9], but not in ECG interpretation. As per the literature, there currently exists no commercial or research-based system that combines the use of eye tracking to provide AI and AR-based training to support and guide beginner interpreters better understand and interpret ECGs. However, the literature contains studies and experiments where the end goal is to explore how eye tracking can be used for medical pedagogy. Authors of some eye tracking experimental research [10, 13] referred to eye-tracking as a means to create tutorials to medical students. The authors [10, 13] achieved the latter by fusing both eye-tracking and audio data in order to create tutorials that visualize and unveil the techniques expert interpreters use to interpret ECGs. The audio recording methodology technique used in the experiments is referred to as a "think aloud" protocol.

3 Investigative Study Description

3.1 Method

The design of the proposed persuasive proactive training system stemmed from extensive interviews conducted with different medical practitioners who have varying expertise years along with medical students [14]. The interviews were semi-structured in the sense that there were questions to guide the interview, but the interviewers were more interested to hear about the experience of ECG interpreters, and what would they expect from a persuasive system to improve in terms of the ECG interpretation experience. Notes from the interviews with each volunteer were recorded. These notes were taken as the foundation of the design of the system described in the following section. The interview was part of a larger empirical eye tracking study that aimed to contrast how do medical practitioners perceive the ECG interpretation process as opposed to how they actually perform the interpretation task [7, 15, 16]. The thematic analysis approach was used as the main method to orient the questions asked during the interview and to conceptualize the training system. The analysis process for the interviews remained faithful to the themes set when designing the questions. Below are the questions that correspond to each theme that guided the interview:

1. *Understanding of one's own ECG interpretation approach:*

   - How do the participants view their expertise with ECGs in general?
   - Do the ECG interpreters follow a certain template or guidelines to proceed through the interpretation of ECGs?
   - Are the participants conscious about their own shortcomings when interpreting an ECG?
   - As they interpreted ECGs over time, did they change their procedure of interpretation?

2. *Persuasive elements that sway someone to consider an alternative ECG diagnosis*

- When interpreting ECGs as a group, do they sometimes get persuaded to change their final interpretation or diagnosis?
- Do they use the automated interval and waveform calculations provided by the digital ECG systems?

3. *Suggestions by medical practitioners about ECG interpretation improvement from the perspective of technologies.*

- What would they wish to have as a supporting persuasive tool to guide the novice or experienced ECG interpreters correctly diagnose the heart abnormality?

3.2 Participants

Twelve participants with different medical roles and varying ECG interpretation years of experience were recruited from a university campus and a cardiac hospital. Participants were selected based their job title/role in clinical practice. The mean age was 27 ± 3 years. The medical categories are defined as follows: Junior medical students - those in a pre-clinical curriculum, Senior medical students - those in a clinical curriculum, Nurses – Nurses either serving in the catheterization laboratory or the cardiac care unit, Technicians - Cardiovascular technologists working in a cardiac catheterization laboratory, Fellows - physicians undergoing post-graduate training in cardiology, Cardiology consultants – Board-certified, independent cardiology practitioners. Out of the 12 participants, four are female while eight are male. Years of experience ranged between 1 and 15 years of ECG interpretation experience.

3.3 Ethics

Conducting the interviews is part of a larger study that can be examined at [7, 15, 16, 14]. The study received institutional review board (IRB) approval from the ethical board of both the Qatar Biomedical Research Institute at Hamad bin Khalifa University [17] as well as the Hamad Medical Corporation. The research protocol reference number for the study is QBRI-IRB-2020–01-009. Approval was granted before the start of the interviews. Institutional review board approval guarantees that all study methods were conducted following the guidelines and recommendations of international regulatory agencies [17]. Participants signed informed consent before being interviewed.

3.4 Results

The below points summarize the essence of the interviews conducted with the participants according to the three themes set in the methods Sect. 3.1.

1. *Understanding of one's own ECG interpretation approach:*
   The ECG is a deeply personalized biomarker: A consistent theme repeating itself through the interview with all the participants suggests that the ECG is a deeply personalized bio-marker, regardless whether it shows a normal sinus rhythm or a heart abnormality.

   Reading an ECG suggests only observing a snapshot of the heart's state in the time of ECG capture. This entails that an ECG does not provide a wholistic view of the patient's heart condition. Most of the medical practitioners, especially the cardiology consultants emphasize on the fact that the ECG, in most cases serves as a starting point to the diagnosis. It may also serve as an ending point where the consultants need to confirm a hypothesis about the patient's heart abnormality.

2. *Persuasive elements that sway someone to consider an alternative ECG diagnosis*
   Healthcare practitioners read ECGs differently depending on different factors. Among these factors is the role the healthcare practitioner holds. A nurse may look for different signs of abnormalities than a technician or a consultant. Moreover, healthcare practitioners with the same role may read the ECG differently if they belong to different departments. A catheterization lab nurse may read the ECG differently than an emergency room nurse. This has also been demonstrated through our experimental eye tracking study [15].

   One factor that persuades medical practitioners to have a nuanced interpretation of the same ECG among each others is the presence or absence of patient' history and follow-up. This has been also demonstrated through different eye-tracking studies [18].

3. *Suggestions by medical practitioners about ECG interpretation improvement from the perspective of technologies.*
   There are several opportunities to improve and digitalize the ECG reading and capture. Among these methodologies is to use guidance in order to orient and tunnel the interpreter towards observing the right heart abnormalities. This guidance could be in the below forms:

   Simplifying the way the ECG is presented. Studies have explored different ways about how an ECG could be presented for more readability and focus on the alarming signs of an arrhythmia. Some of these methodologies refer to pseudo-coloring the ECG's waveform as well as referring to a polar coordinate system [19].

   Adapting the guidance depending on the expertise level as well as the expectation from the diagnosis.

   Providing a dynamic interactive guidance depending on where the interpreter is observing. This was concluded as the interviewers explained the abilities that eye tracking technology can unlock.

3.5 Discussion

The points gathered from interviewing the pool of medical practitioners and students were taken into consideration to propose a blueprint for a proactive system that adopts the elements of persuasive technology to guide and channel ECG interpreters to better examine ECGs and eventually provide a correct diagnosis. The opportunities that machine learning, artificial intelligence, as well as eye tracking technology provide for

ECG interpretation can join forces to design a coherent system to present a plan for better ECG interpretation. The following section discusses the components of the system, and how they can orient a clueless interpreter to better observing the ECG to find hints about what could be the right diagnosis. Each component is detailed separately.

4 Proposed System's Blueprint

4.1 System's Goal

We propose a proactive Artificial Intelligence (AI) and Augmented Reality (AR) based eye tracking system to train cardiology professionals to better interpret electrocardiograms.

4.2 System's Components

Figure 1 depicts a blueprint for the structure of the proposed platform. The platform uses eye tracking technology to record the interpreters' eye movements while they observe the ECG before giving a diagnosis. The eye tracking data serves as an input to the machine learning algorithm that analyses the interpreters' eye movements while they perform the task of interpretation. Using AR, and the support of the analyzed data, the system provides live feedback to guide the interpreters correctly interpret the ECG being observed. The development of the training system is done in three phases. Each phase represents a sub-system working in synergy with the other two sub-systems in order to provide an adaptive coaching platform for medical practitioners who interpret ECGs in their daily practice. Details about each sub-system are below.

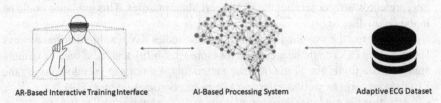

AR-Based Interactive Training Interface   AI-Based Processing System   Adaptive ECG Dataset

Fig. 1. Structure for the AI&AR-based educational platform for ECG interpretation training

The Adaptive ECG Dataset

ECG interpretation is complex due to the existence of several nuanced heart arrhythmias [20]. These arrhythmias are therefore reflected differently on the ECG. However, as the ECG is one of the most versatile and most used tests in medicine [21], large open-source datasets for these arrhythmias are stored for reference and training purposes in medicine. With the affordability of digital storage, many of these ECG databases are digitalized. The proposed system to be developed will base its training dataset on two elements. The ECGs set included in the training sessions will be either from the personal collection of experts in ECG interpretation involved in the design of the system, or from the open ECG dataset available from the PhysioNet database [22].

The AR-Based Interactive Training Interface

The training interface consists of an eye-tracker integrated in the Microsoft HoloLens 2 with a software used to record eye movements with a sampling rate of 60 Hz (± 1 Hz). The software is also responsible to display the ECGs used in the training session. It is also responsible to correlate each collected eye tracking dataset to its corresponding ECG. We envision the AR-based system to have a minimalistic interface. The interface is minimalistic in the sense that the 12-lead ECG image takes up the whole space for the displayed 3D image, and the cues and guidance for a correct interpretation are superposed on top of the image using AR technology. The guidelines will be displayed in real-time to the trainee in the form of heatmaps, eye movement scan paths, as well as indicators to some critical areas on the ECG. The comments as well as the ECG signal's width and intervals, which are two critical measures for identifying abnormalities in the patient's heartbeat, will be displayed on the side of the screen for reference purposes. The AR based interactive training interface will adapt the training according to the interpreter's eye movement as the interpreter moves around the ECG image.

The AI-Based Processing Sub-system

The AI-based processing sub-system is at the center of the eye tracking data processing using machine learning algorithms. The machine learning algorithm's aim is to predict to what extent are the interpretation patterns for medical practitioners interpreting the ECG predictable. The system uses the collected dataset generated by the eye tracking device. The collected dataset grows at around 60 raw observations per second. These observations contain mainly the interpreter's eye fixation data. The aim of the machine learning sub-system is to filter through the raw data, cluster it based on the X,Y coordinates on the ECG image, and based on the time sequence the interpreter follows. This final step then results in obtaining clusters to be analyzed. The obtained clusters will then enable the sub-systems to predict the trajectory of the interpreters based on their current eye movement trends. The clusters will also enable to predict whether the interpreter currently reading the ECG needs guidance and cues in order to move towards the right observation to provide a correct final interpretation.

This process is done continuously on a loop fashion as long as the trainee is requesting for more training programs. As the system keeps running, the collected eye movements information of the trainees serves for the system's unsupervised learning.

5 Conclusion

5.1 Concluding Remarks

We proposed a blueprint for a proactive artificial intelligence and augmented reality-based eye tracking system to train cardiology professionals better interpret electrocardiograms. Prior to introducing its sub-systems, we explored the related works by looking at the conducted studies and experiments that used eye tracking to understand how medical practitioners interpret ECGs. These studies proved that eye tracking technology is an efficient facilitator that enables the understanding of how skilled interpreters reach an accurate ECG interpretation, and eventually contribute towards the training of novice interpreters. We then explained how adding an augmented reality layer on top of eye tracking technology helps for a better training experience for the trainee. The related works was emphasized by using an investigative study in the form of semi-structured interviews to observe first-hand the challenges that medical practitioners face during their daily tasks of ECG interpretation, and how can artificial intelligence powered by eye tracking as well as persuasive technologies help in coaching medical practitioners for an accurate ECG interpretation. We then detailed the sub-systems constituting the AR and AI-based system for training. These are the adaptive ECG dataset, the AR-based interactive training interface, and finally the AI-based processing module.

5.2 Limitations

One main limitation of the paper is that it presents only a high-level overview for the proposed system. Improvements of the paper may include a more detailed and comprehensive class and UML diagrams explaining the classes and workflow of each subsystem along with their hierarchy and interactions. Additionally, an improvement may be to reveal the specifics for the implementation to the eye tracking component, the augmented reality component, and finally the machine learning component of the training system.

5.3 Future Works

In addition to addressing the proposed improvements in the limitations section, we aim to start the implementation of the system by further exploring the concept of an eye scan-path for each trainee using the AR-based interactive training interface. The eye movements of each trainee have the potential to be enablers for a unique unreproducible "eye signature". This refers to the scanning trajectory that the eye of the interpreter takes before making an understanding of an image. This requires a detailed processing and filtering through the collected data frames from the participants of the eye tracking component of the AR-based interactive training interface.

References

1. Cadet, J.V.: Report: Cost savings will drive ECG global market to nearly $160M by 2015 (2009). https://www.cardiovascularbusiness.com/topics/cardiovascular-imaging/report-cost-savings-will-drive-ecg-global-market-nearly-160m-2015#:~:text=%22Savingsof%242per ECG,annuallyintheUnitedStates.%22. Accessed 12 Nov 2020
2. Davies, A., et al.: How do healthcare practitioners read electrocardiograms? A dual-process model of electrocardiogram interpretation. Br. J. Card. Nurs. 14(10), 1–19 (2019)
3. O'Brien, K.E., Cannarozzi, M.L., Torre, D.M., Mechaber, A.J., Durning, S.J.: Training and assessment of ECG interpretation skills: results from the 2005 CDIM survey. Teach. Learn. Med. 21(2), 111–115 (2009)
4. Sqalli, M.T., Al-Thani, D.: AI-supported health coaching model for patients with chronic diseases. In: 2019 16th International Symposium on Wireless Communication Systems (ISWCS), pp. 452–456 (2019)

5. Sqalli, M.T., Al-Thani, D.: Evolution of wearable devices in health coaching: challenges and opportunities. Front. Digital Health **2**, 545646 (2020). https://doi.org/10.3389/fdgth.2020.545646

6. Davies, A.: Examining Expertise Through Eye Movements: A Study of Clinicians Interpreting Electrocardiograms. The University of Manchester (2018)

7. Sqalli, M.T., Al-Thani, D.: On how chronic conditions affect the patient-AI interaction: a literature review. Healthcare **8**(3), 313 (2020). https://doi.org/10.3390/healthcare8030313

8. PwC: Chronic diseases and conditions are on the rise. PwC Consulting (2017). https://www.pwc.com/gx/en/industries/healthcare/emerging-trends-pwc-healthcare/chronic-diseases.html

9. Tang, K.S., Cheng, D.L., Mi, E., Greenberg, P.B.: Augmented reality in medical education: a systematic review. Canadian Med. Educ. J. **11**, e81–e85 (2019). https://doi.org/10.36834/cmej.61705

10. Bond, R.R., et al.: Assessing computerized eye tracking technology for gaining insight into expert interpretation of the 12-lead electrocardiogram: an objective quantitative approach. J. Electrocardiol. **47**(6), 895–906 (2014)

11. Davies, A., Harper, S., Vigo, M., Jay, C.: Investigating the effect of clinical history before electrocardiogram interpretation on the visual behavior and interpretation accuracy of clinicians. Sci. Rep. **9**(1), 11300 (2019)

12. Breen, C.J., Bond, R., Finlay, D.: An evaluation of eye tracking technology in the assessment of 12 lead electrocardiography interpretation. J. Electrocardiol. **47**(6), 922–929 (2014)

13. Bond, R.R., et al.: Novel approach to documenting expert ECG interpretation using eye tracking technology: a historical and biographical representation of the late Dr Rory Childers in action. J. Electrocardiol. **48**(1), 43–44 (2015)

14. Tahri Sqalli, M., Al-Thani, D., Elshazly, M.B., Al-Hijji, M., Houssaini, Y.S.: The journey towards an accurate electrocardiogram interpretation: an eye-tracking study overview. In: 8th International Conference on Behavioral and Social Computing (BESC) (2021)

15. Tahri Sqalli, M., Al-Thani, D., Elshazly, M.B., Al-Hijji, M.: Interpretation of a 12-lead electrocardiogram by medical students: eye-tracking quantitative approach. JMIR Med. Educ. (2021)

16. Tahri Sqalli, M., Al-Thani, D., Elshazly, M., Al-Hijji, M., Alahmadi, A., Sqalli Houssaini, Y.: Understanding cardiology practitioners' interpretations of electrocardiograms: an eye-tracking study. JMIR Hum Factors **9**(1), e34058 (2022). https://doi.org/10.2196/34058. https://humanfactors.jmir.org/2022/1/e34058

17. Qatar Biomedical Research at Institute at Hamad Bin Khalifa. Research Compliance Assurance. https://www.hbku.edu.qa/en/qbri/research-areas/research-compliance

18. Wood, G., Batt, J., Appelboam, A., Harris, A., Wilson, M.R.: Exploring the impact of expertise, clinical history, and visual search on electrocardiogram interpretation. Med. Decis. Mak. **34**(1), 75–83 (2014)

19. A. Alahmadi, A. Davies, J. Royle, Vigo, M., Jay, C.: Evaluating the impact of pseudo-colour and coordinate system on the detection of medication-induced ECG changes. In: Proceedings of the 2019 CHI Conference on Human Factors in Computing Systems - CHI 2019 (2019)

20. Sqalli, M.T., Al-Thani, D., Qaraqe, M., Fernandez-Luque, L.: Perspectives on human-AI interaction applied to health and wellness management: between milestones and hurdles. In: Househ, M., Borycki, E., Kushniruk, A. (eds.) Multiple Perspectives on Artificial Intelligence in Healthcare: Opportunities and Challenges, pp. 41–51. Springer International Publishing, Cham (2021). https://doi.org/10.1007/978-3-030-67303-1_4

21. Cadet, J.V.: Report: cost savings will drive ECG global market to nearly $160M by 2015 (2009). https://tinyurl.com/y3rrguqf. Accessed 10 Aug 2020

22. Goldberger, A.L., et al.: PhysioBank, PhysioToolkit, and PhysioNet: components of a new research resource for complex physiologic signals. Circulation **101**(23), e215 (2000). https://doi.org/10.1161/01.CIR.101.23.e215

Context-Aware Chatbot Based on Cyber-Physical Sensing for Promoting Serendipitous Face-to-Face Communication

Hirokazu Tanaka[1]([⊠]) [iD], Hiromu Motomatsu[1] [iD], Yugo Nakamura[1,2] [iD], and Yutaka Arakawa[1] [iD]

[1] Kyushu University, Fukuoka 819-0395, Japan
[2] JST Presto, Chiyoda-ku, Tokyo 102-0076, Japan

Abstract. To promote the face-to-face communication reduced by COVID-19, we proposed and implemented a context-aware Slack chatbot based on Cyber-Physical sensing that helps colleagues meet more often in the same place. Our system periodically collects the user's internal context through Slack (cyber sensing) and uses small BLE beacons distributed to colleagues and beacon scanners installed in a laboratory to sense physical attendance (physical sensing). In addition, the system notifies the user of recommended actions, such as lunch or coffee break, depending on the context determined by the Cyber-Physical sensors. We deployed the proposed system in a laboratory environment and conducted an initial experiment for six weeks. Experimental results confirmed that our system can encourage serendipitous face-to-face communication during periods when the frequency of attending school and going to work dropped due to COVID-19. It was also found that in an environment such as a laboratory, where a certain level of trust has already been established, the openness of the collected information can further motivate users to participate in the system.

Keywords: Behavior change support system · Chatbot · Collaboration · Cyber-Physical sensing · Serendipitous communication

1 Introduction

Due to the COVID-19 pandemic, the way people work and communicate is rapidly shifting from offline to online. The increase in the number of classes and meetings held using online tools, is causing a decrease in the opportunities for face-to-face communication in laboratories and workplaces. Is this continuous shift to exclusively online communication well-advised? Group Genius research has shown that enhanced face-to-face communication within an organization contributes to the overall knowledge of the organization [15]. It has also been shown that face-to-face communication has an impact on organizational decision-making [1], and

© Springer Nature Switzerland AG 2022
N. Baghaei et al. (Eds.): PERSUASIVE 2022, LNCS 13213, pp. 230–239, 2022.
https://doi.org/10.1007/978-3-030-98438-0_18

that face-to-face communication and serendipitous encounters play a central role in building new collaborative partnerships within organizations. [4].

We consider the following three factors responsible for the decrease in serendipitous face-to-face communication and camaraderie in workplaces such as laboratories during the COVID-19 pandemic.

First, the number of people who choose face-to-face communication, such as going to the laboratory, is decreasing due to the use of increasingly sophisticated online communication tools. This is further exacerbated by the fact that people who do physically come to the workplace now come at different times, reducing the probability of face-to-face meetings in the workspace (Factor 1). Second, even if they are in the same location, it is difficult for people to gauge each other's internal state due to social distancing restrictions. (Factor 2). Third, because they could no longer grasp each other's internal state, the hurdles to suggesting an action increased, and the opportunity to take action together decreased (Factor 3). This study aims to mitigate these factors with the proposed system and to promote people's serendipitous face-to-face communication and thus improve workplace relations. In this study, we propose a context-aware Slack chatbot to facilitate and increase face-to-face communication, which has been reduced by COVID-19, by encouraging people to meet in person at a certain location. The novelty of this system is its ability to sense the user's context using Cyber-Physical sensing, effectively change people's behavior, and deliver context-sensitive message notifications.

2   Related Work

The online and offline communication networks in an employee's workplace interact with and complement each other, and it is important to maintain a balance between the two [17]. Pollmann's study [13] showed that the more participants communicated face-to-face with their partners, the more they understood each other and the more satisfied they were with their relationships. In contrast, text messages did not predict relationship satisfaction. This indicates that face-to-face communication may have a positive impact on trust and relationships, and that a decrease in face-to-face communication also affects workplace performance. It has also been found that people's positive mood lasts longer in events that occur under uncertain conditions, such as contingent communication, which is more likely to occur during face-to-face communication [16].

A significant number of notifications can cause users to be less productive [2,3]. To solve this problem, research on improving both the timing [5,11] and the content [14] of notifications was conducted. Research results show that ensuring both that notifications are sent at times when users switch their behavior, and that they are relevant to the targeted users improves the notification response rate. In addition to visual, auditory, and tactile notifications, it is shown in [9] that olfactory notifications are effective in helping users determine the urgency of a notification. The simplest method of notification is simultaneous notification to all users, but it can be bothersome for individual users to receive notifications about events that don't concern them. Moreover, if a user continues to receive notifications that are not relevant to them, they might be discouraged from using the system. Therefore, it is necessary to identify and notify only users who are the targets of drop-in behavior. In the past, we have proposed a method for detecting groups of people by sending and receiving BLE (Bluetooth Low Energy) signals through a smartphone application [7], a method using BLE beacon tags [6], and a method involving installing sensors on chairs [12]. However, since it is difficult to create an application that runs constantly in the background, and that the increasingly popular practice of hot-desking at work or at school makes it impossible to predict which user will sit at which chair, we adopt a method that uses BLE beacon tags to notify only the users who are exhibiting the relevant behavior.

3   System Design and Implementation

Our proposed system consists of three steps. First, the system uses BLE beacon tags and BLE wireless receivers to detect and visualize the user's school attendance (Step 1). Next, the system uses Slack, a communication tool, to collect and visualize the user's internal state (Step 2). Finally, the system proposes serendipitous events using the Cyber-Physical data, such as the user's school attendance and internal state, obtained in Steps 1 and 2 (Step 3). The configuration diagram and system flow are shown in Fig. 1.

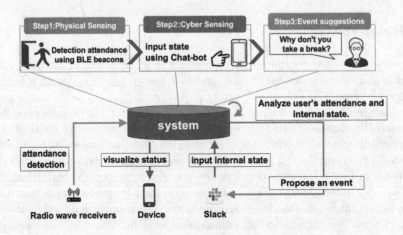

Fig. 1. System diagram

Step 1: Collection and Visualization of School Attendance Status. The BLE beacon signal for attendance detection of each user is polled every 5 min, and if the BLE signal is not detected for 30 min, the user is considered absent. The collected attendance data is stored in a database. This collected school attendance status can be visualized on the web application. The purpose of this visualization is to be able to know if the user is at school on a given day.

Example of understanding the physical information from RSSI (Received Signal Strength Indication) obtained from BLE signal is shown in Fig. 2, where (a) shows the detection of moving outside the university laboratory and (b) shows the same location in the university laboratory.

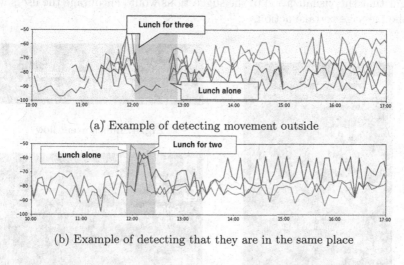

(a) Example of detecting movement outside

(b) Example of detecting that they are in the same place

Fig. 2. Physical relationships estimated from RSSI of BLE beacons

Step 2: Collection and Visualization of Internal States. We defined nine states including six health states and environmental states of the user, which make up the cyber information. First, we defined six health states that the user feels: free, hungry, tired, sleepy, concentrated, and normal. This state was set based on the information obtained from a questionnaire survey on the state that the participants usually felt in the laboratory. In addition, since temperature is an external factor that affects the user's state [8], we defined three environmental states: hot, cold, and comfortable. Users were allowed to select both a health state and an environmental state in their responses. In our system, a button shown in Fig. 3 is sent through Slack to a user who has been detected as being in attendance for them to enter their internal state. We use a button input with Slack to enable one-click input and further facilitate the internal state reporting procedure. The internal state entered by the user is stored in the system's database and visualized by a web application. The system sends notifications to the users to encourage input. Since the target audience of this experiment was students, the notifications were sent at the end of the class, when they would not interfere with the class. Furthermore, to reduce the psychological burden of unnecessary notifications, we designed the system not to send a button to users who were absent.

Step 3: Event Proposal by the System. In Fig. 4 and Fig. 5, the system suggests lunch events and coffee events based on the user's Cyber-Physical information. Lunch events are proposed to users A, B, and C in the Hungry state at 12:00, which is the lunch break time, as shown in Fig. 4. Figure 5 shows how the coffee event works: when there are two or more people in the sleepy state, the system sends a notification to the user asking them to make coffee. These suggestions are made on a Slack channel that can be seen by all other users. We thought that the visualization of the suggestions would encourage the users who saw the message to take action.

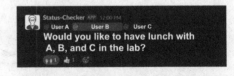

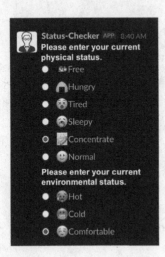

Fig. 4. Lunch event flow

Fig. 3. Internal state input button

Fig. 5. Coffee event flow

4   Experiment

In order for our system to fulfill the requirements for promoting camaraderie, the user's spontaneous participation is required. Therefore, designing a mechanism to keep the user motivated to participate is of utmost importance. We hypothesized that within an organization where people already know each other's names and faces, an internal state, display at the individual level would be more effective in encouraging users to interact with the system than a display summarizing the overall internal state of the laboratory. During this experiment, we continuously collected and displayed data on the school attendance and internal status of each user in the organization under three conditions (a) hidden, (b) pie chart: anonymous, and (c) name and internal status: non-anonymous (twice a week for each condition), and investigated what changes would occur in the number of user responses and user behavior. In addition, we also investigated the impact of the system's event recommendation function on users. This study was conducted for a total of six weeks. The experimental conditions were: 37 people in the Slack experimental channel, and displays set up in three locations in the laboratory so that the users could see the screen. During the experiment, the system recommended two types of events based on the user's context: lunch events and coffee events. We observed the long-term interaction between users.

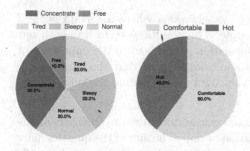

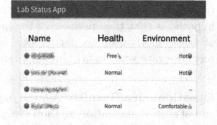

Fig. 6. Pie chart display   **Fig. 7.** Name and states list display

4.1   Results and Discussion

Response Rate. We defined the response rate as an evaluation metric to compare a user's willingness to participate in the system for each of the different visualization methods. The definition of the response rate is shown in Eq. 1.

$$\text{Response rate} = \frac{\text{Number of clicks}}{\text{Total number of notifications sent}} \tag{1}$$

The buttons were sent from Slack to the users attending school when they first arrived at school, and at the end of class at 10:10, 12:00, 14:30, 16:20, and 18:10. In addition, a questionnaire was given to users at the end of each of the three different data visualization method periods. The visualization of condition (b) is shown in Fig. 6. This visualization uses a pie chart to show the number of people inputting their internal states and the percentage of each recorded internal state. The visualization of condition (c) is shown in Fig. 7. In this visualization, the user's name and internal state are displayed.

We investigate changes in user motivation according to different information visualization methods. Tables 1 and 2 show the response rates for each display method.

Table 1. Health state click data   **Table 2.** Environmental state click data

Method	Send [times]	Click [times]	Response [%]
Hidden (1st)	301	146	48.5
Pie (1st)	362	224	61.9
Name (1st)	363	266	**73.3**
Hidden (2nd)	336	201	59.8
Pie (2nd)	244	151	61.9
Name (2nd)	310	209	67.4

Method	Send [times]	Click [times]	Response [%]
Hidden (1st)	301	145	48.2
Pie (1st)	362	211	58.3
Name (1st)	363	244	**67.2**
Hidden (2nd)	336	189	56.3
Pie (2nd)	244	146	59.8
Name (2nd)	310	201	64.8

The results showed that the highest response rates were obtained for (c) name and internal states, (b) pie chart, and (a) hidden, in order, for both the first and second time that a particular visualization method was used. The results show that the display method is effective for organizations where a certain level of trust has been established between people. The results were in line with our hypothesis that the openness of the information would lead to the improvement of users' motivation to participate. In addition, we saw that the health state response rate was slightly higher than the environmental state response rate.

Questionnaire Results. A questionnaire was administered to the users at the end of each visualization method evaluation period. The aim of the questionnaire was to determine whether the different visualization methods triggered specific changes in user behavior.

Hidden. After the use of the non-visualization method, we received comments such as: "I was looking forward to seeing my status reflected on the screen, so I was a little disappointed not to see it displayed.". This would indicate that the display was a motivation for input, and that thus removing it triggered a change in user behavior.

Pie Chart. This visualization method was able to trigger specific behavioral changes, illustrated by comments such as: "Visualizing system status was useful for air conditioning management.".

Name and State. With the name and internal state display method, we received comments such as: "If I know that someone is concentrating, I make sure to work quietly around them", and behavioral changes occurred due to the visualization of the state on an individual basis.

Interview for Events Produced by the System. We built a co-activity recommend system to propose lunch and coffee events and observed the users' behavior. After that, we conducted free answer interviews with two participants in our experiment (P1 and P2) from our university laboratory. Based on the results of this interview, we will discuss whether there was any change in behavior as a result of the event suggestions made by the system.

Lunch-Event. The lunch event caused a direct behavioral change in P1: "We did not usually have lunch together because we were in different years, but the system proposal allowed us to have lunch together. The suggestion of the system itself became a trigger to ask her out for lunch". In this case, the system's suggestions had a positive impact on the ease of face-to-face communication. Contrary to P1, P2 did not experience any direct behavioral changes from the system, saying: "I was not able to attend the event due to not being aware of the notification or the timing of the notification.". This shows that it is necessary to design our system to determine not only a user's status and whether they are in the laboratory, but also the timing and method of notification delivered used by the system. P2 claimed that there was no direct interaction, but said that there was indirect interaction: "I decided to go to school because of a notification of an event in Slack which enabled me to indirectly know that there was someone in the school that I wanted to talk to directly.". This response is an indirect interaction that the original system did not anticipate, and leads us to consider that information about who is currently in the laboratory is a behavior-changing element.

From the results of these interviews, it can be concluded that the system's suggestion of a lunch event has the effect of promoting a certain level of behavioral change, and that it may be able to create an opportunity to promote communication between people who normally have difficulty communicating, such as those who are in different years at university. On the other hand, we received feedback stating that it is difficult to participate in an event when people with weaker relationships are matched with each other.

Coffee-Event. During the experimental period, the system proposed coffee events 13 times, and the number of coffee events conducted was 6. The average number of participants who could be confirmed with Slack was 3.67. In this study, we interviewed a participant from our university laboratory who participated in the coffee event (P1) and one who did not (P2).

P1 said: "I was able to share the work of making coffee with other participants and chat with them over a cup of coffee. In that way, I was able to connect with people I do not usually have the opportunity to connect with." P1 continued, "In the Slack channel, you can check the coffee event and learn about what kind of people want to drink coffee. Therefore, if someone who wants to chat gets notified about the event, they might join in and communicate with me." These comments suggest that the coffee event can promote face-to-face communication.

P2 did not participate in the event, saying: "I did not participate in the event because I do not like coffee and cannot drink it even if the event is recommended." We found that the subject of coffee drinking, which depends on the users' personal tastes, is directly related to the willingness to participate in the event. Therefore, it is important to design events that do not depend on preferences, gender, age, or other factors, or on the contrary, to design personalized events based on user preferences.

5   Conclusion

In this study, we proposed and implemented a context-aware Slack chatbot to facilitate face-to-face communication, which has been reduced by COVID-19. We deployed the system in a university laboratory environment for six weeks to confirm the effectiveness of our proposed system. Experimental results show that the system can encourage serendipitous face-to-face communication while reducing the frequency of coming to school and going to work. We also found that in an organization where a certain level of trust has already been established, such as in a laboratory, the openness of the collected information can increase the user's willingness to participate in the system, which can be evidenced by an improved notification response rate. It was also found that visualizing the internal state of others had an effect on behavioral changes in users, such as being able to pay more attention to air conditioning and adjusting their speaking voice according to the level of concentration around them. In the future, we plan to integrate ambient notification methods based on the IoT (Internet of Things) nudging described in [10] into our system and investigate their impact on user motivation.

References

1. Baltes, B.B., Dickson, M.W., Sherman, M.P., Bauer, C.C., LaGanke, J.S.: Computer-mediated communication and group decision making: a meta-analysis. Organ. Behav. Human Decis. Process. **87**(1), 156–179 (2002)
2. Cutrell, E.B., Czerwinski, M., Horvitz, E.: Effects of instant messaging interruptions on computing tasks. In: CHI 2000 Extended Abstracts on Human Factors in Computing Systems, pp. 99–100 (2000)
3. Horvitz, E.C.M.C.E.: Notification, disruption, and memory: effects of messaging interruptions on memory and performance. In: Human-Computer Interaction: INTERACT, vol. 1, p. 263 (2001)
4. Irving, G.L., Ayoko, O.B., Ashkanasy, N.M.: Collaboration, physical proximity and serendipitous encounters: avoiding collaboration in a collaborative building. Organ. Stud. **41**(8), 1123–1146 (2020). https://doi.org/10.1177/0170840619856913
5. Kandappu, T., Mehrotra, A., Misra, A., Musolesi, M., Cheng, S.F., Meegahapola, L.: Pokeme: applying context-driven notifications to increase worker engagement in mobile crowd-sourcing. In: Proceedings of the 2020 Conference on Human Information Interaction and Retrieval, pp. 3–12 (2020)
6. Komai, K., Fujimoto, M., Arakawa, Y., Suwa, H., Kashimoto, Y., Yasumoto, K.: Elderly person monitoring in day care center using Bluetooth low energy. In: 2016 10th International Symposium on Medical Information and Communication Technology (ISMICT), pp. 1–5. IEEE (2016)
7. Koshiba, R., Hirabe, Y., Fujimoto, M., Suwa, H., Arakawa, Y., Yasumoto, K.: Group detection based on user-to-user distance in everyday life for office lunch group recommendation. In: 2017 31st International Conference on Advanced Information Networking and Applications Workshops (WAINA), pp. 309–314 (2017). https://doi.org/10.1109/WAINA.2017.43
8. Lamb, S., Kwok, K.C.: A longitudinal investigation of work environment stressors on the performance and wellbeing of office workers. Appl. Ergon. **52**, 104–111 (2016)
9. Maggioni, E., Cobden, R., Dmitrenko, D., Obrist, M.: Smell-o-message: integration of olfactory notifications into a messaging application to improve users' performance. In: Proceedings of the 20th ACM International Conference on Multimodal Interaction, pp. 45–54 (2018)
10. Nakamura, Y., Matsuda, Y.: Iot nudge: Iot data-driven nudging for health behavior change. In: Adjunct Proceedings of the 2021 ACM International Joint Conference on Pervasive and Ubiquitous Computing and Proceedings of the 2021 ACM International Symposium on Wearable Computers, pp. 51–53 (2021)
11. Okoshi, T., Tsubouchi, K., Tokuda, H.: Real-world large-scale study on adaptive notification scheduling on smartphones. Pervas. Mob. Comput. **50**, 1–24 (2018)
12. Otoda, Y., et al.: Continuous posture sensing chair for office workers. In: 2018 IEEE International Conference on Consumer Electronics (ICCE), pp. 1–2. IEEE (2018)

13. Pollmann, M.M., Norman, T.J., Crockett, E.E.: A daily-diary study on the effects of face-to-face communication, texting, and their interplay on understanding and relationship satisfaction. Comput. Human Behav. Rep. **3**, 100088 (2021). https://doi.org/10.1016/j.chbr.2021.100088, https://www.sciencedirect.com/science/article/pii/S2451958821000361

14. Saikia, P., Cheung, M., She, J., Park, S.: Effectiveness of mobile notification delivery. In: 2017 18th IEEE International Conference on Mobile Data Management (MDM), pp. 21–29 (2017). https://doi.org/10.1109/MDM.2017.14

15. Sawyer, K.: Group Genius: The Creative Power of Collaboration. Basic Books, New York (2017)

16. Wilson, T.D., Centerbar, D.B., Kermer, D.A., Gilbert, D.T.: The pleasures of uncertainty: prolonging positive moods in ways people do not anticipate. J. Persona. Soc. Psychol. **88**(1), 5 (2005)

17. Zhang, X., Venkatesh, V.: Explaining employee job performance: the role of online and offline workplace communication networks. Mis Q. **47**, 695–722 (2013)

The Utility of Personality Types
for Personalizing Persuasion

Wenzhen Xu[✉] , Yuichi Ishikawa , and Roberto Legaspi

Data Intelligence Division, KDDI Research, Inc., Fujimino, Japan
{we-xu,yi-ishikawa,ro-legaspi}@kddi-research.jp

Abstract. Existing research shows that it is effective for the persuader to personalize persuasion based on the persuadee's personality. However, prior studies overlooked the interactions of multiple personality traits, which undermines the effectiveness of personalization. In this paper, we investigated the utility of personality types for predicting behavioral intention and personalizing persuasion. The personality types are constructed by categorizing subjects based on the interactions of their Big Five personality traits. Using these personality types as predictors, we then examined how they improved model fitting and prediction accuracy compared to personality traits. Specifically, we used the online survey data of 3,116 Japanese participants to build nine prediction models and confirmed that (1) personality type is a significant factor in personalizing strategies and predicting behavioral intention, and (2) personality types should be appropriately applied according to the prediction model's complexity when personalizing persuasive strategies.

Keywords: Personalized persuasion · Personality type · Behavioral intention prediction

1 Introduction

In the last two decades, persuasive technology (PT) has been widely investigated and applied to effect voluntary changes of individuals' attitudes and behaviors in the sales and marketing domain (e.g., to encourage purchasing behavior), health care (e.g., to promote healthy habits) and public management (e.g., to popularize eco-friendly lifestyles). PT professionals have made a consensus that persuasion strategies could not be applied in a one-size-fits-all approach. To produce accurate and effective persuasions, appropriate personalization is necessary [1, 2].

One solution for personalization is to choose persuasive strategies according to individuals' characteristics (e.g., demographic information, personality, preference, and value). Numerous prior works on this approach investigated the association between personality and persuasion strategies and have drawn the conclusion that the interaction between personality and persuasive strategy is an essential predictor of attitude and behavior change [3–5]. However, even though their experimental procedures were sophisticated, and the reasoning processes were logical, two pitfalls remain to challenge the veracity and effectiveness of predicting behavior and individualizing strategies.

© Springer Nature Switzerland AG 2022
N. Baghaei et al. (Eds.): PERSUASIVE 2022, LNCS 13213, pp. 240–254, 2022.
https://doi.org/10.1007/978-3-030-98438-0_19

First, to determine personality, most prior studies adopted the "trait ~~theory~~ approach", which argues that human personality consists of multiple traits and is characterized by being high or low on these traits. They investigated the association between one personality trait (e.g., *Openness* of the Big Five traits [7]) and one persuasive strategy (e.g., *Scarcity* of Cialdini's six principles of influence [8]) without considering the interactions of multiple personality traits. For example, a prior study drew two statements: A) people high on *Openness* are susceptible to the *Commitment* strategy, and B) people high on *Agreeableness* (another Big Five trait) are susceptible to the same strategy [3]. However, it is difficult to infer from these statements if *Commitment* strategy would work effectively when a person is high on *Openness* and, at the same time, low on *Agreeableness*. Not taking into account the interactions among multiple traits may reduce the accuracy of predicting behavior and lead to ineffective personalization.

The second pitfall is that although prior works investigated the association between personality traits and persuasion strategies, it remains unclear how to model such associations to better predict people's intentions and behaviors, especially when considering the multiple trait interaction described above. In general, models become highly complex as they incorporate more and more interactions (e.g., multiple trait interactions, interactions between multiple traits and persuasion strategies), which could degrade model interpretability and generalizability.

In this study, we tackled the two challenges above. To address the first, we investigated the utility of the "type theory" for predicting behavioral intention. So far, personality type Personality type deserves greater attention in PT research since it is another meaningful way to represent personality. Specifically, the type theory states that each person falls into one of several personality types. Based on this statement, researchers have proposed various typologies [2, 11–13]. For example, Gerlach et al. proposed a typology with four types (*Role model, Average, Self-centered and Reserved*) [2] and Robins et al. proposed three types (*Overcontrolled, Undercontrolled,* and *Resilient*) [12]. Among the major typologies are those constructed by categorizing subjects based on the interaction of the personality traits (e.g., Gerlach's types were constructed based on the interaction of the Big Five traits). By using such personality types as predictors, a model can predict behavioral intention with multiple trait interactions being reflected in the prediction. In addition, since the number of types is generally limited, the model can incorporate the interactions without significantly increasing its complexity.

For the second issue, we investigated when and how to use the personality types to predict behavioral intention, i.e., *when* formulating prediction models with different degrees of complexity, *how* should personality types be used together with personality traits or should they be employed independently. While personality traits are represented as continuous variables, personality types are represented as categorical variables. This means that while using the types simplifies the model, it also leads to a reduction of information about personality compared to using the traits. Therefore, whether to use types or traits, or use them together, should be decided depending on the complexity of the model.

To carry out our investigations, we conducted a large-scale online survey in which we asked the participants their behavioral intention after they were shown various persuasive contents. For the first issue, we measured the participants' Big Five scores and then categorized them into personality types based on their scores following the approach proposed by Gerlach et al. [2]. We then examined the predictive utility of the personality types by using them in the prediction models. For the second issue, we prepared multiple prediction models with different levels of complexity (e.g., a model with only the direct effects of personality and persuasive strategy, a model with three-way interaction effects, i.e., personality × persuasive strategy × context) and examined which model should utilize the types.

The rest of this paper is organized as follows: Sect. 2 and 3 discuss the key concepts and research questions of our work, respectively. Section 4 details the experimental method and procedures. Section 5 presents the results, and Sect. 6 discusses the main findings and then concludes.

2 Key Concepts

We introduce in this section the concepts that are relevant to our present study. These include the Big Five personality traits, personality types, and Cialdini's six principles of influence (hereafter, persuasive strategy for brevity).

2.1 The Big Five Personality Traits

The Big Five is a well-examined and widely accepted taxonomy for personality traits. It was conceived on the idea that "most individual differences in human personality can be classified into five broad, empirically derived domains" (i.e., traits) [8], namely, *Openness (O)*, *Conscientiousness (C)*, *Extraversion (E)*, *Agreeableness (A)*, and *Neuroticism (N)*.

2.2 Personality Types and Gerlach Et Al.'s Personality Type

In contrast to the Big Five, the existence of personality types (e.g., Asendorpf–Robins–Caspi [ARC] type [11–13] and Myers–Briggs Type Indicator [MBTI; 14]) remains highly controversial. Although the ARC types are widely supported and applied in clinical psychology, its robustness has been questioned for decades [15–18]. There are two critical opinions: 1) having been developed from small data challenges the reliability of its typologies, and 2) using data collected from individuals with particular attributes and cultural backgrounds challenges the generalizability and reproducibility of the typologies [15, 19].

Gerlach and his colleagues developed a more robust set of personality types by conducting cluster analyses using the self-reported Big Five scores [2]. They resolved the problems of reliability and generalizability by using four large datasets that were comprised of more than 1.5 million participants from different countries with different demographic attributes. Their finding suggests a robust four-type solution, that is, 1) *Role model*, 2) *Average*, 3) *Self-centered* and 4) *Reserved*.

The features of each type are shown in Table 1. As the types are determined by the combination of all the Big Five traits, each personality type variable contains the interactions among the five personality traits. Gerlach et al. first denoted the two most stable clusters as *Role model* and *Average. Role model* displays socially desirable traits as characterized by low *N* scores and high scores in the other traits. *Average* is characterized by the average of the five trait scores. The cluster with low *O, A* and *C* scores is referred to as *Self-centered*, and the cluster with low *O* and *N* scores as *Reserved*. We marked some cells in the table with "-" since the supposedly corresponding trait scores were not clearly described in the original paper.

Table 1. Personality types proposed by Gerlach et al. [2]

Type \ Trait	Openness	Conscientiousness	Agreebleness	Neuroticism	Extraversion
Role model	High	High	High	Low	High
Average	Medium	Medium	Medium	Medium	Medium
Self-centered	Low	Low	Low	-	-
Reserved	Low	-	-	Low	-

2.3 The Six Principles of Influence

Cialdini explored potential factors that could affect decision-making and proposed from his investigations six principles of influence (i.e., persuasive strategies) [9]. These principles that have been widely investigated in previous studies [2, 4, 10] are as follows:

- *Authority*: People tend to believe and obey those in positions of authority.
- *Commitment*: People tend to do things they commit to doing by declaring verbally or in written form.
- *Consensus*: If it is uncertain whether to do something, people tend to look up to those around them as references.
- *Liking*: People tend to accept a request if asked by a person they like or who shares similarities with them.
- *Reciprocity*: People tend to pay back favors done to them.
- *Scarcity*: People are more likely to evaluate or desire a product if they are told it is rare.

3 Research Questions

In recent years, numerous research in the PT field have demonstrated a link between the Big Five and Cialdini's persuasive strategies. The representative works can be generally divided into two categories based on how they assessed the participants' susceptibility to persuasive strategies: 1) collected self-reported preferences for the persuasive strategies and 2) actual behaviors (e.g., click rate) that were monitored when using the persuasive strategies. Two typical examples of the first are Alkis & Temizel [3] and Oyibo et al. [4]. They investigated the correlation between the individual Big Five trait scores and the level of the subjects' susceptibility to each of Cialdini's six persuasive strategies. They confirmed significant correlation between them and concluded that the Big Five personality traits affect the susceptibility to the strategies. On the other hand, an example of the second is Ciocarlan et al. [5]. They monitored participants' decision-making behaviors in a PC game wherein they used system quests to represent persuasive strategies. For example, "This character is a member of the same guild as you" represented the strategy of "Liking". Despite the differences from [3] and [4] in experimental design, Ciocarlan et al.'s conclusion was consistent with [3] and [4] that significant correlations exist between the Big Five scores and susceptibility to the persuasive strategies and their interactions impact behaviors.

However, the studies above did not examine the interactions of personality traits, which we hypothesize could limit the effect of personalized persuasive strategies. Figure 1 exemplifies such a case. As we described in Sect. 1, previous studies found that *Commitment* is effective for people high on O and those high on A. Based on this alone, it is clear that *Commitment* will work well for those high on both O and A (see top-right square of Fig. 1) and will not work for those who are low on both (the bottom-left square). However, it is unclear whether *Commitment* will work for people in the grey squares. These certainty and ambiguity are likely if we take only the above findings into account that do not consider the interaction of O and A. In contrast, the problem could be addressed by using personality types because these types already contain information on the interactions of several personality traits.

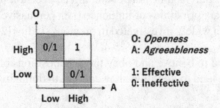

Fig. 1. Certainty and ambiguity on the effectiveness of *Commitment* strategy

To our knowledge, there are but very few previous studies that explored the relationship between personality type and persuasive strategy. For instance, Wall and colleagues showed that Type D personality is susceptible to persuasion [20]. Type D (distress) originated in the field of medical psychological to indicate the tendency to experience negative affectivity and social inhibition occurring jointly [32]. However, we choose Gerlach et al.'s typology since it covers a bigger set of personality types and thereby can accommodate a broader population.

It is also possible to model the interactions of personality traits by using traits directly rather than the types. However, doing so could significantly increase the complexity of the prediction models, as well as degrade their interpretability and generalizability. For example, if we consider the interaction between O and A, the prediction models need to account for a three-way interaction (e.g., $O \times A \times$ "whether to use *Commitment*"). Furthermore, trait interactions that need to be considered can be more than three-way, e.g., five-way interaction at most - $O \times C \times E \times A \times N$, which further increases the complexity of modeling. In contrast, we can keep the models simple by using the personality types, and if trait interactions need to be incorporated in the modeling, then there should be a methodic way to select which traits to use in order for the model not to become complex again.

Based on the above, we set our general research question (GRQ) to explore the feasibility of using personality types, as follows:

GRQ: *Could personality types be used to accurately predict susceptibility to per suasive strategies?*

We break down the GRQ into three sub-RQs that examine how our prediction models can accurately predict behavioral intentions, as follows:

RQ1: *Could personality types be used to represent the direct effect of personality?*
RQ2: *Could personality types be used to represent personality in the two-way interaction of personality and persuasive strategies?*
RQ3: *Could personality types be used to represent personality in the three-way interaction of personality, persuasive strategies, and contexts?*

Although prior studies agree that the persuasive effects of Cialdini's persuasive strategies vary depending on personality, their conclusions are not entirely consistent. Alslaity et al. [2] compared the findings of Oyibo et al. [4], Sofia et al. [10] and Alkis and Temizel [3] and found that only 50% of the results are consistent. For instance, significant correlation between *Openness* and *Authority* was confirmed by Sofia et al. [9], but not by the other two. Alslaity and his colleagues interpreted the inconsistent results across different studies as caused by varying contexts in which the persuasion was carried out. Although the inference of Alslaity et al. was insightful and examined by descriptive statistics, the relationships among personality traits, persuasive strategies and contexts, as well as the impact of their interactions on decision-making were not examined statistically. Thus, we examined a prediction model that incorporates a context variable and added RQ3. However, it is not our objective at this time to analyze the separate effects (only the overall) of the different contexts we considered for this study.

4 Method

4.1 Dataset

We recruited 3,116 participants (female: 1,559, male: 1,557; age ranging from 20 to 60 years old) from seven major cities in Japan. We assessed their Big Five traits using a well-cited Japanese questionnaire (70 items) that was developed by Murakami and Murakami (1970), whose reliability and validity were properly examined in [21].

We then surveyed the participants' behavioral intentions using a web-based questionnaire in which scenarios were explained to them (e.g., takeout promotion), and in each scenario, they were shown six web banner contents to which Cialdini's six strategies were applied. Afterwards, the participants were asked regarding their behavioral intentions after viewing each content. For example, in the takeout promotion scenario, they were asked *"Would you like to order a takeout dish?"* The answer would lie on a five-point Likert scale, ranging from "1. I will never do that" to "5. I will definitely do that". We binarized the answers, specifically, "1-*prefer to do*" and "0-*not prefer to do*" and used them as dependent variable to be predicted. To improve the reliability of the evaluation, we binarized into two patterns. The first counted the "4. I will probably do that" and "5. I will definitely do that" as "1", and the other answers as "0". The second pattern was stricter in that it only treated the "5. I will definitely do that" answer as "1".

4.2 Interventional Materials

We prepared three scenarios in the web-based questionnaire, namely, takeout promotion in an everyday situation, takeout promotion in the pandemic, and traffic congestion reduction in a supposedly normal situation. We chose these contexts for two reasons. First, we aimed to sample from both commercial and non-commercial domains. Alslaity and his colleagues [2] took the first step to explore the effects of contexts on personalized persuasion. They chose two typical recommender systems for commercial use, which are e-commerce and movie recommendation, to represent the context variable. To our knowledge, personalized persuasion is equally important and is being applied to non-commercial use cases, such as traffic congestion reduction [22], public medicine [23], and health management [24]. To further add to Alslaity et al.'s observations, we selected two use cases for commercial use (i.e., takeout promotion) and one for non-commercial use (i.e., traffic congestion reduction) as the contexts.

Second, we consider the nature of context as two-faceted, i.e., having domain and situation. Both facets can influence the effect of personalized persuasion. For example, ordering takeout in a normal situation and during the pandemic belong to the same domain but are different situations. People under different circumstances may have different motivations for ordering a takeout dish, e.g., for convenience in a normal situation and safety in a pandemic. Therefore, the motivation for the same persuasive strategy and the subsequent processes may vary. It is from this point of view that we chose the three contexts mentioned above.

We prepared a total of 18 web banners, i.e., six banners for each scenario (see Fig. 2), which were designed based on the definitions of Cialdini's six principles by three PT professionals and one ad and visuals designer. Each banner consists of one picture and one catchphrase. For example, to express the *Authority* strategy in the context of takeout promotion in the pandemic, we chose a picture of a female nutritionist and a catchphrase that says, "Supervised by a nutritionist! Reform your irregular diet rhythm during this self-restraint period by choosing well-balanced takeout dishes!" (English translation of the Japanese catchphrase). The term "self-restraint" is used to call the policy in Japan that is similar to but less restrictive than a lockdown.

To verify that the banners represented well the corresponding persuasive strategies, we asked three other PT professionals to independently evaluate all the banners. Specifically, these judges were asked to rate each banner, i.e., how well a banner fittingly represents one of the six strategies. The ratings ranged from "1. Not fit at all" to "5. Fit perfectly". The average ratings for 16 of the 18 banners were over 4, and the other two banners reached the acceptable average ratings of over 3. To test the consistency among the three judges, we calculated the in-class correlation coefficient (ICC). The

Fig. 2. An example of the interventional materials

score reached a near perfect level (ICC = 0.967), which indicates the ratings of the three judges reached a notably high consistency.

4.3 Manner of Analysis

We conducted two series of analyses. First, since Gerlach et al. focused on Westerners as participants, we examined if the personality types they proposed could also be seen in a Japanese population. To do so, we conducted a series of hierarchical cluster analyses. Specifically, we first z-normalized the answers to the Big Five questionnaire items and calculated the Big Five scores. Using the scores, we ran a hierarchical cluster analysis using Ward's minimum variance method that minimizes the total within-cluster variance [25]. The classification sensitivity with this method is higher than other distance functions such that the variance within the clusters is minimized [26].

In the second set, we explored the predictive utility of the personality types in predicting behavioral intentions by conducting a series of logistic regression analyses. We built a total of nine prediction models with three different complexities (see Table 2), namely, direct effect models (M1~M3), two-way interaction models (M4~M6) and three-way interaction models (M7~M9), which are formulated as follows:

$$M1{\sim}M3 : P = \sigma(b + DE), DE = \sum_i \beta_i^p p_i + \sum_j \beta_j^S s_j,$$
$$M4{\sim}M6 : P = \sigma\left(b + DE + IE_{2way}\right), IE_{2way} = \sum_i \sum_j \beta_{i,j}^{2way} p_i s_j,$$
$$M7{\sim}M9 : P = \sigma\left(b + DE + IE_{2way} + IE_{3way}\right), IE_{3way} = \sum_i \sum_j \sum_k \beta_{i,j,k}^{3way} p_i s_j c_k,$$

where P, σ, b, DE, IE_{2way} and IE_{3way} respectively denote the probability of a positive intention (i.e., "1-*prefer to do*"), logistic function, intercept, direct effect, two-way interaction effect and three-way interaction effects. In DE and IE, β denotes partial coefficients and p_i, s_j (binary value), and c_k (binary value) denote personality, strategy and context, respectively. A binary value 1 indicates the personality, strategy or context is used in the model, and not utilized if 0. Note, however, that p_i is represented differently in each model (as shown in Table 2). For example, in the direct effect models, we used the Big Five scores (B; continuous values) in M1, the personality types (T; binary values) in M2, and both B and T in M3.

We compared the prediction models in each group to examine whether the inclusion of personality types improved model fit and prediction accuracy. First, we fit the models to the entire dataset and calculated their Akaike Information Criterion (AIC) and Bayesian Information Criterion (BIC), both of which estimate the amount of information loss from the true model, i.e., a model with smaller AIC and BIC values is better. To evaluate the prediction accuracy, we conducted five-fold cross validation using the whole dataset and measured the models' ROC-AUC that ranges from 0.0 to 1.0, and a higher ROC-AUC means a more accurate prediction. In principle, if a model with the personality types has smaller AIC and BIC, and higher ROC-AUC, we can conclude that the types have predictive utility and they should be utilized for prediction.

5 Results

Hierarchical cluster analyses of the dataset we derived from a Japanese population confirmed four personality types that are similar to Gerlach et al. When we examined the possible solution with three, four, five or six clusters, we observed the following. In the three-cluster solution, the distribution of the data was extremely skewed, i.e., 3,114 out of the 3,116 participants were classified to one cluster, which rendered this three-cluster solution not suitable. In the four-cluster solution, the distribution was relatively balanced: 692 in cluster A, 1068 in B, 1022 in C, and 334 in D. In the five-cluster solution, clusters A, B, and D remained, while C broke into clusters C_1 (n = 390) and C_2 (n = 632). In the six-cluster solution, A and D remained, and similar to C, cluster B also broke into clusters B_1 (n = 536) and B_2 (n = 532). These results were consistent with Gerlach et al.'s conclusion that at least four distinct personality types exist.

To examine if the clusters in the four-cluster solution indeed have the same meanings as Gerlach et al.'s personality types, we analyzed each cluster's Big Five trait scores. To classify a trait score, we took the average of all the scores and whether a score is low, medium or high depended on how far it was from the average (i.e., the standard deviation, SD). Our results shown in Fig. 3 largely matched the characteristics of each type shown in Table 1. Specifically, cluster A matched *Reserved* that is low ($< -0.5SD$) on O and N, cluster B matched *Average* with medium scores ($-0.5SD$–$0.5SD$) on all the traits, cluster C only had O, A, and C scores below the average ($\geq -0.5SD$ and $<$ 0SD) that matched *Self-centered*, and finally, cluster D matched *Role model* because it has high scores ($>0.5SD$) on O, E, A and C, but with a low ($<-0.5SD$) N score.

We then proceeded to analyzing the performance of the various prediction models, starting with the results shown in Fig. 4 from comparing the direct effect models M1, M2 and M3. The left graph shows the results when we regarded the behavioral intentions "4" and "5" as "1-*prefer to do*", and the one at the right is when option "5" is regarded as "1-*prefer to do*". In both graphs, M3 best fit the data given its AIC and the BIC are the lowest in both graphs. In addition, looking at the differences of AIC/BIC values among the three models, the relative likelihood that M1 or M2 is closer to the true model is 0.01 less than M3. The result of DeLong's test [27] also showed that ROC-AUC of M3 is significantly higher than M1 (Z $= -3.147$ and $p < 0.01$; Z $= -1.952$ and $p = 0.05$, for the graphs on the left and right, respectively).

Next, we compared in Fig. 5 the performance of models M3 to M6. We took M3 as baseline to validate any improvement from using the two-way interaction of personality and persuasive strategy. The ROC-AUC of M4 to M6 showed no notable improvement

Table 2. Variables in each model

	Model / Variable	DE			IE 2way		IE 3way	
		Big Five (B)	Type (T)	Strategy (s)	B×s	T×s	B×s×c	T×s×c
Direct effect models	M1	✓		✓				
	M2		✓	✓				
	M3	✓	✓	✓				
Two-way interaction models	M4	✓	✓	✓	✓			
	M5	✓	✓	✓		✓		
	M6	✓	✓	✓	✓	✓		
Three-way interaction models	M7	✓	✓	✓	✓	✓	✓	
	M8	✓	✓	✓	✓	✓		✓
	M9	✓	✓	✓	✓	✓	✓	✓

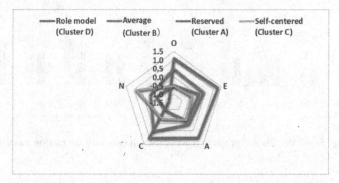

Fig. 3. Four personality types obtained from the Japanese dataset

from M3, and their AIC and BIC values are even poorer than M3. These results suggest that adding the two-way interactions of personality and persuasive strategies has no contribution to improving the predictive capabilities of the models. These findings are contrary to most of the prior studies. We detail our interpretations in the Discussion.

Finally, we looked at the results of comparing models M6 to M9, with M6 as baseline, to check if any improvement came out from the three-way interaction models. The results in Fig. 6 show that while M7 has poorer AIC, BIC and ROC-AUC than M6, M8 is better than M6 on both model fit and prediction accuracy. The difference is whether they use the traits (M7) or the types (M8) to represent personality. Thus, the results suggest that types should be the representation for personality in a three-way interaction (i.e., personality × strategy × context), and not the traits. In addition, the difference between M6 and M8 indicate that the moderation effect of context should be considered when predicting behavioral intention using personality and strategy [2]. This is in line with Alslaity et al.'s observations.

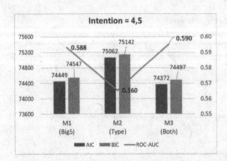

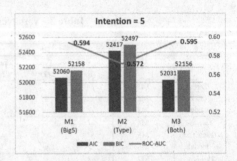

Fig. 4. Model fit and prediction accuracies of the direct effect prediction models

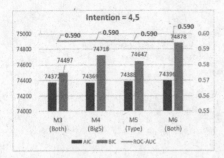

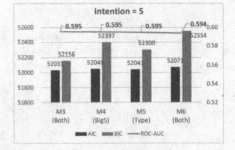

Fig. 5. Model fits and prediction accuracies in two-way interaction models

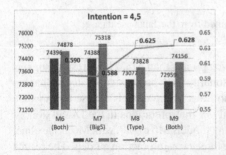

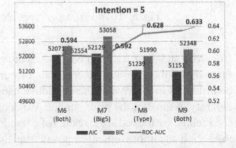

Fig. 6. Model fits and prediction accuracies of the three-way interaction models

6 Discussion

6.1 Empirical Findings and Implications

Our results indicate that representing personality as a combination of the Big Five traits and personality types (M3) improved both model fit and prediction accuracy in contrast to using independently the traits (M1) and types (M2). A plausible reason is that the personality type variable added interaction information to the Big Five traits. Thus, to answer our first research question (RQ1), we consider the best way to represent the direct effect of personality is by using both types and traits. Although adding the personality types helped improve the model fit and prediction accuracy, the contribution was smaller than the Big Five's direct effect. This is because the amount of information captured by a nominal variable (i.e., personality type) is less than that of a continuous variable (i.e., Big Five trait).

In the two-way interaction models, what surprised us is that adding interactions between personality and strategy did not improve the model fit nor prediction accuracy compared to the best direct effect model (M3). Although our results seem inconsistent with numerous prior investigations in which significant correlations between personality traits and susceptibility to persuasive strategies were confirmed, our finding echoes Alasity et al.'s critique on prior studies [2]. As we mentioned in Sect. 2.2, although prior studies reached a general agreement that the persuasive effects of Cialdini's six principles vary among personalities, half of the conclusions (i.e., the correlation between a particular personality trait and a particular persuasive strategy) are not entirely consistent. This suggests that additional factors (i.e., context) would moderate the impact of personality on strategy selection. Informed by the above, to answer our RQ2, we consider that when an association between personality and a persuasive strategy is confirmed, research should then examine for a more conclusive observation whether the association is universal or context dependent.

To further examine Alasity et al.'s observation, we incorporated the three-way interaction among personality, persuasive strategies, and context into the prediction models. Our results showed that when personality is represented by the types (M8), the three-way interaction leads to a notable improvement in model fit and prediction accuracy. On the contrary, the three-way interaction slightly negatively impacts both the model fit and prediction accuracy when the Big Five traits are used (M7).

We consider the possible reasons are the model's complexity, as well as ignoring the interactions of personality traits in M7. The three-way interaction in M7 is represented by a total of 50 variables (the number of $\beta_{i,j,k}^{IE3} p_i s_j c_k$ in IE_{3way} is $5 \times 5 \times 2$), whereas M8 used only 30 variables ($3 \times 5 \times 2$) for IE_{3way}. The lower AIC and BIC, and higher ROC-AUC, of M7 compared to the baseline (M6) that has no three-way interaction suggest that the many variables in M7 made the model overfit and degrade its prediction accuracy. Moreover, interactions of traits were not incorporated in the IE_{3way} of M7, in contrast to M8 that incorporated them. Based on these, to answer our RQ3, we posit personality should be represented by the types rather than traits in the three-way interaction since they lead to less model complexity and higher prediction accuracy.

6.2 Contribution

The primary contribution of this study is that we provided initial evidence to suggest when and how personality type could be utilized for prediction per the nine models we investigated in which each model falls in one of three model complexities. The results we obtained from using the prediction models indicate that representing personality only by the Big Five is insufficient for personalization. Further, personality type is a significant factor for predicting behavioral intentions and should be applied properly according to a model's complexity. Our secondary contribution is that we obtained the same personality types as Gerlach et al.'s using a dataset from a Japanese population. To our knowledge, we achieved the first step to examining the cross-cultural appeal of

Gerlach et al.' s personality typology in an East Asian context. We believe the personality typology has a significant advantage in both academic and practical applications, i.e., with the information on the interactions among multiple personality traits may result to higher prediction accuracy.

6.3   Limitations and Future Directions

Several limitations of this study should also be noted. First, although the three-way interactions among personality types, persuasive strategies and contexts were confirmed, we did not investigate which persuasive strategy is most effective for a particular personality type. Furthermore, we have little knowledge of the robustness and generalizability of the personality-strategy compatibility across contexts. More sophisticated subsequent investigations should be conducted to address these issues. Second, we predicted the behavioral intention rather than actual changes in behavior. Although numerous psychological theories (e.g., theory of planned behavior [28]) and the theory of reasoned action [29] posit intention is a key determinant of behavior, the obstacles between intention change and behavior change should not be ignored. Thus, the impact of three-way interaction on actual behavior should also be examined with viable PoCs. Third, it is most probably infeasible to obtain personality information from all participants with a lengthy questionnaire, let alone in a large-scale deployment. However, some previous works have attempted to predict the Big Five personality traits from various modalities of data, such as activity data (e.g., driving [30]), Internet usage logs, and visual data [31], among others. This is a viable approach for us to adopt. Last but not least, more sophisticated investigation is also needed to explore, validate, and further analyze the personality types of a Japanese population.

7   Conclusion

This study examined the efficacy of personality type on predicting behavioral intention in three types of prediction models. We addressed two methodological pitfalls of prior studies and brought new insights to personalizing persuasions. Overall, this study shows personality type is also a potent predictor of behavioral intention and should be applied properly according to the prediction model's complexity.

References

1. Aisha, M., Orji, R., Oyibo, K.: Personalizing persuasive technologies: do gender and age affect susceptibility to persuasive strategies? In: Adjunct Publication of the 26th Conference on User Modeling, Adaptation and Personalization, 2 July 2018, pp. 329–334. ACM (2018)
2. Alslaity, A., Tran, T.: On the impact of the application domain on users' susceptibility to the six weapons of influence. In: Gram-Hansen, S.B., Jonasen, T.S., Midden, C. (eds.) PERSUASIVE 2020. LNCS, vol. 12064, pp. 3–15. Springer, Cham (2020). https://doi.org/10.1007/978-3-030-45712-9_1
3. Alkis, N., Temizel, T.T.: The impact of individual differences on influence strategies. Person. Individ. Diff. **87**, 147–152 (2015)

4. Oyibo, K., Orji, R., Vassileva, J.: Investigation of the influence of personality traits on Cialdini's persuasive strategies. PPT@PERSUASIVE (2017)
5. Ciocarlan, A., Masthoff, J., Oren, N.: Actual persuasiveness: impact of personality, age and gender on message type susceptibility. In: Oinas-Kukkonen, H., Win, K.T., Karapanos, E., Karppinen, P., Kyza, E. (eds.) PERSUASIVE 2019. LNCS, vol. 11433, pp. 283–294. Springer, Cham (2019). https://doi.org/10.1007/978-3-030-17287-9_23
6. Gerlach, M., Farb, B., Revelle, W.: A robust data-driven approach identifies four personality types across four large data sets. Nat. Hum. Beh. **2**, 735–742 (2018)
7. Cialdini, R.B.: Influence: The Psychology of Persuasion. HarperCollins (2006)
8. Goldberg, L.R.: An alternative description of personality: the big-five factor structure. J. Pers. Soc. Psychol. **59**(6), 1216 (1990)
9. Cialdini, R.: Influence. The Psychology of Persuasion. William Morrowe Company, New York (1984)
10. Sofia, G., Marianna, S., George, L., Panos, K.: Investigating the role of personality traits and influence strategies on the persuasive effect of personalized recommendations. In: 4th Workshop on Emotions and Personality in Personalized Systems (EMPIRE), August 2016, p. 9 (2016)
11. Asendorpf, J.B., Borkenau, P., Ostendorf, F., Van Aken, M.A.G.: Carving personality description at its joints: confrmation of three replicable personality prototypes for both children and adults. Eur. J. Pers. **15**, 169–198 (2001)
12. Robins, R.W., John, O.P., Caspi, A., Moftt, T.E., Stouthamer-Loeber, M.: Resilient, overcontrolled, and undercontrolled boys: three replicable personality types. J. Pers. Soc. Psychol. **70**, 157–171 (1996)
13. Caspi, A., Silva, P.A.: Temperamental qualities at age three predict personality traits in young adulthood: longitudinal evidence from a birth cohort. Child Dev. **66**, 486–498 (1995)
14. Myers, I.B., Myers, P.B.: Gifts Differing: Understanding Personality Type, 2nd edn. Davies-Black Publishing Under Special License from CPP, Inc., Mountain View (1995). ISBN:978-0-89106-074-1
15. Donnellan, M.B., Robins, R.W.: Resilient, overcontrolled, and undercontrolled personality types: issues and controversies. Soc. Pers. Psychol. Compass **11**, 1070–1083 (2010)
16. Costa, P.T., Herbst, J.H., McCrae, R.R., Samuels, J., Ozer, D.J.: The replicability and utility of three personality types. Eur. J. Personal (2002)
17. Herzberg, P.Y., Roth, M.: Beyond resilients, undercontrollers, and overcontrollers? An extension of personality prototype research. Eur. J. Pers. **20**, 5–28 (2006)
18. Altman, N., Krzywinski, M.: Points of signifcance: clustering. Nat. Methods **14**, 545–546 (2017)
19. Specht, J., Luhmann, M., Geiser, C.: On the consistency of personality types across adulthood: latent profle analyses in two large-scale panel studies. J. Pers. Soc. Psychol. **107**, 540–556 (2014)
20. Wall, H.J., Campbell, C.C., Kaye, L.K., Levy, A., Bhullar, N.: Personality profiles and persuasion: an exploratory study investigating the role of the Big-5, Type D personality and the Dark Triad on susceptibility to persuasion. Person. Individ. Differ. **139**, 69–76 (2019)
21. Murakami, Y., Murakami, C.: Scale construction of a "Big Five" personality inventory. Jpn. J. Pers. **6**(1), 29–39 (1997)
22. Xu, W., Kuriki, Y., Sato, T., Taya, M., Ono, C.: Does traffic information provided by smartphones increase detour behavior? In: Gram-Hansen, S.B., Jonasen, T.S., Midden, C. (eds.) PERSUASIVE 2020. LNCS, vol. 12064, pp. 45–57. Springer, Cham (2020). https://doi.org/10.1007/978-3-030-45712-9_4
23. Dai, H., Saccardo, S., Han, M.A., et al.: Behavioural nudges increase COVID-19 vaccinations. Nature **597**, 404–409 (2021). https://doi.org/10.1038/s41586-021-03843-2

24. Weingarten, E., Chen, Q., McAdams, M., Yi, J., Hepler, J., Albarracín, D.: From primed concepts to action: a meta-analysis of the behavioral effects of incidental presented words. Psychol. Bull. **142**(5), 472–497 (2016)
25. Ward, J.H., Jr.: Hierarchical grouping to optimize an objective function. J. Am. Stat. Assoc. **58**, 236–244 (1969)
26. Everitt, B.S., Landau, S., Leese, M., Stahl, D.: Cluster Analysis, 5th edn, Wiley, London (2011) ISBN:978-0-470-97844-3
27. DeLong, E.R., DeLong, D.M., Clarke-Pearson, D.L.: Comparing the areas under two or more correlated receiver operating characteristic curves: a nonparametric approach. Biometrics **44**(3), 837–845 (1988). https://doi.org/10.2307/2531595
28. Schifter, D.E., Ajzen, I.: Intention, perceived control, and weight loss: an application of the theory of planned behavior. J. Pers. Soc. Psychol. **49**(3), 843–851 (1985)
29. Fishbein, M.: A theory of reasoned action: Some applications and implications. In: Howe, H., Page, M. (eds.) Nebraska Symposium on Motivation, vol. 27, pp. 65–116. University of Nebraska Press, Lincoln (1980)
30. Ishikawa, Y., Kobayashi, A., Minamikawa, A., Ono, C.: Predicting a driver's personality from daily driving behavior. In: Proceedings of the 10th International Driving Symposium on Human Factors in Driver Assessment, Training and Vehicle Design: Driving Assessment (2019)
31. Kamisaka, D., Ishikawa, Y.: Personality prediction with cross-modality feature projection. In: Proceedings of the 2021 International Conference on Multimodal Interaction. Association for Computing Machinery, New York, NY, USA, pp. 758–762 (2021)
32. Denollet, J., Sys, S.U., Stroobant, N., Rombouts, H., Gillebert, T.C., Brutsaert, D.L.: Personality as independent predictor of long-term mortality in patients with coronary heart disease. Lancet **347**(8999), 417–421 (1996)

Subliminal Warnings: Utilizing the High Bandwidth of Nonconscious Visual Perception

Feng Zhu[1]($\boxtimes$) (iD), Sandra Carpenter[1] (iD), and Mini Zeng[2] (iD)

[1] University of Alabama in Huntsville, Huntsville, AL 35899, USA
{fz0001,carpens}@uah.edu
[2] Jacksonville University, Jacksonville, FL 32211, USA
mzeng@ju.edu

Abstract. Cybersecurity warnings often fail. A fundamental problem is that existing warnings compete for conscious attention. Human conscious attention has a bandwidth of only 40 bit/s. The human visual perception system, however, has a bandwidth of 10 M bit/s. Cognitive science reveals that perception, evaluation, and motivation can happen without conscious awareness. Our novel idea is to harvest the power of nonconscious processing. To the best of our knowledge, this is the first research attempt to use nonconscious processing for cybersecurity, but the application contexts are very different from typical cognitive science studies. Thus, we first address: Do the subliminal warnings change users' security/privacy behavior? As a proof of concept, we implemented a restaurant table reservation app. When participants input their personal information, we displayed a subliminal warning message, "Privacy." The experimental results showed that participants in the subliminal warning condition disclosed less information than those in a no-warning control condition.

Keywords: Subliminal messages · Nonconscious processing · Warnings

1 Introduction

Numerous experiments and field studies have shown that computer warnings are often not effective. Studies revealed that some warnings failed most of the time [1] and others were as ineffective as no warning at all [2]. A fundamental problem is lack of attention paid to warnings [3]. While all users saw warnings, about 82% of them ignored the warnings [3]. In a large-scale study, up to 70% of the users simply clicked through warnings [4].

Many warning designs attempt to attract more attention [5] and suggest to fully interrupt users' primary tasks [6]. But other researchers indicate that warnings overconsume attention [7]. From users' perspective, they often perceive that the cost of reading a warning is much higher than the potential harm [3]. In terms of the monetized time allotment, reading the warning can be several orders of magnitude more expensive than taking the risk [8].

Our insight is that conscious attention is the bottleneck and can be bypassed. Human conscious attention has an information flow speed of 40 bit/s [9], and can focus on only

N. Baghaei et al. (Eds.): PERSUASIVE 2022, LNCS 13213, pp. 255–271, 2022.
https://doi.org/10.1007/978-3-030-98438-0_20

one thing at a time. The human visual system, however, has an information flow speed of 10 Mbit/s [9]. Much of our visual processing happens without conscious attention and yet shapes our behavior [10]. The last several decades of research in cognitive science reveal that perception, evaluation, and motivation can happen without conscious awareness [11]. Within dozens of milliseconds, the human visual system can accurately process information [12] and understand the semantic meanings of words [13]. Nonconscious processing can achieve the same effects (i.e., overt behavior) as conscious processing [14].

We want to apply nonconscious processing to cybersecurity warnings, specifically using subliminal messages. Cognitive science research indicates that subliminal warning messages can achieve all purposes of warnings. Our context, however, is very different from typical cognitive science studies. Those experiments required participants to look at the center of the screen. Often a participant went through dozens to hundreds of rounds of subliminal messages. In our approach, we present a subliminal warning only once, at the very moment when it is needed.

As our first step to harvest the power of nonconscious processing, we address the following questions.

- Can the subliminal warning message be consistently and accurately displayed in a realistic scenario?
- Does the subliminal warning message work?

Since subliminal warnings and user behavior all occur at the millisecond level, we chose to conduct a lab experiment. It offers the best way that isolates the effect of subliminal warnings [15]. It also enabled us to precisely measure the durations of the warning messages using a scene camera, observe participants' eye movements using an eye tracker, and confirm that the warning is subliminal.

We tested subliminal warnings in the context of privacy protection. People often worry about their privacy, but their behavior does not match their attitudes [16, 17]. Our subliminal warnings remind people their privacy attitudes. Note that different people may have different sensitivity levels, perceptions, opinions, and habits. Our messages assist them to better align their behavior with attitudes. Our hypothesis is that the subliminal warning messages reduce users' privacy disclosure behavior.

As a proof of concept, we created a restaurant table reservation app mimicking one of the very popular mobile apps that asks users for their identity information. Our subliminal warning message, "Privacy," was shown just-in-time as they typed in their personal information. The message appeared once for 50 ms. Thirty participants were in the subliminal warning condition and another thirty participants were in the control condition (no warnings). The results show that participants in subliminal warning condition disclosed less personal information than those in the control condition.

We made the following main contributions in this paper. First, our novel application of nonconscious perception bypasses the bottleneck and requirement of conscious attention in existing warnings, and thus solve the fundamental problem. It goes beyond current warning theories [18] and cybersecurity warning frameworks [19]. Second, we presented the theoretical foundation for subliminal warnings that can achieve the same effect and functions of the supraliminal warnings. Third, we ascertained subliminal warnings can be consistently and accurately displayed in realistic scenarios and do change people's identity disclosure behavior.

The rest of the paper is structured as follows. We first present background information and related work. Afterward, we discuss the theoretical foundation of our approach. Next, we discuss the experimental design. Then, we present our analyses and key findings with respect to the effectiveness of our approach. Last, we outline our future work and conclude by discussing our contributions.

2 Background and Related Work

2.1 Warnings and Warning Frameworks

Warnings have been widely used (e.g., on labels, signs, and product manuals), and much effort has been devoted to warning research since the 1980s [20]. Warnings have four basic purposes [18]: (1) provide information about potential risks, hazards, and/or consequences; (2) influence or change people's behavior; (3) serve as a reminder; and thus (4) increase safety. Our subliminal warning in the experiment serves as a reminder for users about their own privacy attitudes and help them to reduce identity disclosure.

To guide warning designs and to find why warnings fail, researchers may refer to the communication-human information processing (C-HIP) model [18]. In the C-HIP model, a user goes through multiple stages: attention switch (to warnings); attention maintenance (on warnings); comprehension (of warnings); changes in attitudes, beliefs, and affect (about behavior); motivation to change behavior; and behavior (compliance with the warning). These stages appear in Fig. 1, on the right column headed "Traditional warnings." Theoretically, warnings fail if users are blocked at any stage. While the C-HIP model serves as a framework for all types of warnings, computer scientists also use the C-HIP model to evaluate their designs [6]. Our proposed approach bypasses the first three stages and directly reminds users' privacy attitudes. Therefore, the warning does not compete for limited conscious attention.

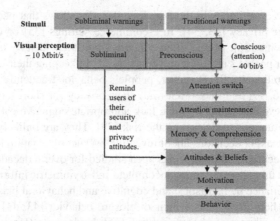

Fig. 1. Comparison of subliminal and traditional warnings.

2.2 No Attention on Cybersecurity Warnings

With the proliferation of web and mobile devices, people face various cybersecurity threats. Thus, there has been an increased interest in cybersecurity warnings in the last decade: warnings on SSL security in browsers [21], phishing attacks [6], and malware downloads [4]. Unfortunately, people do not pay attention to cybersecurity warnings [22] because as soon as people identify the messages as warnings, they often ignore them [3, 6] or simply click through warning messages [4].

Substantial research attempted to address the problem including the application of the warning theories and cybersecurity warning models [18, 19]. Researchers have been investigating two main knowledge gaps: (a) why cybersecurity warnings fail and (b) how to design effective warnings [23]. For the first gap, lab experiments and field studies have observed people's behavior [4] and determined reasons for warning ineffectiveness: lack of attention [21, 23, 24], overconsumption of human attention [7, 8], and habituation [25, 26]. Further analyses via game theoretical models indicate that ignoring warnings is rational if the risk to any specific individual is low [7, 8, 27, 28].

To address the second gap, new designs [5, 6, 21, 24] have been proposed to improve the effectiveness of cybersecurity warnings based on warning theories [28] or cybersecurity warning models [19]. The critical parts in these theoretical models are attention switch, attention maintenance, and comprehension. One approach is to strengthen or force attention switch and attention maintenance. Researchers proposed more salient warning features [29], applied polymorphic forms of warnings [30, 31], and used attractive visual cues [5]. Another approach is to facilitate attention switch and maintenance. We used eye-gaze information to dynamically display warnings (i.e., warnings that appear when needed, and then fade away) [32]. Even these well-crafted warning designs are not optimal, however. In this project, we go beyond current theoretical models and apply nonconscious processing theories.

2.3 Apply Warnings to Privacy and Identity Disclosure

Research on privacy attitudes in the last three decades shows that people, in general, worry about their privacy [33, 34]. In e-commerce settings [35] or unfamiliar computing environments [36], people often concern about their identity information. Our survey found that people's attitudes and concerns about keeping their identity information private are rational [37]. However, people's behavior frequently does not match their attitudes [16, 17] and they often trade their privacy for short-term benefits [38]. Researchers believe that usually people lack appropriate cognitive calculation mechanisms in these situations to determine the risk [39]. They are unlikely to use rational strategies when making decisions about revealing private information [40].

Nudges for security and privacy has been studied for over a decade [41]. They are designed to assist users in overcoming incomplete and asymmetric information, bounded rationality and reliance on heuristics, and cognitive and behavioral biases [42]. Privacy nudges strive to help users reduce their disclosure behavior [43, 44] and avoid apps that aggressively collect personal information [45]. Nudges may have negative effects, however. They may cause ethical objections [46], annoyance [47], and creepiness [48], or it may even be exploited [42].

3   The Theoretical Foundation of Using Subliminal Warnings

The subliminal warnings utilize subliminal visual perception capabilities. The human visual perception may be classified into subliminal, preconscious, and conscious processing [10] (Fig. 1). Subliminal perception occurs when the intensity of a stimulus is so brief or weak that we may not consciously perceive it even if we pay attention. It is below a subjective threshold of conscious awareness [10]. A subjective threshold is defined as half of the people being able to consciously notice a message. When visual stimuli are above the threshold, (i.e., supraliminal), and we focus our attention on them, they are available to our conscious processing. Preconscious processing occurs when stimuli are supraliminal (above a subjective threshold), but we ignore them. (Note that attention and consciousness are two distinct brain processes [49]; nonconscious processing includes both subliminal and preconscious processing [10].)

Subliminal Perception is Ubiquitous. With 100 million photoreceptors and 1 million axons leaving each eye and connected to the brain [50], humans process raw data at about 10M bit/s [49]. Cognitive neuroscience studies show that the human visual system processes information ultra-rapidly (e.g., in only 20 ms, people can differentiate whether a photo contains an animal), and produces reliable response behavior [12, 51]. Our sensory-perceptual system processes stimuli below conscious awareness [52] and even feeds into the brain's error-monitoring system [53]. Subliminal perception has been confirmed and studied using fMRIs [54], eye trackers [55], EEGs [56], event-related potentials (ERPs) [57, 58], and galvanic skin responses (GSRs) [59].

Subliminal Perception Reaches the Semantic Level. While early studies and debate were about the existence of subliminal perception, the focus in the last two decades has shifted to the depth of subliminal perception. Brain imaging technology has clearly shown that subliminal perception occurs at the sematic level and guides the motor process without awareness [60]. A meta-analysis [13], which includes both published and unpublished studies, shows that subliminal messages can be processed semantically.

Subliminal stimuli in research experiments are often in the forms of photos [61], words [62], signs [63, 64], and shapes [65]. They occur for several milliseconds to dozens of milliseconds. Numerous psychological experiments, field studies, and meta-analyses have demonstrated that subliminal messages can enhance persuasion [66], affect people's preferences, attitudes, and behavior [67, 68], influence one's decision making [69, 70], change motor processes [71], and motivate people [72–74]. Subliminal perception has also been studied and shown to be effective in various contexts from learning to political campaigns [67, 75–77].

Activating Mental Representations is the Key. Our brains do not care whether a stimulus is subliminal or supraliminal. What is crucial is that the corresponding mental representation is activated [14]. Studies show that subliminal stimuli can activate the same mental concepts as the supraliminal stimuli. For example, exposure to both subliminal [78] and supraliminal [79] trait terms similarly influenced people's impressions of others. A review of the literature [80] shows that when subliminal and supraliminal stimuli activate the same mental representations, overt behavior is affected in the same way. Experiments comparing the subliminal and supraliminal activations and using the same behavioral measure further demonstrated the same performance [81, 82].

Contemporary research on nonconscious processing indicates that *subliminal messages can achieve all four purposes of warnings* (i.e., provide information, influence behavior, serve as a reminder, and increase safety). In our experiment, we show that subliminal warnings can effectively reduce privacy disclosure.

4   Experimental Design

In this section, we discuss the hardware and software that we used to precisely deliver the subliminal warnings and measure users' behavior at the millisecond level. The experimental settings enabled us to answer our first question – whether subliminal warning messages can be consistently and accurately displayed.

We chose a typical application in which people were asked for their personal information. We created a restaurant table reservation app called ReserveME (a Windows app). It mimics the OpenTable app, a popular reservation mobile app. ReserveME asks for name, email, phone number, street address, city, state, and zip code.

We used a mixed-method design: an experiment and a follow-up questionnaire. We hypothesized that participants in the subliminal warning condition would disclose less of their private information than those in the control condition (without warnings). The participants were assigned to either the control condition or the subliminal condition.

4.1   The Hardware and Software

We used the SMI RED 250 Mobile Eye Tracking System (250 Hz) to record participants' eye gaze information, and a scene camera, ELP mini USB camera, (120 Hz) to ensure the display of subliminal warning messages. We had not seen the usage of scene cameras or other objective measurements of subliminal message in previous experiments, but we wanted to verify that subliminal messages were properly displayed.

One PC ran the eye tracking system and the ReserveME app, whereas the other machine ran the scene camera and software. Besides the ReserveME app and our scene camera software, we built another piece of software that integrated data collection, event synchronization, data processing, and analysis. All three pieces of software were synchronized and recording their respective events. Our tests show that there is less than 1 ms difference in the event logs of the software and hardware.

After the experiment, our software displayed the eye gaze data in videos, which can be played frame by frame. The eye gaze information was displayed and overlaid on the ReserveME pages. The scene camera video could be playing the respective scenes, specifically verifying the display of the subliminal messages.

4.2   The Warning Design and Its Rationale

We chose the key design factors to increase the success rate when there was only one opportunity to present a warning message. Our choices were based on literature review and a meta-analysis [13] which included both published and unpublished studies. Our emphasis was on the effectiveness of semantic processing. We used a short warning word, "Privacy" as the subliminal warning message. Meaningful words are one of the most effective stimuli [13, 16, 83] among all effective subliminal message forms (i.e., photos [61], words [62], signs [63, 64], and shapes/polygons [65]). The subliminal warning was presented just-in-time. That is, after a user clicked the input textbox and right before disclosing information, the subliminal warning was shown directly above the input textbox, as shown in Fig. 2.

Fig. 2. The subliminal warning was shown right above the text field of street address.

Our warning was presented as subliminal priming. Priming refers to activating and making a concept or category of information already in memory more salient by presenting a stimulus from that category. Priming triggers semantic memory that involves cognitive representations of the word [84]. In our case, priming was through the subliminal warning message that prepared people to consider their privacy attitudes when identity information was requested. The benefit of priming is that it activates three interactive systems (the evaluative, motivational, and perceptual systems) and their respective interfaces to the behavior [85]. Literature has shown strong relations between the semantic activation of related primes and their targets (i.e., words about which people are making decisions) [52, 85].

In our experiment, when a user clicked on the street address textbox, the subliminal text message appeared. The message was set to display for 50ms. Participants were not required to look at the subliminal message area. Street address was the only piece of information for which the prime was shown, although we asked for six pieces of information (phone number and email address were on the next page.) We wanted to ascertain the impact of a subliminal warning on disclosure of street address, when we showed the message only once. We hypothesized that the subliminal prime would reduce disclosure of street address (our hypothesized result), and we also wanted to explore the possibility that the prime might affect disclosure of the other five pieces of information.

4.3 Participants

We recruited the participants from the students who were taking introductory psychology classes at our university. This course is a popular general education course, so the students represent a wide diversity of college majors. We posted the experiment on the psychology department's experimental listing website. In the experimental descriptions, we did not mention of privacy or security issues. Instead, we stated that students would evaluate the quality/usability of a new restaurant reservation app. Of the sixty participants who completed the experiment, thirty-eight were women and twenty-two were men. Their ages ranged from seventeen to forty-eight with a median of age twenty. Their ethnic heritage was as follows: forty-five Caucasian, five African, four Asian, and four Hispanic. Two participants reported "other" as an ethnicity.

4.4 Procedure

We conducted the experiment with one participant at a time. Upon arrival, we provided every participant a consent form and a brief overview of the restaurant reservation app. The researchers explained the procedures of the experiment and the devices (eye tracker and scene camera). Participants were guided through the eye tracking calibration. They proceeded at their own paces through the ReserveME app, and they did not interact with our researchers unless there were questions or issues. Once participants finished the table reservation, they completed the post-experiment questionnaire. They usually spent 30 min to complete the entire process. The procedure of the experiment were approved by our university's Institutional Review Board (IRB). At the end of the experiment, during the debriefing, we told them the purpose of the experiment and none of their personal information had been recorded.

4.5 Questionnaire

We started our post-experiment questionnaire by requesting participants' feedback on the ReserveME app, in keeping with our cover story. We asked about some details of the information presented in the ReserveME app to verify whether participants paid attention during their interaction with the app. Then, we asked participants to indicate, for each type of identity information requested by ReserveME, whether they provided true or false information. We followed this with queries as to why they provided accurate or inaccurate information. We also asked their privacy attitudes towards these identity elements. In the last part, we asked participants whether they saw anything on the screenshot of the ReserveME page.

5 Experimental Results and Key Findings

5.1 The Subliminal Warning Was Consistently Displayed

From the scene camera videos, we saw that the subliminal warning message was displayed in all thirty instances in the subliminal condition. We watched the videos and manually played the subliminal warning portion frame by frame to determine the accuracy and consistency of the subliminal warning message.

The average number of frames for the subliminal messages in the scene camera videos was 7.4 frames. The sampling rate of the scene camera was 120 Hz (i.e., about every

8.3 ms). The display durations were relatively consistent. Among thirty participants in the subliminal warning condition, the warning messages lasted seven or eight frames for twenty-seven of them. Two participants' warning message lasted six frames; and one participant's warning message lasted nine frames. Therefore, we believe that the subliminal warning can be displayed consistently and accurately.

5.2 Most Participants Were not Consciously Aware of the Warning Message

In the post-experiment questionnaire, we asked participants to report whether or not they saw any message above the address textbox area (Fig. 2). We asked participants to describe the message if they answered "yes."

Four participants in the subliminal warning condition stated "yes," whereas the rest stated either "no" or "not sure." One participant reported that the message was "secure," which is semantically close to the warning message. One participant saw "something yellow." For the other two participants, one said "list info" and the other said "address line." We speculate that the last two participants were recalling supraliminal information presented on the page.

Likewise, we asked the thirty participants in the control group the same question. There was no message shown around the street address textbox. Four participants answered "yes" in the questionnaire. Two said "read policy;" one said "available time;" and the other said "restaurant time." We speculate that these participants were remembering information shown in a different location in the app.

5.3 The Warnings Were Subliminal

Was it possible that the warning message was not subliminal? Instead participants might "forget" about it because there were several minutes from when they "saw" the message to when they reported their "perception" in the questionnaire.

To address the concern, we conducted another test using the same experimental design, settings, and procedure [86]. Right after the subliminal warning message was shown, our researcher interrupted the experiment and asked participants whether they saw anything in the area where the subliminal message was display. An additional eighteen participants were recruited for the experiment. Twelve of them said that they did not notice anything; three saw a flash; and the other three recalled the message. This test results indicated that 50 ms for the warning message was below the subject threshold. So, we believe that the warnings were subliminal.

5.4 Identity Disclosure Behavior

There were 30 participants in each condition. Table 1 shows the number of participants who provided their real identity information. If a participant did not input in a field or provided fake information, we considered the case as the participant not providing real information.

Compared to those in the control condition, fewer participants in the subliminal warning condition provided their real identity information for all six identity elements.

Table 1. Number of participants who disclosed their real information in the two conditions. *The numbers in parentheses indicate the odds ratios when we compare the control to the subliminal condition (i.e., reciprocals of the odds ratios that compared the two conditions).

	Control	Subliminal	P-value	Odds ratio*
Address	24	18	**0.042**	0.38 (2.67)
City	27	23	0.080	0.37 (2.74)
State	27	26	0.344	0.72 (1.38)
Zip code	27	20	0.011	0.22 (4.50)
Email	28	23	0.032	0.23 (4.26)
Phone	25	24	0.369	0.80 (1.25)

We conducted an omnibus 3-way chi-square with a $2 \times 6 \times 2$ design to test whether the difference was statistically significant. The statistical test included 2 experimental conditions (control vs. subliminal warning), 6 identity elements, and 2 participant choices (disclose vs. not disclose). The overall result was significant ($p\text{-}value = 0.001$). Therefore, the disclosure behavior of two groups was different.

To compare participants' behavior for each of the six elements of identity information, we ran two-proportion Z-tests (left-tailed) to compare the percentage of disclosure in the subliminal and control conditions. We had specifically hypothesized that participants in the subliminal warning condition would be less likely to disclose their street address than those in the control condition. For this comparison, we used the 0.05 significance level for interpreting the results. The Z-test showed that participants in the two conditions behaved statistically different ($p\text{-}value = 0.042$). Thus, our hypothesis that a subliminal warning would reduce personal information disclosure was supported.

For the other five identity elements, we did not specifically predict whether participants would behave differently but were curious whether the subliminal warning affected disclosure beyond the identity element for which it was displayed. Because it is statistically appropriate for such exploratory analyses, we used the Bonferroni correction for these five elements of identity information, dividing the significance level by the number of exploratory analyses, yielding a significance value of 0.01 (0.05/5 = 0.01). Using this significance level, we cannot conclude that participants in the two groups behaved statistically different for those five identity elements.

To determine the impact of the subliminal warnings, we also calculated the odds ratios and compared the subliminal condition to the control condition (Table 1). Participants in the control condition, for example, were about 2.67 times more likely to disclose accurate street address compared to those in the subliminal condition.

Further analysis of participants' behavior showed that participants in the warning and control conditions used the same approaches and strategies to protect their personal identity information. They avoided providing real identity elements that were more sensitive and important (e.g., street address), but were more willing to provide information that was less sensitive. That is, those who provided fake information for city, also provided fake street address and zip code, but might provide real information for state.

5.5 What Do the Eye Tracking Data Show?

Eye tracking data and videos enable us to observe participants' behavior in greater detail. Some participants spent a good deal of time using the app. For example, when a participant reached the Reservation page (Fig. 2), s/he first read the restaurant name, reservation time, all identity elements that were requested then started to type in the information. Next, s/he checked every piece of the information again. Afterward, s/he clicked link and read the policy. At the other extreme, a few participants quickly clicked on the input textboxes and input their information, then moved onto the next page.

Eye tracking data also provide high temporal precision information. Among all information, we were particularly interested in the relative positions of the eye gazes and the subliminal warnings messages. The display of the subliminal warning was triggered when participants moved the mouse to the textbox and clicked the input field of street address. The lines in Fig. 3 show the eye gaze movements of all participants and their relative positions to the warning message (when it was shown in the warning condition). The eye gazes of twenty participants in the subliminal condition were very close to the subliminal warning message (about 50 pixels or less) during the display of the message. Nine participants behaved differently. They moved the mouse to the street address field first, looked at other things on the screen, and then clicked the field. Thus, the warning was not projected into the fovea area of the eyes, but we are not sure that they did not see the prime peripherally. Three of them "noticed" something, and then tried to locate it. Right after the message faded away, their eye gazes quickly moved to the warning message area (right above the text field where the subliminal warning was shown). One participant looked down and started typing when he/she clicked the mouse. Thus, the eye tracker lost track of his/her eyes.

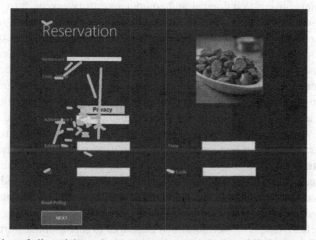

Fig. 3. Depiction of all participants' eye gaze movements in the subliminal condition. Each line represents one participant's eye gaze movement during the display of the subliminal message.

6 Discussion – Is It Ethical to Use Subliminal Warnings?

Over 130 years of the empirical study of subliminal communication [87], two interacting reasons negatively impacted this field [14]: (a) people's discomfort with the concept of nonconscious processing influencing behavior and (b) concern with the ethics of using nonconscious processes to manipulate people's behavior.

Many people feel uncomfortable that human behavior and functioning are, in general, driven by nonconscious processing. In fact, however, external stimuli are automatically processed by our internal psychological processes almost constantly and often without awareness [88]. Social psychology phenomena in everyday life are basically automatic in nature, as opposed to being constantly mediated by conscious attention [85]. Thus, subliminal influences are ubiquitous.

The second negative impact was the false claim that people were manipulated by subliminal messages, "Drink Coke" and "Eat Popcorn," in a theater [14]. This damaged the public's and academia's impression of subliminal perception [14, 89]. Because of the ethical issues, the number of researchers seriously working on subliminal perception dropped dramatically for at least 20 years [14].

Later, researchers looked into the ethics of subliminal communication, especially in advertising and marketing [90–93]. Surveys showed that most people believed that subliminal advertising was unethical and unacceptable [93–95]. But researchers have agreed that subliminal messages are not all bad such as for non-profit and beneficial purposes [96] or to stop shoplifting [90].

7 Conclusions and Future Work

We took an innovative psychological and computer security approach to design warnings. Our major contributions of this research were to explore and use nonconscious processing capability that do not compete for very limited bandwidth of conscious processing and attention. We presented the theoretical foundation that subliminal perception can reach the semantic level and activate people's mental representation of cybersecurity and privacy attitudes and beliefs. The experiment showed that the subliminal warning message did reduce participants' privacy disclosure behavior. The subliminal warning message was also successfully and consistently displayed. We presented eye tracking results and how participants explained their behavior of identity disclosure.

This paper presents our first step to explore the nonconscious perception applied to warnings. Future work will focus on the engineering aspect of the subliminal warning messages, specifically different warning words, durations, the color and background of the message, its location, and the mechanism that triggers the warning. We believe that subliminal warnings will be more reliable, consistent, and effective. We will also compare the effectiveness of the subliminal messages to supraliminal warnings.

In our future research and experiments, we will also study ethical issues of using nonconscious processing in cybersecurity and privacy. We want to understand people's perceptions, feelings, and acceptance of subliminal warning messages as a countermeasure to attacks and as a privacy-preserving approach.

References

1. Dhamija, R., Tygar, J.D., Hearst, M.: Why phishing works. In: Proceedings of the SIGCHI Conference on Human Factors in Computing Systems, CHI 2006, p. 581 (2006). https://doi.org/10.1145/1124772.1124861
2. Wu, M., Miller, R.C., Garfinkel, S.L.: Do security toolbars actually prevent phishing attacks? In: Proceedings of the SIGCHI Conference on Human Factors in Computing Systems, Montréal, Québec, Canada (2006)
3. Krol, K., Moroz, M., Sasse, M.A.: Don't work. Can't work? Why it's time to rethink security warnings. In: 2012 7th International Conference on Risks and Security of Internet and Systems (CRiSIS), pp. 1–8 (2012). https://doi.org/10.1109/CRISIS.2012.6378951
4. Akhawe, D., Felt, A.P.: Alice in warning land: a large-scale field study of browser security warning effectiveness. In: Proceedings of the 22nd USENIX Security Symposium, pp. 257–272 (2013)
5. Bravo-Lillo, C., et al.: Your attention please: designing security-decision UIs to make genuine risks harder to ignore. In: Proceedings of the Ninth Symposium on Usable Privacy and Security, SOUPS 2013, pp. 6:1–6:12 (2013). https://doi.org/10.1145/2501604.2501610
6. Egelman, S., Cranor, L.F., Hong, J.: You've been warned: an empirical study of the effectiveness of web browser phishing warnings. In: Proceedings of the SIGCHI Conference on Human Factors in Computing Systems (2008)
7. Böhme, R., Grossklags, J.: The security cost of cheap user interaction. In: Proceedings of the 2011 Workshop on New Security Paradigms Workshop - NSPW 2011, p. 67 (2011). https://doi.org/10.1145/2073276.2073284
8. Herley, C.: So long, and no thanks for the externalities: the rational rejection of security advice by users. Security, 133–144 (2009). https://doi.org/10.1145/1719030.1719050
9. Zimmermann, M.: the nervous system in the context of information theory. Hum. Physiol., 166–173 (1989). https://doi.org/10.1007/978-3-642-73831-9_7
10. Dehaene, S., Changeux, J.P., Naccache, L., Sackur, J., Sergent, C.: Conscious, preconscious, and subliminal processing: a testable taxonomy. Trends Cogn. Sci. **10**, 204–211 (2006). https://doi.org/10.1016/j.tics.2006.03.007
11. Kihlstrom, J.: The congnitive unconscious. Science **237**, 1445–1452 (1987)
12. Thorpe, S.J., Fize, D., Marlot, C.: Speed of processing in the human visual system (1996). https://doi.org/10.1038/381520a0
13. Van den Bussche, E., Van den Noortgate, W., Reynvoet, B.: Mechanisms of masked priming: a meta-analysis. Psychol. Bull. **135**, 452–477 (2009). https://doi.org/10.1037/a0015329
14. Dijksterhuis, A., Aarts, H., Smith, P.K.: The power of the subliminal: on subliminal persuasion and other potential applications. In: The New Unconscious, pp. 77–106 (2005)
15. Dhami, S.: The Foundations of Behavioral Economic Analysis. Oxford University Press, Oxford (2016)
16. Spiekermann, S., Grossklags, J., Berendt, B.: E-privacy in 2nd generation E-commerce: privacy preferences versus actual behavior. In: Proceedings of the 3rd ACM Conference on Electronic Commerce, Tampa, Florida (2001)
17. Berendt, B., Günther, O., Spiekermann, S.: Privacy in E-commerce: stated preferences vs. actual behavior. Commun. ACM. **48**, 101–106 (2005)
18. Laughery, K.R., Wogalter, M.S.: Designing effective warnings. Rev. Hum. Factors Ergon., 241–271 (2006). https://doi.org/10.1177/1557234X0600200109
19. Cranor, L.F.: A framework for reasoning about the human in the loop. In: Proceedings of the 1st Conference on Usability, Psychology, and Security, pp. 1:1--1:15 (2008)
20. Wogalter, M.S.: Handbook of Warnings. Lawrence Erlbaum Associates, Mahwah (2006)

21. Sunshine, J., Egelman, S., Almuhimedi, H., Atri, N., Cranor, L.F.: Crying wolf: an empirical study of SSL warning effectivenes. In: 18th USENIX Security Symposium, pp. 399–432 (2009). https://doi.org/10.1016/S1353-4858(01)00916-3

22. Zhang, B., Wu, M., Kang, H., Go, E., Sundar, S.S.: Effects of security warnings and instant gratification cues on attitudes toward mobile websites. In: Proceedings of the 32nd Annual ACM Conference on Human Factors in Computing Systems, CHI 2014, pp. 111–114 (2014). https://doi.org/10.1145/2556288.2557347

23. Bravo-Lillo, C., Cranor, L.F., Downs, J., Komanduri, S.: Bridging the gap in computer security warnings: a mental model approach. IEEE Secur. Priv. 9, 18–26 (2011). https://doi.org/10.1109/MSP.2010.198

24. Bravo-Lillo, C., Cranor, L.F., Downs, J., Komanduri, S., Sleeper, M.: Improving computer security dialogs. In: Campos, P., Graham, N., Jorge, J., Nunes, N., Palanque, P., Winckler, M. (eds.) INTERACT 2011. LNCS, vol. 6949, pp. 18–35. Springer, Heidelberg (2011). https://doi.org/10.1007/978-3-642-23768-3_2

25. Kim, S., Wogalter, M.S.: Habituation, dishabituation, and recovery effects in visual warnings. Hum. Factors Ergon. Soc. Annu. Meet. Proc. 53, 1612–1616 (2009). https://doi.org/10.1518/107118109X12524444080675

26. Maurer, M.-E., De Luca, A., Kempe, S.: Using data type based security alert dialogs to raise online security awareness. In: Proceedings of the Seventh Symposium on Usable Privacy and Security - SOUPS 2011, p. 1 (2011). https://doi.org/10.1145/2078827.2078830

27. Anderson, R., Moore, T.: The economics of information security. Science 314, 610–613 (2006)

28. Laughery, K.R., Wogalter, M.S.: Designing effective warnings. Rev. Hum. Factors Ergon. 2, 241–271 (2006). https://doi.org/10.1177/1557234X0600200109

29. Egelman, S., Schechter, S.: The Importance of Being Earnest [in Security Warnings] (2013)

30. Brustoloni, J.C., Villamarín-Salomón, R.: Improving security decisions with polymorphic and audited dialogs. In: Proceedings of the 3rd Symposium on Usable Privacy and Security - SOUPS 2007, p. 76 (2007). https://doi.org/10.1145/1280680.1280691

31. De Keukelaere, F., Yoshihama, S., Trent, S., Zhang, Y., Luo, L., Zurko, M.E.: Adaptive security dialogs for improved security behavior of users. In: Gross, T., et al. (eds.) INTERACT 2009. LNCS, vol. 5726, pp. 510–523. Springer, Heidelberg (2009). https://doi.org/10.1007/978-3-642-03655-2_57

32. Zeng, M., Zhu, F., Carpenter, S.: Eye gaze based dynamic warnings. In: 9th International Conference on Advances in Computer-Human Interactions (ACHI) I, pp. 204–211 (2016)

33. Schneier, B.: Semantic Attacks: The Third Wave of Network Attacks (2000)

34. Sweeney, L.: Uniqueness of Simple Demographics in the U.S. Population. Carnegie Mellon University, Laboratory for International Data Privacy, Pittsburgh (2000)

35. Acquisti, A.: Privacy in electronic commerce and the economics of immediate gratification. In: 5th ACM Conference on Electronic Commerce, New York, NY (2004)

36. Nguyen, D.H., et al.: Encountering SenseCam: personal recording technologies in everyday life. In: Proceedings of the 11th International Conference on Ubiquitous Computing, Orlando, Florida (2009)

37. Zhu, F., Carpenter, S., Kulkarni, A.: Understanding identity exposure in pervasive computing environments. Pervasive Mob. Comput. 8, 777–794 (2012)

38. Acquisti, A., Grossklags, J.: Privacy and rationality in individual decision making. IEEE Secur. Priv. 3, 26–33 (2005)

39. March, J.G.: Risk Taking and Organizational Learning. ICOS, Ann Arbor (1994)

40. Lea, S., Fischer, P.: The psychology of scams: provoking and committing errors of judgement. Office of Fair Trading (2009)

41. The Behavioral Economics: Nudging Privacy (2009)

42. Acquisti, A., Leon, P.G.: Nudges for privacy and security: understanding and assisting users' choices online. ACM Comput. Surv. **50**, 1–41 (2017)

43. Wang, Y., Leon, P.G., Acquisti, A., Cranor, L.F., Forget, A., Sadeh, N.: A field trial of privacy nudges for Facebook. In: ACM CHI Conference on Human Factors in Computing Systems (CHI), pp. 2367–2376 (2014)

44. Almuhimedi, H., et al.: Your location has been shared 5, 398 times! A field study on mobile app privacy nudging (2015). https://doi.org/10.1145/2702123.2702210

45. Choe, E., Jung, J., Lee, B., Fisher, K.: Nudging people away from privacy-invasive mobile apps through visual framing. In: Kotzé, P., Marsden, G., Lindgaard, G., Wesson, J., Winckler, M. (eds.) INTERACT 2013. LNCS, vol. 8119, pp. 74–91. Springer, Heidelberg (2013). https://doi.org/10.1007/978-3-642-40477-1_5

46. Selinger, E., Whyte, K.: Is there a right way to nudge? Pract. Ethics Choice Archit. **10**, 923–935 (2011)

47. Micallef, N., Just, M., Baillie, L.: Stop annoying me! An empirical investigation of the usability of app privacy notifications, pp. 371–375 (2017). https://doi.org/10.1145/3152771.3156139

48. Zhang, B., Xu, H.: Privacy nudges for mobile applications: effects on the creepiness emotion and privacy attitudes, pp. 1676–1690 (2016)

49. Koch, C., Tsuchiya, N.: Attention and consciousness: two distinct brain processes. Trends Cogn. Sci. **11**, 16–22 (2007). https://doi.org/10.1016/j.tics.2006.10.012

50. Bear, M.F., Connors, B.W., Paradiso, M.A.: Neuroscience. Lippincott Williams & Wilkins (2007)

51. Kirchner, H., Thorpe, S.J.: Ultra-rapid object detection with saccadic eye movements: visual processing speed revisited. Vision. Res. **46**, 1762–1776 (2006). https://doi.org/10.1016/j.visres.2005.10.002

52. Kouider, S., Dehaene, S.: Levels of processing during non-conscious perception: a critical review of visual masking. Philos. Trans. Royal Soc. B Biol. Sci. **362**, 857–875 (2007). https://doi.org/10.1098/rstb.2007.2093

53. Pavone, E.F., Marzi, C.A., Girelli, M.: Does subliminal visual perception have an error-monitoring system? Eur. J. Neurosci. **30**, 1424–1431 (2009). https://doi.org/10.1111/j.1460-9568.2009.06908.x

54. Lau, H.C., Passingham, R.E.: Unconscious activation of the cognitive control system in the human prefrontal cortex. J. Neurosci. **27**, 5805–5811 (2007). https://doi.org/10.1523/JNEUROSCI.4335-06.2007

55. Nickel, A.E., Henke, K., Hannula, D.E.: Relational memory is evident in eye movement behavior despite the use of subliminal testing methods. PLoS ONE **10**, 1–28 (2015). https://doi.org/10.1371/journal.pone.0141677

56. Bowman, H., Filetti, M., Janssen, D., Su, L., Alsufyani, A., Wyble, B.: Subliminal salience search illustrated: EEG identity and deception detection on the fringe of awareness. PLoS ONE **8** (2013). https://doi.org/10.1371/journal.pone.0054258

57. Cressman, E.K., Lam, M.Y., Franks, I.M., Enns, J.T., Chua, R.: Unconscious and out of control: subliminal priming is insensitive to observer expectations. Conscious. Cogn. **22**, 716–728 (2013). https://doi.org/10.1016/j.concog.2013.04.011

58. Kiss, M., Eimer, M.: ERPs reveal subliminal processing of fearful faces. Psychophysiology **45**, 318–326 (2008). https://doi.org/10.1111/j.1469-8986.2007.00634.x

59. Lazarus, R.S., McCleary, R.A.: Autonomic discrimination without awareness: a study of subception. Psychol. Rev. **58**, 113 (1951)

60. Dehaene, S., et al.: Imaging unconscious semantic priming. Nature **395**, 597–600 (1998). https://doi.org/10.1038/26967

61. Pessiglione, M., et al.: How the brain translates money into force: a neuroimaging study of subliminal motivation. Science **316**, 904–906 (2007). https://doi.org/10.1126/science.114 0459
62. Capa, R.L., Cleeremans, A., Bustin, G.M., Hansenne, M.: Long-lasting effect of subliminal processes on cardiovascular responses and performance. Int. J. Psychophysiol. **81**, 22–30 (2011). https://doi.org/10.1016/j.ijpsycho.2011.04.001
63. Duarte, E., Rebelo, F., Teles, J., Wogalter, M.S.: Behavioral compliance for dynamic versus static signs in an immersive virtual environment. Appl. Ergon. **45**, 1367–1375 (2014). https://doi.org/10.1016/j.apergo.2013.10.004
64. Reuss, H., Kiesel, A., Kunde, W., Wühr, P.: A cue from the unconscious - masked symbols prompt: spatial anticipation. Front. Psychol. **3**, 1 (2012). https://doi.org/10.3389/fpsyg.2012. 00397
65. Manly, T., Fish, J.E., Griffiths, S., Molenveld, M., Zhou, F.A., Davis, G.J.: Unconscious priming of task-switching generalizes to an untrained task. PLoS ONE **9** (2014). https://doi.org/10.1371/journal.pone.0088416
66. Bermeitinger, C., Goelz, R., Johr, N., Neumann, M., Ecker, U.K.H., Doerr, R.: The hidden persuaders break into the tired brain. J. Exp. Soc. Psychol. **45**, 320–326 (2009). https://doi.org/10.1016/j.jesp.2008.10.001
67. Smarandescu, L., Shimp, T.A.: Drink coca-cola, eat popcorn, and choose powerade: testing the limits of subliminal persuasion. Mark. Lett. **26**(4), 715–726 (2014). https://doi.org/10. 1007/s11002-014-9294-1
68. Winkielman, P., Zajonc, R.B., Schwarz, N.: Subliminal affective priming resists attributional interventions. Cogn. Emot. **11**, 433–465 (1997)
69. Schlaghecken, F., Eimer, M.: Masked prime stimuli can bias "free" choices between response alternatives. Psychon. Bull. Rev. **11**, 463–468 (2004). https://doi.org/10.3758/BF03196596
70. Pessiglione, M., Petrovic, P., Daunizeau, J., Palminteri, S., Dolan, R.J., Frith, C.D.: Subliminal instrumental conditioning demonstrated in the human brain. Neuron **59**, 561–567 (2008). https://doi.org/10.1016/j.neuron.2008.07.005
71. Boulenger, V., Silber, B.Y., Roy, A.C., Paulignan, Y., Jeannerod, M., Nazir, T.A.: Subliminal display of action words interferes with motor planning: a combined EEG and kinematic study. J. Physiol. Paris **102**, 130–136 (2008). https://doi.org/10.1016/j.jphysparis.2008.03.015
72. Aarts, H., Custers, R., Marien, H.: Preparing and motivating behavior outside of awareness. Science (New York, N.Y.) **319**, 1639 (2008). https://doi.org/10.1126/science.1150432
73. Gibson, B., Zielaskowski, K.: Subliminal priming of winning images prompts increased betting in slot machine play. J. Appl. Soc. Psychol. **43**, 106–115 (2013)
74. Schmidt, L., Palminteri, S., Lafargue, G., Pessiglione, M.: Splitting motivation. Psychol. Sci. **21**, 977–983 (2010). https://doi.org/10.1177/0956797610372636
75. Lui, M., Rosenfeld, J.P.: The application of subliminal priming in lie detection: scenario for identification of members of a terrorist ring. Psychophysiology **46**, 889–903 (2009). https://doi.org/10.1111/j.1469-8986.2009.00810.x
76. Radel, R., Sarrazin, P., Legrain, P., Gobancé, L.: Subliminal priming of motivational orientation in educational settings: effect on academic performance moderated by mindfulness. J. Res. Pers. **43**, 695–698 (2009). https://doi.org/10.1016/j.jrp.2009.02.011
77. Westen, D.: RATS, we should have used Clinton: subliminal priming in political campaigns. Polit. Psychol. **29**(5), 631–651 (2008). Published by: International Society of Political 29, 631–651 (2016). Author (s): Joel Weinberger and Drew Westen Source
78. Bargh, J.A., Pietromonaco, P.: Automatic information processing and social perception: the influence of trait information presented outside of conscious awareness on impression formation. J. Pers. Soc. Psychol. **43**, 437 (1982)
79. Tory Higgins, E., Rholes, W.S., Jones, C.R.: Category accessibility and impression formation. J. Exp. Soc. Psychol. **13**, 141–154 (1977)

80. Dijksterhuis, A., Bargh, J.A.: The perception-behavior expressway: automatic effects of social perception on social behavior. In: Advances in Experimental Social Psychology, pp. 1–40. Elsevier (2001)

81. Dijksterhuis, A., Bargh, J.A.: On the relation between associative strength and automatic behavior **544**, 531–544 (2000). https://doi.org/10.1006/jesp.2000.1427

82. Dijksterhuis, A., Bargh, J.A., Miedema, J.: Of men and mackerels: attention, subjective experience, and automatic social behavior. The message within: the role of subjective experience in social cognition and behavior, pp. 37–51 (2000)

83. Bornstein, R.F.: Exposure and affect: overview and meta-analysis of research, 1968–1987. Psychol. Bull. **106**, 265–289 (1989). https://doi.org/10.1037/0033-2909.106.2.265

84. Tulving, E., Schacter, D.: Priming and human memory systems phenomena of prining. Science **247**, 301–306 (1990)

85. Bargh, J.: The automaticity of everyday life. In: Advances in Social Cognition, vol. X. Psychology Press (2014)

86. Agrawal, N., Zhu, F., Carpenter, S.: Do you see the warning? Cybersecurity warnings via nonconscious processing. In: Proceedings of the 2020 ACM Southeast Conference (2020)

87. Kihlstrom, J.F., Barnhardt, T.M., Tataryn, D.J.: Implicit perception (1992)

88. Bargh, J.: The automaticity of social life. Curr. Dir. Psychol. Sci. **2**, 1–4 (2006). https://doi.org/10.1038/nature13314.A

89. Bargh, J.A.: Losing consciousness: automatic influences on consumer judgment, behavior, and motivation. J. Consum. Res. **29**, 280–285 (2002)

90. Gratz, J.E.: The ethics of subliminal communication. J. Bus. Ethics **3**, 181–184 (1984). https://doi.org/10.1007/BF00382916

91. Kelly, J.S.: Subliminal embeds in print advertising: a challenge to advertisng ethics. J. Advert. **8**, 20–24 (1979). https://doi.org/10.1080/00913367.1979.10673284

92. Saegert, J.: Why marketing should quit giving subliminal advertising the benefit of the doubt. Psychol. Mark. **4**, 107–120 (1987). https://doi.org/10.1002/mar.4220040204

93. Zanot, E.J., Pincus, J.D., Lamp, E.J.: Public perceptions of subliminal advertising. J. Advert. **12**, 39–44 (1983)

94. Haber, R.N.: Public attitudes regarding subliminal advertising. Public Opin. Q. **23**(2), 291–293 (1959). https://doi.org/10.1086/266875

95. Rogers, M., Smith, K.H.: Public perceptions of subliminal advertising. J. Advert. Res. **12**, 10–18 (1993)

96. Baruca, A., Saldivar, R., Flores, J.: Is neuromarketing ethical? Consumers say yes. Consumers say no. J. Leg. Ethical Regul. Issues **2**, 77–91 (2014)

Correction to: SortOut: Persuasive Stress Management Mobile Application for Higher Education Students

Mona Alhasani and Rita Orji

Correction to:
Chapter "SortOut: Persuasive Stress Management Mobile
Application for Higher Education Students"
in: N. Baghaei et al. (Eds.): Persuasive Technology,
LNCS 13213, https://doi.org/10.1007/978-3-030-98438-0_2

In an older version of this paper, all figures were erroneously published with low resolution versions of the original images, and figures 8 and 9 were incorrect. These issues have been corrected.

The updated version of this chapter can be found at
https://doi.org/10.1007/978-3-030-98438-0_2

Author Index

Printed in the United States
by Baker & Taylor Publisher Services

Printed in the United States
by Baker & Taylor Publisher Services